ECONOMIC REFORM AND CROSS-STRAIT RELATIONS

Taiwan and China in the WTO

Series on Contemporary China (ISSN: 1793-0847)

Series Editors: Joseph Fewsmith *(Boston University)*
Zheng Yongnian *(University of Nottingham)*

Published

Vol. 1 Legitimacy: Ambiguities of Political Success or Failure in East and Southeast Asia
edited by Lynn White

Vol. 2 China Under Hu Jintao: Opportunities, Dangers, and Dilemmas
edited by Tun-jen Cheng, Jacques deLisle & Deborah Brown

Vol. 3 China's Compliance in Global Affairs: Trade, Arms Control, Environmental Protection, Human Rights
by Gerald Chan

Vol. 4 Political Civilization and Modernization in China: The Political Context of China's Transformation
edited by Yang Zhong and Shiping Hua

Vol. 5 China into the Hu-Wen Era: Policy Initiatives and Challenges
edited by John Wong & Lai Hongyi

Vol. 6 Water and Development in China: The Political Economy of Shanghai Water Policy
by Seungho Lee

Vol. 7 De Facto Federalism in China: Reforms and Dynamics of Central-Local Relations
by Zheng Yongnian

Vol. 8 China's Elite Politics: Political Transition and Power Balancing
by Bo Zhiyue

Vol. 9 Economic Reform and Cross-Strait Relations: Taiwan and China in the WTO
edited by Julian Chang & Steven M Goldstein

Vol. 10 Discontented Miracle: Growth, Conflict, and Institutional Adaptations in China
edited by Dali L Yang

Series on Contemporary China – Vol. 9

ECONOMIC REFORM AND CROSS-STRAIT RELATIONS

Taiwan and China in the WTO

editors

Julian Chang

Harvard University, USA

Steven M. Goldstein

Smith College, USA

World Scientific

NEW JERSEY • LONDON • SINGAPORE • BEIJING • SHANGHAI • HONG KONG • TAIPEI • CHENNAI

Published by

World Scientific Publishing Co. Pte. Ltd.

5 Toh Tuck Link, Singapore 596224

USA office: 27 Warren Street, Suite 401-402, Hackensack, NJ 07601

UK office: 57 Shelton Street, Covent Garden, London WC2H 9HE

British Library Cataloguing-in-Publication Data
A catalogue record for this book is available from the British Library.

Series on Contemporary China — Vol. 9
ECONOMIC REFORM AND CROSS-STRAIT RELATIONS
Taiwan and China in the WTO

ISBN-13 978-981-256-854-0
ISBN-10 981-256-854-9

Typeset by Stallion Press
Email: enquiries@stallionpress.com

Printed in Singapore by World Scientific Printers (S) Pte Ltd

Contents

List of Tables

List of Figures

Acknowledgements

Our thanks go first to the authors of the chapters that follow for their efforts and their patience, as this project found its way to conclusion.

This project was supported by a grant from the Ministry of Foreign Affairs of the Republic of China.

Steven Goldstein would like to thank Maja Gray and Christa Daly for their research assistance. In addition, thanks go to the Chiang Ching-kuo International Foundation for its support for the research on Taiwan.

Julian Chang would like to thank Dimitre Michev for his research assistance at an early stage of this project.

And lastly, we are indebted to Nancy Hearst for doing her usual editorial magic on this manuscript. We, like so many others in the field of Chinese studies, are fortunate to have benefited from her wisdom and skill.

Chapter

1

Introduction: The WTO and Cross-Strait Economic Relations

Julian Chang and Steven M. Goldstein

On January 1, 2002, Taiwan joined the World Trade Organization (WTO) as its 144th member. Membership represented an important watershed in the evolution of an economy which, since the 1970s, had been recognized as one of the "miracles" of East Asia. Although its phenomenal growth had been driven by exports, the island was only selectively-integrated into the world economy. Its industrial policy was vigorously protectionist and its foreign trade, focused on the U.S. and Japan, was hardly multi-lateral.

Taiwan's accession followed that of the People's Republic of China (PRC) that became the 143rd member of the world organization the previous month. Like Taiwan, China's membership in the WTO represented a dramatic reversal of past economic policies. Ambivalence about participation in the world economic system gave way to "deep integration," while the demands of being a part of the global regime required a radical restructuring of the nation's socialist economy.

It was clear that membership in the world organization might provide not only new opportunities for the economies on both sides of the strait, but would also pose formidable challenges as Taiwan and China each sought to adjust to what was literally a new way of doing business. Their respective commitments to globalization under the WTO regime were universally expected to inaugurate periods of transformation and uncertainty.

What was less clear was the impact that common membership would have on the China–Taiwan relationship. Although Taiwan and the mainland shared memberships in non-governmental organizations and in regional governmental organizations such as the Asian Development Bank, their common membership in the WTO that sets the ground rules for world trade was an extraordinary event. Moreover, mutual accession was occurring against the backdrop of a decade characterized by growing cross-strait political and military tensions, and amidst a flourishing economic relationship. Speculation was rife concerning the impact that membership in the WTO might have on the shape and direction of economic ties, as well as concerning the increasing disconnect between these ties and the degenerating political relationship during the 1990s.

This volume draws from a project launched at Harvard University to examine the implications and results of the simultaneous accession of Taiwan and the mainland to the WTO. In the chapters that follow, we examine the commitments made on each side of the strait to secure membership in the organization; the extent to which these commitments have been applied by each side in its economic dealings with the other side; the implications for Taiwan's place in the economic architecture of the region; the impact of the cross-strait trade regime that has evolved since WTO membership on four major sectors of economic interaction (finance and banking, agriculture, automobile manufacturing, and electronics); and the degree to which common membership has contributed to an improvement in the cross-strait political and security relationship.

In this introduction, we endeavor to provide the background to, and context for, these individual analyses. We begin with an examination of the respective accession processes of the PRC and Taiwan; of the motivations behind their applications; and of the general nature of the commitments made by each side prior to accession. We then turn to a description of the cross-strait economic relationship that had evolved during the 1990s. This, in turn, provides the basis for an analysis of the manner in which the commitments made to secure WTO membership interacted with the structure and rationale of the existing relationship to give shape to the specific cross-strait interactions described by the individual authors in the chapters that follow.

THE PATTERN OF ACCESSION

A Global Trade Regime. The WTO emerged out of the General Agreement on Tariffs and Trade (GATT) created in 1947. The stated purpose of this agreement was to arrive at "mutually advantageous arrangements directed to the substantial reduction of tariffs and other barriers to trade and to the elimination of discriminatory treatment in international commerce."[1] Having agreed to begin the process of achieving major tariff reductions in the import of foreign goods, the signatories established two fundamental principles that would continue to guide its successor organization, the WTO: most-favored nation (MFN) and national treatment. The former assured that concessions granted to one member would be available to all, while the latter prevented discrimination (such as taxation) against imported goods in the home market.[2]

By 1986, the GATT had secured accession of additional members. Six more rounds of negotiation had been held, leading to a further reduction of tariffs; the expansion of the agreement to include such items as anti-dumping provisions and dispute resolution procedures; and the beginning of the process to consider the reduction of non-tariff restrictions on imports.[3] Also, in 1986, the so-called "Uruguay

---

[1] "The General Agreement on Tariffs and Trade" [GATT, 1947], Preamble, http://www.wto.org/english/docs_e/legal_e/gatt47_01_e.htm, accessed August 1, 2005.

[2] "The General Agreement on Tariffs and Trade" [GATT, 1947], Articles II and III, http://www.wto.org/english/docs_e/legal_e/gatt47_01_e.htm, accessed August 1, 2005.

[3] Except where noted, the following three paragraphs are drawn from World Trade Organization, *Understanding the WTO*, 3rd ed. (Geneva: World Trade Organization, 2003).

Round" began, which would continue into 1993. With 123 nations eventually taking part, the seven years of meetings produced a new agreement that combined an amended and expanded GATT treaty (GATT 1994) with a General Agreement on Services (GATS) and an Agreement on Trade-Related Aspects of Intellectual Property Rights (TRIPS). These three agreements were to be administered by a newly-established organization, the World Trade Organization, headquartered in Geneva.[4]

The agreements created an international trade regime with far greater complexity and coverage than the GATT. In the first place, during the Uruguay Round, the original GATT agreement was expanded to regulate a wider range of trade instruments, now including subsidies, supports and local content requirements, and covering a broader range of goods — particularly textiles and agricultural products. The GATS extended the scope of the trade regime to include foreign participation in domestic service industries (ranging from finance to telecommunications) which, by the end of the twentieth century, had come to represent 60 percent of global output and 30 percent of global employment. The TRIPS agreement set the ground rules for the international protection of copyrights, patents, designs, and so forth. Finally, the agreements of the Uruguay Round established an enhanced dispute resolution mechanism and provided for periodic reviews of member nations' compliance with the terms of the agreement.

In short, with the establishment of the WTO in 1995, a structure was created that provided a negotiation arena for participants in the global economy; a set of transparent rules for mutual interaction; and a mechanism to settle disputes regarding these rules.[5] Significantly, the expanded agreements reached during the Uruguay Round were guided by the same two basic principles that had been at the center of the GATT — most-favored nation and national

---

[4] For a discussion of some of the issues that led to the transition from the GATT to the WTO, see Hugh Corbet, "Issues in the Accession of China to the WTO System," *Journal of Northeast Asian Studies* 15, no. 3 (Fall 1996), pp. 14–33.

[5] Ibid.

treatment. It is thus no wonder that, for better or for worse, the WTO has become the symbol of globalization.

Accession. Neither the PRC nor Taiwan was a member of the GATT when the Uruguay Round began. Although the Republic of China (ROC) had been one of the founding members, after its defeat in the civil war on the mainland and its retreat to Taiwan, it resigned from the organization in 1950, only to rejoin as an observer in 1965. However, in 1971, when it was replaced by the PRC in the United Nations, it also lost its observer status. In 1990, it decided to re-apply to the GATT, and in 1995, it again became an observer.[6] The PRC became an observer in 1982 and, despite its claim for succession to the ROC's founder status, began the process of formal application in 1986.[7]

With separate applications submitted within a period of six years, it seemed as if the two sides would move on parallel tracks toward membership in the WTO. In fact, from the very beginning, the two applications became not only linked, but also enmeshed in the politics of cross-strait relations. However, due to the GATT's (and later the WTO's) distinctive nature as an inter-governmental organization, the either/or solution that had been reached at the United Nations in 1971 was avoided — much to the frustration of the PRC.

In order to accommodate the accession of colonies, Article XXXIII of the GATT agreement had stipulated that "a government acting on behalf of a separate customs territory possessing full autonomy in the conduct of its external commercial relations and of other matters provided for in this Agreement, may accede to this agreement." Pursuant to this article that spoke of a "government" and not a "state," the ROC applied under the designation of the "Separate Customs Territory of Taiwan, Penghu, Kinmen, and Matsu" (TPKM), asserting that it met the requirement of being "fully autonomous in the conduct of the external commercial relations of

6 "The Republic of China [Taiwan] in 2003 APEC," http://www.gio.gov.tw/taiwan-website/5-gp/apec/ap3_03.htm, accessed July 12, 2005.

7 "Chronology of China's Bid for WTO Accession," http://www.china.org.cn/Beijing-Review/Beijing/BeijingReview/99Nov/bjr99-48e-8.html, accessed July 16, 2005.

the territory."[8] By the time a working party had been appointed to consider its application, the parenthetical expression "referred to as 'Chinese Taipei'" was being used along with the more unwieldy title.[9] In short, the absence of statehood as a requirement made possible Taiwan's initial application and then future membership in the inter-governmental GATT/WTO.[10]

For Beijing, of course, this was a difference without a distinction. When Taiwan applied in 1990, the PRC Foreign Ministry dismissed the application as "utterly illegal and absurd."[11] Article XXVI:5 (c) of the GATT Agreement provided for colonies to gain membership with the sponsorship of the home country once full autonomy was certified by the contracting metropolitan country. Britain had provided such a certification for Hong Kong and the PRC maintained that it had given its consent in the 1984 agreement regarding the handover of the colony. Since Taiwan was a province of China, Beijing argued, it was not entitled to apply for membership on its own. If it were to join, it could only be in a similar manner, i.e., with sponsorship from the PRC.[12]

However, due to the lingering effects of the 1989 Tiananmen crackdown, Beijing was in a weak bargaining position.[13] Concerned that, given the mood of the time, Taiwan might be admitted before

---

[8] For an excellent discussion of the nature of this clause, see Cho Hui-Wan, *Taiwan's Application to GATT/WTO: Significance of Multilateralism for an Unrecognized State* (Westport, CT: Praeger, 2002), pp. 173–179.

[9] "Working Party on the Accession of the Separate Customs Territory of Taiwan," General Agreement on Tariffs and Trade, Document L/7095/Rev. 1, November 6, 1992, www.GATT.Stanford.Edu, accessed July 26, 2005.

[10] For a defense of the appropriateness of Taiwan's application under Article XXXIII, see Y. Qin, "GATT Membership for Taiwan: A Study in International Law," *NYU Journal of International Law* 24 (1992), p. 1059.

[11] James V. Feinerman, "Taiwan and the GATT," *Columbia Business Law Review* 39, no. 1 (1992), pp. 39–60.

[12] Cho Hui-Wan, *Taiwan's Application to GATT/WTO: Significance of Multilateralism for an Unrecognized State* (Westport, CT: Praeger, 2002), p. 179; Tsai Ing-Wen "Taiwan's WTO Accession: Meeting the Requirements," *Journal of Northeast Asian Studies* 15, no. 3 (Fall 1996), pp. 34–44.

[13] This paragraph is based on the discussion in Wei Liang, "China's WTO Negotiation Process and its Applications," *Journal of Contemporary China* 11 (2002), pp. 693–694.

the PRC, the mainland relaxed its opposition. In a letter to the director-general of the GATT and all contracting parties, Premier Li Peng set three conditions for Taiwan's admission: that "the PRC is the only legitimate government of China and Taiwan is a part of China; Taiwan could join GATT as a separate customs territory only after the PRC joins GATT; and Taiwan's application must be consulted [sic] and agreed to by the PRC government." After consultations with both the mainland and Taiwan, as well as with the American and European Union representatives, a compromise was reached.

At a GATT Council meeting in late September 1992, Chairman B.K. Zuchi announced that after "extensive consultations" ... "all contracting parties" ... "acknowledged the view that there was only one China"; that "many ... had agreed with the view of the People's Republic of China ... that Chinese Taipei, as a separate customs territory, should not accede to the GATT before the PRC itself"; and that there was "a general desire" to set up a separate working party to consider the application from TPKM.[14]

This being the case, Zuchi "concluded that there was a consensus among the contracting parties" to establish a working party to consider the island's admission, but the GATT Council would adopt the protocol for the PRC accession before that of Taiwan. The minutes of the meeting note that the Council "agreed" to these conditions. Further, Zuchi informed the Council that:

> ...as a part of the understanding, the representation of Chinese Taipei in the GATT would be along the same lines as that of Hong Kong and Macau during the course of its status as an observer and subsequently as a contracting-party delegation, and that the titles carried by its representative would not have any implication on the issue of sovereignty.

The minutes report that "The Council *took note* [italics in the original]" of this statement (see footnote 14). The careful wording was clearly a result of the complex diplomatic minuet that had preceded the meeting; later on, this wording would become problematic.

---

[14] "Minutes of Meeting Held in the Centre William Rappard on September 29-October 1, 1992," General Agreement on Tariffs and Trade, C/M/259, pp. 3–4, www.GATT.Stanford.Edu, accessed July 26, 2005.

The informal and somewhat ad hoc arrangement launched the process of what had become a parallel, but hardly separate, dual-accession process. This was an extremely fragile basis upon which to resolve the fundamental issue of sovereignty that divided the two sides. The content and the underlying logic of the compromise thus continued to be a contentious issue, despite the fact that in 1995, Taiwan transferred its application to the GATT to its successor, the WTO, in which Article XII of the founding agreement specifically used the wording "any state or separate customs territory" to define eligibility for membership (see footnote 12).

However, although neither side was completely satisfied with the apparent compromise, there were reasons, relating to cross-strait relations, not to belabor the issue. It should be recalled that relations were just beginning to thaw in the early 1990s. Each side had established semi-governmental organizations to manage policy toward the other, economic relations were growing apace, and, by the fall of 1992, preparatory negotiations were taking place for a meeting between representatives of each side for the first time since the end of the Chinese civil war. Here, as in the GATT, the issue of Taiwan's status as a part of "one China" complicated the negotiations. However, both sides were anxious to get on with the meeting. The result was that in fall 1992, the GATT Council arrived at a shaky compromise, an even more tenuous arrangement defining the status of the two sides than the 1992 consensus which, as we shall see later, also became mired in controversy.

Still, the most compelling reason for the two sides to proceed with the process of accession related to the economic and political advantages that each believed would be gained from membership in the GATT/WTO. To be sure, motivations on each side of the strait evolved in the years that ensued from application to accession; after all, as we have seen, by the time they became members, the GATT had been transformed into the more-complex WTO.[15] Still, the underlying motivating factors — a mixture of politics and

[15] Wei Liang, "China's WTO Negotiation Process and its Implications," *Journal of Contemporary China* 11, no. 33 (2002), pp. 683–719.

economics — remained constant on each side throughout the period pending accession.

For Taiwan, the application for membership was part of an initiative begun by Chiang Ching-kuo in the mid-1980s and aggressively continued by his successor Lee Teng-hui to reverse the steady diplomatic isolation of the island, which had followed the PRC's admission to the United Nations and Taiwan's expulsion from most inter-governmental organizations.[16] The combination of Taiwan's strong global economic position, the lack of a requirement of statehood for admission, and the fact that the PRC as a non-member could not effectively oppose Taiwan's application, presented a unique opportunity for Taiwan to enter a flagship inter-governmental organization. Moreover, in addition to the prestige — and the domestic political capital — to be gained from admission, membership in the GATT/WTO would provide opportunities for Taipei also to seek admission to related international organizations; to maintain quasi-diplomatic contacts with countries that recognize the PRC; and, most generally, to increase its international profile and reputation.

The economic motivation for membership was also rooted in developments that had taken place during the previous decade. As the island made the transition from labor-intensive consumer goods to higher value-added and more technologically-sophisticated products, there was a growing awareness that greater openness to international competition and increased access to foreign goods and services were necessary. Indeed, many in Taiwan argued that membership in the WTO would provide an external stimulus for the reform of an economic and industrial system that was becoming increasingly unsuitable for the changing international and domestic environment.

Finally, these domestic pressures and incentives for change were joined by calls emanating from the island's trading partners,

[16] Government Information Office, Republic of Taiwan, "Taiwan's Accession to the World Trade Organization," pp. 1–3, http://www.taipei.org/un2003,html/wto.htm, accessed July 25, 2005; Paul Hsu, "Policy Brief on Taiwan in the WTO," www.epoch.org.tw/pdf/knowledge_ 06.pdf, accessed July 28, 2005.

especially the U.S. During the 1980s, Taiwan had been forced to lower its barriers to international trade and investment and to improve its protection of intellectual property, largely as a result of pressures from Washington. As one author has noted, it began to appear that Taiwan was "following most GATT rules without being a party to the agreement" (see footnote 12). However, the island's efforts were not fully reciprocated. Membership in a multi-lateral international organization based on the principle of MFN would assure such reciprocity. Moreover, contacts in a multi-lateral organization would presumably increase Taiwan's leverage in settling economic disputes with those countries with which it had either no official relationship or only limited contact.

In the future, as Connie Guang-Hwa Yang notes in Chapter 2, with the protection of an international trade regime (in which it would have a voice) and of a system of dispute resolution, Taiwan could now defend itself against "the threat of unilateral sanctions and retaliations" that had been used to pry open its previously highly-protected economy.[17] Finally, of course, membership in the GATT/WTO would provide increased information about global economic opportunities and trends through contacts with delegations from other nations and the rich data provided by the organization itself.

Ironically, the efforts by the PRC to join the GATT/WTO were driven by similar factors.[18] Although the PRC did not suffer from the isolation that characterized Taiwan's international position, the establishment of its nationalist credentials in the international trade

---

[17] Paul Hsu, "Policy Brief on Taiwan in the WTO," www.epoch.org.tw/pdf/knowledge_ 06.pdf, accessed July 28, 2005.

[18] Icksoo Kim, "Accession to the WTO: External Pressure for Industrial Reform in China," *Journal of Contemporary China* 11, no. 32 (2002), pp. 433–458; Joseph Fewsmith, "The Political and Social Implications of China's Admission to the WTO," *The China Quarterly*, no. 73 (2001), pp. 573–591; Leonard K. Cheng, "China's Economic Benefits from WTO Membership," *Economic Analysis and Commentary* [Hong Kong University of Science and Technology], http://www.bm.ust.hk/~ced/nw_benefit.htm, accessed July 23, 2005; Wei Liang, "China's WTO Negotiation Process and its Implications," *Journal of Contemporary China* 11, no. 33 (2002), pp. 683–719.

organization undoubtedly had great symbolic value for a Communist Party seeking to rebuild its image at home after a decade of the Cultural Revolution. Accession, like membership in the United Nations, was an indication of the nation's arrival as a recognized member of the international community. Moreover, after the suppression of the Tiananmen demonstrations in 1989, there was the additional incentive to refurbish its image abroad.

Equally important was the role that membership would play in assisting the development of the national economy. By the 1980s, it had become obvious that the architects of the post-Mao reform program planned to rely heavily on foreign investment and export-driven industrialization to promote economic development. Membership in the GATT/WTO would assure wider and more favorable access to markets abroad — especially those in the U.S. where the granting of most-favored-nation status had become a yearly drama. Moreover, with China committed by treaty to an international regime with binding dispute resolution mechanisms, international investor confidence would grow and bring with it an influx of capital, management techniques, international marketing experience, and technology.

Finally, it was realized by some of China's reformers that membership in the WTO could be an important factor to overcome domestic resistance to the reform of the formerly-planned economy. Although this objective had motivated Zhao Ziyang to sanction the original application in the 1980s, it became a much stronger factor during the mid-1990s when Zhu Rongji took over the premiership and the reform agenda became more complex. By that time, meeting the terms of the more-complicated WTO accession process and inviting the competition of foreign goods and services were seen by many leaders in Beijing as the key to speeding up the process of economic reform.[19]

[19] Joseph Fewsmith, "The Political and Social Implications of China's Admission to the WTO," *The China Quarterly*, no. 167 (2001), pp. 573–591; Ji Chen and Steve Thomas, "WTO and China's Financial Services Sector," *Journal of Contemporary China* 11, no. 33 (2002), pp. 673–682; Wei Liang, "China's WTO Negotiation Process and its Implications," *Journal of Contemporary China* 11, no. 33 (2002), pp. 683–719.

With such strikingly similar motivations, both sides pursued accession. In the process, each side agreed to be bound by the general terms of the WTO trade regime, as well as by the accession agreements on specific issues that had been negotiated with existing members and that, for the most part, were thus extended to all members under the most-favored-nation principle. As the process progressed, the broad outlines of their future relationship to the world economy; of the structural reforms that each would have to implement; and of the impact that membership would have on various sectors of their respective economies, all became apparent.

This is not the place to review the specifics of the accession agreements of Taiwan and the mainland. Tian-jy Chen touches upon some of their highlights in his chapter in this volume. However, in order to pursue the theme of this introduction — the relationship between the commitments to the WTO and the cross-strait trade regime existing at the time of accession — it is necessary to identify the general classes of trade and investment that the organization sought to regulate.

In broad outline, the accession agreements negotiated by Taipei and Beijing had a common format.[20] Both sides agreed to the general rules of trade in goods included in the GATT treaty as supplemented/modified by the 1994 agreements. These included

[20] The accession protocols for each side are lengthy documents that are available at www.wto.org. There are numerous summaries of the terms agreed upon by each side. Among the most useful for the People's Republic of China are: Office of the United States Trade Representative, "Background on China's Accession to the World Trade Organization," December 11, 2001, http://www.ustr.gov/ Document_Library/ Fact_Sheets/2001/Background_Information_on_China's_Accession_to_the_World_ Trade_Organization.html, accessed August 1, 2005 and "What Does China's WTO Accession Mean for Foreign Industry," http://www.china-window.com/china_market/ wto_and_china/what-does-chinas-wto-acce.shtml, accessed July 22, 2005.

For Taiwan, see Republic of China, Board of Foreign Trade, "Trade and Investment Opportunities Presented by Taiwan's Accession to the World Trade Organization," http://www.gio.gov.tw/taiwan-website/4-oa/wto/wto01.htm, accessed August 2, 2005 and Robin J. Winkler, "Taiwan WTO Survey: Getting a Head Start on Reform," http://www.winklerpartners.com/htmlffiles-english/Publications/articles/ 2001-12CLPWTO.PDF, accessed August 1, 2005.

commitments to lower tariff barriers (itemized goods and the extent of tariff reductions were specified in the individual protocols); to reduce the number of non-tariff barriers (such as import licenses or quotas); and to adhere to the TRIMS agreement that disallowed the approval of investments conditional on adherence to regulations that favored domestic products, rules regarding dumping, and so forth.[21] In addition, Taiwan and the PRC agreed to the general terms of GATS, while, in a manner similar to the procedure followed in the GATT agreement, specifying in separate schedules what service industries would be opened and in what manner. Third, both sides agreed to the TRIPS agreement by pledging the protection of intellectual property rights and the punishment of violators. Finally, accession meant that both sides would be subject to dispute resolution proceedings brought by other members and to periodic reviews of their individual trade regimes by other members of the WTO.

As part of the accession process, Taiwan and China each negotiated separate agreements with some members of the organization, which were incorporated in their terms of accession and made available to all WTO members under the most-favored-nation principle. However, of particular significance was the fact that, since both parties were entering the organization at about the same time, they made no commitments to one another. This would later provide an important justification for the distinctive trade regime maintained by Taiwan vis-à-vis the mainland.

However, within the broad areas of the common commitments made by both Taipei and Beijing, there were significant differences. Most prominent among these were their very different tariff schedules and service schedules, and the fact that China entered as a developing economy, thus gaining greater flexibility in meeting the terms of accession, whereas Taiwan entered as a developed economy.

There were also differences that resulted from the special characteristics of each economy or the obstacles to trade perceived by the negotiating partners. Included in the mainland's terms were

[21] For an explanation of TRIMS, see "WTO Related Investment Measures (TRIMs) Agreement," http://www.dti.gov.uk/ewt/trims.pdf, accessed August 3, 2005.

stipulations regarding state-owned enterprises, subsidies, trading rights, and intellectual property rights. For Taiwan, intellectual property rights, the service industries, the discriminatory nature of the government's alcohol and tobacco monopoly, and the agreement to join the Government Procurement Agreement (GPA) of the WTO after accession constituted the principal foci of the agreements.

As many of the chapters in this book suggest, when the terms of accession for each side became apparent, there was considerable speculation on such issues as the scope of the reform challenge faced by each economy; the identification of the winning and losing sectors within the economy; the social and political tensions that might result from these readjustments; and the opportunities presented to outside traders and investors. Generally, there was a consensus that due to previous reforms (for the most part made under pressure from the U.S.), Taiwan would have an easier task in conforming to the terms of accession. However, a common theme in the discussions of the post-accession economies of both sides was the warning about the severity of the short-term adjustments that would be required of certain sectors of the economy, complemented by an enumeration of the benefits that would be derived from greater global integration in the future.

In the end, it was obvious that it would no longer be business as usual with the rest of the world for either the PRC or Taiwan.[22] Policy

[22] U.S. Department of Agriculture, "The U.S.—China Accession Deal: A Strong Deal in the Best Interests of U.S. Agriculture," http://www.fas.usda.gov/info/factsheets/China/deal.html, accessed July 18, 2005; Office of the United States Trade Representative, "Background on China's Accession to the World Trade Organization," December 11, 2001, http://www.ustr.gov/Document_Library/Fact_Sheets/2001/Background_Information_on_China's_Accession_to_the_World_Trade_Organization.html, accessed August 1, 2005; Thomas Weishing Huang, "The Impact of the WTO Treaties on Investments in China," *Harvard Asia Quarterly*, http://www.fas.harvard.edu/~asiactr/haq/200102/0102a002.htm, accessed August 6, 2005; Robin J. Winkler, "Taiwan WTO Survey: Getting a Head Start on Reform," http://www.winklerpartners.com/htmlffiles-english/Publications/articles/2001-12CLPWTO.PDF, accessed August 1, 2005; I.–W. Tsai, "Taiwan's WTO Accession: Meeting the Requirements," *Journal of Northeast Asian Studies* 15, no. 3 (1996).

tools that had been essential to the industrial policies of these two very different economies either would not be permitted or would have to be reduced or phased out. Domestic industries and agriculture could not be protected by an array of high tariff barriers and non-tariff measures. Export subsidies would be eliminated and trade-distorting domestic subsidies reduced. Special trading or distribution privileges for domestic companies and domestic content requirements were no longer allowed. The most-favored-nation principle would end special privileges granted to one partner and requirements for transparency would limit official discretion in manipulating trade regulations. The service sector would undergo a revolution as foreign participation was to be permitted in areas such as telecommunications, insurance, and banking. Finally, accession to the WTO meant the periodic monitoring of the members' trade regimes and the possibility of the imposition of sanctions for violations of the agreement through the organization's dispute settlement proceedings.

What was not so apparent was the impact that common membership would have on the relationship between the two sides. Although the earlier wrangling over the terms of Taiwan's application gave important clues to the future, absent any accession negotiations between Taipei and Beijing, it was difficult to predict what opportunities and problems lay ahead in the relationship. However, there was little question that the complex history of the relationship between the two sides — both economic and political — would create a post-WTO relationship quite different from that which each was expected to maintain with the rest of the world.

BEFORE THE WTO: A FLOURISHING ECONOMIC RELATIONSHIP

Cross-strait relations had their origins in the civil war. When the Republic of China moved to Taiwan in 1949, it declared Taipei to be the temporary capital of a mainland temporarily occupied by the Communist "rebels." The island was to be a staging area for a counterattack that would restore the rule of the Kuomintang (KMT), or the Nationalist Party, to the mainland. Aside from some smuggling, economic contacts were non-existent and political negotiations were off-limits — to take any other posture would constitute a recognition of the illegal regime on the mainland. The fundamental policy of Chiang Kai-shek's government was founded on the principle of "recovering the mainland" (*guangfu dalu*).[23]

After the end of the civil war, the posture of the new government in Beijing was equally confrontational. On the mainland, the slogan was to "liberate Taiwan" (*jiefang Taiwan*). In the 1950s and 1960s, mainland leaders did offer some proposals for a new period of "Kuomintang-Communist cooperation" that would have Taiwan rejoining the mainland, while retaining some autonomy (an offer refused by Chiang). However, the main thrust of Beijing's policy was unyielding — as reflected in the crises of 1954–55 and 1958.[24] In these years, the only thing that both sides of the strait seemed able to agree upon was that Taiwan was a part of China; of course, who ruled that China was another question altogether.

The PRC identifies the January 1, 1979 "Letter to Taiwan Compatriots" as a watershed signaling the change from a policy of liberating Taiwan by force to one of seeking "peaceful reunification" (*heping tongyi*). Although Beijing continued to reserve the right to use force in certain circumstances, the tone and substance of mainland policy changed as it sought to engage both the government and the people of Taiwan. Drawing on the earlier offers for autonomy, in 1983, China's new leader, Deng Xiaoping, offered to negotiate the island's reunification under the terms of a "one country, two systems" (*yiguo liangzhi*) framework (see footnote 24).

[23] Zhang Zhanhe, *Liang'an guanxi bianqian shi* [A Changing History of the Relations between the Two Shores] (Taipei: Shibao wenhua chuban qiye youxian gongsi, 1995), p. 193.

[24] Quanguo Taiwan yanjiuhui, *Taiwan wenti shilu* [Report on the Taiwan Issue] (Beijing: Jiuzhou chubanshe, 2002), pp. 993–1001.

Initially, there was little response from Taiwan. Chiang Ching-kuo, who succeeded his father after the latter's death in 1975, stuck to what had become known as the "three nos" policy — no contact, no compromise, and no negotiation with the mainland. However, in the period immediately preceding his own death in January 1988, in an effort to rebuild the eroding legitimacy of the KMT government, Chiang set into motion a series of policies that relaxed the single-party dictatorship and took a more pragmatic approach to foreign relations.

With regard to cross-strait policy, Chiang initiated three policies that, although they did little to change the politics of cross-strait relations, had an enormous impact on the economic relationship: travel to the mainland was approved for limited categories of citizens (with a humanitarian gloss regarding the need for aging veterans to visit relatives); a general regulation relaxing restrictions on the export of capital was promulgated; and a willingness to turn a blind eye to cross-strait trade through a third country (or colony, in the case of Hong Kong) was apparent in the statements of government officials who did little to discourage the beginnings of such economic contacts.[25] As the Director-General of the Board of Trade put it coyly, the policy was that there would be "no direct trade with the mainland, no direct contact with Communist Chinese representatives, and no interference with trans-shipment trade."[26]

During the decade of the 1990s that followed, cross-strait trade and investment took off dramatically, with an average growth rate of 30 percent per year.[27] In 1990, the total two-way trade was

[25] This refers to the so-called "non-interference principle of indirect trade with the mainland" announced in 1985. See Tung Chen-yuan, *China's Economic Leverage and Taiwan's Security Concerns,* Ph.D. Dissertation, Johns Hopkins University, 2002, p.27.
[26] *Free China Journal,* September 21, 1987; The previous year, Chiang Ching-kuo had told an American reporter, "it is beyond our control to prevent indirect trade through a third country," *Free China Journal,* October 20, 1986.
[27] Luo Qi, "Economic Dynamism and Political Fragility: The Mainland China-Taiwan Relationship Revisited," http://www.future-china.org.tw/csipf/activity/19990606/mt9906_08e.htm, p. 7, accessed August 11, 2005.

US$ 5.2 billion; in 1995, it was US$ 22.5 billion; and in 2001 — the year before accession — it reached US$ 27.9 billion. Moreover, during this same period, trade with China went from 3.31 percent of Taiwan's total trade in 1990 to 12.10 percent in 2001. For the mainland, growth was much lower, rising from 4.47 percent of overall trade in 1990 to 5.46 percent in 2001 — although it had been as high as 8.2 percent in 1996. By the time they entered the WTO the mainland was Taiwan's leading export destination and Taiwan ranked fourth among China's sources of imports.[28]

Looking at these figures, one author has noted three characteristics.[29] The first is their "increasing trade dependence" — especially in the case of Taiwan. During the years from 1990 to 2001, trade with Taiwan averaged 7 percent of the mainland's total trade, with imports from Taiwan at 12.8 percent and exports to Taiwan a mere 1.9 percent. For Taiwan, the average figures were 9.6 percent of total trade, 3 percent for imports from the mainland and 15.7 percent for exports to the mainland. Significantly, in the case of Taiwan, the overall and export figures grew by roughly 300 percent in those years.[30]

The second characteristic suggested by these figures is that in the 12 years between 1990 and 2001, Taiwan consistently ran a large surplus in its trade with the mainland. Indeed, in 2001, the PRC's trade deficit with Taiwan was more than twice that with next trading partner (South Korea).[31] Specifically, in 1990, the deficit was

[28] *Liang'an jingji tongji yuebao* [Cross-Strait Statistical Monthly], no. 112 (December 2001), Tables 6, 7, 8, and 9, http://www.chinabiz.org.tw/chang/Eco/112-2001-12/menu.htm, accessed August 10, 2005.

[29] Luo Qi, "Economic Dynamism and Political Fragility: The Mainland China-Taiwan Relationship Revisited," http://www.future-china.org.tw/csipf/activity/19990606/mt9906_08e.htm, accessed August 11, 2005.

[30] *Liang'an jingji tongji yuebao* [Cross-Strait Statistical Monthly], no. 112 (December 2001), Tables 8 and 9, http://www.chinabiz.org.tw/chang/Eco/112-2001-12/menu.htm, accessed August 10, 2005. We have calculated these percentages from figures supplied by Taiwan's Mainland Affairs Council.

[31] U.S. Department of Commerce, International Trade Administration, Market Access and Compliance, "China Trade 1995–2002," Table 3B, March 2003.

US$ 3.6 billion; in 1995, US$ 16.3 billion; and in 2001, US$16 billion (down from nearly US$ 19 billion in 2000). During this period, Taiwan's trade surplus with the mainland represented respectively 29 percent, 202 percent, and 103 percent of the island's total trade surplus (it had been as high as 266 percent in 1998).[32]

The final characteristic pertains to the composition of the trade. Studies by Tung Chen-yuan and Luo Qi, which examine the content of trade according to the standard international classification code (the "Harmonized System" numbers), tell largely the same story. By 1998, the principal exports from Taiwan to the mainland were machinery and electrical equipment, plastics and rubber, base metals, and textiles — representing 79 percent of total exports. Growth was particularly dramatic in the iron and steel and machinery sectors, which grew by 93 percent and 44 percent respectively in the 1995–98 period.[33] In the year before accession, three of the five top exports from Taiwan were classified as electrical machinery, with "parts and accessories of automatic data machines" and chips and integrated circuits topping the list.[34]

The pattern of mainland exports to Taiwan was strikingly similar. In 1998, machinery, electrical equipment, and base metals constituted approximately 57 percent of mainland exports. During the 1995–98 period, certain sub-categories of machinery and electrical equipment saw strong growth as their volume increased by

---

[32] *Liang'an jingji tongji yuebao* [Cross-Strait Statistical Monthly], no. 112 (December 2001), Tables 8 and 9, http://www.chinabiz.org.tw/chang/Eco/112-2001-12/menu.htm, accessed August 10, 2005.

[33] Tung Chen-yuan, *China's Economic Leverage and Taiwan's Security Concerns*, Ph.D. Dissertation, Johns Hopkins University, 2002, p.30; Luo Qi, "Economic Dynamism and Political Fragility: The Mainland China-Taiwan Relationship Revisited," http://www.future-china.org.tw/csipf/activity/19990606/ mt9906_08e.htm, accessed August 11, 2005. It should be noted that, although there is a slight difference in the way these two authors use the Harmonized System classification system, their results are roughly comparable.

[34] *Liang'an jingji tongji yuebao* [Cross-Strait Statistical Monthly], no. 112 (December 2001), Table 3, http://www.chinabiz.org.tw/chang/Eco/112-2001-12/menu.htm, accessed August 10, 2005.

147 percent and 243 percent respectively.[35] In 2001, they represented four of the five major mainland exports to Taiwan.[36]

The similarity in the composition of exports to the mainland and imports from the mainland provides a clue to the final characteristic of cross-strait trade — what Luo Qi has called "the investment induced effect."[37] As Luo notes, in the late 1990s

> ... about two-thirds of Taiwan's exports to mainland China were actually ordered by Taiwan-invested enterprises (TIEs) in the mainland, which have to import machinery and equipment, semi-products, parts and accessories, and raw materials from Taiwan for their operations on the mainland.[38]

In other words, although over time, upstream and mid-stream suppliers followed industry to the mainland, while local sourcing increased, it remained the case that in the pre-accession period, the bulk of Taiwan's exports to the mainland consisted of machinery and raw materials that were processed by less expensive Chinese labor. The finished products were then exported directly from the mainland to customers abroad.[39] Indeed, by the year 2000, it was estimated that 39 percent of the output of information

---

[35] Tung Chen-yuan, *China's Economic Leverage and Taiwan's Security Concerns*, Ph.D. Dissertation, Johns Hopkins University, 2002, p. 33; Luo Qi, "Economic Dynamism and Political Fragility: The Mainland China-Taiwan Relationship Revisited," p. 14, http://www.future-china.org.tw/csipf/activity/19990606/mt9906_08e.htm, accessed August 11, 2005.

[36] *Liang'an jingji tongji yuebao* [Cross-Strait Statistical Monthly], no. 112 (December 2001), Table 4, http:// www.chinabiz.org.tw/chang/Eco/112-2001-12/menu.htm, accessed August 10, 2005.

[37] Tung uses the term "FDI-driven trade," in C.–Y. Tung, *China's Economic Leverage and Taiwan's Security Concerns*, Ph.D. Dissertation, Johns Hopkins University, 2002, p. 42.

[38] Luo Qi, "Economic Dynamism and Political Fragility: The Mainland China-Taiwan Relationship Revisited," p. 14, at http://www.future-China.org.tw/csipf/activity/19990606/mt9906_08e.htm, accessed August 11, 2005.

[39] In addition to the sources cited above, see also M.S. Chase, K.L. Pollpeter, and J. Mulvenon, *Untying the Knot: Making Peace in the Taiwan Strait*, Chapter 3 (Santa Monica: Rand Corporation, 2004) and B. Naughton, ed., *The China Circle: Economics and Electronics in the PRC, Taiwan and Hong Kong*, (Washington, DC: Brookings Institution Press, 1997), Chapter 1.

products manufactured by Taiwan companies was from companies based in China and that these enterprises were producing about 72 percent of the mainland's total information technology hardware.[40]

Moreover, although the quantities were not the same, mainland imports to Taiwan reflected a somewhat similar pattern. In certain higher-value-added industries, components or semi-processed goods produced in China were returned to Taiwan for finishing and export.[41] Ironically, this kind of activity increased during times of Sino-American trade frictions as the government in Taiwan relaxed rules on the import of semi-finished goods from the mainland so that they could enter the American market with Taiwan as the country of origin.[42]

In short, cross-strait trade and investment were intimately linked. Underlying the dramatic growth of trade in the pre-accession period was a related, and equally significant, evolving cross-strait division of labor, which was driven by a parallel and similarly-rapid growth of investment by Taiwan companies on the mainland, which began in the late 1980s.

At that time, the original drivers of the Taiwan "economic miracle" — the small and medium enterprises producing labor-intensive goods for export — were facing severe challenges. At home, land and labor costs were increasing and a growing environmental movement was complicating production. The appreciation of the Taiwan dollar made Taiwan products more expensive and neo-protectionist sentiment in the island's traditional export markets was growing. When restrictions on investment abroad were reduced in the late 1980s, Taiwan's business people — primarily in

[40] Tung Chen-yuan, *China's Economic Leverage and Taiwan's Security Concerns*, Ph.D. Dissertation, Johns Hopkins University, 2002, pp. 42–45.

[41] Sheng Lijun, *China and Taiwan: Cross-Strait Relations under Chen Shui-bian* (London: Zed Books, 2002), p. 78; Steven A. Y. Lin, "Roles of Foreign Direct Investment in Taiwan's Economic Growth," in *Taiwan in the Global Economy*, ed. Peter C. Y. Chow (Westport, CT: Praeger, 2002), pp. 85–88.

[42] Kelly Her, "Mainland Market Alliance a Risk to Economic Health," *Free China Journal*, June 28, 1996, p. 3.

the labor-intensive "sunset industries" — began to look abroad to areas with lower production costs, more flexible environmental regulations, and larger import quotas in the developed world.[43] Given the cultural affinity and geographic proximity, China was a natural choice.

Indeed, the move to the mainland was made even more attractive by the orientation of mainland foreign economic policy in the late 1980s. It was at this time that Beijing implemented its coastal development strategy that was specifically intended to make the east coast of China an attractive venue for labor-intensive manufacture. Given the "push" factors at work in Taiwan, the "pull" from the mainland dramatically accelerated the movement of the island's firms to the mainland.[44]

Thus, the drivers during the initial period of Taiwan investment on the mainland were industries manufacturing shoes, umbrellas, textiles, and so forth.[45] As the 1990s progressed, the nature of investment changed. Investment in manufacturing remained dominant at more than 90 percent of the total, while agriculture and services represented less than 10 percent.[46] However, the size and technological sophistication of the investments increased over time and upstream suppliers (for example, Formosa Plastics) followed their customers to the mainland and companies producing for the mainland market (such as those in the food industry) established a presence across

[43] Timothy Ka-ying Wong, *The Political Economy of Taiwan's Foreign Policy* (Hong Kong: Hong Kong Institute of Asia-Pacific Studies, Chinese University of Hong Kong, 1999), Occasional Paper No. 92, pp. 17–19.

[44] Chung Chin, "Division of Labor across the Taiwan Strait: Macro Overview and Analysis of the Electronics Industry," in *The China Circle: Economics and Electronics in the PRC, Taiwan and Hong Kong*, ed. Barry Naughton (Washington, DC: Brookings Institution Press, 1997), p. 98; Barry Naughton, "Economic Policy and Reform in the PRC and Taiwan," in Ibid., p. 163.

[45] Yun-wing Sung, *The Emergence of Greater China: The Economic Integration of Mainland China, Taiwan and Hong Kong* (Basingstoke: Palgrave Macmillan, 2005), p. 139.

[46] This is typical for Taiwan's outward investment where services dominate. Y.–W. Sung, *The Emergence of Greater China: The Economic Integration of Mainland China, Taiwan and Hong Kong* (Basingstoke: Palgrave Macmillan, 2005), p. 161.

the strait.[47] Within a decade, there had been a dramatic change in the profile of Taiwan-invested enterprises on the mainland.

Still, the most significant development was the migration of Taiwan's electronics industries to the mainland. On the eve of WTO accession, these industries were the dominant investors, constituting 45 percent of the island's FDI on the mainland, with metals and metal products in a distant second place at 7 percent — a figure that correlates with the dominance of these industries in Taiwan's foreign trade.[48] At that time, 37 percent of Taiwan's information technology hardware was being produced on the mainland.[49]

Measuring the precise amount of investment on the mainland during the pre-accession period is difficult, although its overall magnitude is unquestionable.[50] According to figures provided by Taiwan, between 1952 and 2001, the government approved 24,160 applications for investment on the mainland, worth nearly US$ 20 billion. This made it the leading destination (at 39 percent) for the island's outward investment during that period.[51] The larger

---

[47] In 1995, electronics and information technology took the place of food and labor-intensive goods as the major investments on the mainland. *Free China Journal*, January 6, 1996, p. 3.

[48] *Liang'an jingji tongji yuebao* [Cross-Strait Statistical Monthly], no. 112 (December 2001), Table 12, http://www.chinabiz.org.tw/chang/Eco/112-2001-12/menu.htm, accessed August 10, 2005.

[49] Michael S. Chase, Kevin L. Pollpeter, and James Mulvenon, *Shanghaied?: The Economic and Political Implications of the Flow of Information Technology Across the Taiwan Strait* (Santa Monica: Rand Corporation, 2004), p. 63.

[50] Due to restrictions by the Taiwan government to be discussed below, many potential investors funnel their money to the mainland from subsidiaries abroad, or from accounts in third countries (e.g., the British colonies in the Caribbean). Thus, although both China and Taiwan report figures that are usually quite different, with the mainland's estimates consistently higher, both are thought to under-estimate the true amount.

[51] The next largest approved destination was "British Central America" with 21.24 percent. A large proportion of these funds surely found their way to the mainland (*Liang'an jingji tongji yuebao* [Cross-Strait Statistical Monthly], no. 112 (December 2001), Table 13, http://www.chinabiz.org.tw/chang/Eco/112-2001-12/menu.htm accessed August 10, 2005).

mainland figures claim that, from 1979 to 2001, the mainland was the destination for nearly 50,000 projects from Taiwan, with a contracted value of about US$ 55 billion and US$ 29 billion already utilized. As a result, Taiwan was the fourth-ranked investor on the mainland after Hong Kong, the U.S., and Japan.[52]

In sum, during the 1990s, there was a dramatic change in the economic relationship between the two sides of the Taiwan Strait. The former enemies had become economic partners. The scope and the intensity of the rapid development of their relationship was remarkable. Yet, for many commentators, even more surprising was the contrast between the flourishing cross-strait economic ties and the almost simultaneous deterioration in the political/security relationship. As Richard Bush[53] writes in a recent study:

> Since the late 1980s...the story line has taken two very different paths: economically and socially, what was a no man's land is now a superhighway of cross-Strait trade and travel, while politically and militarily the two sides are locked in a stalemate of mistrust and hostility.

As we shall see in the next section, the political-military tensions surely escalated during these years. However, they did not do so on a "path" apart from the economic developments. In fact, the difference between the two was more apparent than real.

BEFORE THE WTO: GROWING POLITICAL TENSIONS

Despite the lingering impact of the civil war on cross-strait relations after 1949, the two sides always agreed that the conflict was a domestic matter between two political parties within the context of one

---

[52] Once again, the importance of the British territories should be noted. The mainland reports that the Virgin Islands was the source of about US$ 37 billion in contracted investment, with about half of that utilized (*Liang'an jingji tongji yuebao* [Cross-Strait Statistical Monthly], no. 112 (December 2001), Table 28, http://www.chinabiz.org.tw/chang/Eco/112-2001-12/menu.htm, accessed August 10, 2005).

[53] Richard Bush, *Untying the Knot: Making Peace in the Taiwan Strait* (Washington, DC: Brookings Institution Press, 2005), p. 7.

China. As Deng Xiaoping noted in 1983, the KMT and the Chinese Communist Party spoke "a common language" (see footnote 24).

As late as the 1980s, it seemed that Chiang Ching-kuo and his KMT were still speaking the same language. Chiang upheld the notion of Taiwan's inclusion in "one China," affirmed the domestic nature of the relationship with the mainland, and, as we have seen, initiated a process that enhanced the economic contacts between the two sides. However, he also began a reform process that had the effect of reshaping the "central government" in Taipei into a government of the island, rather than of all of China. By doing so, he eroded the island's ties to the mainland, thus laying the basis for a radical change in the dynamics of cross-strait relations.[54]

Chiang initiated a process of political reform that brought large numbers of non-mainlanders into the KMT party and government, and permitted the creation of an opposition party — the Democratic Progressive Party (DPP) — that was committed to the further Taiwanization of the government, as well as independence from the mainland. Moreover, by abandoning the KMT's insistence that other nations and international organizations had to choose between relations with either Taipei or Beijing, Chiang began the process of establishing a separate international identity for Taiwan.

After Chiang's death, his successor, Lee Teng-hui, continued — and even accelerated — these somewhat contradictory trends. On the one hand, the new administration spoke the language of one China, and created political institutions and a legal framework for increased dealings with the mainland. Thus, from 1988 to 1993, the fundamental legislation governing cross-strait relations was promulgated; organizations (both official and semi-official) were created for the management of cross-strait relations; the National Unification Guidelines that laid out a process for Taiwan to rejoin the mainland were established; and the thick economic ties described above

[54] Steven Goldstein, "Terms of Engagement: Taiwan's Mainland Policy," in *Engaging China: The Management of an Emerging Power*, ed. Alastair Iain Johnston and Robert Ross (London: Routledge, 1999), pp. 57–86.

began to develop in an environment of cautious rapprochement. Most dramatically, in 1993, talks were held in Singapore between "unofficial" representatives of both sides — the first such meeting since the end of the civil war.

However, in retrospect, it is clear that this meeting represented not only the high-tide of cross-strait relations during the 1990s, but also the beginning of the end of positive developments in both the economic and political realms.[55] As Taiwan and the mainland edged toward the 1993 talks, the opposition, the pro-independence DPP, accused the KMT of selling out Taiwan in party-to-party talks through a new "united front." These voices challenged the traditional KMT-CCP consensus that Taiwan was a part of China. In the new democratizing Taiwan, these voices could be neither suppressed nor ignored.

Negotiations between the former enemies in the civil war thus no longer defined the nature of cross-strait talks. The KMT was a ruling party within a developing democracy in which the nature of the relationship with the mainland was now a bitterly-contested political issue. If political progress were to parallel the economic progress, it was now necessary to arrive at a new agreement regarding the nature of each side and its relation to the other side.

As the Singapore talks approached, it was evident that although the KMT government still adhered to the principle of "one China" in name, its definition conflicted with that held by Beijing. Even though Taipei noted the mainland's claim that "one China" was the PRC, it maintained that "'one China'... [meant] the Republic of China founded in 1911...with *de jure* sovereignty over all of China [but] jurisdiction only over Taiwan, Penghu, Kinmen, and Matsu." On this basis, Taipei insisted that unification would be a multi-stage process to be negotiated by two equal, sovereign entities.

---

[55] Steven Goldstein, "The Cross Straits Talks of 1993 — The Rest of the Story: Domestic Politics and Taiwan's Relations with the Mainland," *Journal of Contemporary China* 6, no. 15 (July 1997), pp. 259–286; Wang Mingyi, *Bu queding de haixia* [Uncertain Strait] (Taipei: Shibao wenhua chuban qiye youxian gongsi, 1993).

By the mid-1990s, Taiwan was routinely defining itself as an "independent sovereign state since its establishment in 1912." Lee Teng-hui sought to substantiate this claim by increasing Taiwan's international profile through "pragmatic diplomacy" and renewed efforts to enter the United Nations. In 1999, he appeared to erode his commitment to the idea of one China by speaking of the "special state-to-state relationship" (*teshu guo yu guo guanxi*) that existed between Taiwan and China.

The reaction of the leadership on the mainland to the evolution of Lee Teng-hui's cross-strait policy was predictable. Follow-up talks to the Singapore meeting scheduled for the summer of 1995 failed to materialize as a result of Lee's "unofficial" visit to the U.S. Rather, the mainland flexed its muscle with missile tests close to the island — a form of intimidation repeated on the eve of the first presidential election in Taiwan in 1996. From that point on, Lee was seen as an advocate of independence, and when he enunciated his "two-state theory" in 1999, the PRC ended the tenuous political links that had existed between cross-strait organizations and declared that their renewal would require recognition of the "one China principle."

The election of Chen Shui-bian as President of Taiwan in March 2000 and the legislative gains of the DPP in December 2001 exacerbated the situation. Because Chen and his party were closely associated with the independence cause, on the eve of his election, the mainland adopted a threatening posture. Although Chen struck a moderate tone in his inaugural address, he co-opted the KMT view that the ROC was already an independent, sovereign state; continued to refuse to accept the "one China" principle, or the consensus of 1992, as a precondition for talks with the mainland; and accelerated efforts to enhance Taiwan's international profile. Characterizing his approach to cross-strait relations as "insincere" and his efforts to secure a separate international identity for Taiwan as seeking independence, Beijing refused any dealings with Chen or his government and aggressively sought to limit the island's "international space."

In short, after the mid-1990s, the two sides simply ceased to speak "a common language." As a result, negotiations stalled and the political relationship reached a new low point even as economic relations lingered at their apex.

Yet, economic and political policies were not entirely as separate as is so commonly assumed. The spillover of the political conflict into the economic ties was manifest in the dispute over the negotiation of direct shipping links between the island and the mainland. Despite the growing economic presence on the mainland and the wishes of many Taiwan entrepreneurs, Taipei held to its demand that direct transportation links would have to be negotiated by government representatives from each side. Although Beijing was willing to hold such talks if Taiwan accepted the "one China principle" (which it would not), the mainland proposed unofficial talks that were unacceptable to Taipei. Meanwhile, Taiwan's business people on the mainland incurred the extra indirect shipping and travel expenses as cross-strait economics were subordinated to politics.

This very public, and often bitterly-contested, spillover of political concerns (the one China issue) into economic relations seemed an exception in the trade and investment relationship that was developing from strength to strength during these years. In fact, this was more a symptom, rather than an exception. Although lacking the visibility of the dispute over negotiations of direct links, the deep political differences between the two sides were creating a distinctive trade regime that would have to be reconciled — or not — with the requirements of membership in the WTO.

BEFORE THE WTO: A VERY POLITICIZED TRADE REGIME

Almost from the inception of renewed cross-strait economic contacts, Beijing was not shy about making it clear that these policies also had an important political purpose. As Yang Shangkun, then China's President, put it in December of 1990:

> We should make efforts to develop cross-Strait relations. The emphasis should be placed on economic and other exchanges in order to *yi shang wei zheng* [exploit business to exploit politics] and *yi min bi guan* [utilize the public to urge

the official]. We should lead cross-Strait exchanges in the direction to facilitate unification of the motherland and the four modernizations.[56]

In other words, economic relations would create a constituency for unification within the Taiwan business community. Economics would create a united front from below, as China put its "hope in the Taiwan people" (*xiwang yu Taiwan renmin*), rather than in its government. Throughout the 1990s, as cross-strait political relations deteriorated, official dialogue ended, and the issue of direct transport links remained unresolved, mainland statements sought to mobilize this constituency by emphasizing the importance of improved cross-strait relations for Taiwan's economic health. Indeed, this message intensified (especially in respect to the economic benefits of direct shipping) as the island's economy braced for an unprecedented decline on the eve of accession to the WTO during the 2001–2002 period.[57]

In pursuit of these political goals, the mainland created a regulatory framework and political environment for Taiwan's business people on the mainland, which was both exceptionally open and supportive. Paradoxically, at a time when China's opening to the world was still somewhat circumscribed, the privileges granted to Taiwan companies were expansive. In July 1988, the "Regulations of the State Council of the PRC for Encouraging Taiwan Compatriots to Invest in the Mainland" extended regulations pertaining to foreign companies to those from Taiwan; stipulated the types of investment that would be permitted; pledged that Taiwan Invested Enterprises (TIEs) would not be nationalized; permitted remittances abroad, and so forth.

In addition, the compatriots (*tongbao*) of Taiwan also were granted special privileges. In 1994, the "PRC Law on the Protection of Investment by Taiwan Compatriots" that was further elaborated in 1999 in the "Detailed Implementation Rules," according to mainland

---

[56] Tung Chen-yuan, *China's Economic Leverage and Taiwan's Security Concerns*, Ph.D. Dissertation, Johns Hopkins University, 2002, p. 2.

[57] Steven Goldstein, "The Taiwan Strait: A Continuing *Status Quo* of Deadlock?" *Cambridge Review of International Affairs* 15, no. 1 (April 2002), pp. 89–90.

commentators, was intended to ease the concerns of Taiwan's investors. These regulations covered matters ranging from tax status to the schooling of children to the protection of property to the enjoyment of equal rights with Chinese firms with respect to the purchase of materials and utilities.[58]

Taiwan enterprises received special privileges as well. Preferential treatment was initially accorded to Taiwan enterprises investing in the province of Fujian. In the years that followed, other provinces and cities set aside special zones for investment by Taiwan enterprises and provided added incentives such as tax exemptions, duty free imports, land use rights, and so forth — some of which were granted without the approval of the central government.[59] Moreover, according to mainland commentators, special assistance was provided to these Taiwan companies in matters such as obtaining loans or resolving disputes and the local branches of the Taiwan Affairs Office of the State Council were required by law to provide assistance to the Taiwan compatriots.[60]

To be sure, there were occasional suggestions of Taiwan business people being subjected to political pressure and of their

[58] Appendix 52—"Regulations of the State Council of the PRC for Encouraging Taiwan Compatriots to Invest in the Mainland," http//:cns.miis.edu/straittalk/Appendix% 2052.htm, August 9, 2005, accessed June 2, 2006.

[59] Barry Naughton, "Economic Policy and Reform in the PRC and Taiwan," in *The China Circle*, ed. Naughton, p. 101; Michael S. Chase, Kevin L. Pollpeter, and James Mulvenon, *Shanghaied?: The Economic and Political Implications of the Flow of Information Technology Across the Taiwan Strait* (Santa Monica: Rand Corporation, 2004), p. 6; Tian Cheng, "The Political Economy of Taiwan's Investments in China," in *Inherited Rivalry: Conflict Across the Taiwan Straits*, ed. Tun-jen Cheng, Chi Huang, and Samuel S. G. Wu (Boulder, CO: Lynne Rienner, 1995); Wu Yu-shan, "Economic Reform, Cross-Straits Relations, and the Politics of Issue Linkage," in *Inherited Rivalry: Conflict Across the Taiwan Straits*, ed. Tun-jen Cheng, Chi Huang, and Samuel S. G. Wu (Boulder, CO: Lynne Rienner, 1995), pp. 67–96.

[60] Liu Zhengtao, "Cujin liang'an jingji jiaoliu, zaofu Zhonghua minzu" [Promote Economic Exchanges Across the Strait, Benefit the Chinese Nation], in *Cross-Strait Interactions in the New Era: Challenges and Opportunities*, ed. Phillipe Regnier and Wei-wei Zhang (Geneva: Modern Asia Research Center, Graduate School of International and Development Studies, 2003), pp. 2–3.

vulnerability to predatory local officials. However, in a detailed study of the interaction between Taiwan business people and the mainland government, Tung Chen-yuan also found considerable evidence of efforts by Chinese officials both at the center and in the localities to look after the interests of Taiwan investors, and to retain their confidence during times of political or military tension (such as during the 1996 cross-strait crisis).[61]

Finally, the mainland's trade regime for Taiwan was intended not only to favor and nurture investment from the island, but also to keep it quite distinct from the international trade regime. Taiwan businessmen were referred to as *tongbao* (fellow countrymen or compatriots), and although they were *granted* many of the privileges of foreign business people (and sometimes treated as foreign investors), they were clearly in a different category on the mainland.[62] For example, Beijing refused to discuss an investment protection treaty with Taipei because such a treaty would have suggested that relations were international in nature. Rather, investment protection was, as we have seen, legislated as if it were a domestic issue, with the implication that Taiwan companies were domestic in nature.

Taiwan's regulatory framework for trade with the mainland was also shaped by political factors — of both a domestic and international nature. However, here, the orientation was the mirror image of that prevailing on the mainland. At a time when Taiwan was progressively liberalizing its trade regime vis-à-vis the rest of the world, it was seeking to closely regulate interaction with the mainland.

From the inception of cross-strait economic relations in the 1990s, the government in Taiwan was torn between a policy of restricting interactions with the mainland in the interests of limiting perceived damage to the security and the economy of the island,

---

[61] Tung Chen-yuan, *China's Economic Leverage and Taiwan's Security Concerns*, Ph.D. Dissertation, Johns Hopkins University, 2002, Chapters 10 and 11.

[62] Michael S. Chase, Kevin L. Pollpeter, and James Mulvenon, *Shanghaied?: The Economic and Political Implications of the Flow of Information Technology Across the Taiwan Strait* (Santa Monica: Rand Corporation, 2004), p. 87.

and the desire to lessen political pressures emanating from the business community for a more open trade regime.[63] What resulted was not only a fluctuating pattern of regulation, but also, more fundamentally, a paradoxical situation, whereby a highly restrictive trade regime for the management of cross-strait trade existed alongside an apparently flourishing economic relationship.

Although Chiang Ching-kuo had unleashed the forces for cross-strait trade and investment in the late 1980s, it did not take long before the government became alarmed over the potential impact on both the island's economy, as well as on its ability to resist mainland pressures. As early as 1990, there was official concern over what came to be known as "mainland fever," and frequent warnings of the dangers of what, at that time, was a relatively small amount of Taiwan trade and investment with the mainland.[64] Over the next decade, these warnings intensified, culminating in Lee Teng-hui's 1996 direct response to Yang Shangkun's pronouncement of 1990:

> During this year's elections, the Communists ended the close communications channel that had been established. Until now they have practiced techniques of "cold dealings" [*leng chuli*], and methods of "using the people to pressure the officials" [*yi bian bi guan*] and [to] "use business to surround politics" [*yi shang wei zheng*]...to counter this situation we must adopt the great principle of "avoiding haste and being patient" [*jingji yongren*].[65]

Still, although there were occasional suggestions that a constituency sympathetic to mainland demands was indeed developing, and considerable concern that investment flight to the mainland would "hollow out" Taiwan's industry or cause the island to lose its technological edge, the major worry in Taipei, during the 1990s,

---

[63] Leng Tse-keng, *The Taiwan-China Connection: Democracy and Development Across the Taiwan Straits* (Boulder, CO: Westview Press, 1996); Steven Goldstein, "The Cross Straits Talks of 1993—The Rest of the Story: Domestic Politics and Taiwan's Relations with the Mainland," *Journal of Contemporary China* 6, no. 15 (July 1997), pp. 259–286.

[64] Lin Ching-wen, "Mainland Fever Concern Heating Up in Taiwan," *Free China Journal*, August 23, 1990; "Political Ties in M'Land Trade," *Free China Journal*, April 16, 1990.

[65] Zhou Yang-shan, ed., *Li Denghui zhizheng shi nian* [Lee Teng-hui's Ten Years in Power] (Taipei: Luntan chubanshe youxian gongsi, 1998), p. 233.

centered on the political leverage through economic sanctions that the mainland would gain from the island's growing economic dependence.[66] In order to prevent such an outcome, the government initiated several measures to regulate and restrict economic relations with the mainland.

In 1992, the Lee Teng-hui Administration promulgated the "Act Governing Relations between the People of the Taiwan Area and the Mainland Area" that established broad governmental powers for the purpose of "regulating dealings between the people of the Taiwan area and the mainland area." Under the umbrella of this legislation, more specific regulations to govern trade and investment, such as the "Regulations Governing Permission of Trade between Taiwan Area and Mainland Area," were put into effect in order "to implement due control or administration of the trading activities" across the strait.[67]

Four areas were subject to control by the government in Taipei. Incoming investment from the mainland was, by and large, forbidden, as was investment by Hong Kong companies in which mainland companies held more than a 20-percent share.[68] Second, there were regulations limiting the movement of persons across the strait, especially mainland technicians or managers employed by Taiwan or

---

[66] Tung Chen-yuan, *China's Economic Leverage and Taiwan's Security Concerns*, Ph. D. Dissertation, Johns Hopkins University, 2002. For another consideration of the dependence issue, see T.–K. Cheng, "The Political Economy of Taiwan's Investments in China," in *Inherited Rivalry: Conflicts Across the Taiwan Straits*, ed. T.–J. Cheng, C. Huang, and S.S.G. Wu (Boulder, CO: Lynne Rienner, 1995), pp. 153–169. For a report from the mid-1990s, concerning over-reliance on the mainland, see K. Her, "Mainland Market Alliance: A Risk to Economic Health," *Free China Journal*, June 28, 1996, p. 3.

[67] http://www.mac.gov.tw/english/english/law/law1.twm and http://www.mac.gov.tw/english/law/en09.htm, accessed August 19, 2005.

[68] As the chairperson of Taiwan's Mainland Affairs Council noted in 2001, "Currently the [Taiwan] Government in general prohibits inward investment from mainland China and approvals are only granted as exceptions on a case by case basis" (Dr. Tsai Ing-wen, "Current Cross-strait Relationship," speech to the Taiwanese Chamber of Commerce, San Francisco Bay Area, http://www.mac.gov.tw/english/english/foreign/2.htm, accessed August 3, 2005).

foreign companies.[69] Third, imports from the mainland were strictly controlled. For example, in mid-1991, imports of 158 classes of items were designated as permissible (a three-fold increase over 1988); by 1995, the number had increased to roughly 3,900 industrial products and 200 agricultural products; and in the year before accession to the WTO, approximately 5,600 agricultural and industrial items were permitted, representing slightly less than 50 percent of China's classes of exports.[70]

For many in Taiwan, the final area of control was the most critical: the regulation of investment on the mainland. In a manner similar to the regulation of imports, the government sought to identify permissible areas of investment on the mainland. During the 1990s, a complicated regulatory framework for the approval of individual investments, which considered the sizes of the investment, the types of companies that could invest, and the classes of investments that would be permitted, was developed. By 1994, almost half of the 9,000 types of products produced by Taiwan companies could be manufactured on the mainland, with the government noting that approval would be granted only if the manufacture of the products in Taiwan could "no longer be competitive internationally." At the same time, some investment in the service industries on the mainland was also permitted.[71]

After Lee's 1996 exhortation to the business community to limit its investments on the mainland, regulations were tightened, accompanied by threats of more diligent enforcement and severe punishment for violations. Thus, in May 1996, a more stringent screening process went into effect; investments were capped at US$ 50 million (although exceptions were possible), and investments in infrastructural projects on the mainland were banned. Still, despite Lee's rhetoric and encouragement for Taiwan's investors to "go south,"

---

[69] Allen Pun, "Visits Open to Mainland Businessmen," *Free China Journal*, August 26, 1994, p. 3.

[70] "Government Eases Trade Restrictions with China," *Taipei Times*, February 18, 2002.

[71] Deborah Shen, "Investment Channels Increase," *Free China Journal*, September 2, 1994.

the government still classified over 6,600 classes of manufactured goods that could be manufactured on the mainland — only 342 were prohibited.[72] Persistent demands from the influential business community for a less restrictive trade regime, as well as simple evasion, remained at odds with the government policy.

In 2001, on the eve of accession to the WTO, the administration of Chen Shui-bian tried to seize the initiative in managing economic relations with the mainland. It abandoned the "no haste, be patient" policy and replaced it with a policy of "active opening and effective management" (*jiji kaifang, youxiao guanli*), which was both a recognition of the failure of earlier attempts to regulate and a political concession to business on the eve of the legislative elections. In essence, the rules that followed from the new approach retained the principle of government regulation of investments and imports, and enhanced the "security coefficient of the economy" ("effective management"), while simplifying administrative procedures and easing restrictions on the size of investments (for example, the US$ 50 million cap on investment size was eliminated) and on the types of projects that could be initiated ("active opening").[73]

In sum, although the active and often cooperative nature of economic relations between Taiwan and the mainland provided a sharp contrast to the stagnation and conflict of the political relationship, the two tracks were not mutually independent. Although neither side totally succeeded, each sought to shape the cross-strait trade regime in a manner that would serve its respective political ends. The complex intertwining and interaction of these two strands with politics as the dominant factor was the defining characteristic of cross-strait relations as both sides acceded to the WTO.

---

[72] Tung Chen-yuan, *China's Economic Leverage and Taiwan's Security Concerns*, Ph.D. Dissertation, Johns Hopkins University, 2002, p. 36.

[73] David G. Brown, "China-Taiwan Relations: Economics is Still the Story," *Comparative Connections* 3, no. 4 (2001), pp. 64–70. For an official presentation of the new regulations, see Mainland Affairs Council, "Trade and Economic Category," http://www.mac.gov.tw/english/english/macpolicy/qa03.pdf, accessed August 22, 2002.

BEFORE THE WTO: EXPECTATIONS AND OBSTACLES

There was considerable optimism regarding the economic potential of dual WTO membership. During the preceding decade, a foundation had been built for a close and mutually-beneficial relationship between the mainland and Taiwan. This was not due simply to the magnitude of the economic links between the two sides — their quality was also important. A cross-strait division of labor tied to often-complex production chains had emerged, even as Taiwan enterprises on the mainland established roots in the mainland's cultural, legal, and economic systems. For the most part, the existing size and quality of the economic relationship seemed to provide precisely the kind of environment that, after an inevitable period of adjustment, could thrive in the trade regime mandated by the WTO agreements. As Barry Naughton noted, the years before had seen the "close integration of production networks without any institution for fostering overall economic integration and despite significant unresolved political differences."[74] The world organization could provide the institutional framework that was lacking, but the political differences would remain.

While the economic relationship that developed during the 1990s held the promise of dramatic expansion under the new trade regime, the highly-politicized trade regime that had shaped it would have to be radically reformed, if it were to conform to WTO requirements. As we have seen, both Taiwan and the PRC, by seeking to achieve political/security ends through economic means, by parallel, unilateral actions had developed regulatory frameworks for cross-strait trade and investment, that were inconsistent with the WTO and the associated agreements that they had pledged to respect.

Thus, although the lingering ban on direct transportation links did not fall under WTO regulations, Taiwan's restrictions on imports from the mainland; regulations of movement of persons across the strait; and blocking of mainland investments in the island's service industries, which had been motivated by the perceived need to limit the island's vulnerability to political and economic pressures from

[74] Barry Naughton, ed., *The China Circle: Economics and Electronics in the PRC, Taiwan and Hong Kong* (Washington, DC: Brookings Institution Press, 1997), p. 7.

the mainland, were clear violations of the core principles of the most-favored nation and national treatment. Although Taiwan might have invoked the non-application clause (Article XIII) in the WTO founding agreement or used the vaguer rationale of security concerns (Article XXI), it chose not to.[75] These non-conforming elements remained in place as Taiwan entered the WTO.

For the mainland, the areas of possible non-compliance did not revolve around restraints on incoming trade and investment. Expansion, rather than restriction, served the PRC's interests and political goals. However, the special privileges granted to Taiwan investors or favorable treatment on imports in order to increase political capital did run afoul of the WTO's core principles of most-favored nation and national treatment as blatantly as Taiwan's restrictions. Still, although important elements in the mainland's cross-strait policy, these issues were dwarfed by the much larger question of the implications for the PRC's "one China principle" were it to deal with Taiwan within the context of the WTO either by applying its rules to cross-strait trade, or by dealing directly with the island's representatives. To recognize that the WTO agreement applied in any way to cross-strait relations would contradict the claim that these relations were a domestic issue subject to no outside interference and, tacitly, sanction Taiwan's participation in a key international organization. Yet, like Taiwan, the mainland chose not to exercise the exclusion clause or to make claims based on national security.

Thus, the dual accession of Taiwan and the PRC to the WTO presented a paradox. As the result of historical conditions, both were entering the organization against a background of promising economic relations, while still steadfastly holding to fundamental policies vis-à-vis each other which, as a condition of membership, they had solemnly pledged to eliminate from their dealings with all other members.

In the chapters that follow, the contributors to this volume address this dilemma, but they do so within the broader context of

---

[75] Kong Qingjiang, "Cross-Strait Relations: What are the Legitimate Expectations from the WTO?" *Harvard Asia Quarterly* (Spring 2004), pp. 1–2, http://www.fas.harvard.edu/~asiactr/haq/200402/0402a003.htm, accessed August 18, 2005.

the more general impact of accession to the WTO on the economies of Taiwan and China.

OVERVIEW OF THE CHAPTERS

In the first chapter, Tain-Jy Chen provides a survey of the domestic consequences of WTO accession for both Taiwan and China. After reviewing the accession agreements of each party, he examines the concessions in industrial goods, agriculture, and services such as telecom, insurance, banking and securities on Taiwan. In China, he examines the concessions in tariffs, quotas and import controls, trading and distribution rights, and the service industry. He concludes that Taiwan experienced no "major dislocation" due to accession. In fact, Taiwan's industrial sectors were able to make some inevitable adjustments that would have been difficult to make without the cover provided by the WTO accession demands. To some extent, a similar process occurred in China and the perceived fears of the impacts of WTO trade liberalization were cushioned by a variety of technical measures. As has become obvious over the past four years, post-WTO economic growth continued with no major disruptions.

Connie Huang-hwa Yang reviews the domestic legal and structural changes that Taiwan had to make in order to fulfill its commitments. Similar to Chen's analysis, she finds that the long accession process enabled Taiwan to make gradual changes that, in any case, were desirable. Examining the legal history with the knowledge of an insider, Ms. Yang explores how approaches to amending its laws were expected to be used as a precedent for future trade pacts. She also reviews the domestic consultative process for accession; the internal tensions of the administration during the accession process; and the internationalization of different agencies after accession. The role of the foreign business communities was another factor that impacted the redesign of the legal infrastructure. Finally, the chapter presents two cases to illustrate the political difficulties Taiwan has confronted after accession — the stigma attached to WTO accession due to the public's misconception of the merits of the WTO rules and China's refusal to treat Taiwan in the same manner as other WTO members.

In a guardedly-pessimistic conclusion, Yang writes that, for the moment, China has no intention of interacting with Taiwan under the WTO framework, but hopes that China's domestic economic growth will bring China's political conditions closer to those of Taiwan.

In his discussion of Taiwan's accession requirements and their impact on economic policy, Chi Schive looks at the extent of Taiwan's deregulation in trade and investment policies toward the mainland, notably in the commodities area. After introducing a projection of the possible economic impact on both sides of the strait of the policy changes made in accordance with the WTO rules, Schive explores the reasoning guiding Taiwan's current policies to restrict the scope of cross-strait economic ties. He goes on to examine the unilateral import and investment restrictions by Taiwan with respect to the PRC, which resulted from this reasoning, and reviews existing Taiwan regulations regarding investments in and technological collaboration with the PRC. Schive notes that, if Taiwan continued its tight control policy, real GDP was predicted to increase by 0.17 and 0.15 percent in Taiwan and the PRC, respectively, whereas if Taiwan loosened its policy, real GDP was predicted to increase by 0.21 and 0.17 percent respectively. He concludes with a call for Taiwan to continue to liberalize its trade policy in all sectors, including agriculture, which he sees as Taiwan's weakest sector.

Peter Drysdale and Xinpeng Xu use a trade efficiency and intensity analysis to look at the relative benefits for Taiwan and China after WTO accession. They find that, due to political restrictions, Taiwan has not been able to take full advantage of China's economic liberalization and, thus, Taiwan's industrial upgrading has not progressed as quickly as it could have. In part, China's pursuit of Free Trade Agreements (FTAs) on sub-regional or bilateral bases has also pre-empted many of Taiwan's own interests in these arrangements. The authors recommend a strategy for Taiwan of going "loudly and actively globalist," and including China in its liberalization strategy. Taiwan should push for liberalization in goods and services and remove trade discrimination against the mainland.

In his chapter on the political economy of cross-strait relations, Joseph Fewsmith reviews the tight trade and economic links between

Taiwan and China. He asks how such links — the "centripetal forces" of integration — might interact with the "centrifugal pulls of identity and politics" on both sides of the strait. After reviewing the benefits of investment flows for both Taiwan and China, Fewsmith looks at the impact of the investment trends on cross-strait economic and political ties. He examines the case of the steel dispute in 2002 as an example of increased cooperative behavior within an international organization. Unfortunately, as Fewsmith notes, this was the only case of a dispute being adjudicated in such a manner. However, Fewsmith's conclusion is relatively optimistic. He contends that WTO accession has been a "boon" to both Taiwan and China, and that, within a range of politically acceptable options, amelioration of tensions could occur.

In the first of the chapters on sectoral studies, Jih-chu Lee reviews the state of the financial sectors in Taiwan and China. She notes that this sector is commonly regarded as the weakest in both of the two economies. One difference is that Taiwan has allowed foreign financial institutions equal footing with local entities, thus bringing in competition at an earlier stage in Taiwan. Lee identifies the major weaknesses of Taiwan's financial sector as the following: too many banks; increasingly poor quality of assets; lack of innovation in service offerings; and inadequate exit mechanisms. In a cautiously-optimistic prognosis for the long term, however, she notes that Taiwan's reform initiatives in the financial sector, such as the establishment of asset management companies, will create greater efficiency over the next few years. In a similar review of China's financial sector, Lee finds greater cause for concern. Poor supervision, distortions of loan portfolios, higher levels of NPLs, an underdeveloped money and bond market, as well as an undisciplined stock market, remain highly problematic. She predicts an outflow of deposits, human resource problems, and increased competition from new financial instruments. All this may be ameliorated by an acceleration of financial reforms as the WTO regulations kick in. Lee also reviews cross-strait cooperation in the financial sector and offers suggestions for further integration.

Robert Ash notes that the agricultural sectors in both Taiwan and China are vulnerable to foreign competition. However, the potential costs of WTO accession are not the same for each side. In China, the possible dislocation of millions of farmers was seen as a real threat to regime stability, whereas in Taiwan, the "age structure of its farm population, its more comprehensive social security provisions and the greater cohesiveness of its social fabric promised to cushion the impact of more intense foreign competition." After a review of the accession requirements and negotiated settlements, Ash analyzes the implications of the accession agreements for China and Taiwan. His wide-ranging discussion of crop distribution, employment, and regional implications concludes that the significance for agricultural restructuring and intensified economic reform may be the most important results of accession. In terms of cross-strait consequences, although Taiwan's economy has generally become more integrated with the Chinese economy, in the agricultural sector, the data are not conclusive.

Charles Trappey presents an optimistic scenario for the future of the electronics and the ICT sector. After reviewing the histories of the electronic industries in both Taiwan and China, he compares the WTO accession terms for each side. He notes that China had a longer way to go than Taiwan to meet the terms of accession, but still has made great progress. Trappey is confident that WTO accession will continue to be the primary driving force for positive trade policy changes in both China and Taiwan during the next few years.

Chwo-Ming Joseph Yu looks at the WTO's impact on the auto sector in Taiwan and China, and examines the types of cross-strait cooperation, as well as the future prospects. Automakers on both sides of the strait have increased their links with foreign companies, but cross-strait trade has been limited due to political tensions. After reviewing the world automobile industry and the many joint ventures formed by major automakers in China, Yu proceeds to describe the market characteristics in Taiwan and China. He assesses the impact of WTO accession, examines joint ventures between automakers from Taiwan and China, and summarizes the development of cross-strait cooperation for firms in the automobile industry. Yu finds that Taiwan and China automakers have become integrated into the global automobile industry over the past few years. But, with the exception of parts trade, they have not achieved the kind of cross-strait integration once thought possible due to political conflicts.

Chapter

2

WTO Commitments by Taiwan and China and the Domestic Consequences

Tain-Jy Chen

INTRODUCTION

Taiwan first applied to join the General Agreement on Tariffs and Trade (GATT), the forerunner of the World Trade Organization (WTO), in 1990, and was finally admitted into the WTO at the beginning of 2002. Taiwan's application was formally processed by the GATT in 1992, with bilateral negotiations beginning in 1994 and 30 members of the GATT participating in the process. These negotiations determined the concessions and reforms that Taiwan was to make in its tariff and trade structures.

Following Taiwan's accession, its economic performance has remained stable (although not as remarkable as it had been in the 1990s); thus, there seems to have been no major dislocation of industries caused by WTO membership. Although the unemployment rate shot up in 2001 — Taiwan registered its first-ever negative GDP growth — these events were mainly caused by industrial restructuring prompted by rising wages and massive capital outflows. WTO membership may have actually provided an opportunity for Taiwan's industries to smoothly implement inevitable adjustments that were needed, regardless of WTO membership.

China applied to join the GATT in 1986, and was admitted to the WTO in December 2001. During 15 years of negotiations, China was pressured to make a wide range of commitments, promising a sea change in the Chinese economy. Not only was China forced to substantially reduce tariffs and lift all existing quotas, it also agreed to open its grossly underdeveloped service sector and offer trading and distribution rights to foreign firms. Furthermore, China allowed other WTO members to invoke special safeguard measures against Chinese imports for 12 years and to impose quotas on Chinese-made textiles even after the Multi-fiber Agreement expired in 2005.

Surprisingly, the Chinese economy remained robust after WTO entry, attracting more foreign-direct investment that aided capital accumulation. Although Chinese state-owned enterprises and banks faced difficult challenges, large-scale dislocation did not occur. The Chinese government used a variety of technical measures to cushion the impact of trade liberalization that had already been set in motion and is expected to be completed by 2008.

This chapter examines the commitments that Taiwan and China made prior to WTO entry and the impacts of these commitments on their respective economies immediately after accession. In addition, we will briefly discuss the effect of WTO membership on cross-strait economic relations. Both China and Taiwan have benefited from WTO membership and they have also deepened their economic interdependence.

TAIWAN'S CONCESSIONS

Concessions on Industrial Goods

Prior to WTO entry, Taiwan's average tariff rate for industrial goods was 6.03 percent. Taiwan promised to cut average tariff rates to 5.78 percent in 2002, the first year of accession. More tariff cuts were to be made in the following years, eventually leading to an average tariff rate of 4.15 percent. Most tariff cuts were to be implemented over a five-year period, albeit with a few exceptions, such as automobiles, where the tariff was to be reduced gradually over a ten-year period, until it reaches the final target of 17.5 percent. Although, in proportional terms, the reduction from 6.03 percent to 4.15 percent does seem substantial, given that average tariff rates were fairly low to begin with, the degree of protection afforded to Taiwan's industry will not change dramatically.

During the bilateral negotiations leading to WTO accession, Taiwan accepted a zero-for-zero tariff scheme for spirits, medicine, medical equipment, furniture, paper, steel, and beer with the EU (with a very strong interest in spirits), and for medicine and medical equipment with the U.S. Taiwan also agreed to allow free importation of certain types of machinery, in which the EU has a competitive edge, such as that used in mineral exploration and processing. In the areas of furniture and toys, Taiwan had formerly been a major exporter to both the United States and Europe. Although these industries have now lost their competitiveness, the export-oriented structure of the industry has allowed Taiwan to face import competition without affecting the vested interest groups. Taiwan also accepted the principle of tariff harmonization imposed on chemical products. All chemical products were to be categorized into three groups, with a uniform tariff rate being applied to each group, that is, 0 percent for raw materials, 5.5 percent for intermediate goods, and 6.5 percent for final products.

In 1997, following the Asia Pacific Economic Cooperation (APEC) initiative, Taiwan signed the Information Technology Agreement (ITA), which by the time of Taiwan's WTO accession, had succeeded in eliminating tariffs on most information products, such as computers, telecommunications equipment, semiconductors, and semiconductor equipment.

During the bilateral negotiations, the major concern of the Taiwan government was the automobile industry, to which Taiwan had consistently applied very high tariffs, for example, 30 percent on passenger cars with an engine capacity of 3.0 liters or below, and 42 percent on cars with an engine capacity exceeding 3.0 liters. (In comparison, China's tariffs were 70 percent and 80 percent, respectively.)

Furthermore, only cars produced in North America and Western Europe were allowed to be imported, and cars manufactured elsewhere were prohibited. This geographical trade preference constituted a conspicuous violation of the most-favored-nation principle.

Prior to WTO entry, a total of 11 automobile manufacturers operated on the island, all of which were involved in joint ventures with Japanese auto manufacturers. The notable exceptions were Ford (Taiwan) and Ching-Chung that is a joint venture with Volkswagen. Given Taiwan's small market, each of these automobile manufacturers produced only a small number of cars, and as such none had the economies of scale that would enable it to compete in the global market. They survived only because of trade protection.

The Taiwan government decided to abandon tax incentive schemes on local-design-and-content requirements in exchange for the preservation of high tariffs. To a certain extent, the tactic worked, largely because U.S.-based Ford held a strong position in the Taiwan market and elimination of the local content requirement reduced its production costs. The repeal of the tax incentives on model designs also favored Ford as this put it on a level playing field with other manufacturers in which local partners had majority ownership since this gave them a stronger incentive to design their own models.

In the bilateral negotiations that concluded on August 6, 1998, the U.S. agreed to Taiwan's proposal to cut automobile tariffs from the existing levels to 20 percent within ten years of WTO accession, provided that Taiwan would also agree to repeal the tax incentive for model design and eliminate local content requirements upon accession. In fact, the U.S. requested and Taiwan accepted that it cut the local content ratio from 50 percent to 40 percent prior to WTO entry, effective January 1, 1999. The United States also demanded that Taiwan unify the commodity tax at 25 percent for cars and trucks with different engine capacities. Taiwan had previously applied higher tariff rates and higher commodity tax rates on cars and trucks with larger engine capacities, a category to which most U.S.-made vehicles belong. This demand was also satisfied. The U.S. further demanded that Taiwan regulate the used-car market, which until then had been ungoverned. In particular, the U.S. demanded that the same business tax that was applied to new cars should also be applied to used-car transactions.

Although negotiators in Taiwan appeared to be satisfied with these compromises in exchange for the U.S. agreement that Taiwan could maintain 20 percent tariffs after a ten-year adjustment period, at subsequent negotiations, EU negotiators then dropped a bombshell. They demanded that import tariffs be reduced further to 15 percent. With the exception of one small operation by Volkswagen in the form of licensed production, the EU did not have any presence in the Taiwan market, and therefore did not have any market share to protect.

Agricultural Concessions

Prior to WTO accession, Taiwan applied regional trade preferences to the importation of fruit, including pears, lemons, apples, grapes, plums, and grapefruit, with the major beneficiary from this trade preference being the U.S. that enjoyed full market access, whereas many other countries were totally excluded. Since such preferential treatment was a conspicuous violation of the MFN principle, Taiwan agreed to remove these discriminatory measures upon accession to the WTO.

Taiwan had also previously prohibited the importation of a whole range of agricultural products, for which Taiwan now offered to impose a tariff-quota scheme. In the end, 21 agricultural products were placed under the tariff quota, including mushrooms, garlic, day lilies, peanuts, red beans, betel nuts, oriental pears, pomelos, coconuts, persimmons, longans, pineapples, mangoes, bananas, pork, chicken, liquid milk, and a list of fish species. With the notable exceptions of pork and chicken, the production volume of all these items, in fact, was quite small. Taiwan further agreed to allow less sensitive agricultural products, such as tea leaves, onions, plums, oranges, lemons, apples, papayas, and grapefruits, to be imported under the tariff regime free of quota restrictions. The latter group is the area in which major U.S. interests reside, and after removing regional preferences, the U.S. demanded a reduction in tariffs to compensate for the loss of import privileges.

The United States was also interested in Taiwan's markets for chicken and red meat since importation of chicken had been prohibited before the bilateral negotiations began. After a series of confrontational negotiations that involved 301 actions by the U.S. Trade Representative in the late 1980s, turkeys were allowed to be imported. In concluding its bilateral negotiations with the U.S., Taiwan pledged to allow U.S. chicken meat to be imported into Taiwan prior to the island's WTO accession. A quota of 10,000 metric tons was granted for the first year after signing the bilateral agreement, with the quota to be renewed on an annual basis. This quota was to be raised to 19,163 metric tons upon WTO accession, and to 45,990 metric tons by 2004. The quota controls were to be completely removed in 2005, thereafter allowing unrestricted imports.

In the area of red meat, Taiwan agreed to establish a quota for the U.S. of 7,500 metric tons of pork offal and 5,000 metric tons of beef offal, at the then-applied tariff rates. Upon WTO accession, the quotas were to be removed and replaced by a tariff rate of 25 percent, which was to be phased down to 15 percent by 2004. At the time of its WTO accession, Taiwan was also to establish a tariff quota for 10,000 metric tons of pork hocks, feet, stomachs, skirts, intestines, and rectums. The size of this quota would grow incrementally to reach 27,500 metric tons by 2004. Similarly, an annual quota of 5,000 metric tons of pork bellies and other pork cuts was to be established prior to accession. The quota on pork cuts would be removed upon accession and replaced by a tariff. The quota on port bellies would increase to 6,160 metric tons upon WTO accession, increasing in further increments to 15,400 metric tons by 2004. The quota on pork bellies was also set to be replaced by a tariff beginning on January 1, 2005. In other words, quotas were established for red meat prior to accession, and were to be replaced by tariffs in subsequent years.

Similar pre-accession quota arrangements were made with the EU. Taiwan agreed to establish quotas for the EU of 3,000 metric tons of apples and 1,500 metric tons of oranges. Taiwan also agreed to establish a global quota of 1,160 metric tons of pork bellies,

9,163 metric tons of chicken offal, 2,500 metric tons of pork offal, and 5,000 metric tons of beef offal from all countries, with the exception of the U.S. This was aimed at providing equal access to EU meat products.

Pre-accession quotas were also established for agricultural products from Australia and New Zealand. A quota of 2,400 metric tons of apples, 1,000 metric tons of peaches and plums, and 600 metric tons of oranges was established for Australia. It was also offered a reduction in specific tariffs on its beef from NT$ 30 to NT$ 27 per kilogram, bringing it on an even keel with the specific tariffs applied to American Prime and Choice, and Canadian AAA beef. This was to be implemented prior to WTO accession. It is clear that Australian beef has suffered from tariff discrimination since the mid-1980s. Nevertheless, the United States subsequently negotiated a tariff margin for its Prime Choice beef at NT$ 20 per kilogram, while Australian beef remains subject to a tariff of NT$ 25 per kilogram.

For New Zealand, quotas of 8,000 metric tons were established for apples and quotas of 500 metric tons for peaches and plums. In addition, Taiwan pledged to establish a separate tariff line for New Zealand's blue cod at a 25 percent tariff rate.

Prior to WTO accession, Taiwan's average tariff rate on agricultural products was 20.02 percent. Upon accession, the average rate was cut to 14.01 percent, and was to be further reduced to 12.86 percent by 2011. Prior to accession, 41 tariff lines were either prohibited from importation, or were allowed to be imported only with special permission. Of these, 21 were put under a tariff-quota scheme, and rice was given special treatment, while the rest were rendered freely importable. Special safeguard measures were established for 14 sensitive items in order to guard against any dramatic rise in imports after accession.

Concessions in the Service Sectors

Taiwan proposed its initial offer of commitments to trade in services in July 1994, in accordance with the General Agreement on Trade in Services (GATS), thus setting the stage for the ensuing bilateral negotiations. Again, the greatest hurdle was negotiations with the U.S., which ended in February 1998. Although the U.S. had broad interests in Taiwan's service industry, one of the foci of the bilateral negotiations was telecommunications, where the U.S. demanded that Taiwan reduce access fees to basic telecommunications networks monopolized by the state-owned Chunghwa Telecom. The United States also required that Taiwan allow foreign participation in ownership of telecommunications operations, with Taiwan subsequently agreeing to a 20-percent limit on foreign ownership. The United States also demanded market access to professional services, particularly in the case of legal services, as it wanted foreign law firms practicing foreign law in Taiwan to be allowed to hire local lawyers. Finally, the U.S. also required that foreign lawyers be allowed to become partners in law firms in Taiwan. Taiwan agreed to amend related laws within three years of WTO accession to accommodate these demands. These bilateral negotiations with the U.S. involved 11 sessions, and the two sides eventually reached agreement in 1998.

Hong Kong was also an active participant in the service-trade negotiations with Taiwan. Hong Kong's major concerns were in the areas of banking, insurance, securities, telecommunications, maritime transportation, and foreign investment in equity markets. Taiwan's major concession was a pledge to remove the upper limit on foreign investment in Taiwan's stock markets.

Bilateral negotiations between Taiwan and Japan focused on the areas of legal services, courier services, financial services, maritime transportation, and construction services. Particular attention was paid to Taiwan's restrictions on Japanese films, which Taiwan duly removed in October 1994.

Bilateral negotiations with the EU took place during nine separate sessions until final agreement was reached. The focus of these negotiations was on financial services, maritime transportation, inland transportation, telecommunications, and legal services. The major concessions made by Taiwan included the abolition of the requirement that there be a two-year waiting period for a foreign-owned bank to establish a new branch in Taiwan; a commitment to open the market for basic telecommunications services; and permission for foreigners to operate car-leasing businesses in Taiwan.

In sum, major commitments made by Taiwan in service-trade negotiations included the following:

Telecommunications services. Foreigners are allowed to provide telecommunications services if they establish a locally-incorporated company in which their direct ownership is limited to 20 percent. With the notable exception of the state-owned provider, Chunghwa Telecom, foreigners may increase their share of ownership in these companies through a third party, up to 60 percent. Foreigners are not allowed to serve as chairmen on the boards of telecommunications companies and the number of foreign nationals on the boards of directors may not exceed half the total number of directors.

Insurance services. Foreign insurance companies are allowed to provide cross-border insurance policies covering sea-going vessels and planes, including the commodities carried by them. Cross-border consumption by Taiwan nationals is allowed for life-insurance policies, but the advertisement of such trade in Taiwan by foreign-based insurance companies is not. Foreign insurance companies are allowed to take part in Taiwan's insurance market in the form of a subsidiary, branch, joint venture, or representative office. Foreigners are also allowed to establish business operations to serve as insurance agents, brokers, notary-service providers, or salespersons.

Banking services. The cross-border supply of banking services is allowed, but the advertisement of such trade is allowed only for foreign banks with a local establishment in Taiwan. Upon WTO accession, Taiwan nationals were allowed to open overseas bank accounts and transfer funds into them. Foreigners were allowed to establish locally-incorporated banks, foreign bank branches, branches of international banking services, foreign-exchange dealerships, credit-card issuers, bill-financing companies, and investment-trust companies (with certain ownership restrictions). Foreign-owned banks could also participate in policy-loan consortia organized by the government.

Securities industry. Foreign securities firms are allowed to participate in the trading of stocks, over-the-counter shares, futures contracts, and their derivatives. Cross-border supply of services, however, is not allowed. Foreign securities firms may also engage in the underwriting of newly-issued shares and fund-raising operations. They are also allowed to provide asset-management services (including pension fund and trust management) and clearance services in Taiwan.

CHINA'S CONCESSIONS

Tariffs

In 2001, China's average tariff on industrial goods stood at 12.59 percent, and on agricultural goods at 19.28 percent. China pledged to reduce average tariffs on industrial goods to 8.92 percent by 2008, and to 15.02 percent on agricultural goods by 2010. Concessions on both industrial and agricultural goods were substantial. China agreed to put all tariff lines under binding constraints and all tariffs were to take the ad valorem form. This commitment means substantial tariff cuts were to be made in industries that had been previously designated by the Chinese government as import-substitution industries, including consumer electronics, textiles, bicycles, motorcycles, automobiles, and liquor, among others. For example, in the automobile industry, import tariffs ranged from 70 percent to 100 percent in 2001. These were to be sliced to 25 percent in 2006. Import tariffs on auto parts were to be reduced from 30 percent to 80 percent in 2001 to a mere 10 percent in 2006. For information-technology products, China agreed to sign on to the Information Technology Agreement, whereby tariffs on computers, semiconductors, telecommunications equipment, and semiconductor-making machinery, among others, were to be eliminated by 2005. In fact, China agreed to eliminate tariffs on 117 information-technology products upon accession and on another 93 items in the following year. When fully implemented, more than 90 percent of information products will be imported free of duty.

China committed to even more drastic tariff cuts in agricultural trade, where the U.S. has a strong interest and China has a large farming population to protect. For example, tariffs on beef cuts were scheduled to be reduced from 45 percent to 12 percent by 2004, and on beef carcasses from 45 percent to 20 percent. Tariffs on butter were to be cut from 50 percent to 10 percent, on milk and cream products from 25 percent to 10–15 percent, on grapes to 13 percent, on citrus products to 12 percent, and on apples and pears to 10 percent.

QUOTAS AND IMPORT CONTROLS

Before WTO accession, China applied import quotas on various products targeted under the import-substitution policy. Most quotas were allocated to state-owned enterprises by administrative discretion. China agreed to eliminate all quotas by 2008, except for a few items that will remain under the tariff-quota regime, including wheat, corn, rice, cotton, wool, sugar, vegetable oils, and fertilizers — all related to agriculture. The in-quota tariffs for the above items are in the range of 1 percent to 9 percent and the volume of the quota is to increase over time. Moreover, each year, a portion of each tariff quota is to be reserved for importation by non-state trading entities. In the industrial sector, at least 240 products were targeted for quota removal, including refrigerators, cathode ray tubes (used in televisions and computers), tape recorders, crude oil, refined oil, tires, cameras, watches, and motorcycles. Even import quotas on automobiles that were considered a strategic industry and protected by market-entry restrictions were to be eliminated as early as 2005. Along with the removal of import quotas, the once-tedious import-licensing procedures were to be either simplified or abolished. China also agreed to abide by the WTO Agreement on Import Licensing Procedures to ensure the transparency and predictability of license approval.

TRADING AND DISTRIBUTION RIGHTS

Before WTO accession, foreign-owned enterprises were denied the right to import and distribute goods, except in the case of materials needed for production in China. Foreign-owned enterprises were also denied the right to export goods from China, except for their own production. In fact, China reserved most trading rights for its state enterprises. Upon accession to the WTO, China committed to making full trading rights available to all enterprises within three years, including for joint ventures and wholly foreign-owned enterprises. China also agreed to remove eligibility requirements for obtaining trading rights, such as for export performance, trade balancing, foreign-exchange balancing, and prior-experience requirements.

China also agreed to offer foreign-owned enterprises the right to distribute products and to provide related services in China within three years of WTO accession, subject to limited product exceptions. During the transition period, China would offer distribution rights to different enterprises progressively: first to Chinese-owned enterprises, then to minority foreign-owned joint-ventures, then to majority foreign-owned joint ventures, and finally to wholly foreign-owned enterprises. The product exceptions included chemical fertilizers, processed oil, and crude oil, which were to be eliminated within five years. Only salt and tobacco will remain inaccessible to foreign-owned companies. But China reserved the rights to impose geographic and quantitative restrictions on retail services until 2005.

THE SERVICES INDUSTRY

Until WTO entry, China's services industry had been heavily-protected and regulated. Foreign service providers were only allowed to operate in restricted areas, such as Shanghai and Shenzhen, under the terms of experimental licenses. As a result of the WTO negotiations, China committed to a substantial opening in a broad range of services sectors, such as banking, insurance, telecommunications, and professional services, through the elimination of many of the existing limitations on market access. These commitments were considered by the U.S. Trade Representative (USTR) as "far-reaching," compared with commitments by other WTO members.[1] One estimate put the coverage of market access commitments at 57.4 percent, higher than the commitments offered by any other group of countries in the Uruguay Round.[2]

For example, before WTO accession, China allowed foreign banks to conduct only foreign-currency business in selected cities. China also allowed some foreign banks to conduct local currency business on an experimental basis, but this was limited to foreign customers. Upon WTO accession, China committed to a five-year phase-in for foreign banks to provide full banking services. Immediately following accession, China would allow foreign banks to provide foreign-currency services to foreign enterprises and foreign individuals, subject to some geographic restrictions. Within two years of WTO accession, foreign banks would be allowed to conduct domestic-currency business with Chinese enterprises. Within five years, foreign banks would be allowed to conduct domestic-currency business with Chinese individuals and all geographic limitations would be removed.

Similar restrictions were imposed on the insurance sector before WTO entry. China committed to phase-out all geographic restrictions on all types of insurance operations during the first three years after accession. Ownership restrictions on insurance operators would also be lifted within the same time-span. Upon accession, foreign life-insurance companies would be allowed to hold up to 50 percent equity shares in joint ventures. Foreign property, casualty, and other non-life-insurance companies would be allowed to establish a branch or to hold 51-percent equity shares in a joint venture. Wholly-owned foreign insurance operators would be permitted within two years of WTO accession.

---

[1] USTR, *Report to Congress on China's WTO Compliance* (Washington, DC: USTR, 2002), 62.

[2] Aaditya Mattoo, "China's Accession to the WTO: The Service Dimension," *Journal of International Economic Law* 6, No. 2 (2003), 299–339.

IMPACT OF THE WTO COMMITMENTS ON THE DOMESTIC ECONOMIES

Impact on Taiwan

Taiwan's economy underwent immense structural changes in the 1990s as a result of reforms aimed at securing the island's accession to the WTO. Due to the rising wages and outward investment, the share of national production accounted for by the island's manufacturing industry fell. In its place, the services sector now accounts for a majority of the island's GDP. However, although services accounted for 66 percent of GDP in 2002, the sector was generally outmoded and was largely incompatible with Taiwan's open economy that had largely become integrated with the global economy. Government initiatives to develop Taiwan into a regional operations center were put in place in 1995, coinciding with the drive toward WTO accession. This initiative highlighted the themes of liberalization and deregulation, with concessions made in the island's WTO negotiations serving as its commitment to this goal.

In fact, the liberalization of the financial sector was under way as early as the late 1980s when, after a 30-year moratorium, new licenses for private banks, insurance companies, and security firms were issued, and competition intensified. Although Taiwan's WTO commitments have further opened financial markets to foreign competition, the impact has not been too severe. The banking industry, for example, has essentially been in recession since the mid-1990s, due to the bursting of the real estate bubble that created a flood of non-performing loans. The situation was exacerbated by an excessive number of newly-established private banks fighting for the already stagnant loan market that was dominated by state-owned banks. Beginning in 2000, domestic banks entered a phase of consolidation by merging with non-banking financial institutions, such as securities houses and insurance companies, to form financial-holding companies. This was in line with the global trend toward universal banking and with government aspirations to increase the size of local financial institutions in preparation for intensified foreign competition. With the exception of some merger-and-acquisition opportunities, foreign banks found little room in the saturated sector.

More positive developments were observed in the equity market. Although bank credits stagnated due to structural problems within the industry, nevertheless, the local stock market began to expand and take up the slack. The government first allowed foreign-based institutional investors to invest in the Taiwan Stock Exchange under strict restrictions with regard to capital flows. The regulatory scheme, referred to as the Qualified Institutional Investors (QFII) scheme, required foreign investors to apply for an investment-funds quota and to remit funds under the supervision of the Ministry of Finance and the Taipei-based Central Bank of China. In August 2003, the government removed the quota restrictions to allow free movement of investment funds and abolished the QFII scheme altogether in November 2003. This allowed all foreign investors to participate in Taiwan's stock markets.

The Taiwan government assessed the possible WTO impact on the manufacturing sector and identified automobiles, consumer electronics, electric equipment, and paper as the sectors that were most likely to lose out. All were domestic-market-oriented and lacked the ability to export. Consumer electronics, where tariffs were to be lowered in several stages, had been on the decline since Taiwan first opened its domestic market to imports in 1986. Since then, Japanese and South Korean TVs and refrigerators had swamped the Taiwan market with new models at low prices, and local producers of consumer electronics started investing in China in an attempt to reduce costs.

Following WTO accession, local producers began importing mostly semi-finished products from China in an attempt to fight off Japanese and South Korean competition. At the same time, they exported key components of consumer electronics, such as CRTs used in TV receivers and air compressors used in air conditioners, to China. These components became an important weapon in the fight against Japanese and South Korean imports by Chinese producers.[3]

[3] Chen Tain-Jy, "Will Taiwan be Marginalized by China?" *Asian Economic Papers* 2, No. 2 (2003), 78–105.

Also beginning in 2003, flat-panel-TV receivers, made from Taiwan-manufactured flat panels and assembled in China, began entering the Taiwan market at ultra-low prices, which surprised even the South Korean producers. The industry is still struggling through this new phase of competition, but seems to have found a niche.

Data on automobile production and sales since January 2002 show that Taiwan's auto deals have been very effective in protecting local car manufacturers. U.S. and European car manufacturers have been unable to consume their quotas, while the Japanese have been consuming the global quota in addition to their country quota. In 2002, U.S. cars imports totaled 1,526 units, equivalent to 1 percent of the U.S. quota, whereas cars imported from the EU totaled 26,872 units, equivalent to 17 percent of the EU quota. Meanwhile, Japan exported 11,683 units of cars to Taiwan, equivalent to 117 percent of the country quota (see Table 2.1). Japanese car manufacturers have pursued a market-segmentation strategy that allows ample room for the survival of local joint ventures. A typical strategy for Japanese car manufacturers is to import full-sized and luxury cars from Japan to complement locally-produced small- and mid-sized cars. Toyota, for example, exports the Lexus brand to Taiwan, while allowing its local subsidiary in Taiwan to produce the Camry, Corolla, and Tercel models. Nissan also exports its Infiniti luxury model from Japan, while allowing its local subsidiary to produce the Cefiro and Sentra models in Taiwan.

Table 2.1 Automobile Imports to Taiwan, 2002

Source of Import	Units Imported	Country Quota	Quota Utilization Rate (%)
U.S.	1,526	159,220	1.0
EU	26,872	159,220	16.8
Canada	679	12,912	5.3
Japan	11,683	10,000	116.8
South Korea	5,160	10,000	51.6
Other	2,281	10,000 per country	–
Total	48,201		

The country quota for Japan was allocated among Japanese car manufacturers by the Japanese government with the overall aim of maximizing the utilization rate. Car manufacturers that use the quota more efficiently are awarded more cars. Toyota, for example, was given just over 1,000 units in 1997, but its quota for 2003 was raised to 4,565 units. The global quota, on the other hand, is allocated by the Taiwan government, which distributes it to local producers in proportion to the local production volume so as to minimize the impact on local industry. For example, when Honda ceased production in Taiwan in 2002, its global quota was also removed (see Table 2.2).

However, factors that have had the greatest impact on Taiwan's automobile industry since its accession to the WTO have not been the concessions made by the government, but rather the rise of China as a rapidly-growing market for automobiles. As all major auto manufacturers rushed to invest in China and produce vehicles there, Taiwan's auto industry was in a strategic position to provide support to vehicle manufacturing in China. Taiwan car manufacturers, such as Yulong (allied with Nissan of Japan) and Chunghwa (allied with Mitsubishi of Japan) took full advantage of this strategic

Table 2.2 Distribution of Quota Allocations among Japanese Car Manufacturers, 2003

Car Manufacturers	Country Quota	Global Quota	Actual Imports*
Toyota	4,565	1,563	5,079
Mazda	3,499	1,051	3,753
Nissan	634	1,688	512
Mitsubishi	680	2,007	1,159
Honda	160	–	–
Suzuki	1,196	281	981
Daihatsu	627	–	573
Isuzu	50	141	33
Subaru	229	–	209
Total	11,700	7,800	

Note: * Figures refer to cumulative number of units from January 2003 to August 2003.
Source: Shen Mei-shin, "Fengtian yu Mazda ying zai bei'e celue" (Toyota and Mazda Won by Quota Strategies), *Commercial Times*, September 29, 2003.

position. Together with Nissan, Yulong formed a joint venture with the Chinese auto manufacturer, Dongfeng, while Chunghwa, along with its Japanese partner, Mitsubishi, invested in China's Southeast Autos. Both have enjoyed remarkable success in terms of market penetration in the largely-segmented Chinese market. Through their production bases in China, Yulong and Chunghwa have been able to enlarge the scale of parts production and are now able even to design a portion of the new car models in cooperation with the Japanese partners, thus facilitating a division of labor among Taiwan, China, and Japan. China's concessions on the importation of auto parts and eventual elimination of local content requirements appear to have become more important for the future of Taiwan's car manufacturers than the concessions made by Taiwan itself.

Despite Taiwan's commitment to liberalization of the local car market, Honda of Japan, after leaving its previous joint-venture partner, invested in a new plant in southern Taiwan in 2002. It is obvious that the local market is not the key to Honda's decision, but rather the production capabilities that Taiwan had accumulated over the years under heavy trade protectionism. These capabilities may be useful to Honda's overall production network in Asia, encompassing production bases in China, Thailand, and elsewhere.[4]

The government estimated a loss in agricultural output valued at NT$ 24.7 billion for the first year (2002), equivalent to 6.8 percent of total production. This production loss was estimated to increase to NT$ 54.2 billion by 2004, equivalent to 14 percent of the total production volume for 2000. The opening of agricultural trade will inevitably lead to a general shrinkage of farming area which, according to government estimates, was reduced by 53,000 hectares in the first year after WTO accession — a figure that was expected to rise to 86,000 hectares by 2004.

The greatest impact was on rice farming. Taiwan has agreed to allow trading under the special treatment defined by the WTO Agriculture Agreement in accordance with the Japanese model,

[4] See Chwo-Ming Joseph Yu's chapter in this volume for a case study of the impact of WTO accession on the automobile sector.

whereby minimum access, equivalent to 8 percent of domestic consumption, is to be set aside for imported rice. The government also pledged to lift the ban on selling government-owned buffer rice on the domestic market. Buffer rice comes mainly from the government's price-guarantee program that offers rice farmers above-market prices. Previously, any over-accumulated buffer rice was discharged by the government only in export markets, often at low prices; this was considered an export subsidy by U.S. officials. Discharging this excess on the domestic market depresses the domestic price of rice, thereby reducing the actual subsidy to domestic rice farmers. Since the minimum market access of 8 percent, or 144,720 metric tons of rice, had to be imported in 2002, this alone would have reduced the overall rice farming area by 30,000 hectares.

Several measures have been introduced to help the agricultural sector adjust to the new trading regime. First, the government has encouraged farmers to reduce the area of rice cultivation by providing a subsidy to farmers who do not grow a second crop — Taiwan's rice farmers normally grow two rice crops per year. In particular, the government has provided NT$ 46,000 for each hectare of rice paddies that is turned over to leaf vegetables, instead of rice. Second, the government has amended the law to allow non-farmers to own farmland and to reclassify some farmland as industrial or commercial land. The plan is to release 160,000 hectares of farmland by 2011. Third, the government has encouraged the development of the tourist-farming industry to combine tourism with farming; notable examples are fruit-picking farms, vineyards, and recreational farms. The idea is to develop some non-tradable elements of the farming industry so as to protect the sector from foreign competition. Fourth, the government has provided pensions to elderly farmers ahead of the national pension program. A minimum living support of NT$ 4,000 per month was considered necessary because this sector of the population is aging much more rapidly than the rest of society.

Some segments of the farming industry, notably aquaculture, underwent restructuring long before WTO accession. Shrimp and fish farming was an important export sector in Taiwan before the 1980s, but this industry suffered from both rising wages and land sinkage due to the over-extraction of underground water. Some farmers began to migrate to Southeast Asia, with their technology, capital, and market connections, and the prospects for WTO accession accelerated the process.

The sector has been further squeezed since WTO accession by the importation of high-quality foreign-sourced fish. Although the average tariff on imported fish was only modestly reduced from 28 percent to 20 percent, along with a tariff-quota scheme to protect certain kinds of fish that are important to Taiwan fishermen, imports have increased substantially in some high-price fish categories that were not traditional catches for Taiwan fishermen, for example, imports of salmon increased from 11,000 metric tons in 2001 to 14,000 metric tons in 2002, trout from 13,000 metric tons to 35,000 metric tons, and halibut from 14,000 metric tons to 16,000 metric tons. This essentially took away the domestic market share from local fish farmers. However, the industry has shown a significant restructuring effort toward high-quality fishing, particularly toward export markets. For example, from 2001 to 2002, there were significant increases in the export value of eel, tilapia, and garoupa, mainly due to an increase in per-unit export value. Tilapia — a cultivated fish geared toward the domestic market — saw its per-unit export price increase from NT$ 37.61 per kilogram in 2001 to NT$ 47.69 per kilogram in 2002. Therefore, it appeared that WTO accession guided the industry toward international markets.

China was the most attractive destination for farmers who wished to migrate and invest overseas. The migration of eel farmers made China an important platform for eel exports to Japan, which previously had been dominated by products from Taiwan. A similar pattern was observed for flower and fruit plantations. Some of this investment is aimed at the local Chinese market, some for export to third countries. As a result of overseas investment, protection of species and agricultural know-how has now become an important issue in Taiwan.[5]

[5] See Robert Ash's chapter in this volume for a more detailed analysis of the impact on agriculture.

IMPACT ON CHINA

After accession to the WTO, the greatest impact on China was felt in agriculture and the service sectors. A modest impact was expected on manufacturing where capital and technology-intensive industries would be adversely affected by surging imports, whereas labor-intensive industries were expected to gain from increasing access to foreign markets. At the firm level, state-owned enterprises were expected to be hard hit, whereas foreign-invested enterprises were expected to gain from the rights to trade and distribute goods in the Chinese market.

Three years after WTO accession, the outcomes largely fell in line with expectations, except for agriculture. It was expected that after WTO accession, Chinese agricultural land would decrease by 18.38 percent and the income of rural residents would fall by 2.05 percent by 2005.[6] But from 2001 to 2003, this gloomy picture did not emerge. Grain imports actually decreased. Although imports of palm oil, sugar, and oil increased, they still fell short of set quotas. Apparent improvements in agriculture technologies and the switch from grains to cash and feed crops helped to dampen imports.[7] The decrease in grain production also led to an expansion in livestock and aquatic products.[8]

WTO membership had an impact on capital-intensive industries, most obviously steel, which had been targeted by the Chinese government for import substitution. Imports increased substantially following WTO accession, but this surge was fueled more by increased domestic consumption that, in turn, was driven by a booming economy, rather than by tariff reductions. China's steel consumption was 114 million metric tons in 2000. It increased to 182 million metric

[6] Lian Xiao, "China in the WTO: Impact to Its People and Asia," 2004, http://www.daga.org/ds/dsp00/dl3m-g.htm (accessed January 1, 2005).

[7] China Internet Information Center, "Domestic Industry Feels Impact of WTO Membership," 2002, http://www.china.org.cn (accessed December 11, 2002).

[8] Liu Zhenwei, "Agricultural Policy Adjustment in China after WTO Accession," in *Agricultural Policies in China after WTO Accession* (Paris: OECD, 2002).

tons in 2002 and was estimated at 260 million metric tons in 2003. State-owned steel companies were hit hard by imports in higher-value segments of steel products, such as cold-rolled plates, hot-rolled plates, stainless-steel plates, cold-rolled magnetic-silicon steel, and special seamless pipelines. State-owned steel companies jointly brought an anti-dumping case against imports from Taiwan, South Korea, Russia, Ukraine, and Kazakhstan in 2001, and the Chinese government concurred. But later on, the investigation into anti-dumping was suspended and replaced by safeguard measures as retaliation against tariffs imposed by the Bush administration on imported steel in March 2002. When the U.S. lifted tariffs after they had been declared illegal by the WTO, China reopened the case and imposed anti-dumping duties. Despite the protectionist measure, imports of steel continued to pour into the Chinese market, which in turn spurred feverish domestic investment in steel mills. Beginning in late 2003, worldwide steel prices were bid up by the skyrocketing Chinese demand. Prices of cold-rolled steel sheets, for example, rose from U.S.$ 390 per ton in December 2003 to U.S.$ 460 in February 2004.[9]

The impact of imports on the auto industry has yet to be felt because, as of this writing, imports are still restrained by quotas. After China's WTO entry, a rush of international automakers invested in China to gain a foothold in the rapidly-growing market. They quickly increased production capacity in China, and vehicle sales in China reached 3.3 million units in 2002, further increasing to 4.6 million in 2003, making China the fourth-largest automobile-producing country in the world. Vehicle imports reached 172,683 units in 2003, almost doubling the volume in 2001, but the import share of total consumption actually fell. Chinese quotas from 2001 to 2004 are stipulated in terms of value, rather than volume; so imported vehicles consist mainly of high-priced large-sized cars. The Chinese government still only allowed joint ventures, and foreign automakers were not allowed to enter as fully-owned

[9] Jeffrey Sparshott, "US Steel Makers are Alarmed by Spiraling Costs," *Knight Rider Tribune News*, March 10, 2004, 1.

subsidiaries. Major domestic automakers, such as Shanghai Auto, First Auto, and Dongfeng, paired with various foreign automakers. After WTO entry, there was an increase in the degree of market concentration as established firms expanded capacity to capture market share. Tariffs on auto parts were also reduced significantly, which induced a substantial increase in imports. China agreed to comply with the Trade-Related Investment Measures (TRIMS) regulations immediately following WTO accession, whereby local content regulations were removed. This encouraged the import of auto parts.

In labor-intensive industries, the most apparent beneficiary has been the textile and garment industry. Prompted by the phase-out of MFA quotas, China's exports of textiles and garments to the U.S. surged 125 percent in 2002 over the previous year, surpassing exports from Mexico. For the first time since NAFTA took effect in 1994, China became the top exporter of textile products to the U.S. For example, as the quota on infant garments was removed in 2001, U.S. imports from China increased 9 times in 2002.[10] In response to a petition from the domestic textile industry, the U.S. government imposed quotas on Chinese-made bras, dressing gowns, and knit fabrics, invoking special safeguard measures that the U.S. had arranged with China as a part of the WTO accession package.

In the high-technology industries, China won enthusiastic support from foreign investors who saw China as a low-cost manufacturing base whose access to foreign markets had been guaranteed by China's WTO membership. This was particularly evident in the case of information-technology products. Taiwan computer makers, along with competitors from South Korea and Japan, began to invest in China in 2001. Following the infusion of foreign capital, China quickly emerged as the world's third-largest producer of IT products after the U.S. and Japan, while Taiwan fell to fourth place. It is

[10] Tony Mecia, "Textile Imports from China Double," *Knight Ridder Tribune News*, February 21, 2003, 1.

estimated that over 70 percent of IT exports from China were made by multinational firms.[11] Even products oriented toward local markets were largely made locally, instead of being imported, despite China's agreement to sign the ITA by 2005.

In the services sector where a huge impact was expected, the outcome was not as severe as previously thought. In the retail, banking, and insurance industries, the Chinese government used geographical restrictions on foreign operators to protect domestic firms. In terms of market share, domestic firms still dominate the industries, but there is no telling whether this market position will be maintained after China abolished geographical restrictions in 2005. For example, U.S.-based Walmart and France-based Carrefour are taking larger and larger stakes in local retail joint ventures and quickly expanding their market reach. After Carrefour opened two stores in Shanghai, three state-owned retailers folded.[12] It was feared that these multinational conglomerates would overwhelm small Chinese retail stores through mergers and acquisitions. The Chinese government planned to consolidate local retailers into 15 to 20 business groups to counter the foreign forces.

On the other hand, as of December 2003, foreign banks were allowed to conduct foreign-currency business across China, whereas renminbi business was restricted to four cities: Shanghai, Shenzhen, Tianjin, and Dalian. Chinese banks still dominate the market at the present time, but the number of foreign banks is increasing rapidly, despite China's strict capitalization requirements that are set above international standards.

With China's commitments to liberalize its trade regime, it was expected that China's trade with the rest of the world would increase substantially after WTO accession, and indeed that has

[11] Jiang Xiaojuan, "FDI in China: Contributions to Growth, Restructuring and Competitiveness," paper presented at the Korea Institute for International Economic Policy, 2004.

[12]China Economic Information Network, "One Carrefour Made Three State Enterprises Bankrupt: A Hard Time for Domestic Retailers," 2004, http://www1.cei.gov.cn/hottopic/ (accessed February 2, 2004).

occurred. China's total trade exceeded U.S.$ 800 billion in 2003, making China the fourth-largest trader in the world, behind only the U.S., Japan, and Germany. Although China has invented some technical barriers to protect its domestic industry, it has complied with its WTO commitments to a large extent. In the industrial sector, tariffs have been reduced and quota controls lessened. But some foreign traders have complained about a lack of transparency in quota allocations. Accusations raised by foreign traders include: delays in announcements of quota applications; insufficient time allowed for preparation for quota allocation requests; lack of open-bidding processes to earn quotas; apparent priority given to exporting firms vis-à-vis domestic consumers in receiving quotas; false fulfillment of quota allowances by counting auto-parts imports as automobile imports by the Chinese authorities; and the like.[13] Although China had committed to allow quota-holders, most of which were state-owned companies, to transfer quota rights to private firms, the government discouraged them from doing so.

In addition to the erection of procedural barriers, China also used domestic taxes to distort trade. China applied a heavy 17 percent value-added tax (VAT) on domestically-traded commodities, but various degrees of rebate were given to certain products used in export-processing. This created a tax distortion in favor of the export industry. In the case of the semiconductor industry, for example, China imposed a 17 percent VAT on ICs traded in China, but 14 percent of the VAT was rebated if the ICs were domestically-made or designed. Tax discrimination negates the impact of the zero tariffs applied on information products in accordance with China's commitment to the ITA. The Chinese government also required end-user certification for imported information products to qualify for zero tariffs. In other words, only products consumed in China qualify for duty-free import, whereas imports for export processing still require payment of duties. After WTO entry, VAT manipulation has become

[13] USTR, *Report to Congress on China's WTO Compliance* (Washington, DC: USTR, 2003), 23–24.

an important tool in China's industrial policy. VAT rebates are also offered to some types of fertilizers produced domestically.

In anticipation of its eventual WTO entry, China gradually adjusted its import-substitution policies in the 1990s. In 1992, China lifted import surcharges and lowered tariffs on more than 3,000 items. Further tariff cuts were made in 1996 and 1997. In 2000 and 2001, China enacted legal changes to eliminate local content requirements for foreign investment, which were aimed at protecting domestically-made intermediate goods. Upon WTO accession, China waived privileges of developing-country status to comply immediately with TRIM rules that prohibit investment measures that distort trade, such as local content requirements.

Prior to WTO entry, China had turned its attention to the development of high-tech industries, which may be unfit for an import-substitution policy. China's tenth five-year economic development plan called for an increase in China's semiconductor output from U.S.$ 2 billion in 2000 to U.S.$ 24 billion in 2010. To boost the semiconductor industry, an 11-percent VAT rebate was offered to domestically-designed or made ICs in 2000. After WTO accession, the Chinese government further raised the VAT rebate to 14 percent in 2002. China also mobilized government resources to jump-start local semiconductor companies.

Technical barriers were also installed to protect domestic producers in the telecommunications equipment industry. Before WTO accession, China used a licensing scheme to limit foreign enterprise rights to sell branded cellular phone sets in China, even if sales were handled by Chinese distributors and the products were made in China. In order to obtain licenses to market products, foreign enterprises were often required to make large investments or critical technology transfers to prevent excessive competition in the local market. Upon WTO accession, China committed to lifting this restriction by 2005, but, at present, it still encourages telecommunications companies to buy components and equipment from domestic sources. Recently, the Chinese government announced that foreign computer and chip makers that want to sell certain kinds of wireless devices in China are required to use Chinese encryption software and to co-produce products with a Chinese company from a designated list.[14]

Despite efforts to lessen the impact of its WTO commitments, Chinese industry was apparently significantly affected by the new trade regime. Rising imports have pushed struggling state enterprises into dire straits. The Chinese government has resorted to anti-dumping and other safeguard measures to aid domestic industry. China enacted an anti-dumping law in 1997, and before joining WTO in 2001, it initiated 32 anti-dumping cases. After joining WTO, in 2002 alone, China initiated 30 anti-dumping cases. Taiwan had never been targeted in the pre-WTO cases, but in the post-WTO era, five cases were brought against Taiwan. Virtually all cases were filed by state-owned enterprises.

CROSS-STRAIT COMPARISONS

China joined the WTO on December 11, 2001 and Taiwan followed on January 1, 2002. After entry, Taiwan has taken major steps to liberalize the cross-strait trade regime, although China has so far refused to negotiate with Taiwan under WTO auspices. On February 15, 2004, the Taiwan government announced that China could be a legal entity as an export destination or import source on trade documents. Previously, China could not be designated as an official trade partner. However, shipments to and from China still have to go through third ports. The government also increased the number of products on the eligibility list for importation from China. Before WTO entry, only 56.3 percent of tariff lines were allowed to be imported from China. Since WTO entry, the eligibility list has been reviewed every six months, and the proportion of importable items exceeded 75 percent by December 2003.

Bilateral trade has increased substantially since WTO accession. Taiwan exported U.S.$ 29.4 billion worth of goods to China in 2002, an increase of 22.4 percent from 2001, making China the largest

[14] *New York Times*, January 15, 2004.

consumer of Taiwan's exports, surpassing even the U.S. In 2003, Taiwan's exports to China further increased to U.S.$ 35.5 billion, accounting for 24.6 percent of total exports. Imports from China also increased dramatically, despite existing restrictions. In 2003, Taiwan imported U.S.$ 11.0 billion worth of Chinese goods, accounting for 8.6 percent of Taiwan's total imports.

Taiwan also liberalized certain services sectors for Chinese investors. In April 2002, Taiwan amended the "Cross-Strait People's Relations Act" whereby Chinese residents were allowed to invest in Taiwan real estate. The government also proposed opening 58 sectors for investment from China within 108 service sectors that Taiwan had committed to offer market access to WTO members. But the law has yet to be enacted. The government expedited visits by Chinese engineers and professionals to Taiwan by shortening waiting-day requirements for visa applications. Significant liberalization also took place in Taiwan's regulations on outward investment in China. Except for a few high-tech industries, Taiwan FDI into China is free of prohibitions. The capital ceiling of U.S.$ 50 million in each investment project was lifted in 2001. According to official Chinese statistics, by 2003, a total of U.S.$ 70 billion had been invested in China by Taiwan enterprises. In 2002 alone, Taiwan invested U.S.$ 52.7 billion in China, and in 2003, despite the outbreak of severe acute respiratory syndrome, it invested U.S.$ 53.5 billion.

Although Taiwan's dependence on China has deepened, Taiwan businesses are less important to China because of the latter's rapid growth. Although China's share of Taiwan's exports has increased significantly since WTO accession, Taiwan's share of China's imports has not increased. Taiwan ranked as China's second-largest import source, accounting for 11.9 percent of China's total imports in 2003, but its share fell from 12.9 percent in 2002. China had been the predominant recipient of Taiwan's capital exports, but Taiwan's position as China's capital supplier has diminished. In recent years, China regularly took 50 percent of Taiwan's outward FDI, but Taiwan's position in China's inward FDI has fallen from second place to sixth place. This implies that Taiwan's bargaining power with China has declined.

CONCLUSIONS

Prior to WTO accession, Taiwan's import-competing sector suffered more from resource competition in domestic export industries than from imports. As the export industry thrived through policy inducements, the import-competing sector lost in attractiveness in its bid for human and financial resources. The trade surplus created by strong exports led to a currency appreciation that automatically reduced the level of protection to the import-competing sector. Most import-control measures, such as quotas and import licenses, were eliminated prior to 1994, when Taiwan began bilateral negotiations with the U.S. pursuant to WTO accession.[15]

With the imminent prospect of WTO accession and following in the footsteps of the export industries, the import-competing industries became more active in foreign direct investment, partly to penetrate local markets, and partly to manufacture goods with low-wage labor for re-export back to Taiwan. The fact that Taiwan and China joined the WTO at the same time made such re-exportation possible. Although Taiwan still banned a substantial proportion of Chinese-made goods, products made by Taiwan firms in China entered Taiwan in the form of semi-finished goods or by being rerouted through third countries. More importantly, Taiwan-made components and parts were exported in large volumes to China to constitute a vertically-integrated production network across the Taiwan Strait. WTO accession has indeed facilitated a division of labor between the two sides of the strait, for example in the case of consumer electronics and automobiles.

In the meantime, WTO accession had been expected to have an immense impact on China's import-competing industries. Vehicles for import-substitution industrial development, namely state-owned enterprises, were expected to be the immediate losers. This indeed occurred, but the Chinese government took advantage of a

[15] Chen Tain-Jy, "Democratization and Trade Liberalization," in *Taiwan's Economic Success Since 1980,* ed. Chao-Cheng Mai and Chien-Sheng Shih (Cheltenham, UK: Edward Elgar, 2001), 312–346.

rapidly expanding domestic market, partially supported by growing exports whose access to foreign markets was guaranteed under the WTO, to create new opportunities for the ailing import-substitution industries. State-owned enterprises were encouraged to form joint ventures with multinational firms to deepen capital investments and to upgrade technologies to survive. Joint ventures became prevalent in the automobile, petrochemical, steel, and retail sectors.

China also launched a high-tech industry drive to jump-start the computer and semiconductor industries. This has succeeded to a large extent. The fear that the Chinese market would be monopolized by multinational firms and flooded with imported goods did not come to pass. Lacking famous brands, Taiwan firms have found it difficult to penetrate the newly-opened Chinese markets through joint ventures. They have chosen to establish a looser form of cooperation with Chinese firms, namely strategic alliances. The record so far suggests that Taiwan firms have lost this game to Western multinationals. The cooperative relationship between Taiwan and Chinese firms before WTO accession has gradually given way to a competitive, and sometimes confrontational relationship, manifested by an increasing number of anti-dumping cases brought against Taiwan firms by China's state-owned enterprises. Taiwan firms still maintain the ability to produce in China for export, using Taiwan-made components and parts, but they have not been able to penetrate local markets, despite China's offer of trade and distribution rights to foreign firms.

Until now, Taiwan still restricts a large proportion of Chinese goods from being imported and enjoys a sizable trade surplus. If this restriction is lifted, imports from China will increase substantially, but most imports will probably be products made by Taiwan firms in China. This implies that although the current trade surplus that Taiwan enjoys will shrink, the cross-strait division of labor will be further enhanced and production by Taiwan firms will be further rationalized.

Chapter

3

The Legal and Political Implications of Taiwan's WTO Accession

Connie Guang-Hwa Yang

INTRODUCTION

It has been several years since Taiwan became a member of the World Trade Organization (WTO) in January 2002. Given the broad coverage of accession commitments Taiwan made for both rules compliance and market opening, it was assumed that upon accession, its trade and economic regime would have to be changed substantially. Specifically, major modifications of relevant laws and regulations would be required, as the WTO demands that new members liberalize trade to open potential markets.

Indeed, some in Taiwan soon placed the blame for their business problems on WTO membership, suggesting a kind of "WTO-syndrome," i.e., to seek compensation from the government by attributing business losses to WTO accession; or to sabotage the reputation of the government for political reasons by linking irrelevant problems to WTO accession; or even to lobby for their own interests by asserting WTO mandates, regardless of whether such requirements exist in the WTO agreement.

However, little evidence can be found to support these claims. The impact of WTO accession in Taiwan during the past several years has not been significant. In fact, Taiwan was already largely prepared to integrate into the multi-lateral trading system when it applied for WTO membership. Moreover, the long accession process provided a good opportunity for it to make gradual adjustments.

In order to demonstrate that Taiwan had been prepared to a large extent prior to its application for membership, this Chapter begins with the historical background to Taiwan's application for GATT/WTO membership, especially its trade and economic liberalization in the 1980s and 1990s. Taiwan's early efforts at liberalization strengthened its later attempt to join the GATT/WTO, but, given the broad coverage of the accession commitments, there were difficulties that could not be ignored. This discussion is followed by a summary of the commitments and review of the required legal and structural changes for Taiwan to fulfill these commitments — changes that are expected to create precedents for future trade pacts.

We then turn to a discussion of the political implications of Taiwan's WTO accession with an analysis of the consultative process and tension among the different agencies regarding accession. Two cases are used to exemplify the political difficulties Taiwan has encountered since accession. They are the rice wine tax incident and China's interference in Taiwan's GPA (Government Procurement Agreement) accession. The former illustrates how the public might not favor WTO membership or might question the merits of liberalization and globalization if the underlying rationale of the measures to implement WTO commitments failed to be conveyed. The latter case study demonstrates how unrealistic it is at the present time to use the WTO forum to resolve cross-strait trade problems. In conclusion, the Chapter indicates that there is still a possibility that WTO membership will narrow the differences on each side of the strait if, in the long run, the liberalization prompted by membership can facilitate the democratization process in China.

TAIWAN'S NEED AND READINESS FOR GATT/ WTO MEMBERSHIP

Taiwan's economic development has taken a track similar to that of most Asian economies. Land reform and a series of four-year plans undertaken during the 1950s and 1960s drastically reduced the inflation of the postwar years and rapidly increased the island's productivity. When government leaders recognized the economic bottlenecks caused by the narrow base of Taiwan's domestic economy, they quickly opted for an export-promotion strategy. As a resource-poor, but labor-rich country, Taiwan began to manufacture for export light industrial goods produced by labor-intensive industries. As Taiwan gradually lost its labor competitiveness in the 1980s, it turned to capital-intensive industries and concentrated on high-tech and exports of chemical products. Between 1962 and 1985, Taiwan's economy grew by an average of 9.3 percent per year, over two times the average economic growth rate of the industrialized countries during this period.

Although Taiwan's economy has been heavily dependent on external trade (about 50 percent of its GDP is attributed to exports),[1] its trade relations have long been limited to bilateral trade. More than 20 years ago (1983), 45 percent of its exports went to a single country, i.e., the U.S.[2] This geographic concentration is understandable since the U.S. is one of the largest trading nations in the world. Moreover, at the initial stage of Taiwan's development after World War II, aid from the U.S. was one of the most essential factors stabilizing the economy. In addition, the U.S. was one of Taiwan's most important allies, despite the severing of diplomatic ties at the end of the 1970s.

This intensity of the geographical concentration of exports could only be reduced through efforts to diversify the export market. Businessmen who realized the risk of overdependence on a single

---

[1] Department of Statistics, Ministry of Economic Affairs (ROC), www.moea.gov.tw/gnweb/english/indicators/reports/A01.xls (accessed June 1, 2006).

[2] Council for Economic Planning and Development, Executive Yuan (ROC), *Taiwan Statistical Data Book, 2005*, www.cepd.gov.tw/upload/Statis/TSDB/2005DataBook (accessed June 1, 2006).

market would take the initiative to do so without government approval as long as they could afford the diversifying costs. The question for Taiwan was whether it could have access to as many markets as it wanted so as to achieve sufficient diversity. The answer was not always positive.

If Taiwan's exports were to be competitive enough to compete with locally-made products or with foreign imports in the export markets that it wanted to enter, it had to have a level playing field. Taiwan's industrial development plans at different phases explain such efforts. But Taiwan's lack of access to foreign markets was not always a problem of its capacity. Sometimes, the lack of access was due to biases against Taiwan.

At this stage of export-oriented development, Taiwan usually was not entitled to tariff concessions or any other favorable treatments available for GATT-contracting parties. Due to its international status, Taiwan was, by and large, excluded from any official multi-lateral network.[3] It had very little leverage in bargaining for favorable treatment and very limited access to official trade talks aimed at solving trade problems. During its early stage of economic development, Taiwan did receive the Generalized System of Preference (GSP) from some leading countries, which, to a certain extent, offset the disadvantage of being excluded from the multi-lateral trading system. The GSP, however, did not last forever. As Taiwan became more competitive, it soon "graduated" from such treatment, thus facing more unfair requirements.

It was against this background that Taiwan submitted a formal application for accession to the GATT in 1990, and after the WTO was established in 1995, the application was transferred to the WTO. Taiwan's commitments for accession sometimes are characterized as "GATT/WTO plus" obligations. This is probably the case for all acceding members because they are always regarded as "demandeurs" and they have little leverage in their negotiations with the incumbent

[3] Among more than 100 trading partners, Taiwan had diplomatic ties with fewer than 30 countries. It did not have official ties with any of its major trading partners.

members.[4] For Taiwan, the benefits derived from entry into the GATT/WTO seemed worthy of such high costs.

The reasons were clear. The principles of most-favored-nation (MFN) and national treatment (NT) embodied in the GATT would allow Taiwan exports to compete with those from other economies on a level playing field. Moreover, Taiwan could have recourse to formal consultations with its trading partners, or in the case of trade disputes, could even bring its partners to formal settlement procedures within a multi-lateral framework. Entry into the multi-lateral system also meant that comprehensive trade and economic information about its trading partners would be made available as would the opportunities to participate in the multi-lateral rule-making process and the rounds of negotiations for market access. Such opportunities would ensure that Taiwan's trade interests would be fully taken into account as the world trading system evolved.

Not only did the benefits derived from GATT/WTO membership attract Taiwan, the cost of entry at Taiwan's initial assessment was also affordable because Taiwan believed that its trade regime was already sufficiently open to meet GATT requirements. Such confidence was not without basis. Although Taiwan's economy was quite protected in many sectors in the 1950s and 1960s, many of the trade barriers had been reduced or dismantled during its bilateral negotiations with the U.S. in the 1980s. These had included negotiations on textiles, machinery, and agricultural products such as turkey meats, tobacco, and wine products. In fact, Taiwan had continuously implemented tariff reduction plans since 1980. Thus, by the time the GATT application process began in 1992, tariffs had been lowered by some 50 percent,[5] and the nominal average tariff was only 8.89 percent, which was comparable to the level of the average tariff of

---

[4] Bernard M. Hoekman and Michel M. Kostecki, *The Political Economy of the World Trading System: The WTO and Beyond,* 2nd ed. (London: Oxford University Press, 2001), 67.

[5] Report of the Working Party on the Accession of the Separate Customs Territory of Taiwan, Penghu, Kinmen and Matsu, WTO Doc. WT/MIN(01)/4, November 11, 2001, para. 23.

the developed economies.[6] In addition to efforts to reduce tariffs, which greatly liberalized commodities trade, Taiwan's earlier bilateral consultations with the U.S. on IPR protection and liberalization of the banking market, as well as the exchange rate, had not only improved Taiwan's overall foreign trade regime, but also adjusted its trade regulations so that they were more in line with international standards. For these reasons Taiwan was less seriously impacted by its GATT/WTO accession.

TAIWAN'S ACCESSION COMMITMENTS

Taiwan initially planned to accede to the GATT prior to the conclusion of the Uruguay Round (December 15, 1993) so that it could avoid the hassle of negotiating any commitment related to the Round, of which it had only limited understanding because it had had no chance to participate in it. This plan did not work out. In addition to the political shadow cast by China (the PRC), which made Taiwan's early accession impossible, the contracting parties also had high expectations of Taiwan, considering it to be a mature and sophisticated economy. Before Taiwan, especially its agricultural sector, could meet the degree of openness demanded by some negotiating counterparts, the Uruguay Round had already concluded. Therefore, the accession negotiations were extended to the areas of trade in services and trade related to intellectual property, in addition to the traditional GATT area, i.e., trade in goods.

Even for trade in goods, the requirements after the Uruguay Round were more extensive and profound. First, there was a comprehensive agreement that was aimed at agricultural reform, thus putting Taiwan's most sensitive sector under enormous unexpected pressures. In addition, the insistence by some members that Taiwan sign the pluri-lateral trade agreements, namely, the Agreement on Government Procurement, the Agreement on Trade in Civil Aircraft, and the Information Technology Agreement (concluded after the

---

[6] Taxation and Tariff Committee, Ministry of Finance (ROC), *Guide to ROC Taxes 2005*, www.ttc.gov.tw/public/Attachment/56231657471.pdf.

Uruguay Round), was also unexpected. In short, the multi-lateral review of Taiwan's trade regime held in the Working Party meetings, as well as the bilateral process of negotiations for access to Taiwan's goods and services market, became more complicated than they had been under the GATT.

For its WTO accession, Taiwan agreed to reduce tariff rates on a total of 4,491 items and to open up its market in all 11 service sectors as categorized by the Uruguay Round service negotiations. In addition, Taiwan also committed to observe all WTO disciplines, including: reducing non-tariff barriers; enforcing the protection of intellectual property rights; and ensuring the transparency of all its laws and regulations in conformity with the letter and spirit of the WTO agreements. It also committed to sign the Agreements on Government Procurement and Trade in Civil Aircraft.[7]

In the previous chapter, Dr. Chen Tain-jy presents a detailed discussion of Taiwan's commitments upon accession to the WTO. Here, we need only briefly outline the scope of these agreements before turning to an analysis of the legal adjustments required for their implementation.

Tariff Reduction. Prior to membership, Taiwan had already joined the WTO Information Technology Agreement (ITA) at the request of some members and had agreed to eliminate tariffs on IT imports upon accession. Taiwan also agreed to accept the Uruguay Round zero-for-zero proposal to eliminate tariffs on another ten groups of products, including pharmaceuticals (that were already subject to zero tariffs in 1995), spirits, furniture, paper products, toys, medical equipment, farm and construction equipment, steel products, and beer. With the exception of the latter two, all had been tariff-free since 2002, the first year after accession. Tariffs on steel products were zero in 2004, and tariffs on beer were zero in 2005. Taiwan also included in its concession package the Chemical Tariff

[7] Report of the Working Party on the Accession of the Separate Customs Territory of Taiwan, Penghu, Kinmen and Matsu, WTO Doc. WT/MIN(01)/4, November 11, 2001, para. 166, 222.

Harmonization Agreement that had been agreed to by only some two dozen WTO members.

Reducing Controls on Agricultural and Industrial Imports. Prior to accession, Taiwan maintained certain import restrictions in some sectors, either because of their sensitivity, e.g., the agricultural sector, or because of policy, e.g., industrial policy or state monopoly. For accession, Taiwan agreed to change these measures and observe the WTO discipline.

Commitments in the Services Trade. Taiwan had undertaken the liberalization of its service sectors long before accession, partially due to government plans to establish the Asia-Pacific Regional Operations Center (APROC) in Taiwan.[8] As a result, it was able to meet the demand of its trading partners that its services schedule included all 11 sectors as identified by the Uruguay Round. These were: 1. business services (that cover professional services), 2. communication services, 3. construction and related engineering services, 4. distribution services, 5. education services, 6. environmental services, 7. financial services, 8. health-related and social services, 9. tourism and travel-related services, 10. recreational, cultural, and sporting services, and 11. transport services.[9]

Commitments on Trade Related to Intellectual Property. Partially due to pressure from past trade sanctions intended by one of its trading partners to protect intellectual property rights, Taiwan's intellectual property legislation almost met the requirements of the relevant international norms prior to accession.[10] With membership, Taiwan further committed to extend to all WTO members the intellectual

---

[8] The APROC, announced in 1995, included plans for six different centers: a Manufacturing Center, Sea Transportation Center, Air Transportation Center, Financial Center, Telecommunication Center, and Media Center, www.cedi.cepd.gov.tw/aproc/html/index_e.html (accessed June 10, 2006).

[9] GATT Doc. MTN.GNS/W/120, July 10, 1991.

[10] James V. Feinerman, "Taiwan and the GATT," *Columbia Business Law Review*, no. 1 (1992), 39–60.

property rights protection that previously had only been offered on a reciprocal basis. Moreover, Taiwan committed to enhance its enforcement of the relevant legislation, which was deemed by some WTO members as the source of its failure to deter piracy.

Other Significant Commitments. From 2002, the Commercial Harbor Construction Dues were replaced with the commercial port service fees in accordance with the user-pay principle embodied in Article VIII of the GATT. This was intended to resolve the long controversy over the nature of such levies and their consistency with WTO rules. For various types of financial assistance that had been or would be provided to the agricultural and industrial sectors as policy tools, Taiwan also committed to either eliminate them or adjust them in accordance with the relevant subsidies disciplines of the WTO.

LEGAL IMPLICATIONS OF THE GATT/WTO ACCESSION

In order to implement these accession commitments and to comply with existing WTO practices, certain legislative changes had to be made. In addition, legislative appropriations of funds for structural adjustments in response to the impact caused by the accession were also required. Taiwan's Constitution requires respect of all international treaties into which the government enters (Constitution [ROC], Article 141). Some, therefore, argued that the international agreements should have a "direct effect" on Taiwan. Although some court cases held that self-executing agreements could have a direct effect, the question of whether or not the WTO agreements were self-executing was not easily settled.[11] Taiwan's Administration decided not to take

[11] Court decisions No. 23 Shan-Zu 1074, which refused the jurisdiction based on a treaty explicitly allocating jurisdiction (1934); No. 73 Tai-Fe 69 and No. 74 Tai-Fe 137 (1984, 85), which both upheld the standing of the complainant based on the Taiwan-U.S. bilateral Friendship Commerce Navigation Agreement (FCN Agreement); and No. 79 Shan-Gan-Yi-Zu 128 (1990), which affirmed Encyclopedia Britannica's standing in a copyright case by holding the FCN Agreement over its later-enacted Copyright Law.

the chance of asserting a "direct effect" of the WTO agreements, but rather to amend existing legislation, or to add new legislation to accommodate the legal changes required by the WTO disciplines.

Approaches to Amending the Laws

It was not easy to incorporate all the accession commitments into relevant laws. In the first place, a thorough comparison of the WTO disciplines with existing legislation and administrative practices was required. It was also a challenge to draft the legal texts to prevent any possible deviation in the interpretation of Taiwan's commitment. Taiwan did not intend for its accession process to go on for ten years, but this additional time did reduce some of the difficulties involved in the task of amending the relevant laws.

However, it was still impossible to avoid errors in the amendment process. For example, the Customs Law was revised for accession, but the amendment failed to change the word "reciprocity" in the provision of Article 3 (1), which refers to Taiwan's two columns of duty rates applied respectively to imports from countries entitled to reciprocity treatment and to imports from countries not entitled to such treatment. Fortunately, this gave no rise to violations of the MFN principle, because, in practice, the Customs Law has applied the reciprocal rate to all WTO members since accession, as if it were prescribed as a MFN rate, despite the omission in the text change.

Pact or Omnibus Bill. When Taiwan started to prepare to incorporate all of its accession commitments into laws, the Administration thought it could put all required legal changes into one single bill, i.e., a pact or an "Omnibus Bill."[12] Given that all the legal changes were required for accession, having them all reviewed and passed at the same time so that they could be promulgated and implemented simultaneously would, it believed, ensure legislative consistency in

[12] Lo Chang-fa, *GATT/WTO yu Woguo Maoyi* [GATT/WTO and Our External Trade] (Taipei: Yong Ran Publisher, 1996), 17–18.

the consideration of Taiwan's WTO accession and avoid the repetition of similar reviews, e.g., amendments to delete reciprocal requirements in a number of laws.

Although this proposal made sense, it was quite difficult for the legislature to accept it. The Legislative Yuan of Taiwan is made up of subcommittees responsible for diplomatic affairs, economic affairs, finance, education, interior affairs, national defense, the budget, and so forth. If the executive branch submitted an omnibus bill, it would be necessary to first decide which subcommittee would be responsible for the first reading of the bill. If no subcommittee were willing to give the first reading, then all the subcommittees would have to jointly review the bill in the first reading. Under such a circumstance, there emerged the issue of how to distinguish such a review from the second reading that all members would also attend. Another more real problem was that there would have been no way to have effective debates over the provisions of the bill if all the subcommittees attended the first reading (see footnote 12).

Could the legislature break the omnibus bill into parts and have each provision of the bill reviewed by the relevant subcommittees based on the division of work among the legislative members? The answer was negative because there was no precedent for the legislature to follow in determining what fraction of the legislature would be qualified to divide the bill into parts. Although there was a special taskforce of the legislature designated to hear periodic reports of the accession negotiations from the Administration, this taskforce did not have any genuine power to break the omnibus bill into parts and to assign each part to the relevant subcommittee.

The special taskforce of the legislature mentioned above was established purely for communication purposes. Taiwan does not have any trade legislation similar to the fast-track mechanism of the U.S. trade laws, which grants prior authorization for trade negotiations. As a result, the legislature might not ratify the accession pact without reservation. In fact, some legislative members had intensely complained about the low transparency of the negotiation process and threatened to block the deal. In order to ease such anger, the Administration agreed to brief a special taskforce of the legislature on the accession negotiations as long as such a taskforce comprised only a small group of legislative members, so that the confidentiality of the negotiation strategies would not be compromised. Given its ad hoc nature and informal operation, the special taskforce could not facilitate the first reading of an omnibus bill or rearrange the bill for each subcommittee.

Series of Bills or Simultaneous Bills. To facilitate the review process of the subcommittees, the Administration withdrew the omnibus bill and reorganized the draft amendments in the format of a series of bills for resubmission to the legislature. In addition to the WTO-related series of bills, there were also some bills submitted to the legislature at different stages and labeled as "Simultaneous Bills." The reason for designating them as simultaneous bills was that their promulgation was required no later than Taiwan's accession.

Such simultaneous bills included those not suitable to be organized as a "Series of Bills," such as those involving large-scale changes or changes that were greater than those required by the accession. The former consisted of new legislation, such as the Government Procurement Law, the Tobacco and Wine Administration Law, the Tobacco and Wine Tax Law, and so forth. The latter included the Telecommunications Act, the Organization Statute of the Council of Agriculture, and so forth.

In total, there were 55 legislative bills, including series and simultaneous bills. Some laws even had two separate amendment bills. If the early implementation of the bills would not radically affect domestic interests or affect Taiwan's leverage in the accession negotiations, the legislation usually took effect right after the passage or after the required enforcement scheme was established. Otherwise, the implementation of such bills was postponed to a date no later than accession through a provision by which the legislature would delegate to the Administration the authority to determine the effective date. A summary of these bills, including their respective promulgation and effective dates, is in Appendix 1.

MAJOR CATEGORIES OF LEGAL CHANGES

In addition to the aforementioned 55 WTO-related bills, there were more than 100 administrative regulations amended or added to implement the legal changes required by Taiwan's WTO membership. These legal changes either abolished the existing provisions that were inconsistent with the letter and spirit of the relevant WTO agreements, or provided a legal basis for the Administration to take action to fulfill Taiwan's accession commitments. The latter included some statutes of organizations, such as the "Statute Governing the Organization of the National Treasury, Ministry of Finance" and the "Statute Governing the Organization of the Bureau of Animal and Plant Health Inspection and Quarantine," which were to have authority in the post-accession regulatory regime. The former included the legal changes required for compliance with: (i) the MFN principle; (ii) the national treatment principle and market opening obligation; and (iii) the transparency requirement.

Compliance with the MFN Principle. The most common type of legal change among the 55 WTO-related bills was to abolish the reciprocity requirements. Under a reciprocity requirement, Taiwan could not grant any foreigner the kind of right reserved for its nationals unless the home country of the foreigner also granted Taiwanese the same right—for example, the right to acquire real estate. The requirement applied similarly in the case of the import of foreign products.

Such requirements had been in place for a long time and were regarded as equitable when bilateral trade relations were Taiwan's only external ties. However, after Taiwan became a member of the WTO, it was argued that such requirements might conflict with the MFN principle. If Taiwan's exports were denied access to a WTO member's market not because the member discriminated against Taiwan's exports, but because it did not open that market to all WTO members pursuant to the MFN principle, Taiwan could not prohibit imports from that member as reciprocity required, provided that Taiwan had already committed to open its market for such imports. For this reason, reciprocity requirements had to be removed to comply with the MFN principle. However, this resulted in increased opposition from domestic and foreign enterprises that formerly had been protected. This was especially so in the case of the heavily-protected automobile industry where the U.S., formerly enjoying preferential access, was concerned about Japanese competition after Japan auto exports were no longer prohibited from Taiwan's market under the MFN principle.

Compliance with the NT Principle and Market Opening. Strictly speaking, market opening is different from the NT requirement. The latter does not apply until the foreign products are able to enter the local market. However, without NT, the former cannot deliver meaningful market access or really level the playing field for foreign products. In other words, these two disciplines are similar, at least, in that they both relate to market access and expose domestic products and producers to foreign competition.

Prior to accession, Taiwan often employed local content requirements, tax incentives, interest subsidies, industrial cooperation plans, and so on to encourage the use of domestic industrial products and to discriminate against foreign imports. Such measures are inconsistent with the spirit of the NT principle and are explicitly prohibited by the Agreement on Trade-Related Investment Measures (TRIMs), the Agreement on Subsidies and Countervailing Measures (SCM), and even the Agreement on Government Procurement. The abolition of these measures, however, inevitably clashed with domestic vested interests and with the paternalistic philosophy of some bureaucrats, a fact that was particularly evident in regard to the agriculture sector.

Transparency. Transparency is a very basic requirement of the WTO. It generally requires prior publication and notification of relevant laws, regulations, decisions, rulings, and measures as provided in GATT: X, General Agreement on Trade in Services (GATS): III, and Agreement on Trade-Related Aspects of Intellectual Property Rights (TRIPs): 63. But in some agreements like the

Agreement on Technical Barriers to Trade (TBT Agreement): 2.9, it even requires prior comments by other members. Compliance with such a requirement does not adversely affect any local interests. On the contrary, it benefits local interests in the same way as it benefits foreign interests. However, this inevitably involved reform of the bureaucratic system and a possible revolutionary change.

The publication of relevant legal instruments and administrative measures before entering into force had long been common practice in Taiwan. After its official gazettes and court report became easily accessible on the Internet, the degree of transparency was further enhanced. However, when the transparency involved the translation of a legal text into one of the official WTO languages (in Taiwan's case, English), Taiwan required a substantial amount of capacity-building, just like any other WTO member whose official language was neither English, French, nor Spanish. Although Taiwan only committed to translate and publish in English the laws, regulations, judicial decisions, and administrative rulings of general application relating to trade in goods and measures subject to the transparency provisions of the GATS and TRIPs Agreement no later than 90 days after enactment or issuance,[13] the burden was still quite heavy. Regarding the prior comment provision, Taiwan's commitments went beyond the requirement of the TBT Agreement. It committed to provide a period, except in cases of extreme emergency, for all other WTO members to comment on "all laws, regulations, and other measures pertaining to or affecting trade in goods, services, or TRIPs of at least sixty days before the implementation of such measures."[14]

To accommodate prior comments on legislative bills in effect was not at all difficult for Taiwan because after proposing legislation, the Administration usually conducts wide consultation to perfect the bills and secure support. In addition, the legislature also often holds

[13] Report of the Working Party on the Accession of the Separate Customs Territory of Taiwan, Penghu, Kinmen and Matsu, WTO Doc. WT/MIN(01)/4, November 11, 2001, para. 217.

[14] Report of the Working Party on the Accession of the Separate Customs Territory of Taiwan, Penghu, Kinmen and Matsu, WTO Doc. WT/MIN(01)/4, November 11, 2001, para. 219.

hearings to seek public views on relevant bills. However, seeking prior comments openly on proposed administrative measures of general application is not so common and, therefore, was more difficult. However, in 1999, legislation was passed, which provided the legal basis for the process of prior comments on administrative rules or measures (Administrative Procedures Law, Article 154).

CROSS-STRAIT TRADE NORMALIZATION

Another important category of legal changes involves those made to normalize cross-strait trade. Taiwan did not invoke Article XIII of the WTO Agreement for the non-application of any WTO agreements with China. Therefore, it cannot control its trade with China unless justified by the relevant WTO provisions. In some respects, such a normalization can be seen as compliance with the MFN principle, but it deserves separate treatment, given the political complexities involved.

Taiwan was aware of its MFN obligation. However, prior to accession, it never had any chance to hold official trade talks with China, its fourth-largest trading partner. Also, China had never renounced its use of force against Taiwan or suspended its intelligence activities against Taiwan. Furthermore, Taiwan resented the denigration of its status in the international community by the People's Republic of China. Because of these security issues, Taiwan could never be too careful in dealing with its trade relations with China. On the other hand, China's cheap labor and large market had already induced many Taiwan businesses to set up establishments in China. Taiwan's businesses would have to bear the extra costs of using China as a manufacturing base, if the trade closure continued at previous levels.

In response to the needs of its businesses in China, Taiwan cautiously, but progressively, began the legal changes required for the normalization of cross-strait trade, while taking into account the impact on its security and societal interests. The process began long before accession, but accelerated after accession.

Cross-Strait Trade in Goods. Taiwan changed its practice of regulating imports from mainland China from a positive list approach to a negative list approach in 1996. In other words, after 1996, items not on the list were allowed to be imported from China. The negative list was also constantly reviewed and shortened. After accession, as discussed in Chi Schive's chapter in this volume, Taiwan removed a significant number of items from the negative list. As of mid-2005, there were more than 8,700 items that could be imported from China, most of which did not require licensing. This represented almost 80 percent of Taiwan's tariff lines.[15]

For items permitted to be imported, direct trade is allowed between cross-strait traders, but the shipments must go through a third place. Negotiations for direct shipping links have not begun because the Chinese government insists that Taiwan first recognize the one-China principle. Facing such an insurmountable hurdle, Taiwan began to set up some off-shore zones to accommodate products shipped directly to Taiwan. To a certain extent, this also facilitated Taiwan's goal of becoming a regional transshipment center.

Cross-Strait Trade in Services. In 2001, Taiwan replaced the "No Haste, Be Patient" policy that restricted China-bound investments with a policy of "Proactive Liberalization with Effective Management." Since then, the Taiwan authorities gradually removed most restrictions on China-bound investments.[16] Currently, only postal, telecommunications, IC design, banking and futures brokerage, and railway transport service industries cannot invest on the mainland.[17] The financial industry usually is regarded as very sensitive due to its relation to the stability of Taiwan's own financial system. However, now not only securities and insurance businesses can invest on the mainland, banking businesses also can have commercial establishments there, as noted in Lee Jih-chu's chapter. In fact, since

[15] Board of Foreign Trade, Ministry of Economic Affairs (ROC), *Statistics for Items of Agricultural and Industrial Imports from Mainland, 2005,* www.trade.gov.tw.

[16] Government Information Office (ROC), *The Republic of China Year Book 2002,* www.gio.gov.tw/taiwan-website/5-gp/yearbook/2002/index.htm.

[17] Investment Commission, Ministry of Economic Affairs (ROC), *Negative List for Investment on the Mainland,* www.moeaic.gov.tw/system_external/ctlr?PRO=DownloadFile&t=3&id=15.

its cross-strait policy change of 2001, Taiwan has started planning to allow banks to invest on the mainland, even though the authorities there only grant them representative office status because cross-strait talks to ensure the "home country supervision" principle is observed have not been arranged yet due to China's insistence on the "one China" principle as a premise.[18] Off-shore banking units in Taiwan can now engage in direct business with Chinese financial institutions. In addition to the liberalization of China-bound investment restrictions, Taiwan's authorities have also opened the services market for inbound investment from China, although some investments are required to abide by relevant regulations.

In October 2003, the most important piece of legislation governing cross-strait relations, the Statute Governing Relations between Peoples of the Taiwan Area and the Mainland Area, was amended substantially in order to reflect the above policy change and to provide a more easily-implemented legal framework for the normalization of cross-strait exchanges.[19] The amendments adjusted the current regulations of cross-strait negotiations, people movement, transportation links, investments, cross-strait trade, commercial and financial activities, including currency exchange, and the education of children of Taiwan businessmen in China. These amendments have provided the basis for continuing the work of normalizing relations with China.

It should be noted that the process of normalizing cross-strait trade has not been prompted entirely by WTO accession. Taiwan and the PRC joined at almost the same time. Therefore, there were no accession negotiations between the two sides and, thus, no commitments made toward one another, besides the general obligations

[18] Financial Supervisory Commission, Executive Yuan (ROC), "The Policy and Current Status of Cross Strait Financial Business," www.fscey.gov.tw/news_detail2.aspx?icuItem=30697&ctNode=1545, December 30, 2004.

[19] The amendments were, by far, the most extensive since the implementation of the Act. The Act originally contained 102 articles, and amendments were made to 83 articles. After being amended, the Act now contains 132 articles. More than 80 percent of the Act was amended, www.mac.gov.tw/english/english/macpolicy/act9211.htm (accessed June 10, 2006).

assumed by their accession to the WTO. However, in light of the circumstances described above and the mainland's generally hostile attitude, Taiwan could not treat the PRC in the same manner that it treated the other members, despite the unlikely risk of being challenged by the PRC for its denial of MFN by doing so.

Why then has normalization accelerated since 2001? The Taiwan government believed that the WTO could be a good platform for resuming a formal dialogue with the PRC on trade issues. It has thus been willing to expedite the normalization process so that it was prepared for such trade talks. In other words, it has been Taiwan's cross-strait policy and not the requirements of WTO membership, which has determined the pace and the scope of the cross-strait trade normalization process. For the past decade, this policy has been reviewed from time to time and has evolved in line with changes in cross-strait relations, as well as changes in the global environment. For example, when Taiwan changed its cross-strait policy to "Proactive Liberalization with Effective Management," only one of the considerations that motivated the change was the WTO membership of both sides.[20] In this way, cross-strait trade normalization that would continue anyway, with or without WTO membership, has moved in an independent, but parallel, path to WTO accession.

THE DOMESTIC POLITICAL IMPLICATIONS OF ACCESSION

In order to make the required legal changes and ensure the successful implementation of such changes, domestic political support was essential. Although some argued that because Taiwan's WTO accession was more or less politically-motivated, it would be accomplished, regardless of the costs involved, or of the views of domestic constituencies. Such a presumption overlooked the influence of the industry constituencies on the Administration. General welfare could

---

[20] Mainland Affairs Council, Policy Statement for "Proactive Liberalization with Effective Management," November 7, 2001, www.mac.gov.tw/big5/cnews/empl01.htm (accessed June 10, 2006).

be expected to improve as the entire economy moved toward full competition, but individual sectors of the economy might suffer a loss of jobs or profits. Unfortunately, the general public is often less aware of the general welfare advantages and tends to be silent in enjoying the benefits. In addition, the size of the general public makes it less organized than the industry groups. As a result, the consumers who will benefit usually fail to show sufficient political support to the Administration to counterbalance the industry's opposition.

THE CONSULTATIVE PROCESS

In 1990, the Ministry of Economic Affairs began an educational campaign to disseminate information about the expected impacts that accession to the GATT would have on the domestic economy. After the WTO was established, the government placed increased emphasis on sharing information about the various Agreements covered under the WTO framework. Efforts were also directed toward encouraging the private sector to implement measures designed to minimize the impact of accession, such as upgrading itself, as well as reallocating resources to more promising sectors. This campaign continued even after accession. According to the government's own estimates,[21] the educational programs that accompanied the accession included the following:

Cross-Sectoral. Between November 2000 and March 2001, the Board of Foreign Trade, Ministry of Economic Affairs, together with the Council of Agriculture, the Industrial Development Bureau, the Council for Economic Planning and Development (CEPD), and other related government agencies conducted more than 70 seminars, hearings, and meetings on GATT and WTO matters. These sessions were aimed at securing industry support for accession and encouraging the private sector to take advantage of the opportunities created by accession to the WTO.

[21] BOFT, "Background Information on Taiwan's WTO Accession," January 14, 2002, at 210.34.17.189/WTO/WTO_enrollment/wto_history5.htm.

Sector-Specific. In addition to the general education campaign, the Council of Agriculture, recognizing that the agricultural sector would be the most seriously affected, hosted a total of 28 seminars for individual farmer groups throughout the island between August and September 2001. Another 150 seminars were held with local governments from December 2001 to January 2002. These seminars were designed to increase understanding among farmers, industry groups, and local agricultural groups of the potential impact of accession and of the adjustment measures available to producers following accession.

Like agriculture, the services industry was also a complex sector. Before the conclusion of the Uruguay Round, there was no international regime for the services trade. Not only were the disciplines new, the number of ministries, departments, and agencies in charge of the services trade was also large, ranging from the least trade-related authorities, such as the Ministry of Justice, in charge of lawyer services, to the most trade-related, such as the Ministry of Economic Affairs. Thus, internal consultation in this sector could be very complicated. During the accession process, the Council for Economic Planning and Development was designated to coordinate the ministries, departments, and agencies responsible for each individual services industry. It hosted 25 seminars and informal meetings between June 1999 and July 2001 for different services industries to discuss the anticipated impact of WTO accession on the respective industries.

With regard to specific services industries, the Ministry of Transportation and Communications (MOTC) hosted three informational meetings in northern, central, and southern Taiwan in December 1999 to consider the implications of accession for the domestic tourism industry. Between June 2000 and July 2001, the MOTC hosted another four informal meetings to discuss the implications of accession for the air-transportation and maritime sectors.

Government Procurement. Between June 1997 and December 2001, the Public Construction Commission held approximately 53 courses to provide education and training to procurement officials on the rules of the GPA.

Unfortunately, these education programs were not successful in clearing up some serious misunderstandings about accession, as illustrated by the following discussion on the rice wine incident. There were several reasons for this: the highly technical and diplomatic nature of the WTO agreements, which defied easy explanation; the failure of the education campaigns that were aimed primarily at industry groups to reach the general public, as well as many small firms; and provocative media reports on WTO accession, which were intended to incite emotion in order to increase circulation.

Public mistrust of the government's ability to protect the interests of domestic constituencies through diplomatic or legal channels also sabotaged the Administration's relations with the market. Without accurate feedback from the market and the cooperation of the public, the adjustment measures did not bring satisfactory results. Public mistrust not only made the implementation of the commitments very costly, as illustrated in the rice wine case, but also limited the Administration's ability to fully participate in future WTO activities, specifically, the possibility of making new concessions in the next round.

THE INTERNAL TENSIONS IN THE ADMINISTRATION

In the past, Taiwan's economy had been less market-oriented. The Administration tended to take the lead in industrial development. This was quite successful for the establishment of the IT industry, but less so for the automobile industry. In some strategic areas, such as the agricultural sector, the government even took a protectionist stance to guard domestic sectors from foreign competition. When Taiwan applied for GATT/WTO membership, the trade authorities were aware of the contribution of foreign competition to its economic welfare. However, such a realization did not automatically lead to unreserved acceptance of changes. Some ministries and departments, especially those not responsible for trade policy, were less enthusiastic about trade liberalization and more concerned about the interests of those sectors under their supervision. When interest groups were well-organized and demonstrated powerful opposition to market opening, paternalistic bureaucrats who favored stability generally hesitated to pursue liberalization. This was evident not only during the accession negotiation phase, but it also continued into the post-accession phase.

There were also many conflicts between different ministries, departments, and agencies over various accession issues. It is difficult to determine whether the conflicts arose from paternalism or from self-interested concerns over a loss of bureaucratic power. The internal tensions between the different ministries, departments, and agencies over the WTO accession are exemplified in the conflict between the Central Bank and the Securities and Futures Commission under the Ministry of Finance[22] over the opening of the portfolio investment market; the disagreement between the trade authorities and industrial authorities over the liberalization of auto imports; the high-profile battle between the banking authorities and the CEPD over the opening of the financial market in the services trade negotiations; and the differences among trade authorities, agricultural authorities, and the Treasury and the monopoly bureau (TTWMB) over the reduction of subsidies on tobacco leaves and wine grapes, as required by the liberalization of tobacco and alcohol products.

The authorities in charge of coordinating the negotiations were inclined to favor the free market and were most eager to conclude the negotiations successfully. The authorities directly responsible for particular sectors were more alert to the sectoral impacts and political liabilities of the accession. For example, the agricultural authorities argued that the farming industry, consisting of 787,407 farm families,[23] played an important role in domestic politics, and that large agricultural concessions would deprive the ruling party of

---

[22] After the Financial Supervisory Commission, Executive Yuan (ROC), was established on July 1, 2004 to consolidate financial supervision in Taiwan and to respond to the development of financial conglomerates, the Securities and Futures Commission was changed to the Securities and Futures Bureau and like the other financial supervisory agencies was under the Financial Supervision Commission.

[23] Council of Agriculture (ROC), "2000 Yearly Report of Taiwan's Agriculture," http://eng.coa.gov.tw/content_print.php?catid=9260 (accessed June 10, 2006).

support from farmers. Import controls on rice were favored for the same reason, as well as in the belief that price fluctuations in major foodstuffs would seriously affect consumers and, thus, disrupt social stability.

Nonetheless, the tensions among different ministries, departments, and agencies were reduced after the accession. Not only did the trade authorities realize that the frictions affected their ability to coordinate and lead, but the other authorities also made efforts to comply with the relevant WTO rules. The latter may not have fully eliminated their paternalistic attitudes because of the serious political consequences, but they came to understand the costs of not participating in global liberalization and tried to cooperate with other economies to protect their sectoral interests. This increase in the degree of internationalization of the bureaucracy may well be the greatest benefit derived from the WTO accession.

THE ROLE OF THE LOCAL FOREIGN COMMUNITY

In Taiwan's liberalization process, including its accession to the WTO, the local foreign community always played an important role. The business people in the foreign community had the opportunity to identify possible barriers to liberalization and to share such knowledge with their home governments that later used this information to negotiate with the authorities on Taiwan for the removal of the barriers. However, when local foreign interests differed from the industry interests back at home, the issues were much more complicated.

Local foreign interests are the incumbent interests because they already have access to the Taiwan market. They may not feel completely satisfied, but they have an advantage over their counterparts at home. The conflicts between their interests and the interests of their home countries' domestic counterparts may have been problematic for their home governments, but not so serious for the authorities on Taiwan, which sometimes used such conflicts to successfully block the demands of their trading partners. In doing so, the authorities encouraged local foreign interests to lobby their home governments to withdraw those requests that only favored the interests of the industry at home, despite their vested interests in Taiwan. The negotiations in the auto industry offer such an example. For the Ford Motor Company that had investments in Taiwan for some time, the market opening accompanying Taiwan's membership brought no benefit. Therefore, it could not accept Washington's market-opening request that had been prompted by General Motors that sought to penetrate the Taiwan market through trade, rather than investment.

DIFFICULTIES OF COMPLIANCE AFTER ACCESSION

After accession, Taiwan had to face difficulties similar to those encountered by most new members: the heavy notification burden; insufficient experience in negotiations; and the dispute settlement procedures, to name only a few areas. All these required capacity-building. In response, Taiwan established its own WTO Center, encouraged the education system to increase WTO-related training, and actively participated in various WTO activities, including joining dispute settlement procedures as a third party.

In addition to the lack of capacity, which is common to most new members, there were also some difficulties specific to Taiwan, such as the general public's frustration caused by the misrepresentation of the government's failure to protect its constituencies and the ongoing tensions between Taiwan and China. These issues are discussed below.

Rice Wine

Taiwan had long planned to reform its tobacco and alcohol monopoly system, but the reform was delayed because it was subsequently linked to the WTO negotiations for wine and tobacco market access. Before accession, whenever the media reported that Taiwan would soon become a WTO member, there would be a cornering of alcohol stocks, especially of those whose prices were to be increased under the new tax system. Such cornering resulted in temporary shortages of supply, thus rapidly driving up prices. After the expectation of early accession failed to materialize, those who had illegally cornered the market had not gained anything. However, market order had been damaged.

But those who cornered the market did not always lose. In 2001, they happened to bet on the right side since the accession process was finally concluded. The alcohol product that would have the largest percentage increase in its selling price under the new tax system required by accession, rice wine, became a favorite to be cornered.[24] Many shops stocked up on rice wine before it would be taxed, and after the new tax system came into force with Taiwan's WTO accession, they sold their stocks at much higher prices, as if the tax had been levied on them. As a result, the price of rice wine in Taiwan increased before, not after, accession, thus arousing the consumers' ire.

Motivated by the lucrative profits from the sale of non-taxed rice wine, after the cornered stocks were depleted, some merchants even started to make fake rice wine from industrial alcohol and to fill recycled rice wine bottles that had fake tax-paid labels. Then they either sold the fake wine at the same price as the genuine rice wine, or at lower prices to attract more business. Some people died from consuming the fake rice wine and the government was severely criticized. Even before the accession, the hike had angered consumers. Their criticism became quite irrational, attributing the deaths to the government's weakness in protecting Taiwan's interests when it negotiated with the U.S. over the tax on rice wine during the WTO accession process.

The government did not effectively or forcefully rebut such allegations. It was hard to explain to the general public that was unfamiliar with the technicalities of the WTO rules that rice wine, used not only for cooking, but also consumed as a beverage by aborigines and low-income people, could not be clearly distinguished from other spirits and, therefore, could not be favored in regard to taxation

[24] In the first year after accession, the tax on rice wine without salt added was NT$ 150/L, and in the second year it was NT$ 185/L. Compared to the pre-accession selling price of NT $24/0.6/L, this tax was very significant. Because of the high tax, a bottle of rice wine (0.6L) had to be priced at NT$ 114 to levy a tax of NT$ 90. This represented a large price jump.

under the national treatment principle. Furthermore, the government did not want to exempt the rice wine for fiscal reasons. In other words, if Taiwan had been willing to tax other spirits less, then the tax on rice wine would have been reduced. However, the result would have been a great loss in revenues.

The reaction to the accidental deaths caused by the fake rice wine was huge. Some legislative members proposed a bill to only lower the tax on rice wine. The Administration was then mandated to re-negotiate a possible tax reduction with its major trading partners. The Administration was well aware of the views of its trading partners, but it still requested a consultation in order to ease the public's anger. The trading partners, like the U.S., reacted positively to the tax reduction on rice wine, but requested no differential treatment on other spirits. Such a reaction was expected based on the WTO rules.

Rice wine is not a strategic product or related to a sensitive industry. Although the reform of the tobacco and wine monopoly system faced many difficulties, the rice wine incident was unexpected. The people's outrage was surprising. It arose from the long-term frustration over shortages of rice wine, which had occurred yearly before Taiwan's accession due to the government's failure to prevent sellers from cornering the market. The outrage was also caused by the public's misconception about the reason why a cheap cooking wine had become a trade issue. All the negative experiences accumulated from the 1980s relating to U.S. requests to open Taiwan's market for wine and tobacco led the public to believe that this was just another example of the lack of capability of the government in protecting the people's interests during its trade negotiations with the U.S.

The dissatisfaction of the general public suggests that the Administration in Taiwan did not prepare the public as well as it prepared the industrial groups for the impact of accession. As discussed above, different ministries, departments, and agencies organized numerous briefings and seminars, but these were for industrial groups, not the general public. It is true that the liberalization of market access is ultimately beneficial to consumers, but it does not mean that the public will not be adversely affected by the WTO accession in the short run.

Accession involves both market opening and rules compliance. The latter may require changes in the behavior and the sense of fairness on the part of the public. For example, the public's respect for IPR required compliance with TRIPs. If the public could not appreciate the merits of the WTO discipline and the importance of such discipline in securing Taiwan's own interests, any change requiring the cooperation of the public to comply with WTO rules would be implemented at very high political costs or would fail altogether.

GPA Accession

Another difficult aspect of implementing Taiwan's commitments after WTO accession involved relations with the PRC. Regardless of whether the two sides across the strait could reach some consensus on political issues, Taiwan had always felt that trade issues could be settled in a more equitable and effective way if both sides were to make better use of the WTO platform, as pointed out in the previous section. Unfortunately, China appeared not to share this view.

Taiwan's efforts to normalize cross-strait trade did not result in China treating Taiwan equally as a WTO member. Under the WTO framework, there should be no reason for China to treat Taiwan differently from the other members because of the MFN principle. As the discussion in Joseph Fewsmith's chapter makes clear, China has been very concerned about the possible political implications of direct contacts with the authorities on Taiwan. As a result, even with regard to the notification and consultation procedures mandated by WTO rules, China either chose not to observe them, until contact was unavoidable, or tried to make the contact as informal as possible.

The difficulties that Taiwan encountered in its interactions with China in the WTO also affected Taiwan's ability to implement its own accession commitments. As mentioned before, Taiwan agreed to join the GPA even though such adherence is optional for WTO members. In order to fulfill this commitment, Taiwan had to take a separate accession track for the GPA since it is not a multi-lateral, but a pluri-lateral agreement providing for a separate accession process independent of the WTO. In other words, Taiwan could not become a GPA signatory automatically, after it acquired the WTO membership.

When Taiwan became a WTO member, it had almost concluded all of its bilateral market access negotiations for the GPA, and therefore it seemed likely that it would complete its accession process at the first GPA Committee meeting of 2002, thus fulfilling its obligation.[25] Unfortunately, this did not occur. By June 2006, Taiwan still had not joined the GPA, not because of any market opening insufficiency or failure of its legal regime to conform to the GPA rules, but rather because of China's objections regarding issues of nomenclature.

The nomenclature problem arose from the market-opening list Taiwan was required to prepare for GPA accession. This list provides the names of the government agencies and institutions that are committed to open their procurement above certain thresholds to foreign suppliers. The sovereign flavor attached to the names of these ministries, departments, and agencies, such as the Presidential Office, the Ministry of National Defense, and so forth, was simply too strong for China to accept, even though China was not yet a signatory of the GPA.[26] Beijing's continued objections have held up Taiwan's accession.

With Taiwan's entry into the GPA seemingly deadlocked, the local foreign business communities in Taiwan began to criticize the government for its failure to observe its accession commitments to open up the government procurement market. However, opening up its government procurement market without becoming a GPA signatory put Taiwan in a disadvantageous situation because it was

---

[25] Report of the Working Party on the Accession of the Separate Customs Territory of Taiwan, Penghu, Kinmen and Matsu, WTO Doc. WT/MIN(01)/4, November 11, 2001, para. 166.

[26] Lin Mei-fang, "Zhongguo Zunao Wo Jiaru WTO Zhengfu Caigou Xieding" [China Obstructing Our Accession to the WTO Government Procurement Agreement], *Ziyou Shibao* [Liberty Times], February 23, 2002, www.libertytimes.com.tw/2002/new/feb/23/today-p7.htm (accessed June 1, 2006).

not able to gain access to the other GPA signatories' procurement markets through the GPA arrangement. Moreover, unilateral liberalization would make the likelihood of Taiwan joining the GPA even more remote because no member would be interested in helping Taiwan resolve the problem caused by the PRC's unreasonable insistence on "one China" in the WTO, once the other WTO members obtained free access to Taiwan's procurement market. In other words, in spite of the benefits to government procurement by unilateral liberalization, Taiwan could not help but be reluctant to open up its procurement market unilaterally, if it was to secure a fair playing field for its industries in other countries' government procurement by means of accession to the GPA.

Whether it is fair to blame the authorities on Taiwan for the failure of fulfillment is unclear. However, the real problem is that this case is just the tip of the iceberg. Taiwan continues to face such issues, and even substantive blockages, from the mainland, its fourth-largest trading partner.[27] The greatest challenge for Taiwan as a WTO member is to prevent such political and diplomatic conflicts with the mainland from interfering with its implementation of its accession commitments.

CONCLUSION

Taiwan made substantial commitments for its WTO accession. However, the changes after accession do not appear very significant due to its early liberalization efforts and the long accession process. Regardless, the way in which Taiwan incorporated the negotiation commitments into its existing legal system, the challenge of the MFN and NT requirements to its relationship with its long-time trading partners and domestic vested interests, the complex and large internal consultative process, the tensions among different ministries, departments, and agencies due to accession, and the new

[27] Jiang Qizheng, "WTO Neng Huajie Liang'an Zhengzhi Duizhi Ma?" [Can WTO Resolve the Cross-Strait Political Deadlock?], *Zhongguo Shibao* (China Times), April 29, 2004.

cross-strait problems arising from interaction with China in the WTO forum are all good lessons for Taiwan. These experiences help Taiwan to continue its pursuit of liberalization with legal support; to further integrate itself into the world trading system without overdependence on bilateral relations; to be more accountable to its constituencies on trade and economic issues; and to expedite unilaterally the normalization of cross-strait trade.

The political problems from China over Taiwan's WTO membership show that, despite expectations in Taiwan, for the moment, China has no intention of interacting with Taiwan under the WTO framework. As pointed out previously, Taiwan has a separate trade regime for its trade with the PRC, which is not completely guided by WTO rules, but rather directed by the assessment of the authorities in Taiwan of the cross-strait and global environment. Therefore, when the authorities in Taiwan realize that its unilateral trade normalization efforts have failed to encourage the PRC to use the WTO as a platform for mutual dialogue, it cannot but pause to reflect on whether the PRC is prepared to treat Taiwan as an equal WTO member. Despite WTO accession, the PRC still attempts to block Taiwan's important trade activities, such as GPA accession and the pursuit of free trade agreements, and refuses to enter into any formal or proper dialogues with Taiwan within the WTO. As a result, Taiwan cannot but be more cautious in dealing with its trade relations with the PRC.

On the surface, it appears that there is no hope at all for Taiwan to use the WTO framework to normalize its overall relations with China. However, the possibility that the economic and trade liberalization driven by China's WTO membership may further the democratization process there, and thus, in the long run, narrow the political differences on each side of the strait should not be ruled out. This certainly would be a positive development for future cross-strait relations.

Appendix 1

Authorities	Title of Law	Summary of Amendments	Promulgation	Effective
Ministry of Interior Affairs	Architects' Law	The amendment is to delete the reciprocity requirement for foreigners to take the architects' examination and become qualified to practice in Chinese Taipei.	1997.05.07	1998.11.10
	Architecture Law	The amendment is to provide a legal basis for foreign construction service suppliers to set up businesses in Taiwan.	2001.11.14	2002.01.01
Ministry of Foreign Affairs	Statute Governing Privileges and Immunities of the Foreign Missions and their Personnel in Chinese Taipei	This addition to the Law is to extend privileges and immunities to WTO-related personnel for purposes of Article 8 of the Marrakesh Agreement Establishing the World Trade Organization.	1997.11.14	2002.01.01
Ministry of Finance	Customs Law	This set of amendments is to achieve the following objectives: (i) to provide a legal basis for the application of tariff-quotas negotiated by Chinese Taipei as substitution measures for existing restrictions;	1997.05.07	2002.01.01

(Continued)

Appendix 1 (*Continued*)

Authorities	Title of Law	Summary of Amendments	Promulgation	Effective
		(ii) to provide for a duty of secrecy to customs personnel with respect to information submitted for the assessment of import duties, so as to meet the requirement of Article 10 of the Agreement on Customs Valuation; (iii) to provide a legal basis for the establishment of the rules of origin and the authority to require the submission of the certificates of origin; (iv) to revise the customs valuation rules according to the Agreement on Customs Valuation; (v) to delete the provisions that limit the drawbacks of import duties to imports of machinery by certain high-tech or important companies whose products are solely for export; and (vi) to revise the provision relating to the determination of normal value for purposes of anti-dumping administration so as to make it consistent with Article 2 of the Anti-dumping Agreement.		
	Customs Import Tariff and Classification of Import & Export Commodities	The amendment is to implement the ITA to lower the tariffs on 260 information technology/ electronic products.	1998.06.17	2002.01.01

(*Continued*)

Appendix 1 (*Continued*)

Authorities	Title of Law	Summary of Amendments	Promulgation	Effective
	Customs Import Tariff and Classification of Import & Export Commodities	The amendment is to lower the tariffs on 13 items, such as beef and salmon, and to add a tariff line for fresh blue cod (*parapercis colias*).	1998.06.17	2002.01.01
	Customs Import Tariff and Classification of Import & Export Commodities	Amended in accordance with the Schedule of Concessions, an annex to the Working Party Report.	2001.11.14	2002.01.01
	Business Tax Law	The amendments are to exclude harbor construction dues from the tax base of the business tax, and to require that the business tax base shall include the tobacco and alcohol tax, as provided in the new Tobacco and Alcohol Tax Law.	1997.05.07	2002.01.01
	Statute for Commodity Tax (The first bill)	The amendment is to delete rules relating to tobacco and alcohol products, as this part of the law will be replaced by the new Tobacco and Alcohol Tax Law, a separate body of law.	1997.05.07	2002.01.01
	Statute for Commodity Tax (The second bill)	The amendment is to eliminate the tax deduction provided to manufacturers of automobiles and motorcycles using domestically-developed and designed parts.	2001.10.31	2002.01.01

(*Continued*)

Appendix 1 (*Continued*)

Authorities	Title of Law	Summary of Amendments	Promulgation	Effective
	Tobacco and Alcohol Tax Law	The new legislation is to achieve the following: (i) to provide definitions of tobacco and alcoholic beverages; (ii) to establish a new tax system in light of the reform of the tobacco and alcohol monopoly to facilitate tax collection; (iii) to establish tax collection procedures to facilitate the enforcement of the new tax regime.	2000.04.19	2002.01.01
	Statute Governing the Organization of the National Treasury, Ministry of Finance	The amendments reflect the administrative modifications made with the reform of the tobacco and alcohol monopoly. A department will be added to the current organizational structure to implement administrative rules established in the new Tobacco and Alcohol Administration Law.	2000.04.19	2000.04.21
	Tobacco and Alcohol Administration Law	Following the tobacco and alcohol reform plan, the new law is to provide a legislative mandate to the administrative authorities for the trade liberalization of tobacco and alcohol products.	2000.04.19	2002.01.01
	Banking Law	This amendment is to complement the amendment of Article 23 of the Central Bank Act with respect to authority in the setting of the deposit reserve ratio and reserves for other liabilities.	1997.05.07	1999.07.07

(*Continued*)

Appendix 1 (*Continued*)

Authorities	Title of Law	Summary of Amendments	Promulgation	Effective
	Securities and Exchange Law	This amendment is to delete the requirement that certain business personnel of securities firms be Taiwan residents.	1997.05.07	2001.01.15
	Certified Public Accountants Law (The first bill)	The amendment is to delete the reciprocity requirement for foreigners to take the examination and be qualified as certified public accountants in Taiwan.	1997.05.07	Integrated into the second bill.
	Certified Public Accountants Law (The second bill)	The amendment is to abolish the restriction on cross-district practicing.	2001.11.14	2002.01.01
Ministry of Justice	Lawyers' Law (The first bill)	The amendment is to delete the reciprocity requirement for foreigners to take the bar examination and become qualified to practice ROC law.	1998.06.24	2002.01.01
	Lawyers' Law (The second bill)	The amendment is to allow foreign lawyers to have partnerships with, or hire Taiwan (ROC) lawyers.	2001.11.14	2002.01.01
Ministry of Economic Affairs	Company Law	The amendment is to delete the reciprocity requirement for the recognition of foreign companies and the public offerings of foreign companies' shares and corporate bonds so as to fulfill Taiwan's commitments under the GATT.	1997.06.25	2002.01.01

(*Continued*)

Appendix 1 (*Continued*)

Authorities	Title of Law	Summary of Amendments	Promulgation	Effective
	Foreign Trade Act	Article 6: The amendment is to remove previous authorization to take restrictive trade measures when encountering bilateral imbalances of trade. The new version changes the condition for taking such actions to imbalances in international payments. Article 18: The amendment deletes the words "drastic or large" in describing the amount of increase in imports as a condition to initiate domestic safeguard actions. This is to follow the use of the language in the Safeguard Agreement. The amendment also provides a legal basis for the authority to set rules to initiate safeguard actions as contemplated in the Agreement on Textiles and Clothing. Article 20.1: This is a new addition to the Law, which is intended to provide the legal basis for the authority to regulate the pre-shipment inspection activities of firms mandated by foreign governments.	1997.05.07	1999.01.01

(*Continued*)

Appendix 1 (*Continued*)

Authorities	Title of Law	Summary of Amendments	Promulgation	Effective
		It also provides binding effects of the decisions of the dispute resolution panel of the WTO Preshipment Inspection Agreement on the private parties concerned, namely, the pre-shipment inspection company and the exporter.		
	Commodity Inspection Law	The amendment exercise is to achieve the following three objectives: (i) to incorporate international standards in the domestic standard-setting process, so as to ensure that domestic inspection standards follow international trends, and the inspection regime meets the requirements of the TBT Agreement;	1997.05.07	1998.12.01
		(ii) to accord national treatment to foreign products, in terms of the application of simplified procedures and exemptions that were previously available only to domestic products; and (iii) to accept and recognize foreign inspection certificates in order to be in line with the spirit of the TBT Agreement, particularly those calling for mutual recognition.	1997.05.07	1998.12.01

(*Continued*)

Appendix 1 *(Continued)*

Authorities	Title of Law	Summary of Amendments	Promulgation	Effective
	Standards Law	The amendment is to be in harmony with the TBT Agreement of the WTO.	1997.11.26	1997.11.28
	Trademark Law	To broaden the scope of reciprocal granting of the right of priority; to include combinations of colors in the group of items eligible for trademarks; to extend administrative protection to well-known marks by providing that no applications may be filed for the registration of a trademark design that is identical, or similar to another person's well-known trademark or mark, and likely to cause the public to have a mistaken impression.	1997.05.07	1998.11.01
	Patent Law (The first bill)	To amend the judicial apparatus that may treat the objects infringing intellectual property rights with noncommercial means; to provide patent owners and his/her exclusive licensees the right to request the destruction, or other necessary disposition of the infringing goods, raw materials, or instruments used, in connection with the infringement; to provide for longer terms of protection for industrial design; to delete the requirement of reciprocity with respect to the granting of patents for micro-organisms, extension of patent protection terms, and the granting of exclusive import rights.	1997.05.07	2002.01.01

(Continued)

Appendix 1 (*Continued*)

Authorities	Title of Law	Summary of Amendments	Promulgation	Effective
	Patent Law (The second bill)	To provide the term of protection for patents still in effect upon accession to the WTO 20 years and 12 years from the date of filing for invention patents and new design patents respectively.	2001.10.24	2001.10.26
	Copyright Law (The first bill)	To amend the definitions for public broadcasts and public performances; to delete provisions concerning compulsory licenses for translations in accordance with TRIPS; and to ensure the performances of the performer.	1998.01.21	1998.01.23
	Copyright Law (The second bill)	The term of protection for computer program copyright is extended to the lifespan of the author plus 50 years.	2001.11.12	2001.11.14
	Copyright Intermediary Organization Act	The new legislation is to promote and to facilitate the use of copyrighted works by the general public through well-established professional copyright intermediary organizations.	1997.11.05	1997.11.07
	Statute for Optical Disk Management	This new legislation adds punishment against the illegal manufacturing of optical disks, including criminal penalties, the revocation of production permits, administrative fines, and the confiscation of machinery.	2001.11.14	2001.11.16

(*Continued*)

Appendix 1 *(Continued)*

Authorities	Title of Law	Summary of Amendments	Promulgation	Effective
	Law for the Administration of State-Owned Enterprises	The amendment is to eliminate the preferential treatment on the procurement of locally-produced material and equipment by state-owned enterprises.	1998.01.07	1999.05.27
	Statute for the Establishment and Management of Economic Processing Zones (The first bill)	The amendment is to delete the provision that excludes duty drawbacks on imported machinery sold to in-zone enterprises by firms located in areas where tariffs were levied in order to eliminate the possible tendency to encourage the purchase of locally-produced machinery.	1997.05.07	1997.05.09
	Statute for the Establishment and Management of Economic Processing Zones (The second bill)	The amendment is to abolish the requirement to export, and limitations on the percentage of local sales.	2001.05.30	2001.06.01
Ministry of Transportation and Communications	Commercial Port Law (The first bill)	The amendment is to levy harbor construction dues on goods transported on domestic routes via harbors.	1997.05.07	Integrated into the second bill.

(Continued)

Appendix 1 (*Continued*)

Authorities	Title of Law	Summary of Amendments	Promulgation	Effective
	Commercial Port Law (The second bill)	The amendment is to eliminate harbor construction dues that were levied on an ad valorem basis, and collect harbor service fees based on, inter alia, the gross registered tonnage of vessels entering the harbor, the weight of cargo loaded and unloaded in the harbor, and the number of departing passengers, in order to be consistent with Article 8 of the GATT 1994.	2001.11.21	2002.01.01
	Navigation Industry Law	The amendment is to open the market for maritime freight transport agencies, cargo handling and forwarding services, and stacking yard services to foreign service suppliers.	1999.02.03	1999.02.05
	Highway Law	The amendment is to permit authorized foreign service suppliers to supply car rental, trucking, and container trucking services.	1997.05.07	1997.11.01
	Telecommunications Act	The amendment is to relax the percentage of foreign equity ownership of local telecommunications businesses for direct and indirect investment in accordance with the commitments made in the Service Schedule.	1999.11.03	1999.11.05

(*Continued*)

Appendix 1 (*Continued*)

Authorities	Title of Law	Summary of Amendments	Promulgation	Effective
	Civil Aviation Law	The amendment is to abolish the ceiling limit on foreign equity and the number of foreign directors in air cargo forwarding and stacking yard businesses.	2001.11.14	2001.11.16
Ministry of Examination	Examination Law for Professionals and Technical	The amendment is to permit foreigners to take the examination for real estate surveyor, certified agent for real estate registrations, real estate broker, and insurance professional, and to eliminate the reciprocity requirement in allowing foreigners to take the professional and engineer examinations.	2001.11.14 Personnel	2001.11.14
Gov't Information Office	Publication Law	This law was repealed on January 25, 1999, to allow the unregistered publication of copyright protection.	1999.01.25	1999.01.27 Repealed
	Law Governing Motion Pictures	The amendment is to delete the legal basis that mandates a minimum percentage of the screening of domestic motion pictures, and authorizes the levy of domestic motion picture assistance dues against imported motion pictures.	2001.11.14	2001.11.16
Department of Health	Law of Pharmaceutical Affairs	This amendment is to lift the restriction on and provide the rules for regulating the repackaging of imported pharmaceutical products.	1997.05.07	2002.01.01

(*Continued*)

Appendix 1 *(Continued)*

Authorities	Title of Law	Summary of Amendments	Promulgation	Effective
	Law Governing Food Sanitation	The amendment is to provide the labeling of food products with an option to use the date of manufacture or the expiry date as a code for product identification.	1997.05.07	1998.08.01
National Science Council	Statute for the Establishment and Administration of a Science-Based Industrial Park	To delete the provision that excludes duty drawbacks on machinery sold in this zone, in order to eliminate the possibility of encouraging park-based enterprises purchasing locally-produced machinery.	2001.01.20	2001.01.20
Veterans Affairs Commission	Statute of Veterans Affairs	The amendment is to abolish the preference in favor of the organizations under the Veterans Affairs Commission in the government procurement of construction projects.	1997.05.14	1997.05.14
Council of Agriculture	Statute Governing the Organization of the Council of Agriculture	The amendment is to provide that the Council of Agriculture is in charge of national agriculture policy.	1998.06.24	1998.06.26
	Statute Governing the Organization of the Bureau of Animal and Plant Health Inspection and Quarantine	The statute is to provide a legal basis for the establishment of a competent authority in charge of animal and plant health inspection and quarantine.	1998.06.24	1998.06.26

(Continued)

Appendix 1 (*Continued*)

Authorities	Title of Law	Summary of Amendments	Promulgation	Effective
	Livestock Husbandry Law	The amendment is to provide a basis to regulate livestock imports resulting from the market opening.	1998.06.24	1998.06.26
	Food Management Law (The first bill)	The amendment is to lift the ban on rice imports and provide a basis for the collection of mark-ups from imported rice under the quota system.	1997.05.30	1997.06.01
	Food Management Law (The second bill)	The amendments to this law are to minimize the price differential between domestic and imported goods. Japan's "mark-up" approach to imports of cereal, rice, and processed rice products will be adopted, consistent with Article 4(2) of the WTO Agreement on Agriculture.	2001.11.07	2001.11.09
	Statute for Agriculture Development	The amendments to this statute are to achieve the following: (i) to introduce a competitive pricing system by deleting "uniform pricing" for exported agricultural products, and to complement the enforcement of the Fair Trade Law and open-market mechanisms;	2000.01.09	2000.01.26

(*Continued*)

Appendix 1 (*Continued*)

Authorities	Title of Law	Summary of Amendments	Promulgation	Effective
		(ii) to expand the statute to include special safeguard provisions consistent with the WTO Agreement on Agriculture; and (iii) to introduce measures to prevent the monopolization of the market.		
	Veterinarians' Law	The amendment is to delete the reciprocity requirement.	2001.11.07	2002.01.01
Public Construction Commission	Government Procurement Law	This legislation is to mandate that the government procurement procedures be consistent with the rules of the WTO Government Procurement Agreement, and institute the dispute settlement procedures in the context of government procurements.	1998.05.27	1999.05.27
The Central Bank	Central Bank Act	The amendment is to replace current limitations on foreign liabilities of banks operating in Chinese Taipei with reserve requirements.	1997.05.21	1999.07.07

Chapter

4

Economic Prospects from Cross-Strait WTO Membership

Chi Schive

INTRODUCTION

Despite a dramatic increase in economic links across the Taiwan Strait since the late 1980s, the easing of official restrictions by the Taiwan side was gradual. In most areas, only "indirect" links were permissible, and trade and investment were closely regulated. After both sides entered the WTO, it was expected that Taiwan would adjust these policies in conformity with WTO rules, and, in particular, with the nondiscrimination principle. This chapter examines the extent to which this has been the case.

Given that commodity trade is a major component of Taiwan's WTO commitments, the focus of this discussion is on policies related to commodity trade with the PRC. Other areas, such as the movement of natural persons and capital, are not immediate concerns, although they are of growing interest. Moreover, no concrete agreement has been reached in the area of maritime and air transportation, which does not fall directly under WTO guidance.

In this chapter, the first section introduces a projection of the possible economic impact on both sides of the strait of policy changes made in accordance with WTO rules. The next section explores the reasoning guiding Taiwan's current policies to restrict the scope of cross-strait economic ties. Section three discusses the unilateral import and investment restrictions by Taiwan with respect to the PRC, that result from this reasoning. Section four reviews existing regulations on Taiwan regarding investment in and technological collaboration with the PRC. The conclusion explores the implications of the arguments presented here.

PROJECTED IMPACT

According to simulations by a GTAP model, real GDP in Taiwan and the PRC was predicted to increase 0.17 percent and 0.15 percent, respectively (see Table 4.1) as a result of WTO membership if direct shipments across the Taiwan Strait remained highly-regulated during the modeling period.[1] However, the model also suggested an increase of 0.21 percent in Taiwan and 0.17 percent in the PRC, if

Table 4.1 Impact of Taiwan and PRC WTO Entry (Static Simulation)

	GDP percent	Investment percent	Exports percent	Imports percent	Welfare US$ million
Strict regulations on cross-strait shipments					
Taiwan	0.17	0.56	2.41	3.16	524
China	0.15	4.76	−0.36	6.31	4,044
Cross-strait shipments and fewer restrictions on Taiwan's investment in the PRC					
Taiwan	0.21	1.18	2.70	4.37	1,942
China	0.17	7.02	−1.89	8.21	7,291

Source: See Footnote 1.

[1] Chou Ji, Shiu-Tung Wang, Kun-Ming Chen, and Nai-Fong Kuo, "Trade and Direct Investment across the Taiwan Strait: An Empirical Analysis of Taiwan and China's Accession into the WTO," paper presented at the Cross-Strait Industrial Development and Cooperation under the WTO Framework Conference, Taipei, December 2002.

Taiwan adopted a more liberalized approach by opening cross-strait shipments and relaxing investment restrictions toward the PRC.

The simulated impact on individual sectors after entry by each side showed that Taiwan would see an expansion in areas where it had a comparative advantage. The beneficiaries would be capital-intensive and technology-intensive industries, including textiles, chemicals, petroleum, metal products, electronics and machinery equipment, as well as the relevant supporting industries, such as transportation and communications. Other sectors, especially beverages and tobacco, motor vehicles, clothing, agriculture, and mining, would see contractions. In the PRC, the non-heavy manufacturing sector was expected to see an expansion.

Despite lower production in some sectors, imports were expected to expand on both sides, while the PRC's exports were expected to decline. Hsu, Chang and Lin[2] estimated that Taiwan's exports to and imports from the U.S. would increase by 0.38 percent and 8.09 percent, respectively. The PRC's exports to and imports from the U.S. would increase 6.31 percent and 8.83 percent, respectively. Clearly WTO entry was expected not only to further intensify the division of labor across the Taiwan Strait, but also to extend this trend to the U.S.

Chou's GTAP model also predicted a trade diversion from other areas to the PRC. Under the more restricted regulatory case on shipping links, it was estimated that the PRC's share of Taiwan's exports would increase by 0.89 percent from 21.13 percent. Should shipping and investment regulations be relaxed, the change might then be 3.85 percent. It is worth noting that it was predicted that Taiwan's share of the PRC's market would change little in the strict case, although in the more liberalized case, it would increase 0.35 percent. An intuitive explanation for the smaller change in Taiwan's share in the PRC market relative to the PRC's share in the Taiwan market is that this is due to the liberalized treatment already granted. Before

[2] Hsu Shi-hsun, Jin-jen Chang, and Huan-sherng Lin, "Quantitative Analysis of Taiwan-United States Economic Interlinks," *Industry of Free China*, January 2003 (in Chinese).

entering the WTO, Taiwan had more restrictions on PRC products than vice versa. Therefore, in order to implement the WTO rules, Taiwan had much more to do to open to the PRC. Since the PRC market was already open to Taiwan as a "domestic" actor, there were fewer changes required on the mainland side.[3]

THE RATIONALE BEHIND TAIWAN'S POST-WTO CROSS-STRAIT ECONOMIC POLICIES

Theoretically and empirically, common membership in the WTO will bring remarkable economic benefits to both sides of the Taiwan Strait by pursuing greater efficiency in resource allocation through a division of labor. Beyond economic welfare, increasing economic links will create opportunities for dialogue, cooperation, and friendly interchanges, thus helping to promote a peaceful and stable development of cross-strait relations.

However, given the vast differences between Taiwan's current regulatory system for cross-strait economic links and a WTO-conforming framework, the impact of a comprehensive implementation of the WTO rules would be immense. The immediate impact would be on the domestic market and production due to the influx of low-priced imports from the PRC. Imports from Japan, Korea, and the U.S. would be crowded out, as would certain domestic agricultural and industrial goods. Goods produced and brought in by Taiwan firms investing in the PRC were expected to be very competitive due to their better marketing position and cultural proximity, resulting in a loss of employment in comparable industries on the island.

The services sector, the financial markets, and especially the stock and real estate markets, would be vulnerable to fluctuations, if exposed to PRC investors without an effective firewall. This would increase the financial risks.

[3] Because of this, it has been argued that with dual entry, Taiwan would be even worse off because it would no longer enjoy differential treatment according to the national treatment principle.

Finally, if PRC investment were permitted without any restrictions, the inflow of managerial and technical professionals from the PRC would have a lasting impact on Taiwan's employment structure.

IMPACT ON ECONOMIC SECTORS

The agricultural sector will be under the greatest threat should the domestic market be opened to products from the mainland. Many agricultural goods can be grown on the mainland where weather conditions and consumer tastes are similar to those on Taiwan at much lower costs. Fresh vegetables and certain fruits, fishery products, and livestock meats would be most affected. However Taiwan producers of some products with a competitive advantage, such as fruits, flowers, and agricultural products in shortage in the PRC, would benefit from increased exports to the mainland.

In the short run, the import of some fishery and livestock products from the PRC will be strictly prohibited because of quarantine problems. However, trade in fishery products via off-shore fishing boats has existed for some time and is well-known. In the long run, the impact will increase as the quarantine problems are solved and the flow of goods produced by Taiwan firms that have invested in the PRC grows.

The impact on the industrial sector will be mixed. Some groups of labor-intensive products, traditional industries, and lower-quality products might be affected by low-priced imports from the mainland. These include automobiles, beverages, tobacco, iron and steel, electrical home appliances, and consumer electronics. Some industries, however, could lower production costs, and thus increase price competitiveness by using low-priced inputs of raw materials and parts from the PRC. These include export-oriented industries such as textiles, informatics, electronics, and auto parts.

The impact on the service industries will be profound. As Taiwan's service industry still enjoys a comparative advantage over the counterpart on the mainland in the area of operational and management skills, no immediate impact is foreseen if the PRC's investment in services is allowed to enter the domestic market. In the medium to long run, however, PRC investors may plan strategically to develop specific service industries, thus threatening local rivals. In addition, the authorities on Taiwan need to address those issues arising from the inflow of managerial and professional nationals due to the PRC's investment in services.

TRADE AND INVESTMENT ACROSS THE STRAIT

In terms of direct trade, Taiwan's exports to and imports from the PRC increased 109.8 percent and 34.7 percent, respectively, in 2002 — the first year after both sides formally joined the WTO. The jump in Taiwan's export figure is, to a large extent, attributable to the reclassification of data from indirect trade to direct trade. If indirect trade is included as before, the figures are estimated to be 22.4 percent and 34.7 percent, respectively. Imports from the PRC are expected to grow considerably as Taiwan reduces prohibitions of such imports (see Table 4.2). In 2002 alone, Taiwan relaxed prohibitions on one-fifth of the tradable items for import from the PRC.

High expectations of a more open goods and services market in the mainland will attract more Taiwan investment, further securing the cross-strait economic link. Such increasing interdependence will weigh more heavily on Taiwan's part because of its relatively more open economy, higher income, better-quality products, and more advanced technology.

Table 4.2 Trade before and after WTO Accession

	Estimation of Taiwan Exports to Mainland China		Taiwan Imports from Mainland China	
	US$ million	Change %	US$ million	Change %
1998	19,841	−11.6	4,111	5.0
1999	21,313	7.4	4,522	10.0
2000	25,010	17.3	6,223	37.6
2001	21,946	−12.3	5,902	−5.2
2002	29,446	34.2	7,947	34.7
2003	35,358	20.1	10,962	37.9

Source: Mainland Affairs Council.

ECONOMIC AND NON-ECONOMIC CONCERNS

There is a growing fear that the domestic economy in Taiwan is being "marginalized" and losing its industrial base due to the PRC's fast-growing economic power and expanding influence in the region. Therefore, the challenge for policymakers has been to formulate a strategy that will promote globalization while, at the same time, improving Taiwan's deeply rooted basic industrial strength, so as to ensure sustained growth.

Most troubling to Taiwan's leaders are the non-economic aspects of cross-strait relations. The administration foresees a risk of fading national sovereignty in dealing with the PRC on WTO issues as globalization deepens and broadens. For this reason, national security issues have in the past — and will continue in the future — to trump the putative economic benefits that might accrue from cross-strait contacts.

INITIAL GUIDELINES GOVERNING TAIWAN POLICY AFTER ACCESSION

Shortly before accession by both sides, Taiwan was hopeful that there would be a breakthrough in cross-strait relations. In December 2001, the Mainland Affairs Council (MAC) Chairperson Ing-Wen Tsai reduce foresaw "a real opportunity to jointly develop a framework and a set of rules between themselves in regulating the cross-Strait trade and investment; despite that, both sides had limited dialogue on the so-called 'functional issues' in the 1990s."[4]

Taiwan understood that the intensity and the volume of trade and investment flows between the two sides were such that, without proper joint efforts, there would always be a danger of disorder and damage to the interests of traders and investors. Taiwan anticipated that WTO trade rules, to a large extent, would apply to cross-strait trade, as both parties made adjustments or committed to

[4] Tsai Ing-Wen, "A New Era in Cross-Strait Relations? Taiwan and China in the WTO," Washington DC: The Heritage Foundation, December 13, 2001.

making adjustments to their trade regimes to make them compatible with WTO standards. Taiwan was, initially, very optimistic about a closer "direct/formal" economic relationship with the mainland that would result, despite an inevitable transition, from efforts to "bring the bilateral trade relations fully in line with the WTO requirements." Most importantly, under the WTO, there would be mechanisms for consultation between the two sides, which had not existed previously.

It was acknowledged that a transition was required because of the great divide between the economic institutions on the two sides.[5] Moreover, while there was a willingness to follow WTO rules and regulations, and WTO commitments regarding the opening of Taiwan markets to Chinese products and services, any liberalization with regard to economic links with the mainland would be permitted, only if it did not jeopardize national security (see footnote 4). This explains the discrepancy that has continued to exist between Taiwan's WTO commitments and Taiwan's regulatory system governing economic policies toward the mainland.

With these general principles in mind, on January 16, 2002, in the wake of Taiwan's accession to the WTO, the Executive Yuan (the Cabinet) adopted the "Implementation Plan for Adjusting Cross-Strait Trade and Economic Policies in Line with Accession to the WTO." The intent was to pave the way for direct transactions in cross-strait trade; the step-by-step opening up for mainland investment in Taiwan; and direct remittances, mail, and communications between the two sides. Areas to be adjusted under the plan included the review mechanism and the safeguard mechanisms for Chinese imports (in particular, textile imports); the services trade; the inflow of Chinese capital; and the flow of personnel. The principles governing these adjustments included:

1. Step-by-step development of cross-strait economic links on the grounds of stability and security.

[5] Executive Yuan, *Implementation Plan for Adjusting Cross-Strait Trade and Economic Policies in Line with Accession to the WTO*, January 2002.

2. Vigorous promotion of cross-strait consultations to reduce cross-strait economic uncertainties.
3. An initial focus on matters that could be determined solely on Taiwan's part.

Following the adoption of the implementation plan, direct trading was allowed between businessmen on each side of the strait in February 2002, accompanied by cross-strait direct remittances. At the same time, the number of mainland goods permitted to be imported into Taiwan was expanded to 73.15 percent of the overall total of product items. Compared to 56.92 percent in December 2001, this indicated the extent of the impact that WTO accession had already had on Taiwan policy. A regular evaluation mechanism every six months was established; in December 2002, the proportion grew to 75.80 percent and in December 2003 to 77.11 percent.

The percentage of permitted items was lower for agricultural products than for industrial products (61.48 percent versus 76.27 percent in February 2002).

For investments in the mainland, the rationale behind the policy adjustment was later termed "active liberalization with effective management." "Effective management" is required to manage the risks possibly arising from relaxation. "Active liberalization" relaxed restrictions on 8,163 agricultural and industrial products, accounting for 93.82 percent of the total by August 2002.

Investment in the infrastructure sector and the services sector was relaxed to include 68 general items in the services sectors, such as the insurance industry. However, as we shall see below, in certain sensitive areas, such as naphtha cracker plants, semiconductor design, packaging testing, real estate development, industrial park development, and incineration plants, there still has been no relaxation, though, optimistically, one might expect some relaxation to be forthcoming.

With regard to effective management, the emphasis was placed on the risk diversification of business capital. Equally important, a mechanism had to be established to encourage the return flow of profits and funds. To improve knowledge about mainland investments by Taiwan businesses, the government revised regulations to require Taiwan investors to register so as to legally invest in the mainland.

The opening for the inflow of mainland capital-investment in Taiwan was planned to be carried out gradually. In the first stage, the real-estate sector was opened in August 2002. In the second stage, it was anticipated that 58 out of 108 items in the service sector already opened to other countries would be opened for mainland capital-investment in Taiwan. Eventually, the list would be extended to include every sector. However, these changes were contingent upon the revision of Article 73 of the "Statute Governing Relations between the People of the Taiwan Area and the People of the Mainland Area."

Because there are few problems in the manufacturing sector, this sector is also part of the initial consideration. Above all, the government is cautious about possible risks of mainland investment.

The securities market will not be considered until a firewall is established that can adequately prevent "any unmanageable risk from occurring in the country's financial market once it is opened up to Mainland capital," as opening the securities market involves a complicated management problem of short-term capital flow.[6]

In expanding cross-strait financial flows, the government also took a gradualist approach. In the first stage, the OBUs (off-shore banking units) were allowed to process credit grants and account receivables. At the same time, direct remittances between the DBUs (domestic banking units) and mainland financial institutions were permitted. In the second stage, banks and insurance companies were allowed to set up branch offices on the mainland. For the third stage, the government is considering setting up an off-shore capital market to assist Taiwan businessmen on the mainland to raise funds in the local capital market, by encouraging trading in the emerging stock market and relaxing the terms in the issuance of Taiwan Depository Receipts (TDR).

---

[6] Tsai Ing-Wen, "Current Cross-Strait Trade and Economic Policy," speech to the Chinese National Federation of Industries, August 28, 2002.

With regard to cross-strait personnel exchanges, a trial implementation of allowing mainland tourists and category-2 mainland people began in 2002.[7] The government also relaxed restrictions to allow mainland high-tech personnel to travel to Taiwan. Mainlanders will be allowed to go to Taiwan to engage in business activities, in accordance with the policies concerning direct trade and mainland capital-investment in Taiwan. This will also permit multinational corporations in Taiwan to employ mainland personnel.

To sum up, the cautious tone of Taiwan's adjustments after WTO accession was due to both economic and non-economic concerns. Economic concerns focused on the competition following the opening of Taiwan's markets to the PRC and the survival of domestic businesses. Further economic dependency on the mainland deviated from the principle of economic diversification, and was also believed to narrow the space for Taiwan to maneuver politically. On the one hand, Taiwan needed to avoid the risk of being "marginalized" as the PRC emerged as a global production factory. On the other hand, liberalization in trade, investment, and services related to the PRC intensified the fear of a hollowing-out effect or endangering national security as a result of the magnetic effect of the mainland economy.

RESTRICTIONS ON IMPORTS FROM AND INVESTMENT BY THE PRC AFTER ACCESSION

The list of products allowed to be imported from the PRC has been continuously lengthened with each six-month review (see Table 4.3). The greatest progress occurred in 1996, prior to WTO entry, when the number of industrial products permitted for import was increased 23.89 percentage points from 28.67 percent to 52.56 percent. The second greatest change occurred in the year of its WTO entry.

[7] People from the mainland area who travel overseas for tourism or for business purposes will be permitted to visit Taiwan on the condition that they do not violate the laws and regulations of the mainland.

Table 4.3 Permitted Items for Import from the PRC, by Chinese Classification of Commodities, February 2004

		Agricultural Classification Chapters 1–24	Industrial Classification Chapters 25–97	Total
No. of items		2267	8485	10725
Permitted	No. of Items	1362	6945	8307
	% of total	12.7	64.75	77.45
	% of sectoral total	60.08	82.11	–
Prohibited	No. of items	905	1513	2418
	% of total	8.44	14.11	22.55
	% of sectoral total	39.92	17.93	–
Exempt from licensing	No. of Items	1349	6435	7784
	% of total	12.58	60.00	72.58
	% of permitted sectoral total	99.08	92.66	93.70

Source: Board of Foreign Trade, Ministry of Economic Affairs, http://www. trade. gov.tw

Table 4.4 lists permissible items for import. Some categories are very restrictive, with restricted items constituting a significant proportion: Section 1 (live animals and products), 44.9 percent; Section 2 (vegetable products), 39.7 percent; Section 4 (prepared foodstuffs, beverages, spirits, tobacco), 40.2 percent; Section 11 (textiles), 38.9 percent; Section 13 (articles of stone, ceramic products, glass, and glassware), 29.3 percent; Section 15 (basic metals and products), 35.7 percent; and Section 17 (vehicles, aircraft, vessels), 35.3 percent.

Other categories are less restrictive, with restricted items accounting for less than 10 percent: Section 3 (fats and oils), 10.3 percent; Section 5 (mineral products), 5.8 percent; Section 6, (chemicals), 8.7 percent; Section 7 (plastics and products), 3.8 percent; Section 9 (wood and products), 1.1 percent, Section 10 (pulp), 1.3 percent; Section 12 (consumer non-durables), 0 percent; Section 14 (jewelry), 4.9 percent; Section 16 (machinery), 12.0 percent; Section 18 (optical), 6.6 percent; Section 20 (miscellaneous), 0 percent; and Section 21 (works of art), 0 percent.

Table 4.4 Commodities Prohibited from Importing from the PRC (July 2003)

Section	Description	MW0	MP1	Sub-total	Total items	% of Prohibited
1	Live animals; animal products (ch. 1–5)	374	7	381	834	44.8
2	Vegetable products (ch. 6–14)	278	18	296	700	39.7
3	Animal or vegetable fats and oils and their cleavage products; prepared edible fats; animal or vegetable waxes (ch. 15)	8	0	8	78	10.3
4	Prepared foodstuffs; beverages, spirits, and vinegar; tobacco and manufactured tobacco substitutes (ch. 16–24)	296	30	326	737	40.2
5	Mineral products (ch. 25–27)	14	1	15	241	5.8
6	Products of the chemical or allied industries (ch. 28–38)	155	10	165	1788	8.7
7	Plastics and articles thereof; rubber and articles thereof (ch. 39–40)	15	0	15	397	3.8
8	Raw hides and skins, leather, fur skins and articles thereof; saddler and harness; travel goods, handbags, and similar containers; articles of animal gut (other than silk-worm gut) (ch. 41–43)	0	0	0	143	0
9	Wood and articles of wood; wood charcoal; cork and articles of cork; manufactures of straw, of esparto, or of other plaiting materials; basket ware and wickerwork (ch. 44–46)	2	11	13	188	1.1
10	Pulp of wood or of other fibrous cellulose material; recovered (waste and scrap) paper or paperboard; paper and paperboard and articles thereof (ch. 47–49)	4	15	19	298	1.3
11	Textiles and textile articles (ch. 50–63)	490	295	785	1260	38.9
12	Footwear, headgear, umbrellas, sun umbrellas, walking-sticks, seat-sticks, whips, riding-crops, and parts thereof; prepared feathers and articles made therewith; artificial flowers; and articles of human hair (ch. 64–67)	0	0	0	175	05

(Continued)

Table 4.4 (*Continued*)

Section	Description	MW0	MP1	Sub-total	Total items	% of Prohibited
13	Articles of stone, plaster, cement, asbestos, mica, or similar materials; ceramic products; glass and glassware (ch. 68–70)	76	32	108	259	29.3
14	Natural or cultured pearls, precious or semi-precious stones, precious metals, metals clad with precious metal and articles thereof; imitation jewelry; and coins (ch. 71)	4	3	7	82	4.9
15	Base metals and articles of base metal (ch. 72–83)	468	69	537	1312	35.7
16	Machinery and mechanical appliances; electrical equipment; parts thereof; sound recorders and reproducers, television image and sound recorders and reproducers, and parts and accessories of such articles (ch. 84–85)	184	58	242	1532	12.0
17	Vehicles, aircraft, vessels, and associated transport equipment (ch. 86–89)	94	1	95	266	35.3
18	Optical, photographic, cinematographic, measuring, checking, precision, medical, or surgical instruments and apparatus; clocks and watches; musical instruments; parts and accessories thereof (ch. 90–92)	28	7	35	423	6.6
19	Arms and ammunition; parts and accessories thereof (ch. 93)	5	0	5	26	19.2
20	Miscellaneous manufactured articles (ch. 94–96)	0	0	0	235	0
21	Works of art, collectors' pieces, and antiques (ch. 97)	0	0	0	14	0
	Tariff quota goods (ch. 98)	199	0	199	200	99.5

Source: Board of Foreign Trade, Ministry of Economic Affairs, http://www.trade.gov.tw

Agricultural products are subject to more restrictions for protective and sanitary and phyto-sanitary reasons. The most prominent case of a phyto-sanitary concern took place after the outbreak of the SARS epidemic. As the disease spread widely and rapidly during April and May 2003, the number of prohibited items in Section 1 (animals and products) increased continually. By July, it had risen to 374 from 130 before the outbreak of the disease.

Fabrics and textile products are subject to higher import barriers for protective reasons and to meet the rules of origin of third countries. The prohibited proportion of cotton is 91.4 percent; man-made filament, 80.2 percent; man-made staple fibers, 90.1 percent; spinner-woven fabrics, 71.1 percent; knitted fabrics, 87.1 percent; knitted apparels, 78.6 percent; and non-knitted apparels, 70.9 percent.

Iron and steel, and other metal products, are relatively highly-restrictive. Among iron and steel items, 59.4 percent are prohibited; copper and products, 51.2 percent; and aluminum products, 46.8 percent. Given that Taiwan's metal industries are adequately competitive and strong, it is unnecessary to impose protective restrictions on these products. It is suspected that the purpose of these restrictions is to raise the bargaining price.

INVESTMENT

Table 4.5 provides a list of permissible areas for Taiwan investment in the PRC. However, despite the government's "proactive (or active) liberalization" policy, no investment has yet taken place, except in the real-estate sector, due to the lack of supplementary regulations. In 2003, a special set of administrative measures was made available to govern investment from the PRC in real estate and rental/leasing services to boost the weak domestic market. Again, the response from the PRC was cold.[8]

Although the permissible list was said to be extended to include every sector, the government admitted that these changes were

[8] It was reported that only one case had occurred by mid-2004.

Table 4.5 Sectors Permitted for PRC Investment

1. BUSINESS SERVICES
A. Professional services
   b) Accounting, Auditing, and Bookkeeping Services (862)
      i. Certified public accountants
      ii. Other public accountants
   c) Taxation services (863)
   d), e), f), g) Architectural services, engineering services (8671), integrated engineering services (8673), urban planning and landscape architectural services (8674)
      i. Architects
      ii. Professional Engineers
      iii. Other (excluding architect and professional engineer certification services)
B. Computers and related services (excluding computerized airline reservation system services)(841, 842, 843, 844, 845, 849)
C. Research and development services (851, 852, 853)
E. Rental/leasing services without operators
   c) Financial leasing of private cars (83101**)
   d) Other machinery and equipment (83106-83109)
   e) Other (832)
F. Other business services
   a) Advertising services
      ii. Other advertising services (871*)
   c) Management consulting services (865)
   d) Services related to management consulting (866) (including management and operation by contract of health-care facilities on a "for fee" basis, but not including practices of the medical profession)
   e) Technical testing and analysis services (8676)
   h) Services incidental to mining (883, 5115)
   i) Services incidental to manufacturing (excluding 88442 publishing and printing) (884**, 885)
   n) Maintenance and repair of equipment (633, 8861-8866) (excluding maritime vessels, aircraft, and other transportation equipment)
   p) Photographic services (875)
   q) Packaging services (876)
   s) Convention services (87909*)
   t) Other
      i. Telephone answering services (87903)
      ii. Duplicating services (87904)

(*Continued*)

Table 4.5 (*Continued*)

iii. Translation and interpretation services (87905)
iv. Mailing list compilation and mailing services (87906)
v. Specialty design services (87907)

2. COMMUNICATION SERVICES
B. Land-based international courier services: all ground services arising as part of an international shipment being handled by an air express carrier for delivery to a consignee, except for those currently specifically reserved for local postal authorities by law
D. Audiovisual services
Sound recording services

3. CONSTRUCTION AND RELATED ENGINEERING SERVICES
3. Construction and related engineering services (511–518) (including dredging)

4. DISTRIBUTION SERVICES
A. Commission agents' services (621)
B. Wholesale trade services (excluding firearms and military equipment) (622)
C. Retail services (631, 632, 6111, 6113, 6121) (excluding firearms and military equipment)
D. Franchising (8929)

6. ENVIRONMENTAL SERVICES
B. Consulting services incidental to nature and landscape protection (9406**)

7. FINANCIAL SERVICES
A. Insurance and insurance-related services
ii.
b) Re-insurance and retrocession service

8. HEALTH-RELATED AND SOCIAL SERVICES
Other
– Leasing or rental services concerning medical devices without an operator

9. TOURISM AND TRAVEL-RELATED SERVICES
A. Hotels and restaurants (including catering)
b) Hotels (limited to tourist hotels) (excluding food and beverage serving services) (64110**)
c) Food serving services (642) (including related beverage serving services)

10. RECREATIONAL, CULTURAL, AND SPORTING SERVICES (OTHER THAN AUDIOVISUAL SERVICES)
D. Sporting and other recreational services (96411, 96412, 96419)

(*Continued*)

Table 4.5 (*Continued*)

11. TRANSPORT SERVICES
B. Air transport services
   a) Maintenance and repair of aircraft
   b) Selling and marketing of air transport services
   c) Computer reservation systems
F. Road transport services
   a) Passenger transportation (limited to car rental services)
   b) Transport and export of freight that has an origin or destination outside of Taiwan (7123**, excluding regular route freight transportation as currently defined in the Highway Law and those services currently specifically-reserved for postal authorities by law)
   d) Maintenance and repair of road transport equipment (6112, 8667)
H. Services auxiliary to all modes of transport
   c) Freight transport agency services (7480)
   d) Other supporting and auxiliary transport services (excluding local pick-up and delivery) (7490**)

Source: Mainland Affairs Council.

contingent upon the revision of Article 73 of the "Statute Governing Relations between the People of the Taiwan Area and the People of the Mainland Area." The revision was promulgated on October 29, 2003, with a changed tone from totally forbidden to conditionally permitted: "Unless permitted by the competent authorities, any individual, juristic person, organization, or other institution of the Mainland Area, or any company it invests in any third area may not engage in any investment activity in the Taiwan Area."

Previously, the government had no mandate to allow inward investment by the PRC. Now, inward PRC investing is to be permitted at the government's discretion (see Table 4.6). The criteria, however, are not clear, and for this reason, policy uncertainty remains high for businesses. Moreover, rules governing the qualifications of investors, permission requirements, procedures, investment means, business items and amount limits, investment percentage, foreign exchange settlement, review and determination, re-investment, filing items and procedures, application format, and any other requirements, are yet to be drafted and approved.

Table 4.6 Prohibited Sectors for PRC Investment

1. BUSINESS SERVICES

A Professional services
- a) Legal services
  - i. Attorneys of foreign legal affairs (AFLA)
  - ii. Foreign legal assistants or consultants
  - iii. Veterinary Services

D. Real estate services (82203**, 82205)

E. Rental/leasing services without operators
- b) Concerning aircraft (excluding cabotage) (83104**)

F. Other business services
- a) Advertising services
  - i. TV and radio advertising services (871**)
- b) Market research and public opinion polling services (864)
- f) Consulting services incidental to agriculture, animal husbandry and forestry (88110**, 88120**, 881140**)
- k) Placement and supply services of personnel (872)
- m) Engineering-related scientific and technical consulting services (8675)
- o) Building-cleaning services (874)
- r) Publishing services (88442**)
- t) Other

2. COMMUNICATIONS SERVICES

C. Telecommunications services
- (A) BASIC TELECOMMUNICATIONS SERVICES
  - Facilities-based and public switched telecom services
  - Mobile data services (7523**)
  - Resale-based services
- (B) VALUE-ADDED TELECOMMUNICATIONS SERVICES

D. Audiovisual Services
- a) Video tape/motion picture production and distribution services (9611**)
- b) Motion picture projection services (96121)
- c) Radio and television services (96131, 96132)
- Sound recording services

5. EDUCATION SERVICES

Student placement services for overseas studies related to education services as described in CPC 9222,9223,9224, 923, 924, and 929

Education services (9222, 9223, 9224, 923, 924, 929)

6. ENVIRONMENTAL SERVICES
- a) Sewage services (9401); refuse disposal services (9402); sanitation and similar services (9403); others (9404, 9405, 9409)

(*Continued*)

Table 4.6 (*Continued*)

7. FINANCIAL SERVICES
A. Insurance and insurance-related services
   a) Direct insurance—life, accident, and health insurance, non-life insurance
   c) Insurance intermediation (including agent, broker, adjuster, and insurance solicitor)
   d) Insurance auxiliary services (including claim settlement, actuarial services and consultancy services)
B. Banking and other financial services (excluding insurance, securities and futures)
C. Securities and futures

8. HEALTH-RELATED AND SOCIAL SERVICES
   Human health services (931)

9. TOURISM AND TRAVEL-RELATED SERVICES
B. Travel agencies and tour operator services
C. Tourist guides services (7472)

10. RECREATIONAL, CULTURAL AND SPORTING SERVICES (OTHER THAN AUDIOVISUAL SERVICES)
B. News agency services (962)
D. Sports and Other Recreational Services (limited to 96411, 96412, 96419)

11. TRANSPORT SERVICES
E. Rail transport services
H. Services auxiliary to all modes of transport
   a) Cargo handling services (excluding ramping services provided in airports) (741**)
   b) Storage and warehousing services (742)

Source: Mainland Affairs Council.

Table 4.7 is a list of banned investment in the PRC, which is not subject to WTO rules. The forbidden areas focus on the high-tech industries, public utilities, infrastructure, and finance. The high-tech industries are the most profitable, with the highest competitive edge in Taiwan. As these industries are well-integrated in clusters in Taiwan, a move by one manufacturer will generate chain reactions in the industry. Therefore, the government sees outward investment to the PRC as highly sensitive. The banning of investment in most financial sectors is for the sake of financial stability, which is a concern not aimed specifically at the PRC.

Table 4.7 Prohibited Areas for Investment and Technical Collaboration with the PRC

INDUSTRIES	
Wafer and related materials*	42
TFT-LCD and related materials	2
Aircraft	12
Petrochemicals	15
Opium and drugs	21
Nuclear equipment	4
Turbines	2
Aerospace	3
SERVICES	
Postal services	
Telecommunications	
Financial services	
Securities and futures	
IC design	
PUBLIC UTILITIES AND INFRASTRUCTURE	
Highways	
Water resources	
Railways	
Harbors	
Tap water	
Sewage	
Airports	
Rapid mass transportation	
Incinerators	
Power plants	
Power transmission	
Power distribution	
Industrial parks	
AGRICULTURAL PRODUCTS	436

Source: Mainland Affairs Council.

*Conditions for approval: No more than three 8-inch wafer plants will be approved by 2005. The investor should have completed a 12-inch wafer plant in full operation for at least six months.

TAIWAN'S RESTRICTIONS: THE VIEWS OF THIRD COUNTRIES

From the viewpoint of European and American businesses in Taiwan, Taiwan bans about 2,000 imports from the PRC, but not from other WTO members. "In many cases, items from the PRC are only allowed on the condition of domestic industry approval."[9] The foreign business community argues that although there is direct discrimination only against the PRC, third countries also suffer by not being able to fully operate on a regional basis and receive the benefits as they should under a "WTO compliance system."

The third countries are not satisfied with Taiwan's excuses about national security risks and the prevention of injury to domestic industry. For example, the large number of vehicle parts that fall under the import restrictions is a matter of serious concern. The foreign business community also criticizes Taiwan's regulations governing PRC business visitors to Taiwan. Although there has been some change in this area, the regulations only allow large multinational companies to receive PRC visitors. The many small- and medium-sized multinational foreign firms are generally not eligible to receive PRC visitors under the regulations. These regulations are seen as discriminatory against not only the PRC, but also against the small and medium multinationals.

CONCLUSIONS

Taiwan's development over the last half-century is well-known for its market nurturing and opening strategy. During the last two decades, Taiwan has upgraded her industrial structure by investing actively in the region, and it has entered its latest development stage led by both the tertiary sector as well as the high-tech industry. However, Taiwan still does not have normal economic relations with the PRC. The common WTO membership across the Taiwan

---

[9] European Chamber of Commerce Taipei (ECCT), *Monitoring the Implementation of Taiwan's WTO Commitments, Quarterly Report*, various issues, 2004.

Strait presents new possibilities for economic development on both sides. Given the already-close cross-strait economic ties, the new setting provides further opportunities, as well as difficulties. Nevertheless, Taiwan may face the greatest challenges.

Quantitative studies show that both sides can gain from their common membership in the WTO. There are also additional gains for Taiwan from its further liberalization vis-à-vis the mainland. However, this will depend on how well Taiwan can adjust to capitalize on the opportunities. In other words, the benefits from liberalization hinge on Taiwan's flexibility and adaptability to the new situation, not to mention its need for economic reform and the uncertainties presented by cross-strait political issues.

Whereas the PRC's economic growth is a matter of expansion, with some sectors growing more quickly than others, Taiwan's growth is a matter of upgrading, with some sectors on the rise and others on the decline. This explains why the post-WTO pressures and challenges are more acute for Taiwan than for the mainland.

In Taiwan's adjustment process, the most sensitive area is the agricultural sector. Yet the benefits might be the greatest if Taiwan's agricultural sector is modernized, providing services for recreational, residential, conservation, and cultural purposes. In the services sector, a more balanced two-way flow of capital in the financial and real- estate markets with an appropriate firewall is in both sides' interests. Facing an increasingly more open and larger PRC market, Taiwan will benefit greatly from a more liberal investment policy toward the mainland.

In closing, from Taiwan's perspective, "WTO" might also refer to "Watch Taiwan Open." As Taiwan becomes a full-fledged open economy, the normalization of its economic relations with the PRC will be all the more important. From the PRC's perspective, the challenge of developing a more open economy is to continue its ongoing institutional reforms to meet international norms, while maintaining stability. Common membership in the WTO provides a new platform for both sides to build more constructive relations, which will improve economic welfare on both sides of the strait and contribute to the prosperity of the entire region.

Appendix 1

Chapter	Item	MW0	MP1	Total	% of Total
1	Live animals	32	0	73	43.8
2	Meat and edible meat offal	203	1	208	97.6
3	Fish and crustaceans, mollusks, and other aquatic invertebrates	58	5	362	17.4
4	Dairy products; birds' eggs; natural honey edible products of animal origin, not elsewhere specified or included	62	1	73	86.3
5	Products of animal origin, not elsewhere specified or included	19	0	118	16.1
6	Live trees and other plants; bulbs, roots, and the like; cut flowers and ornamental foliage	97	1	124	79.0
7	Edible vegetables and certain roots and tubers	54	6	128	46.9
8	Edible fruit and nuts; peels of citrus fruit or melons	57	4	119	51.3
9	Coffee, tea, mate, and spices	9	0	46	19.6
10	Cereals	13	0	20	65.0
11	Products of the milling industry malt; starches; insulin; and wheat gluten	32	2	51	66.7
12	Oil seeds and oleaginous fruit; miscellaneous grains, seeds, and fruit; industrial or medicinal plants, straw, and fodder	13	1	157	8.9
13	Lac; gums, resins, and other vegetable saps and extracts	0	0	25	0
14	Vegetable plaiting materials; vegetable products not elsewhere specified or included	1	3	30	13.3
15	Animal or vegetable fats and oils and their cleavage products; prepared edible fats; animal or vegetable waxes	8	0	78	10.3
16	Preparations of meat, of fish, or of crustaceans, mollusks, or other aquatic invertebrates	82	1	202	41.1
17	Sugars and sugar confectionery	14	0	32	43.8

(*Continued*)

Appendix 1 *(Continued)*

Chapter	Item	MW0	MP1	Total	% of Total
18	Cocoa and cocoa preparations	14	0	28	50.0
19	Preparations of cereals, flour, starch, or milk; pastry cooks' products	46	3	61	80.3
20	Preparations of vegetables, fruit, nuts, or other parts of plants	65	18	198	41.9
21	Miscellaneous edible preparations	9	3	51	23.5
22	Beverages, spirits, and vinegar	50	2	100	52.0
23	Residues and waste from the food industries; prepared animal fodder	9	3	46	26.1
24	Tobacco and manufactured tobacco substitutes	0	0	19	0
25	Salt; sulphur; earth and stone; plastering materials, lime, and cement	14	1	112	13.4
26	Ores, slag, and ash	0	0	47	0
27	Mineral fuels, mineral oils, and products of their distillation; bituminous substances; and mineral waxes	0	0	82	0
28	Inorganic chemicals; organic or inorganic compounds of precious metals, of rare-earth metals, of radioactive elements, or of isotopes	0	0	311	0
29	Organic chemicals	24	0	710	3.4
30	Pharmaceutical products	71	6	173	44.5
31	Fertilizers	5	0	39	12.8
32	Tanning or dyeing extracts; tannins and their derivatives; dyes, pigments, and other coloring matter; paints and varnishes; putty and other mastics; and inks	23	2	116	21.6
33	Essential oils and resinoids; perfumery, cosmetics, or toilet preparations	0	1	68	1.5
34	Soap, organic surface-active agents, washing preparations, lubricating preparations, artificial waxes, prepared waxes, polishing or scouring preparations, candles and similar articles, modeling pastes, "dental waxes' and dental preparations with a basis of plaster	3	1	45	8.9

(Continued)

Appendix 1 (*Continued*)

Chapter	Item	MW0	MP1	Total	% of Total
35	Albuminoidal substances; modified starches; glues; and enzymes	3	0	45	6.7
36	Explosives; pyrotechnic products; matches; pyrophoric alloys; and certain combustible preparations	3	0	23	13.0
37	Photographic or cinematographic goods	0	0	81	0
38	Miscellaneous chemical products	23	0	177	13.0
39	Plastics and articles thereof	0	0	265	0
40	Rubber and articles thereof	15	0	132	11.4
41	Raw hides and skins (other than fur skins), and leather	0	0	78	0
42	Articles of leather; saddlery, and harness; travel goods, handbags, and similar containers; and articles of animal gut (other than silkworm gut)	0	0	40	0
43	Fur skins and artificial fur; manufactures thereof	0	0	25	0
44	Wood and articles of wood; wood charcoal	2	11	162	8.0
45	Cork and articles of cork	0	0	9	0
46	Manufactures of straw, of esparto, or of other plaiting materials; basket ware and wicker work	0	0	17	0
47	Pulp of wood, or of other fibrous cellulosic material; and recovered (waste and scrap) paper or paperboard	0	0	22	0
48	Paper and paperboard; and articles of paper pulp, of paper or of paperboard	3	8	243	4.5
49	Printed books, newspapers, pictures, and other products of the printing industry; manuscripts, typescripts and plans	1	7	33	24.2
50	Silk	0	0	17	0
51	Wool, fine or coarse animal hair; horsehair yarn and woven fabric	16	0	42	38.1
52	Cotton	160	0	175	91.4
53	Other vegetable textiles	0	0	37	0

(*Continued*)

Appendix 1 *(Continued)*

Chapter	Item	MW0	MP1	Total	% of Total
54	Man-made filaments	63	6	86	80.2
55	Man-made staple fibers	120	8	142	90.1
56	Wadding, felt, and non-wovens; special yarns; twine, cordage, ropes, and cables and articles thereof	6	0	62	9.7
57	Carpets and other textile floor coverings	0	0	43	0
58	Special woven fabrics; tufted textile fabrics; lace; tapestries; trimmings; and embroidery	59	0	83	71.1
59	Impregnated, coated, covered, or laminated textile fabrics; and textile articles of a kind suitable for industrial use	9	4	49	26.5
60	Knitted or crocheted fabrics	53	1	62	87.1
61	Articles of apparel and clothing accessories, knitted or crocheted	2	145	187	78.6
62	Articles of apparel and clothing accessories, not knitted or crocheted	0	129	182	70.9
63	Other made-up textile articles; sets; worn clothing and worn textile articles; and rags	4	0	93	4.3
64	Footwear, gaiters, and the like; and parts of such articles	0	0	120	0
65	Headgear and parts thereof	0	0	36	0
66	Umbrellas, sun umbrellas, walking-sticks, seat-sticks, whips, riding-crops, and parts thereof	0	0	9	0
67	Prepared feathers and down and articles made of feathers or of down; artificial flowers; and articles of human hair	0	0	10	0
68	Articles of stone, plaster, cement asbestos, mica, or similar materials	29	8	97	38.1
69	Ceramic products	16	14	58	51.7
70	Glass and glassware	31	10	104	39.4

(Continued)

Appendix 1 (*Continued*)

Chapter	Item	MW0	MP1	Total	% of Total
71	Natural or cultured pearls, precious or semi-precious stones, precious metals, metals clad with precious metal, and articles thereof; imitation jewelry; and coins	4	3	82	8.5
72	Iron and steel	384	29	695	59.4
73	Articles of iron or steel	33	7	166	24.1
74	Copper and articles thereof	26	18	86	51.2
75	Nickel and articles thereof	0	0	24	0
76	Aluminum and articles thereof	17	12	62	46.8
77					
78	Lead and articles thereof	0	0	14	0
79	Zinc and articles thereof	1	0	20	5
80	Tin and articles thereof	0	0	14	0
81	Other base metals; cermets; articles thereof	2	0	75	0
82	Tools, implements, cutlery, spoons and forks, of base metal; and parts thereof of base metal	0	0	111	0
83	Miscellaneous articles of base metal	5	3	45	17.8
84	Nuclear reactors, boilers, machinery, and mechanical appliances; and parts thereof	32	4	874	4.1
85	Electrical machinery and equipment and parts thereof; sound recorders and reproducers, television image and sound recorders and reproducers, and parts and accessories of such articles	125	47	576	29.9
86	Railway or tramway locomotives, rolling-stock and parts thereof; railway or tramway track fixtures and fittings and parts thereof; and mechanical (including electro-mechanical) traffic signaling equipment of all kinds	0	0	30	0

(*Continued*)

Appendix 1 (*Continued*)

Chapter	Item	MW0	MP1	Total	% of Total
87	Vehicles other than railway or tramway rolling-stock, and parts and accessories thereof	78	0	179	43.6
88	Aircraft, spacecraft, and parts thereof	0	0	25	0
89	Ships, boats, and floating structures	16	1	32	53.1
90	Optical, photographic, cinematographic, measuring, checking, precision, medical, or surgical instruments and apparatus, parts and accessories thereof	28	7	328	10.7
91	Clocks and watches, parts thereof	0	0	59	0
92	Musical instruments, and parts and accessories of such articles	0	0	36	0
93	Arms and ammunition, parts and accessories thereof	5	0	26	19.2
94	Furniture; bedding, mattresses, mattress supports, cushions, and similar stuffed furnishings; lamps and lighting fittings, not elsewhere specified or included; illuminated signs, illuminated name-plates, and the like; and prefabricated buildings	0	0	74	0
95	Toys, games, and sports requisites; parts and accessories thereof	0	0	80	0
96	Miscellaneous manufactured articles	0	0	81	0
97	Works of art, collectors' pieces, and antiques	0	0	14	0
98	Tariff quota goods	199	0	200	99.5

Source: Board of Foreign Trade, Ministry of Economic Affairs, http://www.trade.gov.tw

Chapter

5

Taiwan's Role in the Economic Architecture of East Asia and the Pacific

Peter Drysdale and Xinpeng Xu

INTRODUCTION

The accession of China and Taiwan to the World Trade Organization (WTO) is an important achievement in their international economic diplomacy,[1] and has important implications for China itself, for cross-strait relations, as well as for East Asia, the Pacific, and beyond.[2]

For China, accession to the WTO delivers a significant long-term commitment to economic liberalization and, more importantly, to

[1] The People's Republic of China became a WTO member on December 11, 2001, after more than 15 years of negotiation, and Taiwan became a member of the "Separate Customs Territory of Taiwan, Penghu, Kinmen, and Matsu" on January 1, 2002, having launched its application 12 years earlier.

[2] Jeffrey D. Sachs and Wing Thye Woo, "China's Growth after WTO Membership," *Journal of Chinese Economic and Business Studies* 1, no. 1 (2003), 1–32; Wing Thye Woo, "Recent Claims of China's Economic Exceptionalism: Reflections Inspired by WTO Accession," *China Economic Review* 12, no. 2/3 (2001), 107–136; Xu Xinpeng, "Have the Chinese Provinces Become Integrated Under Reform?" *China Economic Review* 13, no. 2/3 (2002), 116–133.

economic and political reforms.[3] It provides a huge stimulus for the continuation of fast economic growth and transformation, and for the mobilization of resources to support rapid growth. The accumulation of capital and technology is expected to accelerate, particularly because accession has provided an impetus for the inflow of foreign capital, already averaging around US$ 45 billion annually. Productivity gains will flow from trade gains through cheaper imports, their impact on import and export sector efficiency, and also from technology spillover through foreign investment. Domestic liberalization and reform, and a more transparent regime, are expected to reduce transaction costs and correct the distortions that were prevalent in a less liberal and less open economy. Taken together, such effects suggest that, barring accident or policy miscalculation, China's growth rate will continue to increase for a significant period to come.[4]

China is already a major element in East Asia's rising share of world output. With a little over 7 percent economic growth, China could double its income every ten years. This prospect gives confidence that the East Asian economy will continue to increase in importance in the long term. The WTO commitments strengthen the corollary structural trend for China to be increasingly important in the East Asian economy and for the continuation of the already-evident relative decline of Japan (see Figures 5.1 and 5.2).

China's accession to the WTO provides enormous trade and investment opportunities.[5] It has set in train a new wave of trade and industrial transformation, and a new regional and international division of labor. These changes will affect the East Asian, Pacific, and world economies for many years. Accession will have a direct

---

[3] Peter Drysdale and Ligang Song, *China's Entry to the WTO: Strategic Issues and Quantitative Assessments* (London: Routledge, 2000).

[4] The discussion here assumes that China will be able to manage the risks associated with WTO entry and subsequent liberalization in its capital account, in particular the challenges that arise from the present vulnerability in the domestic banking system. These risks are discussed in more detail later.

[5] Peter Drysdale and Ligang Song, *China's Entry to the WTO: Strategic Issues and Quantitative Assessments* (London: Routledge, 2000).

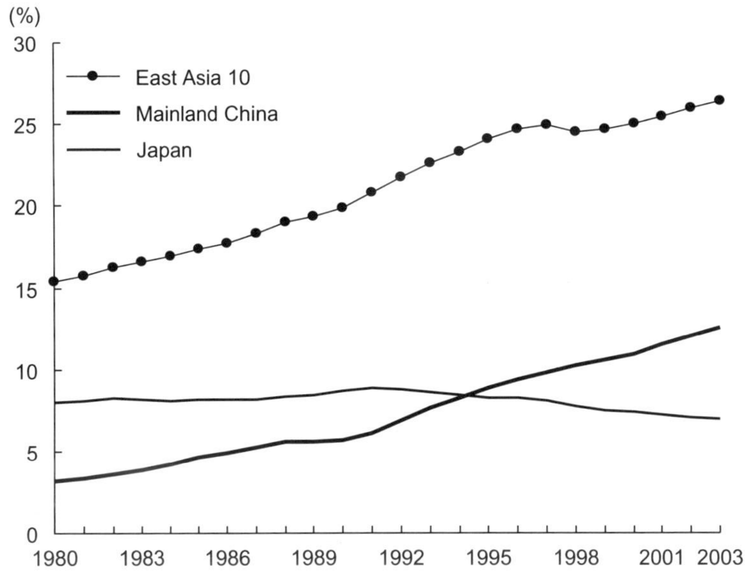

Figure 5.1 China and East Asia in the world economy: Output share valued at PPP (percent)

Notes: Shares of aggregate GDP based on purchasing power parity (PPP) valuation of country GDP. East Asia 10 includes Japan, South Korea, mainland China, Taiwan, Hong Kong, Thailand, Malaysia, Indonesia, Singapore, and the Philippines.

Sources: Authors' calculations based on data from International Monetary Fund, *World Economic Outlook Database*, April 2004.

impact on growth and the structure of growth, but will also have indirect effects. For example, changes in the investment location strategies of multinational firms in the East Asian economy will result in changes in both intra-industry and intra-regional trade patterns, and in changes in the pattern of foreign direct investment (FDI) flows in the region. There has been a huge increase in FDI into China since the mid-1990s — a sizable part of it coming from Taiwan (see Tables 5.1 and 5.2). Increasing integration within East Asia, and the rise of China within the East Asian economy, are now established long-term trends in the world economy.

These developments are at the heart of the evolving East Asian cooperation idea, of which Taiwan is yet to become a part. In particular, the move away from multilateral-oriented regional arrangements

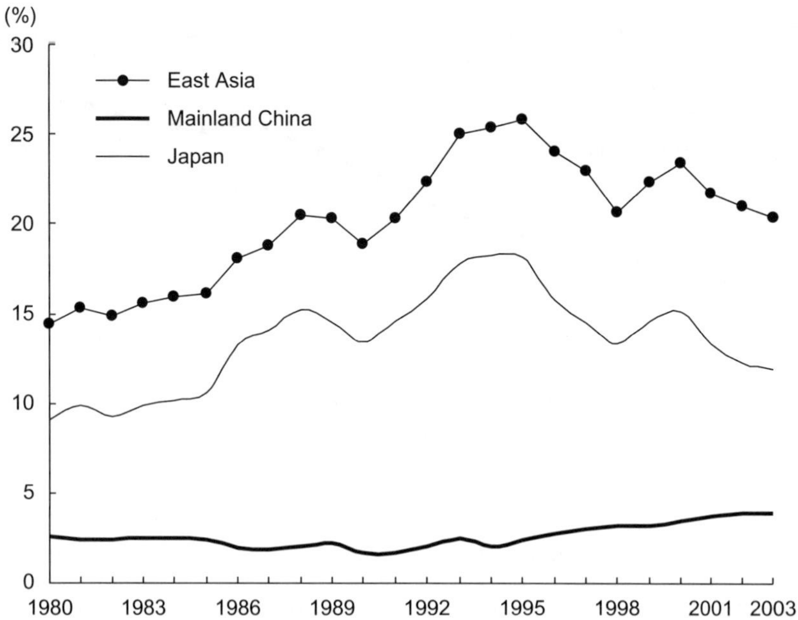

Figure 5.2 China and East Asia in the world economy: Output share valued at market exchange rates (percent)

Notes: Shares of aggregate GDP based on current market exchange rate in US dollars. East Asia 10 includes Japan, South Korea, mainland China, Taiwan, Hong Kong, Thailand, Malaysia, Indonesia, Singapore, and the Philippines.

Sources: Authors' calculations based on International Monetary Fund, *World Economic Outlook Database*, April 2004.

like the Pacific Economic Cooperation Council (PECC) and Asia Pacific Economic Cooperation (APEC), and toward bilateral free trade agreements (FTAs) and ASEAN+3 arrangements, complicates Taiwan's involvement in the regional economy and the economic policy dialogue. Moreover, Taiwan has yet to reap the full advantage of WTO accession, ironically because accession has not resolved its trading problems with China. A coherent and effective Taiwan strategy in response to this new circumstance is yet to emerge. Taiwan continues to discriminate against a significant range of imports from the mainland. These restrictions, and the indirect trading links between Taiwan and the mainland, truncate Taiwan's ability to add

Table 5.1 China's Top Sources of Foreign Investment (cumulative FDI) to 2003

	Cumulative FDI (US$ billion)	Share (%)
Hong Kong	222.6	44.4
United States	44.1	8.8
Japan	41.4	8.3
Taiwan	36.5	7.3
Virgin Islands	30.2	6.0
Singapore	23.5	4.7
South Korea	19.7	3.9
United Kingdom	11.4	2.3
Germany	8.9	1.8
France	6.1	1.2
Others	57.1	11.4
Total	501.5	100.0

Note: FDI=foreign direct investment.
Sources: Data up to 2002 are from China's official FDI Website, Ministry of Commerce, People's Republic of China (www.fdi.gov.cn). Data for 2003 are from *China Economy and Statistics Express*, National Bureau of Statistics, July 2004.

Table 5.2 China: Changing Structure of FDI Inflows (percent)

	1986–1990	1991–1995	1996–2000	2001–2003
Hong Kong	61.3	59.6	42.9	34.2
Japan	12.5	7.6	8.1	8.9
United States	10.9	7.0	9.0	9.2
Taiwan	2.2	10.0	6.8	6.7
European Union	5.0	4.1	9.3	7.8
Others	8.1	11.7	23.8	33.2

Note: Figures are period averages.
Sources: Ministry of Commerce, People's Republic of China; *China Statistical Yearbook* (Beijing: China Statistical Press, various years).

value to cheap components and intermediate goods imported from China. This calls for a drastic shift in Taiwan's trade policy strategy. If Taiwan were to open up its markets to Chinese imports as part of a general liberalization of trade, its income and welfare would be boosted, without any obvious compromise to its security interests.

The aim of this chapter is to assess how Chinese accession to the WTO affects Taiwan's regional role and strategies. We start by examining how Chinese accession to the WTO affects regional trade, investment, and growth, and discuss the implications for the roles of China and Taiwan in the regional economy. We identify problems and challenges for Taiwan in taking advantage of the opportunities made possible by the WTO membership on both sides of the Taiwan Strait. We then discuss challenges for Taiwan's regional diplomacy, setting out some options that have been canvassed. Finally, we offer some thoughts on alternative strategies that may serve Taiwan better than the strategies advocated thus far, both in economic and political terms, and suggest some possible ways forward.

REGIONAL TRADE, INVESTMENT, AND GROWTH

To understand Taiwan's role in the economic architecture of East Asia and the Pacific following China's accession to the WTO, we must first look at the impact of the accession on regional trade, investment, and growth.

Various modeling exercises have been conducted, for example, by Drysdale, Zhang, and Song and Wang,[6] Ianchovichina and Martin,[7] McKibbin and Tang,[8] which measure the effects of China's WTO accession on the Chinese and regional economies. Most results suggest that China is a big beneficiary of accession to the WTO.[9]

---

[6] Peter Drysdale, Yunling Zhang, and Ligang Song, eds., *APEC and Liberalisation of the Chinese Economy* (Canberra: Asia Pacific Press, 2000); Wang Zhi, "WTO Accession, 'Greater China' Free Trade Area and Economic Integration across the Taiwan Strait," *China Economic Review* 14, 316–349.

[7] Elena Ianchovichina and Will Martin, "Economic Impact of China's Accession to the WTO," *World Bank Policy Research Working Paper No. 3053*, World Bank, 2003.

[8] Warwick J. McKibbin and K. K. Tang, "Trade and Financial Reform in China: Impacts on the World Economy," *World-Economy* 23, no. 8 (2000), 979–1003.

[9] Ramesh Adhikari and Yongzheng Yang, "What Will WTO Membership Mean for China and its Trading Partners?" *Finance and Development* (International Monetary Fund) 39, no. 3 (2002), 22–25.

According to Ianchovichina and Walmsley,[10] accession added around US$ 10 billion to GDP in 2001 (an increase of 1 percent). But China's accession to the WTO is significant for more than the measured gain in GDP. At the core of China's WTO membership are long-term commitments to economic liberalization and reform, and to a more transparent regime that will be open to all of China's trading partners. Recent studies by development economists have identified three factors — openness, institutions, and geography — as fundamental forces that drive economic growth.[11] It is China's commitment to liberalization, reform, and openness, which draws it politically, as well as economically, closer to the world's major centers of economic power in North America, Europe, and East Asia, and that provides the foundations for substantial and sustainable economic growth at home.

Reductions of tariffs and non-tariff barriers correct distortions that have been in place for a long time; their removal is expected to generate sizable increases in productivity. The greatest productivity gains arise from opening sectors that have been highly-protected, such as the service sector, because foreign firms bring in advanced technology and managerial expertise.[12] For China, accession will spur on the rapid accumulation of capital and improvement in productivity, promising higher growth rates for a considerable time to come.

China is now established as an engine of growth in East Asia, through its rising share in regional production and trade, and through

---

[10] Elena Ianchovichina and Terrie Walmsley, "Impact of China's WTO Accession on East Asia," *World Bank Policy Research Working Paper No. 3109*, World Bank, 2003.

[11] Dani Rodrik, Arvind Subramanian, and Francesco Trebbi, "Institutions Rule: The Primacy of Institutions over Geography and Integration in Economic Development," *NBER Working Paper No. 9305*, National Bureau of Economic Research, 2002.

[12] A. Matto, "China's Accession to the WTO: The Services Dimension," paper presented at the "Workshop on WTO Accession, Policy Reform, and Poverty Reduction," World Bank, Beijing, 2001; Elena Ianchovichina and Terrie Walmsley, "Impact of China's WTO Accession on East Asia," *World Bank Policy Research Working Paper No. 3109*, World Bank, 2003.

Table 5.3 China and East Asia: Share in World Exports (percent)

	1991–1993	1994–1996	1997–1999	2000–2003
East Asia 10	22.8	23.9	22.9	23.8
China and Hong Kong	3.7	4.1	4.4	5.9
Japan	9.3	8.5	7.4	6.7
South Korea	2.2	2.5	2.5	2.6
Taiwan	2.6	2.7	2.6	2.5
ASEAN	5.0	6.1	6.0	6.1

Notes: Figures are period averages. East Asia includes Japan, South Korea, China (including Hong Kong exports net of intra-Hong Kong–China trade), Taiwan, Thailand, Malaysia, Indonesia, Singapore, and the Philippines. Exports are merchandise exports only. ASEAN includes Thailand, Malaysia, Indonesia, Singapore, and the Philippines.
Sources: Authors' calculations based on data from International Economic Databank, The Australian National University.

its close structural links with other economies in the region (see Figures 5.1 and 5.2 and Table 5.3). In terms of current output, the economic size of China has been rising and is now almost one-third that of Japan — even based on the market exchange rate calculated output measures (Figure 5.2). The contrast is even more striking if the comparison is based on Purchasing Power Parity (PPP) calculated output measures, whereby China has already surpassed Japan, and after 1993 became the second largest economy in the world (Figure 5.1). With growth rates averaging more than 8 percent per annum since 1990, China has been the most important new player in the regional and world economies, and this is expected to continue.

CROSS-STRAIT TRADE: A ONE-WAY STREET

Trade across the Taiwan Strait has been increasing steadily; from just over US$ 5 billion in the early 1990s, it rose to US$ 46 billion in 2003 (see Table 5.4). However, it has been a one-way street, with Taiwan ostensibly enjoying a growing trade surplus over the last decade, amounting to over US$ 24 billion in 2003. In that year, almost 35 percent of Taiwan's exports (worth US$ 35 billion) went to Hong Kong

Table 5.4 Trade across the Taiwan Strait (US$ billion)

	Taiwan's exports	Taiwan's imports	Trade surplus
1982	0.2	0.1	0.1
1985	1.0	0.1	0.9
1990	4.4	0.8	3.6
1991	7.5	1.1	6.4
1992	10.5	1.1	9.4
1993	14.0	1.1	12.9
1994	16.0	1.9	14.2
1995	19.4	3.1	16.3
1996	20.7	3.1	17.7
1997	22.5	3.9	18.5
1998	19.8	4.1	15.7
1999	21.3	4.5	16.8
2000	25.0	6.2	18.8
2001	21.9	5.9	16.0
2002	29.5	7.9	21.5
2003	35.4	11.0	24.4

Sources: Estimates by Mainland Affairs Office, Taiwan, http://www.chinabiz.org.tw (accessed August 5, 2004). See note 13 for alternative estimates.

and China (Table 5.5), and under 10 percent of its imports were drawn from Hong Kong and China (Table 5.6).[13]

CHINA AS A DRIVER OF GROWTH IN THE REGION

The new wave of trade and industrial transformation, which is sweeping the East Asian and international economies, has been

[13] There are many statistical discrepancies in the data for Taiwan's export trade with China. For example, Taiwan's total exports to China in 2002 were US$ 9.9 billion according to Taiwan's customs statistics, but US$ 38.1 billion according to mainland China's customs statistics. According to Hong Kong customs reports, Taiwan's exports to mainland China were US$10.3 billion for the same year. Taiwan's customs data under-estimate Taiwan's exports to China because some Taiwan exporters report their destination as Hong Kong when, in fact, the final destination is mainland China via Hong Kong.

Table 5.5 Taiwan: Geographic Structure of Exports (percent)

	Hong Kong and China	EU-15	Japan	South Korea	United States	ASEAN-5
1980	7.9	14.4	11.0	1.4	34.3	11.2
1985	8.3	8.9	11.3	0.8	48.4	7.7
1990	12.8	16.3	12.4	1.8	32.5	14.1
1991	16.1	16.1	11.9	1.7	28.9	13.0
1992	19.0	15.3	10.9	1.4	29.0	13.8
1993	21.8	13.5	10.6	1.5	27.7	14.5
1994	23.2	12.5	11.0	1.9	26.4	15.9
1995	23.8	12.5	11.7	2.3	23.8	17.0
1996	23.7	12.9	11.8	2.3	23.3	16.4
1997	24.1	13.3	9.5	1.9	24.5	16.1
1998	23.4	15.8	8.4	1.3	26.7	12.3
1999	23.8	14.8	9.7	2.1	25.4	13.4
2000	24.4	14.2	11.1	2.6	23.5	14.0
2001	26.6	14.2	10.3	2.7	22.3	13.4
2002	30.9	13.0	9.1	2.9	20.3	11.8
2003	34.5	12.5	8.3	3.2	18.0	10.0

Sources: Authors' calculations based on data from *Direction of Trade*, International Monetary Fund; International Economic Databank, The Australian National University.

driven significantly by the commitment to more liberal trade and investment regimes in China. China's growing and more open market provides opportunities for countries in the region to participate further in the regional and international division of labor. Already more than half of China's imports are sourced from other countries in East Asia, with 30 percent from Northeast Asia and 20 percent from the ASEAN countries. Lardy[14] suggested that "(w)ithin a decade China's trade is likely to surpass that of Japan and Germany, making China the world's second largest trader." When trade is properly measured, by including Hong Kong's trade together with China's trade net of intra-Hong Kong–China trade, China is already the fourth-largest single trading nation in the world, after the U.S., Germany, and Japan.

[14] Nicholas R. Lardy, *Integrating China into the Global Economy* (Washington DC: Brookings Institution Press, 2002).

Table 5.6 Taiwan: Geographic Structure of Imports (percent)

	Hong Kong and China	EU-15	Japan	South Korea	United States	ASEAN-5
1980	1.3	8.8	27.2	1.0	23.7	10.6
1985	1.6	10.9	27.5	0.9	23.8	10.4
1990	2.4	13.8	30.2	2.5	23.8	10.3
1991	3.6	13.4	29.9	2.8	22.6	10.8
1992	3.6	14.1	30.1	3.2	22.0	11.6
1993	3.6	14.1	30.0	3.3	21.8	12.2
1994	4.1	15.0	29.3	3.6	21.4	13.9
1995	4.8	14.2	29.2	4.2	20.1	13.4
1996	4.7	14.1	26.8	4.1	19.6	14.1
1997	5.2	13.0	25.3	4.4	20.3	14.9
1998	5.9	13.2	25.7	5.4	18.9	15.6
1999	6.1	12.6	27.5	6.5	17.9	16.9
2000	6.1	10.8	27.4	6.4	18.0	18.2
2001	7.4	11.0	24.0	6.2	17.0	18.8
2002	8.8	11.4	24.8	7.0	16.4	15.0
2003	9.9	10.3	25.6	6.9	13.2	13.4

Sources: See Table 5.5.

A central feature of deeper East Asian economic integration has been the remarkable growth of trade in intermediate goods and components. China is now a major player in this process. A growing feature of the international division of labor, especially in East Asia, has been the location of relatively labor-intensive component production and assembly processes within complex, integrated international production chains.[15] The process began in the electronics and textile industries, but is now common in many other industries as well.

[15] Gerald K Helleiner, "Manufacturing Exports from Less Developed Countries and Multinational Firms," *Economic Journal* 83, no. 329 (1973), 21–47; Michael Sharpton, "International Subcontracting," *Oxford Economic Papers* 27, no. 1 (1975), 94–135; Robert Feenstra, "Integration of Trade and Disintegration of Production in the Global Economy," *Journal of Economic Perspectives* 14, no. 4 (1998), 31–50; Prema-chandra Athukorala, "Product Fragmentation and Trade Patterns in East Asia," *Working Paper No. 2003/21*, The Australian National University.

This process is sometimes called international product fragmentation. A recent and careful study of fragmentation trade in East Asia by Athukorala[16] demonstrates just how important it is to the growth of the region and economic integration within it. Athukorala (see footnote 16) reports that the intra-regional share of final trade was 48.3 percent, compared to 52.3 percent of total trade. In 2000, over 60 percent of "final exports" from developing Asia went to countries outside the East Asian region (particularly North America and Europe), up from 55 percent in 1992 (see footnote 16). The fragmentation of the supply chain accelerates the growth of trade in components and makes the region more heavily-dependent on extra-regional trade for "growth dynamism" than is suggested by data that do not net out the trade in components.[17] Athukorala (see footnote 16) shows that the most notable feature of international product fragmentation in recent years has been the rapid integration of China into regional production networks. He argues (see footnote 16) that this development is an important counterpoint to the popular belief that China's global integration would crowd out opportunities for export-led growth for other economies within the region.

In the manufacturing sector, FDI has been the driver of the substantial intra-industry and intra-regional trade growth, and the role of FDI is expected to rise, fostering deeper integration of the regional economies. The effort to cut production costs through greater productivity, and more efficient procurement and outsourcing, has led to the relocation of some segments of the production processes of multinational firms within East Asia. The effect on trade and investment flows is significant. The increased fragmentation, and specialization in production and trade, which has been promoted by the activities of multinational firms in the

---

[16] Prema-chandra Athukorala, "Product Fragmentation and Trade Patterns in East Asia," *Working Paper No. 2003/21*, The Australian National University.

[17] Christopher Findlay, "China and the World Economy: The FTA Strategy," in *China: New Engine of World Growth*, ed. Ross Garnaut and Ligang Song (Canberra: Asia Pacific Press, 2003); Christopher Findlay, "China and the FTA Route to Reform," paper prepared for the Fifth Australian Studies Conference in Taiwan, National Chengchi University, Taipei, 2003.

region, presents enormous opportunities for the East Asian economies to become integrated into international production chains and markets. It increases productivity, output, and trade growth. There are also challenges in developing policies to take advantage of these opportunities. In particular, there may be more intense competition among economies with similar output levels, factor endowments and export structures. A similarity with China's export structure, it might be argued, for example, is likely to increase the intensity of competition faced in taking advantage of the growth of fragmentation in regional trade in manufactured goods.[18] McKibbin and Woo[19] suggest that China's accession to the WTO could create significant welfare losses in ASEAN-4 countries, if FDI is significantly directed away from these countries toward China, and if they are unable to take measures to prevent losses from the reduced FDI inflow. If the ASEAN-4 countries are not to fall behind technologically, they will have to find niches within lengthened international production chains. The evidence suggests that this is, indeed, what is happening, and that China is providing a positive boost to Southeast Asian trade in the process.[20]

Opening up the service sectors such as banking, transportation and communications, professional services, and distribution services to international participation and competition, is also offering enormous opportunities. Trade and income growth built on exports from the more labor-intensive segments of these industries for the less-developed economies and the more human capital-intensive

[18] Xu Xinpeng and Ligang Song, "Export Similarity and Pattern of East Asian Development," in *China in the Global Economy*, ed. Peter Lloyd and Xiao-guang Zhang (Cheltenham, UK: Edward Elgar, 2002), 145–164.

[19] Warwick J. McKibbin and Wing Thye Woo, "The Consequence of China's WTO Accession for its Neighbours," *Asian Economic Papers* 2, no. 2 (2003), 1–38.

[20] Deutsche Bank Research, *China as Potential Superpower: Regional Responses*, special report on China (Singapore: Deutsche Bank, January 15, 2003); The McKibbin and Woo conclusion follows from a simulation exercise that they undertake. See also Tiklak Abeysinghe and Ding Lu, "China as an Economic Powerhouse: Implications on its Neighbors," *China Economic Review* 14, no. 2 (2003), 164–185.

segments for the more advanced economies is generally faster than the growth of industrial goods trade and output, within the region and globally.

THE COSTS TO TAIWAN FROM TRADE DISCRIMINATION AGAINST CHINA

Despite the increase in cross-strait trade, there are still no direct official trade links between Taiwan and China, and Taiwan continues to place important restrictions on imports from China. These restrictions severely constrain China's share of Taiwan's imports, which was under 10 percent of total Taiwan imports in 2003 (Table 5.6). At the end of 2000, only 56 percent of all 10,724 ten-digit commodities under the Harmonized Tariff Schedule (HS) system were permitted imports from mainland China. On February 15, 2002, shortly after the WTO accession, Taiwan removed import restrictions on Chinese imports for 2,058 products, and on November 18, 2002, it removed restrictions on an additional 316 items. However, 2,418 items (22 percent of the 10,724 items categorized under the HS ten-digit tariff code) may still not be imported from mainland China.[21]

Taiwan's restrictions on imports from China affect a wide range of components and other products, including automobile components and parts, and constitute a significant barrier to the growth of Chinese exports to Taiwan. Restrictions on imports from, and investments in, mainland China prevent Taiwan from fully participating in the regional and international division of labor and moving further up the value-added chain.

Theoretically, China's small share in Taiwan's import market could result from commodity specialization or the geographic structure of trade, rather than from official Taiwan barriers to trade with China. Here, we gauge the extent to which Taiwan's import specialization with China is distorted by Taiwan's import restrictions that discriminate against China. We take South Korea as a benchmark; its trade

[21] This information is from the Ministry of Economic Affairs (Taiwan) website, at www.moea.gov.tw.

structure is not dissimilar to that of Taiwan and it is located in the same economic space, but it does not impose on China any special or discriminatory barriers of the kind that Taiwan has in place.

Trade intensity analysis is a well-established technique for analyzing the determinants of bilateral trade flows and the factors that influence them.[22] Table 5.7 shows the trade intensity, bias, and complementarity coefficients for trade between Taiwan and South Korea and China. Here, China is defined as China including Hong Kong minus intra-Hong Kong–China trade so that the effect of Taiwan's indirect trade with the mainland can be taken into account. The coefficients are computed from a vast amount of data to provide a summary comparison of the structure of trade.

Complementarity in bilateral trade is derived from the relation of one partner's commodity specialization in exports (relative to the rest of the world) to the other's specialization in imports; thus, a higher value indicates higher matches between the reporting country's commodity export structure and the partner country's import structure. Country bias derives from the relative closeness of the two partners, in terms of geography, policy treatment, and cultural or other factors that affect economic space.

The striking result from the analysis set out in Table 5.7, as can be seen by comparing columns 5 and 8, is that China's overall pattern of export specialization matches the patterns of import specialization of both South Korea and Taiwan to a remarkably similar degree. For both economies, the complementarity coefficient is between 0.77 and 0.92. For Chinese trade with both South Korea and Taiwan, complementarity has steadily increased over the last few years. This reflects China's growing role as an export-processing zone for all the higher-income economies of East Asia. Yet the import trade intensity between South Korea and China is much greater than that for between Taiwan and China. The South Korean import trade intensity ranged between 0.97 and 1.82 over the 1992–2002 period, suggesting that South Korea takes almost twice the

[22] Peter Drysdale, *International Economic Pluralism: Economic Policy in East Asia and the Pacific* (New York: Columbia University Press, 1988), 86–88.

Table 5.7 China, South Korea, and Taiwan: Trade Complementarity, Bias, and Intensity Indexes

	Exports to								
	China			South Korea			Taiwan		
Exports from	**b**	**c**	**i**	**b**	**c**	**i**	**b**	**c**	**i**
	(1)	(2)	(3)	(4)	(5)	(6)	(7)	(8)	(9)
China									
1992				1.25	0.78	*0.97*	0.87	0.77	*0.67*
1994				1.52	0.78	*1.19*	1.19	0.78	*0.93*
1996				1.74	0.84	*1.46*	1.22	0.80	*0.98*
1998				2.29	0.78	*1.79*	1.39	0.80	*1.11*
2000				1.94	0.83	*1.61*	1.07	0.86	*0.92*
2001				2.16	0.84	*1.82*	1.21	0.88	*1.07*
2002				1.96	0.89	*1.75*	1.16	0.92	*1.07*
South Korea									
1992	1.22	1.62	*1.97*				1.24	1.16	*1.45*
1994	1.33	1.60	*2.14*				1.15	1.19	*1.37*
1996	1.72	1.46	*2.51*				1.19	1.16	*1.38*
1998	2.00	1.37	*2.75*				1.66	1.25	*2.09*
2000	1.82	1.33	*2.42*				1.74	1.22	*2.12*
2001	1.90	1.31	*2.49*				2.00	1.11	*2.20*
2002	1.88	1.35	*2.54*				1.93	1.15	*2.23*
Taiwan									
1992	2.16	1.56	*3.37*	0.75	0.84	*0.63*			
1994	2.26	1.49	*3.37*	0.80	0.93	*0.75*			
1996	2.39	1.48	*3.53*	0.85	0.94	*0.80*			
1998	2.61	1.46	*3.82*	0.83	0.97	*0.81*			
2000	2.33	1.48	*3.46*	0.96	1.09	*1.05*			
2001	2.34	1.51	*3.52*	1.08	1.07	*1.16*			
2002	2.37	1.61	*3.81*	1.04	1.16	*1.21*			

Notes: China here includes the trade of Hong Kong and mainland China net of intra-Hong Kong–China trade; *b* is the bias index; *c* is the complementarity index; *i* is the intensity index; *i* equals *c* times *b*. For detailed definitions, refer to Peter Drysdale, *International Economic Pluralism: Economic Policy in East Asia and in the Pacific* (New York: Columbia University Press, 1988), 86–88.

Sources: Authors' calculations based on data from International Economic Databank, The Australian National University.

value of imports from China, which could be expected from both countries' shares in world markets. By comparison, Taiwan's trade intensity ranges between 0.67 and 1.11; in most years, Taiwan did not import as much from China as would be expected from their world trade shares, despite their high degree of trade complementarity and their proximity in the international economy. It appears that South Korea's trade policy regime has allowed it to take fuller advantage of the opening up of the Chinese economy and the utilization of comparative advantage with China than Taiwan has been able to do.

The issue can be further examined using another technique. Drysdale, Huang, and Kalirajan[23] apply a stochastic gravity model to examine trade efficiency, which is defined as the ratio of actual to potential trade flows. Their results indicate that, although the average efficiency index for Taiwan's export trade between 1991 and 1995 is 0.52 and the average efficiency index for its import trade is 0.41 (an index of 1 indicates that the trade potential is being fully realized), its efficiency index for bilateral trade with mainland China is very low (less than 0.15 for both exports to and imports from the mainland). This suggests that, in actuality, Taiwan's trade is less than 15 percent of the potential trade with China, and that its trade with the rest of the world is only half of its potential trade or less (see footnote 23). We have updated these results for the trade data from 1996 to 2001. During that period, the average efficiency index for Taiwan's export trade rose to 0.60, and that for its import trade to 0.53. But efficiency in its bilateral trade with China remained very low, despite a sharp rise in the efficiency of its bilateral export trade. The index rose to 0.32 for bilateral exports, but was still only 0.17 for imports from China. This will not have changed significantly since then. By comparison, there was an export efficiency of 0.51 in South Korea's export trade with China and 0.48 in its import trade from China. Taiwan's exports to China were only 32 percent of their full potential on this estimate, and

---

[23] Peter Drysdale, Yiping Huang, and K. P. Kalirajan, "China's Trade Efficiency: Measurement and Determinants," in *APEC and Liberalisation of the Chinese Economy*, ed. Peter Drysdale, Yunling Zhang, and Ligang Song (Canberra: Asia Pacific Press, 2000).

imports a mere 17 percent. This is a disturbingly low figure, not reflected in the figures for the efficiency of any other country's trade flows with China.

This analysis treats Taiwan's trade through Hong Kong as if it were not related to China. However, much of it is. A more accurate picture of the extent to which the Taiwan–China trade potential is under-realized can be obtained by running the same analysis on Taiwan's trade with China but including Hong Kong as part of China, net of intra-China–Hong Kong trade. The results of this analysis reveal a stronger Taiwan–China trade relationship because of the importance of indirect trade through Hong Kong.

By contrast, the bilateral export and import efficiency coefficients for South Korea do not change significantly when trade with Hong Kong is included in China's trade. The efficiency index for South Korean exports to China and Hong Kong, net of China–Hong Kong trade, falls to five percentage points to 0.46; on the import side, it falls to even less, also to 0.46. The comparable numbers for Taiwan rise substantially, more than doubling the efficiency numbers when trade with China is measured to include Hong Kong. The export efficiency of Taiwan exports to China and Hong Kong, net of intra-China–Hong Kong trade, rises to 0.65, compared to 0.32 when Hong Kong is not included. And the import efficiency jumps from 0.17 to 0.40 when trade through Hong Kong is included, confirming that a large amount of China–Taiwan trade is being channeled through Hong Kong. Significantly, however, the efficiency of South Korean importing from China (including Hong Kong) is higher than that of Taiwan importing from China (including Hong Kong). This reflects not only the costs of Taiwan trading indirectly through Hong Kong, but also the distortion to this trade caused by Taiwan's bans on imports from China.

The underdevelopment of Taiwan's import trade with China has a major detrimental effect on Taiwan's overall trade performance. The analysis above shows clearly that the restrictions on cross-strait trade, especially on imports from mainland China, have prevented Taiwan from fully specializing in sectors in which it has a comparative advantage, and thus from taking full advantage of China's early-stage processing capacity. These effects are stunting Taiwan's industrial upgrading. Taiwan's restrictions on trade with China prevent it from capturing both sides of the benefit from the emergence of a huge reprocessing zone in China — the opportunity for low-cost production in China and the opportunity for value adding to low-cost Chinese imports in Taiwan.

This chapter does not examine in-depth the political-security implications of this foreign economic policy choice of Taiwan. But there is no obvious political-security rationale for a policy approach that, in effect, denies Taiwan competitiveness in the international marketplace. More specifically, there is no political-security rationale for a strategy that prevents Taiwan from developing an important and closer set of economic, trade, and investment ties through more extensive international production chains with its neighbors, including China, and with major industrial economies outside the region. If Taiwan is to capture the full economic benefits of what is happening in China, it will need to develop such ties.

PROLIFERATION OF FREE TRADE ARRANGEMENTS

Regional Trade Policy Environment

Since the late 1990s, there has been a surge of interest in preferential regional trading arrangements, or so-called free trade areas (FTA), in East Asia and the Pacific.[24] The rich countries in the region, such as Japan, South Korea, Singapore, Australia, New Zealand, and the U.S., have all signed at least one FTA with their trading partners in recent years. Developing countries in the region, such as China and the ASEAN countries, have also shown growing interest in FTAs, and a China–ASEAN FTA is already under negotiation.[25]

---

[24] For a detailed analysis of the effects of FTAs, see J.N. Bhagwati and A. Panagariya, *The Economics of Preferential Trade Agreements* (Washington, DC: AEI Press, 1996).

[25] China and ASEAN reached agreement on a framework to establish a FTA at the end of 2001. Japan also declared its interest in forming a FTA with ASEAN countries. (Information on Japan's FTA strategy is available at Japan's official Ministry of Foreign Affairs of Japan website, http://www.mofa.go.jp/policy/economy/fta/strategy 0210.html [accessed October 31, 2003].)

The motivations for participating in FTAs vary from country to country.[26] The East Asian countries have a longstanding commitment to, and continuing fundamental strategic interest in, the non-discriminatory liberalization of trade, but economic and political circumstances, instead, have led them down the track of discriminatory trade liberalization. This shift in policy-thinking has arisen against the background of the long-term rise in East Asian economic interdependence, even though East Asian trade and economic interests remain more globally-oriented than those of any other major economic area in the world.[27] The proximate causes were related to the East Asian financial crisis (and the sense of economic diplomatic isolation that flowed from it). Other factors included the failure of the Seattle Ministerial Meeting to launch a new WTO round and the political circumstances (affecting Beijing's and Tokyo's dealings with Washington) that led to the formation of ASEAN+3 at the end of the 1990s.[28] In economic diplomacy, the multilateral-oriented institutions appeared to falter and failed to move forward quickly within either the WTO or APEC frameworks. However mistakenly, given the complex structure of the regional economy, countries in the region began to see FTAs as a way to more rapid progress. There was a decisive move away from working through multilateral-oriented regional arrangements like APEC and toward the proposal and negotiation of bilateral FTAs, and the regional grouping, ASEAN+3, also emerged in East Asia.

In Japan, the move toward the bilateral negotiation of FTAs had its recent origins in East Asia. The first move was to forge an agreement with South Korea as part of the process of political rapprochement in the late 1990s. The proposal emphasized industrial

---

[26] Christopher Findlay, Haflah Piei, and Mari Pangestu, "Trading with Favourites: Risks, Motives and Implications of FTAs in the Asia Pacific," paper prepared for the East Asia Trade Strategy Conference, The Australian National University, March 20–21, 2003.

[27] Peter Drysdale and Kenichi Ishigaki, eds., *East Asian Trade and Financial Integration: New Issues* (Canberra: Asia Pacific Press, 2002).

[28] For an alternative view, John Ravenhill, "The Move to Preferential Trade in the Western Pacific Rim," *Asia Pacific Issues* (East-West Center), no. 16 (2003).

integration, and deliberately avoided hard agricultural trade issues. Thus far, there has been no substantive progress toward a deal with South Korea, but negotiations have recently resumed. The second involved Singapore. The "New Economic Partnership Agreement with Singapore" (where there were no major agricultural trade issues to deal with, except the famous issue of goldfish and cut-flower exports from Singapore to Japan) was negotiated and legislated in 2002. The Singapore agreement broke Japan's long commitment to the principle of non-discriminatory trade. The agreement had a trivial impact on the Japanese economy, but in Japan, it came to be rationalized as a way of pushing the domestic reform agenda. However, like almost all such arrangements, it was an extremely limited instrument for achieving that objective. The third bilateral agreement involved Mexico, with which Japan concluded the negotiation of an FTA in 2004, although the impact of the agreement is also very modest.

The Japanese policymakers who initiated these moves did not understand how other countries in the region would react to them. Most importantly, China, in dealing with Southeast Asian sensitivities about its economic rise, was freed to propose an FTA with ASEAN. Because of a more open approach to agricultural trade, it was able to trump Japan in its Southeast Asian diplomacy and move forward with a bolder and more attractive schedule for negotiations (see footnote 27). Beyond Japan, South Korea was flirting with a broader bilateral FTA strategy, but even negotiations with Chile bogged down. Australia moved rapidly to mimic Japan's deal with Singapore, then Thailand, and more significantly, entered into formal negotiations of an FTA with the U.S. — a development made possible in the aftermath of September 11 and Australian support for the Bush administration's campaign in Iraq.[29] At the Bali ASEAN+3 summit in 2003, China again

[29] Ross Garnaut, "Requiem for Uldorama: A Plain but Useful Life," paper presented to the Committee for Economic Development of Australia (CEDA) Conference on "New Horizons in Trade: The WTO Round and Australia's Free Trade Negotiations," Adelaide, June 5, 2003.

seized the initiative in pressing for a broader East Asian trade arrangement, supporting the ASEAN strategy for deepening Southeast Asian integration, and outflanking Japan's initiatives for more divisive bilateral agreements with the Southeast Asian countries. China is now considering FTAs with Australia and New Zealand. The U.S. has done its own deal with Singapore and has mooted bilateral agreements with other ASEAN countries.

Both economic and political considerations have influenced thinking among the Chinese leadership about the change in trade policy strategy. Findlay[30] provides the best interpretation of the background to China's evolving FTA strategy. He suggests that, in the face of other countries' fears that they would be crowded out by China's growth in Southeast Asia, China offered FTAs as way of providing reassurance and as a vehicle for cooperation. Zhang[31] suggested that a FTA, involving all the ASEAN economies, would make the entire region more attractive to foreign investors: this could allay the concerns of ASEAN members about the effect of China's WTO entry on patterns of FDI flows (see footnote 31).

Zhang (see footnote 31) argued that an agreement between China and ASEAN could accelerate moves for Japan and South Korea to form their own bilateral agreements with ASEAN; could push China, South Korea, and Japan toward further progress on bilateral arrangements of their own; and could encourage a broader East Asian regional arrangement. Some people thus see the China–ASEAN FTA as a building block for wider regional cooperation. Zhang (see footnote 31) argued that interest in a more formal institutional arrangement follows from the concern about the vulnerability of market-based integration, and from the

---

[30] Christopher Findlay, "China and the World Economy: The FTA Strategy," in *China: New Engine of World Growth*, ed. Ross Garnaut and Ligang Song (Canberra: Asia Pacific Press, 2003).

[31] Zhang Yunling, "East Asian Cooperation and Integration: Where To Go?" in *East Asian Cooperation: Progress and Future*, ed. Yunling Zhang (Beijing: World Affairs Press, 2003).

emergence of institutionally-based integration in Europe and the Americas.

ASEAN+3 "provides a framework for demonstrating East Asian leadership and influence on regional and international affairs."[32] In addition to the establishment of an East Asian Free Trade Area, the ASEAN+3 agenda includes cooperation on macro-economic policy and financial market strengthening, and joint action on the provision of regional public goods. Zhang (see footnote 31) referred to the common interest in responding to drug trafficking, piracy, illegal migration, environmental disasters, money laundering, international terrorism and other trans-boundary problems. Beyond these areas, there might be interaction in relation to defense and military affairs, but that cooperation involves an even longer time horizon.[33]

From this perspective, the FTA strategy can be seen as designed to contribute to China's capacity to "form at some point a counter-power comparable to the U.S. and Europe by unifying Asian countries." Based on this interpretation, the strategy is part of an attempt by China to build a "strategic partnership" within East Asia, a partnership that can be used to "work closely on regional and international issues."[34] It is not clear that the FTA component is actually required to achieve this goal, but certainly that is how it is presently viewed widely, both in China and Japan.

Zhang (see footnote 31) admitted that it is too early for China to consider a fully-institutionalized East Asian arrangement. One reason is that neither Japan nor South Korea is yet ready to negotiate an

---

[32] Peter Drysdale, "China, the WTO and East Asian Economic Diplomacy," in *East Asian Trade and Financial Integration: New Issues*, ed. Peter Drysdale and Kenichi Ishigaki (Canberra: Asia Pacific Press, 2002), p. 141.

[33] Christopher Findlay, "China and the World Economy: The FTA Strategy," in *China: New Engine of World Growth*, ed. Ross Garnaut and Ligang Song (Canberra: Asia Pacific Press, 2003).

[34] Naoko Munakata, of the Research Institute of Economy, Trade and Industry in Tokyo, quoted in the *Far Eastern Economic Review*, July 17, 2003, p. 29.

agreement with China and vice versa. Another reason is that the region cannot confront the issues that would arise from the treatment of Taiwan in a larger arrangement. For the immediate term, the agenda is actually a subregional one, with the focus on China and ASEAN. We have yet to see how that will finally influence the shape of broader regional cooperation arrangements, but certainly there is limited room for Taiwan (and presently, we might add, Australia) in the growing institutionalization of regional cooperation arrangements in East Asia.

The other important Chinese regional initiative is the Closer Economic Partnership Arrangement (CEPA) with Hong Kong, signed at the end of June 2003.[35] This arrangement is still evolving, but it provides for duty-free access to a broad range of imports that qualify in terms of specified rules of origin and designated service providers. The agreement is deepening the integration of Hong Kong into the economy of South China.

The stalling of the Doha Round of WTO negotiations at Cancun in 2003 gave further impetus to the surge of preferential bilateralism in East Asian and international trade diplomacy. But none of the bilateral agreements that have been put in place so far has made a substantial contribution to trade liberalization.[36] In East Asia, there is

---

[35] So far, 273 tariff items are covered under the agreement. Other exporters of these products to China are subject to tariffs that range from 5 percent to 35 percent. Additional products will be added to the list at the request of manufacturers. In the initial phase of the agreement, the rules of origin requirements were spelled out for each product. The rules of origin requirements were not settled until September 2003. The criteria are that processing must involve either a change in the tariff heading or 30 percent value-added in processing. There is also accelerated access under the WTO accession obligation for service providers in 18 sectors, including telecommunications, a provision added after the conclusion of the initial agreement. See Christopher Findlay, "China and the World Economy: The FTA Strategy," in *China: New Engine of World Growth*, eds. Ross Garnaut and Ligang Song (Canberra: Asia Pacific Press, 2003), pp. 5–7.

[36] Richard Adams, Philippa Dee, Jyothi Gali, and Greg McGuire, "The Trade and Investment Effects of Preferential Trading Arrangements: Old and New Evidence," *Productivity Commission Staff Working Paper*, Canberra, 2003.

an emerging mess of arrangements with more and more complicated rules of origin, which have the potential to distort and derail, rather than encourage and promote broader and deeper economic integration.[37]

Economic and Political Costs to Taiwan

For both political and economic reasons, the proliferation of FTA initiatives and the emergence of ASEAN+3 complicate Taiwan's involvement and interests in the region immensely. The political deadlock across the Taiwan Strait remains. Nor can we underestimate the impact of the rise of China and its dramatic success in integrating into the international economy. A key characteristic of FTAs is that they involve political preference and political, as well as economic, choice. An environment in which FTAs dominate international economic diplomacy is not congenial to Taiwan's economic and political interests. An understanding of this reality does not come easy in Taipei, where the policy instinct still tends to favor preferred and special dealing of the sort that FTAs typically involve. We shall return to this issue at the end of this chapter. Beijing's diplomatic initiative prevents Taiwan's automatic participation in the new international diplomatic game that is being played out in the East Asian region.

---

[37] Ross Garnaut, "Requiem for Uldorama: A Plain but Useful Life," paper presented to the Committee for Economic Development of Australia (CEDA) Conference on "New Horizons in Trade: The WTO Round and Australia's Free Trade Negotiations," Adelaide, June 5, 2003; Ross Garnaut, "America, Australia and Asia after Cancun," Chicago Conference on the Global Economy, Chicago, Council for Foreign Relations, September 16, 2003; Ross Garnaut and Jagdish Bhagwati, "Say No to This Free Trade Deal," *The Australian*, July 11, 2003; Christopher Findlay, Haflah Piei, and Mari Pangestu, "Trading with Favourites: Risks, Motives and Implications of FTAs in the Asia Pacific," paper prepared for the East Asia Trade Strategy Conference, The Australian National University, March 20–21, 2003; Christopher Findlay, "China and the World Economy: The FTA Strategy," in *China: New Engine of World Growth*, ed. Ross Garnaut and Ligang Song (Canberra: Asia Pacific Press, 2003); Gordon de Brouwer, "Financial Markets, Institutions and Integration in East Asia," *Asian Economic Papers* 2, no. 1 (2003), pp. 53–80.

Taiwan's response to this new circumstance has been to seek its own preferential trading deals. As discussed below, it has made a huge diplomatic and policy effort to seal FTAs with other countries in the region and beyond, but has had limited success.

In October 2002, Taipei and Washington began a series of talks at the working-group level with a view to negotiating a trade and investment framework agreement (TIFA). However, formal talks never materialized. The United States complains that Taiwan has been slow to resolve issues concerning the protection of intellectual property rights and opening markets to foreign rice and foreign telecommunications companies. The United States has been quick to use Taiwan's protection of its services sector and agricultural products as excuses for lack of progress on an FTA with Taiwan, but it has deep political reservations about going down the FTA path with Taiwan. Taiwan continues to seek an FTA with the U.S., but would probably receive only a small overall economic benefit from an FTA with the U.S.[38] The political leverage of an agreement, however, would be great.

We call this a "back-to-the-future" policy strategy. It hankers after a return to political and economic circumstances that no longer exist in the relationship between Taipei and Washington because there is now so much at stake in Washington's relationship with Beijing.

After its accession to the WTO in 2002, Taiwan also sought FTAs with other countries, including Japan, New Zealand, Singapore, Panama, and South Korea.

Negotiations with Singapore bogged down over Taiwan's insistence on negotiating a deal as a political entity, not an economic

[38] A report released by the International Trade Commission of the United States concludes that an FTA between the U.S. and Taiwan would likely have a "negligible impact" on the U.S. economy and only a "small impact" on Taiwan, with Taiwan's GDP increasing by 0.3 percent, as a result of the complete elimination of trade barriers under an FTA. For details, see International Trade Commission of the United States, "U.S.–Taiwan FTA: Likely Economic Impact of a Free Trade Agreement between the United States and Taiwan" (2002). Available at http://www.usitc.gov/wais/reports/arc/w3548.htm (accessed September 17, 2003).

entity.[39] The controversy over the visit of Lee Hsien Loong, then Singapore prime minister-in-waiting, to Taipei in 2004, ended any prospect of success on that front.

FTAs with Japan and New Zealand are at an early stage. During the APEC meetings in Bangkok, in October 2003, Taiwan's Minister of Economic Affairs, Lin Yi-fu, announced progress in commitment by Japan's Economic, Trade, and Industry Minister, Shoichi Nakagawa, to an academic study of the feasibility of an arrangement with Japan. He also announced that Taiwan was approaching New Zealand about the possibility of an FTA. It would be difficult for Taiwan to sign an FTA with ASEAN as a whole, so it seems that Taiwan is seeking individual pacts with its individual member-states.[40]

Taiwan has completed one FTA — signed with Panama in August 2003. This FTA agreement went into effect on January 1, 2004. Both countries agreed to open markets for agricultural and industrial products, and to open the service and financial sectors. However, the Panama agreement symbolizes the failure, rather than the success of Taiwan's FTA strategy, because Panama ranks 70th among Taiwan's trading partners, with bilateral trade of less than 1 percent of Taiwan's total trade.[41]

The economic benefits that would derive from any of the FTAs that Taiwan has sought to pursue, including with the U.S., are far outweighed by the benefits that would derive from multilateral or unilateral liberalization of trade in goods and services. A multilateral or unilateral liberalization strategy would also sensibly include the removal of trade discrimination against the mainland. Proponents of the FTA strategy believe that it has an overriding political advantage, but that apparent advantage would seem to be a chimera, given the new economic and political circumstances surrounding China's emergence in East Asia and the Pacific.

---

[39] *Washington Times*, http://washingtontimes.com/upi-breaking/20031014-070643-9566r.htm (accessed October 30, 2003).

[40] See http://news.tradingcharts.com/futures/8/3/41093538.html (accessed October 30, 2003).

[41] See http://www.yonhapnews.co.kr/Engnews/20030829/300200000020030829173243E8.html.

LINKING GLOBALIZATION TO CROSS-STRAIT INTEGRATION

Unilateral Initiatives

Taiwan has achieved tremendous economic success since the 1960s due to a combination of domestic and international factors, such as the accommodation of an export-oriented labor-intensive growth strategy in a favorable international economic environment. The challenge now is industrial upgrading, with labor-intensive industries no longer at the core of Taiwan's comparative advantage. Whether Taiwan can successfully transform itself into a technology- and capital-intensive economy depends on how it manages two major external forces that are overwhelming the region — the emergence of China and the proliferation of preferential trade agreements and sub-regional arrangements.

How should Taiwan use its international economic diplomacy to respond to the rise of China? How can Taiwan relate to the evolving economic dialogues and associations in East Asia, including ASEAN+3, the Manila Framework Group, and the various FTAs and economic partnership arrangements that are under contemplation? We argue that, both economically and politically, the best way for Taiwan is to go loudly and actively globalist. There is no future for Taiwan — or only a most uncertain and divisive future — if it focuses on the FTA route.

"Globalization" is a word that has resonance across the political spectrum in Taiwan. It is a popular idea for two reasons. It is used by people who believe that Taiwan should maintain its protectionist measures against China and discriminate against China, while being open to everyone else. It also appeals to people who believe that Taiwan's globalization must include China as a key element, but not the sole element, in its openness toward the world.[42] It is not yet clear which course Taiwan will take in its globalization strategy.

[42] Jane Skanderup, "China and Taiwan in the WTO: Economic, Political, and Security Implications," paper presented to the Pacific Forum, CSIS, October 2002.

As discussed earlier, China's accession to the WTO delivers a long-term commitment to a more liberal and open regime, and provides tremendous economic and business opportunities for the region. A new wave of trade and industrial transformation is taking place across the region, as multinational firms rationalize their production processes and the way in which they deploy capital and other resources. China is leading the third great wave of regional transformation. The first wave took place in the 1960s and 1970s, when there was an industrial transformation very similar to that of today, with the impact of Japan's growth on the region (and later its shedding of labor-intensive industries to the newly-industrial economies, including Taiwan). The second wave occurred in the late 1980s, when newly-industrial economies began to relocate labor-intensive industries to mainland China and Southeast Asia (see Figure 5.3).

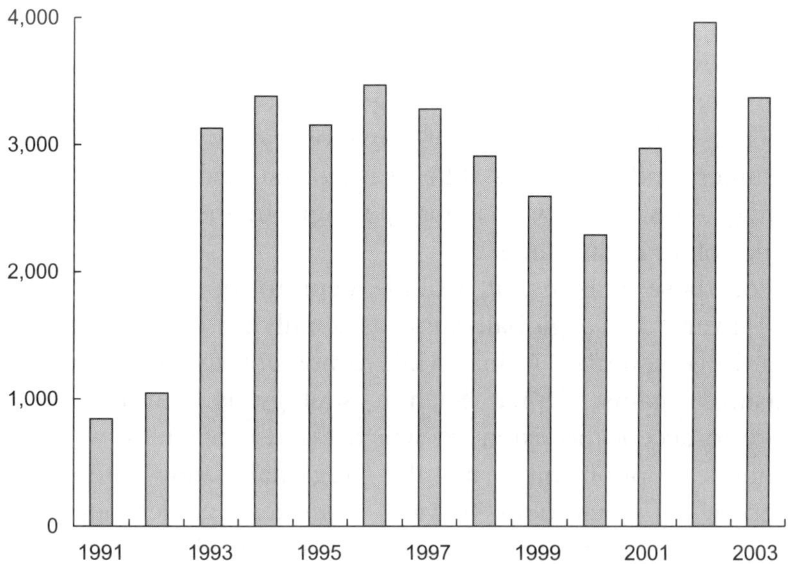

Figure 5.3 Taiwan's investment in mainland China (US$ million)
Sources: Official statistics of the Ministry of Foreign Trade and Economic Cooperation, China. See *China Statistical Yearbook* (Beijing: China Statistical Press, various years). Data for 2003 are from *China Economy and Statistics Express,* National Bureau of Statistics, July 2004.

As we have explained, the current wave of industrial relocation involves both inter-sectoral and, more importantly, intra-sectoral re-specialization in international trade and production. It involves upstream parts of an industry located in one or more countries, while downstream parts of the same industry are located in another country or in several other countries. A most-favored-nation trade policy regime provides the best platform for multinational firms to rationalize their operations through the relocation of different parts of their production processes, if they are to do so on the basis of efficiency, rather than preferential trading arrangements with particular source countries.

This observation applies particularly to China — now the main destination for early-stage processing activities in East Asia. Taiwan's trade policy of discrimination against China severely limits its ability to benefit from the most important positive force sweeping the East Asian economy, or even cuts it out altogether. Taiwan's investment and trade have been on a large scale and have shown impressive growth rates, but they are truncated by the present regime, and this damages economic welfare in Taiwan and cuts off the supply of low-cost goods and inputs to consumers and producers alike. It is an irrational economic policy strategy — a strategy that has its logic in the economics and politics of an earlier time.

For these reasons, it would seem to be a great mistake for Taiwan to use globalization as a rallying call for openness toward everyone but China, while continuing to use protectionist measures against China. Such a strategy is founded on the failure to accept the extent to which the rise of China will create economic opportunity in the regional and international economies. It would deny Taiwan's industries a golden opportunity to move further up the value chain — and would deny them this opportunity at greater and greater costs. This conclusion is not based on the assumption that there are no risks in the third wave of Chinese and regional transformation. However, as we shall argue, the choice of policy strategy for Taiwan will minimize the risks.

The FTA route (back to the future of a cosseted relationship with the U.S.) is equally unpromising, both economically and politically. It makes no sense to channel large and very-scarce policy and diplomatic resources into a strategy that is doomed to failure or to lose international cachet. As mentioned above, in the short term, it is unlikely that Taiwan will negotiate an FTA that would yield more than trivial economic benefits in the short term, and that in the long term would lead to a path of painful adjustment when it eventually confronted the reality of China. Moreover, the FTA route invites increasing diplomatic ridicule. Taiwan is truly between a rock and a hard place with respect to trade and foreign economic policy strategy.

A Common Market without External Tariffs

It has been argued that Taiwan could seek a common market with China. This is a radical idea, given current economic and political relations. It can be seen as a way to define a political association that addresses the key interests of both Beijing and Taipei. However, it has a fatal flaw: it presumes a huge amount of trust in what would be a fundamental and early commitment to close political cooperation. This would be clearly harder for Taipei than for Beijing within a concord in which the ballast of other partnerships was lost. It might succeed if Beijing responded in a way that encouraged a greater degree of political goodwill, but it would exacerbate the schizophrenic attitude toward the mainland by the body politic in Taiwan and, therefore, would fail. For economic reasons, Taiwan must deal with China sooner rather than later, but the traditional common market strategy is too up-front too soon. Taiwan is not Hong Kong and is unlikely to be in such a position for some time.

There is an alternative route by which Taiwan could secure and maximize the economic benefits of deeper integration with mainland China at the same time that it manages the political complexities. The arrangement would require a commitment to deeper integration with the mainland through a unilateral liberalization that applied equally to all of Taiwan's trading partners, not only the mainland. This strategy could have two main elements, one focused on cross-strait integration, the second focused on developing a leading role for Taiwan in the multilateral WTO agenda. A globalization strategy that encompasses both the China factor and the global factor is likely to be the best way to serve Taiwan's economic interests, as well as its political interests. We call this strategy a global integration strategy.

A program of unilateral liberalization should not be restricted to the liberalization of trade in goods and services across the Taiwan Strait and beyond. Importantly, it should also include the liberalization of capital flows. The best way for Taiwan-based businesses to take advantage of growing opportunities in mainland China is for Taiwan to allow its business community to invest freely there. And the liberalization of trade and investment is only one aspect of the strategy. The other is a program directed at facilitating trade and investment — application of the APEC agenda — a priority that should include all elements of trade and commercial linkages, which have yet to be established between Taiwan and the mainland.

The merit of the common market idea is that it encompasses the element of trade facilitation, as well as the element of liberalization, both of which are central to opening up direct and efficient dealings across the Taiwan Strait.[43] The long-established consensus is that geographical proximity, common language and culture, and complementary factor endowments offer big gains when countries remove barriers to the movement of goods and services, capital, and people, and that these gains would apply to both Taiwan and mainland China. Unraveling the political deadlock remains the key.[44] Global integration without a common

---

[43] Vincent Siew proposed a China common market in May 2001, according to a CNN report; "Taiwan Ex-PM Seeks to Build China Common Market," http://edition.cnn.com/2001/WORLD/asiapcf/east/05/08/taiwan.expremier (accessed September 18, 2003).

[44] Xu Xinpeng, "Taiwan's Economic Cooperation with Fujian and Guangdong: The View from China," in *Taiwan in the Asia Pacific in the 1990s*, ed. Gary Klintworth (Australia: Allen & Unwin, 1994), pp. 142–153.

market may be one way forward. It has the potential to lift Taiwan's leverage through constructive participation in the WTO. It would also define a new role for Taiwan, which would help to bring the focus of regional arrangements back to the broader global agenda in which, as we have argued, Taiwan can be more comfortable about pursuing greater openness with China.

Market-driven integration among China, Hong Kong, and Taiwan is already strong, though it is an incomplete triangular relationship. More than half of China's cumulative FDI inflows during the reform period (up to 2003) have come from Taiwan and Hong Kong (Table 5.2). The conclusion of the CEPA between Hong Kong and China brings still deeper integration to one side of the triangle. However, cross-strait trade is still very limited (Tables 5.3 and 5.7) and Taiwan investment in China above a certain level is still restricted. Even small and medium-sized firms that already have operations in China face an array of problems — for example, double taxation, investment protection, and safety and security issues — that prevent both sides from enjoying the full benefits of integration. In developing a global integration strategy for Taiwan, the starting point is to give priority to the facilitation element of the common market proposal. Dealing with these issues does not require the creation of a common external tariff, as is required for a common market, or preferential trading arrangements, as are required for an FTA. The issues can be dealt with perfectly well in a global integration strategy that commits to a scheduled package of liberalization and facilitation measures at the same time.

A dynamic, prosperous Chinese economy will benefit all stakeholders across the Taiwan Strait. So too will a dynamic, prosperous economy on Taiwan. Beijing's guiding principle for managing cross-strait relations is "pursuing common interests by leaving alone disagreement." From this perspective, a common market might be acceptable to Beijing. Yet the element of exclusion in a common market framework would make Taipei beholden to Beijing in a way that would present too many risks on the way to political transition on the mainland and across the Taiwan Strait. In addition, a "closed" common market might accommodate less productive and efficient players, creating new distortions and new interest groups begging for retaliation by major players outside — for example, the U.S., that remains one of the most important export destinations for the Chinese economies. The choice of an open global integration strategy by Taiwan, therefore, would seem to offer a promising way forward.

Regional Strategies with a Global Face

A global integration strategy might provide just the right response to the challenging external environment that now confronts Taiwan.[45] But a number of questions have to be considered and conditions met, if it were to do so. The questions relate to Taiwan's and China's positions in the WTO and Taiwan's position in the regional East Asian arrangements. The conditions relate to the domestic political platform and policy capacities that are required for success.

The first question is whether the membership of the PRC and Taiwan in the WTO can deliver an agenda for deeper integration across the Taiwan Strait and within the region. Taiwan and China have yet to develop member-to-member working relationships within the WTO. There is no articulated agenda for cooperation on the intersection of bilateral issues in multilateral negotiations, or on common interests in third-party dialogues. This situation has arisen for substantial political reasons — and the politics have become more complicated since the Taiwan's presidential election on March 18, 2000 — but also because of limitations in the process, capacity, and experience in the centers of policymaking in Taipei and Beijing. Both Taipei and Beijing are new to the process, and their policy and negotiating capacities are severely overstretched. The development of policy capacity will take time, but there are quicker ways to

[45] Ross Garnaut, "Requiem for Uldorama: A Plain but Useful Life," paper presented to the Committee for Economic Development of Australia (CEDA) Conference on "New Horizons in Trade: The WTO Round and Australia's Free Trade Negotiations," Adelaide, June 5, 2003.

acquire it and more effective ways to engage. There are informal second and one-and-a-half track mechanisms that channel bilateral policy dialogue between the two capitals, but there is no adequate mechanism for the policy shift called for here. Moreover, bilateral channels alone are not a suitable way to deal with issues that involve third-party interests in the region and beyond.

This leads to the second question. What are the implications of joint membership in the WTO for Taiwan's role in APEC and associations with other partners in the region — for example, with ASEAN? The short answer is that there are none. This flows inexorably from the answer to the earlier question. Membership in the WTO has not established any basis of common interest that carries through to regional dealings. That is not to say that common interests could not flow through to regional dealings, but they have not yet done so.

The first step could be to define the opportunities. The argument above suggests that an overarching priority for Taiwan is the global agenda and how to relate regional initiatives and actions to that global agenda. This is the core APEC agenda, and Taiwan has space to play there. It also could seek to promote these broader interests within the East Asian region through less formal initiatives with countries, such as Australia, which have no interest in disturbing cross-strait relationships, but have every interest in forging broader and more open links within the region.

The deeper question is this: If a global integration strategy presents such a good way forward to deal with Taiwan's international economic diplomatic challenges, why has Taiwan shown no sign of adopting it with alacrity? The answer to that question lies in the allusion earlier to policy instinct and political focus. Policy instinct in Taiwan is rooted in the problems and solutions of the past. There is little or no understanding of what lies outside that box. The development of a new set of policy dialogues within Taiwan, and between Taiwan and her neighbors, could help chart the way forward. This could be a precursor to an initiative of the kind suggested here, and to an escape from the atavisms of another era. That needs to be combined with strenuous efforts to strengthen its policy capacity and build a comprehension of the reality that now confronts Taiwan.

TAIWAN'S REGIONAL ROLE AND CHINA'S GLOBAL CHOICE: A WAY FORWARD

Is an actively multilateralist and globalist role for Taiwan compatible with the evolution of the foreign economic policy strategies in China and within the region? China is presently embarked upon a number of initiatives — including the ASEAN FTA enterprise and ASEAN+3 — that could entrench exclusionary policies within the region. These initiatives are largely the product of political and foreign policy considerations, but there is a powerful constraint on their extension beyond the Southeast Asian sub-region. China is comfortable with a multilaterally-oriented TIFA with Australia, for example, but is now contemplating an FTA with Australia, and examining whether and how it would cut across its many global interests, including the interests of America.

China is already a big economy, and it will not be easy to serve trade and foreign economic policy interests by confining them to special ties with particular countries or regions. China is rapidly outgrowing even the East Asia region. It is steadily becoming more and more important to its neighbors in East Asia; in turn, they will become less and less important to China as China extends its global reach. Under these circumstances, the protection of the WTO framework and open regional arrangements will assume greater and greater importance to China's partners in East Asia as time goes by. In brief, if its development ambitions are to stay on course, China must make a global choice.

The challenge is to turn China's positive political and strategic initiatives within East and Southeast Asia into a project of regional economic integration that is wholly consistent with the main game of China's multilateral global interests and the vision of a strong and open East Asian economy. This challenge will come into sharp relief, if China enters into formal negotiation of an FTA with Australia, as now seems likely.

Clearly, the best way forward will be to develop a broad cooperative agenda on trade liberalization, investment cooperation, trade facilitation, and infrastructure development. Trade liberalization with ASEAN, for example, would sensibly contribute to the goals of China and East Asia for the multilateral freeing of trade. Taiwan's interest is in reinforcing that idea through its role in APEC, initiatives within the WTO, and its own active and independent support of policy dialogue directed to that objective within the region.

Earlier, we noted the risks in the Chinese wave of industrial and trade transformation within East Asia, and most importantly, in the management of the economics and politics of the process within China itself. In this period of trade and policy transition in China, the dangers are real. Chinese leaders know that it will be at least two decades before transparent market institutions are fully entrenched in the national economy. During this period, China's major partners in the WTO will, correctly, subject to extra and rigorous scrutiny any special trading deals that China seeks to make with partners within the region or, especially, outside the region.

The Chinese economy is not yet like that of the economies of North America or Europe, even as they were 50 years ago. The challenge for China's domestic reform relates to the fact that what made sense for North America or Europe does not necessarily make sense for China in East Asia today. Whatever value traditional FTAs had in building modern Europe, or in dealing with particular political and economic problems, in late-twentieth-century North America (and they had large costs even to these economies), they are reflective of another place and another age. The needs of East Asia in the twenty-first century are different. East Asia has its own characteristics. The ASEAN+1 and ASEAN+3 groupings make sense, even if they are not organized around the substructure of traditional discriminatory trading arrangements.

Taiwan's commitment to a global integration strategy at this time can support cross-strait interests and help to shape a regional framework that is compatible with the sweep of history, rather than battling against it. That will help to advance the evolution of an economy in China, that genuinely conforms to WTO principles and that occurs within a multilateral economic framework that encourages economic and political openness and transparency. This will contribute both to East Asia's trade and political goals and to a stronger WTO system. In this way, Taiwan's strategic foreign economic policy interests within the East Asian region would be well-served.

Chapter

6

The Political Economy of Cross-Strait Relations: Economic Interdependence, the WTO, and Security

Joseph Fewsmith

Over the past two decades, Taiwan and China have been increasingly bound by economic ties as businesses from Taiwan invested heavily in the mainland and commodity trade (mostly from Taiwan to the mainland) and personal travel (now, the taking up of residence) increased dramatically. Much of the literature on interdependence posits that such thick economic relations will spill over into "high politics," promoting stability between the two sides of the Taiwan Strait.[1] Such literature cannot be dismissed, and there is much evidence that the growing economic integration across the strait has ameliorated political conflict. Nevertheless, continuing security concerns in Taiwan, the growth of a Taiwanese identity, and politics have propelled efforts to fundamentally redefine cross-strait

[1] Robert O. Keohane and Joseph S. Nye, eds., *Power and Interdependence*, 3rd ed. (Boston: Little Brown, 2001).

relations at the same time that growing wealth, military prowess, and nationalism have inclined the PRC to be more assertive about its claim that "Taiwan is a part of China." The centripetal forces of economic ties are thus posed against the centrifugal pulls of identity and politics, making it uncertain at best whether low politics will spill over into high politics, or contrarily, whether the interests and emotions of high politics will lead to increased tensions and perhaps military conflict.

Globalization is a major part of this story. Global competition has increasingly forced businesses in Taiwan to seek lower production costs and diversification as a way to maintain global competitiveness. At the same time, it has largely forced Taiwan to abandon its original strategy of developing vertical integration across the strait (keeping technological know-how located in Taiwan and re-locating production to the mainland) in favor of becoming integrated into global production chains, in which Taiwan companies are frequently only one part of the global enterprises that stretch from North America and Europe to Taiwan to China and elsewhere.

Taiwan investment in the mainland, which was virtually nil in the early 1980s, has now reached an estimated cumulative total of about US$ 70–100 billion,[2] and continues to increase by approximately US$ 4 billion per year. This figure constitutes approximately 70 percent of total Taiwan outward investment. Similarly, trade across the strait continues to grow rapidly. Taiwan is a major beneficiary of this trade, exporting substantially to the mainland (mostly for the processing trade), while, at the same time, restricting imports. Thus, Taiwan has run up a cumulative trade surplus since 1979 of some US$ 230 billion, generating substantial complaints from the mainland.[3] These trade and investment flows have helped Taiwan to grow and prosper, moving its economy up the ladder from labor-intensive to capital-intensive industries. In the late 1980s, Taiwan invested heavily in labor-intensive industries in the PRC as labor costs in Taiwan

[2] Figures on Taiwan investment in the mainland are notoriously difficult to pin down.

[3] *China Daily*, August 20, 2004.

increased. Beginning in the early 1990s, however, Taiwan investment concentrated in capital-intensive industries, particularly consumer electronics, allowing Taiwan's industries to continue to grow and to hire more and better-educated workers.[4]

The mainland has also benefited from this trade and investment. The US$ 70 billion that Taiwan has invested in the mainland constitutes approximately 14 percent of the total FDI in the PRC. Estimates of the number of jobs created by this investment are difficult to come by. According to PRC figures, 6.71 million workers are employed in "foreign invested" enterprises, but this figure is clearly too low. Kao Charng estimated that in 1995 — when cumulative Taiwan investment in the PRC stood at US$ 11.5 million — some 3.9 million workers were employed in Taiwan-invested enterprises (TIEs).[5] On the basis of Charng's figures, Chen-yuan Tung estimated that TIEs employed 8.2 million Chinese workers in 1999 (when cumulative investment stood at US$ 23.8 billion).[6] If Taiwan's businesses continue to invest in the PRC at approximately the rate of US$ 4 billion per year, there will have to be at least 10 million Chinese workers — perhaps more — employed in the TIEs — about 5 percent of China's total urban labor force. These TIEs not only employ a significant number of the Chinese workforce, they also generate a very significant percentage of China's total exports — about 20 percent (see footnote 6). Given that China exported US$ 238 billion of goods to the world in 2003, this means that TIEs accounted for about US$ 48 billion dollars of PRC exports.

---

[4] Chen Tain-Jy and Ying-Hua Ku, "The Effect of Foreign Direct Investment on Firm Growth: The Case of Taiwan's Manufacturers," *Japan and the World Economy* 12, no. 2 (2000), 153–172.

[5] Charng Kao, *Liang'an jingmao guanxi zhi tantao* [An Exploration of Cross-Strait Economic Relations] (Taipei: Tianyi, 1997), cited in Chen-yuan Tung, *China's Economic Leverage and Taiwan's Security Concerns with respect to Cross-Strait Economic Relations*, Ph.d dissertation, 2002, 56–57.

[6] Chen-yuan Tung, *China's Economic Leverage and Taiwan's Security Concerns with respect to Cross-Strait Economic Relations*, Ph.d dissertation, 2002; Chen-Yuan Tung, "Economic Relations between Taiwan and China," *UNISCI Discussion Paper*, http://www.usc.cuhk.edu.hk/wk_wxdetails.asp?id=2861.

ECONOMIC IMPACT OF WTO ACCESSION

The nearly-simultaneous accession of the PRC, on December 11, 2001, and of Taiwan — under the name "Separate Customs Territory of Taiwan, Penghu, Kinmen, and Matsu" — on January 1, 2002, to the WTO has created a complex mixture of economic and political pressures on each side. In economic terms, WTO accession marked an acceleration of globalization, forcing the PRC to drop tariff protection on many goods and to revamp its legal structure, and compelling Taiwan to continue to adjust to external pressures and adjust its policies vis-à-vis the mainland. Economic models suggest that joint membership in the WTO will continue to accelerate this process. As Zhi Wang concluded, "It is evident ... that WTO entry would increase the complementarities of manufacturing industries across the Taiwan Strait, allowing for the combination of Taiwan's capital and know-how with the efficient use of the huge reservoir of low-cost labor in China, making both China and Taiwan stronger competitors in the world of manufactured goods market."[7] Such economic forces will pressure the two sides — Taiwan willingly and the PRC less so — to look to the WTO as a channel to normalize trade relations and possibly also political relations.

Overall, WTO accession has proven such economic expectations to be on the mark for both sides — PRC foreign trade expanded 21.8 percent in 2002 (to reach US$ 620 billion), 37.1 percent in 2003 (to reach US$ 851 billion),[8] 35.4 percent in 2004 (to reach $ 1.15 trillion);

---

[7] Zhi Wang, "WTO Accession, the 'Greater China' Free-Trade Area, and Economic Integration Across the Taiwan Strait," *China Economic Review* 14, no. 3 (2003), 344.

[8] Wen Jiabao, "Government Work Report," Xinhua, March 16, 2004 (translated in FBIS CPP20040316000088); Zeng Peiyan, "Report on the Implementation of the 2002 Plan for National Economic and Social Development and on the 2003 Draft Plan for National Economic and Social Development," Xinhua, March 20, 2003 (translated in FBIS CPP20030320000143); "Report on the Implementation of the 2004 Plan for National Economic and Social Development," Xinhua, March 15, 2005 (translated in FBIS CPP20050315000121); and "Report on the Implementation of the 2005 Plan for National Economic and Social Development," Xinhua, March 15, 2006 (translated in FBIS 20060315039002).

and another 23.2 percent in 2005 (to reach $ 1.42 trillion). FDI into China increased 12.5 percent in 2002 to US$ 52.7 billion, and another 1.5 percent to U.S.$ 53.5 billion in 2003. FDI subsequently increased 15.3 percent to U.S.$ 60.6 billion in 2004, and then dipped slightly to U.S.$ 60.3 billion in 2005 (see footnote 8). Taiwan's exports to China increased 34.3 percent in 2002 and another 28.3 percent in 2003, while imports from the mainland grew 34.7 percent in 2002 and 37.9 percent in 2003, suggesting the great potential for further growth, if and when Taiwan lessens its restrictions on imports from the mainland. Altogether, cross-strait trade was US$ 37.41 billion in 2002 and US$ 46.32 billion in 2003, making the mainland Taiwan's single most important trade partner (it surpassed the U.S. in 2002). This trade has continued to grow and it reached U.S.$ 64.4 billion in the first nine months of 2006.[9] Tain-Jy Chen stated flatly, "Taiwan has benefited from China's WTO entry and its trade liberalization measures more than any other WTO member."[10]

Perhaps ironically, one reason that Taiwan has benefited so much from China's entry into the WTO is that China's trade regime remains quite imperfect, and Taiwan businesses, with their extensive knowledge of local conditions in China and their language advantage, have been able to exploit a liberalizing, but not yet transparent, trade and investment environment in the PRC (see footnote 10).

Of course, Taiwan's investment in the PRC and the burgeoning of cross-strait trade have raised fears in Taiwan that its manufacturing sector will be "hollowed out." Between 1990 and 2000, manufacturing as a share of GDP fell from 33.3 percent to 26.3 percent, and Taiwan's unemployment rate was 4.8 percent in 2001 and above 5 percent in 2002 (see footnote 10). Nevertheless, in a careful study published in 2000, Tain-Jy Chen and Ying-Hua Ku showed that outward investment was beneficial to domestic employment and

[9] Agence France-Presse, November 29, 2006.

[10] Chen Tain-Jy, "Will Taiwan Be Marginalized by China?" *Asian Economic Papers* 2 (Spring-Summer 2003), http://web.lexis-nexis.com/universe/document?_m=9a66ad48b516646048084b8c2a9d5261&_do.

even to domestic investment. One of the interesting findings of this study is that those firms that invested only in China had the lowest increase in domestic employment — 1.7 percent — whereas those firms that invested elsewhere, as well as in China, expanded their domestic employment by an average of 20 percent. The explanation is that those firms investing only in China were smaller firms that were extending their lease on life — thus maintaining domestic employment and earnings — as opposed to more vigorous larger firms that were investing in China as one part of a global development strategy.[11] Thus, to date, hollowing out effects have not hurt Taiwan's domestic employment and investment. But Chen and Ku warned that, in the future, agglomeration effects will begin to work in China's favor as more firms will be forced to relocate to the mainland to be near their suppliers and customers (see footnote 10). What can be said at this point is that WTO accession has increased, not decreased, Taiwan's economic prosperity, while also benefiting the growth of the Chinese economy.

PRESSURES FOR LIBERALIZATION

The same sort of economic opportunities and pressures, which led to expanded cross-strait trade and investment in the wake of WTO accession, also compelled Taiwan to take a number of steps to lessen restrictions on cross-strait relations, either in anticipation of China's accession or following it. This positive impact seems surprising in the face of political concerns on both sides of the strait. On the one hand, the PRC was clearly suspicious of Chen Shui-bian following his 2000 election as President of Taiwan, adopting a policy of "listening to what he says and watching what he does," while, on the other hand, Taiwan's concerns over its increasing economic dependence on the mainland had led the then-President Lee Teng-hui to adopt a policy of "going slow" (*jieji yongren*) on investment

[11] Chen Tain-Jy and Ying-Hua Ku, "The Effect of Foreign Direct Investment on Firm Growth: The Case of Taiwan's Manufacturers," *Japan and the World Economy* 12, no. 2 (2000), 153–172.

in the mainland. In 1994, Lee adopted a "southward strategy" to encourage investment in Southeast Asia. This policy was not very successful as increasing numbers of Taiwan businesses evaded government control by investing in the mainland through subsidiaries set up in the Virgin Islands and elsewhere. By mid-2003, the Virgin Islands had become China's fifth-largest investor, with an accumulated investment of US$ 27.7 billion. The Asian financial crisis in 1997 further stimulated the shift in Taiwan investment to the mainland.

However, in the fall of 2001, as accession to the WTO approached, the Chen Shui-bian government relaxed the *jieji yongren* policy by adopting "active opening, effective management" (which had been proposed at the Economic Development Advisory Conference in August 2001). This change in policy lessened restrictions on amounts that could be invested in the mainland and suggested the degree to which the government was aware of the economic pressures that would accompany accession.

In January 2002, just as Taiwan was entering the WTO, the government announced that 2,126 products from the mainland would be removed from the list of restricted mainland imports. Such restrictions are in violation of the WTO rules, unless a member chooses to invoke Article 13, according to which one member can restrict imports from another member on national security grounds. Interestingly, Taiwan chose not to invoke this article, but, nevertheless, banned about 56 percent of the over 10,000 items on the customs schedule. The January decision thus reduced the number of restricted imports to about 2,500 — 24 percent of the scheduled items. Leaving 20 percent of the goods on the restricted list was still in violation of WTO provisions — something that the PRC has yet to challenge formally, apparently because it does not want to add legitimacy to Taiwan's role in the WTO — but the opening of Taiwan markets to these 2,126 products brought Taiwan closer to compliance.[12] This decision was quickly

[12] Chang Maubo, "Taiwan to Lift Ban on Advertising for Mainland Goods, Services," Central News Agency, January 18, 2002.

followed by the lifting of the ban on advertising products from the mainland.[13] Shortly thereafter, Taiwan loosened restrictions on investments from the PRC.[14]

POLITICAL INTERACTION

Although most people anticipated that the accession to the WTO would increase economic interactions across the strait, the political effects attracted the most attention. For over a decade, after Ye Jianying had called for improved relations across the strait in his "nine points" delivered in 1979, the two sides had found ways to reduce, or at least to control, the hostility that had marked relations over the preceding three decades and to expand commerce and contact. Nevertheless, the dramatic political changes that took place in Taiwan, beginning in the late 1980s, introduced new elements of tension, as the mainlander-led Kuomintang (KMT) began to lose control, first to a Taiwanese-led KMT (under Lee Teng-hui), and then to the opposition Democratic Progressive Party (DPP) under Chen Shui-bian. Still, in 1993, the "unofficial" organizations set up by the two sides — the Association for Relations Across the Taiwan Straits (ARATS) in Beijing and the Straits Exchange Foundation (SEF) in Taipei — were able to meet in Singapore for the Koo-Wang talks, the first time the two sides met together openly since 1949. Following a series of secret contacts, in early 1995, Jiang Zemin laid out his "eight points" for improving cross-strait relations (in which he declared that "Chinese should not fight Chinese"). Taiwan countered with its "six points" that demanded that the PRC drop its right to use force prior to negotiations (a demand known in Taiwan to be unacceptable to Beijing). Shortly thereafter, Lee Teng-hui traveled to his alma mater, Cornell University, and delivered a speech that made no

[13] Deborah Kuo, "Taiwan Opens to Direct Import of 2,126 Products from Mainland China," Central News Agency, January 16, 2002.

[14] "Taipei to Lift Ban on Investment from the Mainland," *The Straits Times*, March 28, 2002.

reference to "one China," and generally acted as a visiting head of state, rather than a person making a "private visit" (the pretext on which his visa was granted). The tentative trust that had begun to emerge since the Koo-Wang talks of 1993 was greatly undermined, and the PRC responded with a show of military force — further undermining the trust.[15]

In short, the politics that had led to a reduction of tensions in the 1980s were replaced by a new politics that generated conflict, as Taiwan sought to redefine its place in the world. But neither the domestic upheaval of the Tiananmen crackdown nor the international storm created by Lee Teng-hui's visit to Cornell, and the subsequent PRC military exercises in the Taiwan Strait, could quell the thirst for economic exchanges across the strait. The two economies were too complementary, the linguistic and cultural comparative advantages of Taiwan business too great, and the desire to cultivate commercial ties for political reasons (mostly on the part of Beijing) too substantial to hamper the growth of investment and trade. As a result, investment and trade continued almost uninterrupted by these political upheavals.

The question was: Would common membership in an important international economic organization ameliorate the political tensions that had built up across the strait, or would such tensions overwhelm the economic forces that had proven so resilient despite them? Expectations were generally high. President Clinton argued at the time that "if both Beijing and Taiwan are in the WTO, it will increase their interdependence and therefore the cost to Beijing of confrontation."[16] Deputy Assistant Secretary of State Susan Shirk elaborated, "A China that plays by the rules internationally is more likely to be a predictable cross-Strait partner... Once the PRC and Taiwan enter the WTO, both sides will be governed by a common enforceable trade

---

[15] Zhao Suisheng, ed., *Across the Taiwan Strait: Mainland China, Taiwan and the 1995–1996 Crisis* (New York: Routledge, 1999).

[16] "Statement by the President," April 11, 2000, http://hongkong.usconsulate.gov/uscn/state/2000/041101.htm.

regime."[17] The views of the Clinton Administration have been shared by the Bush Administration. U.S. Trade Representative Robert Zoellick[18] noted cautiously, but optimistically, that China and Taiwan could "employ the WTO as a channel for communication and negotiation, mutually observe its rules, and use its disciplines to accelerate the course on which they have already embarked." Similarly, William Lasch, the U.S. Assistant Secretary of Commerce for Market Access and Compliance, expressed the belief that cross-strait tensions would be reduced as the two sides repeatedly met with each other in the context of the WTO.[19]

The PRC had sought membership first in the GATT, and then in the WTO, for both economic and political reasons. Politically, the GATT/WTO was the most important international organization of which the PRC was not yet a member, and accession would not only demonstrate the passing of the quasi-pariah status that the PRC had acquired in the aftermath of the Tiananmen crackdown, but also would be indicative of a certain "coming of age." Economically, membership in the GATT/WTO was a way of using external pressure to bring about the sort of far-reaching market-oriented reforms that would be difficult to sustain without international competition.[20]

The PRC, however, was clearly unhappy about the prospects of Taiwan's admission as an equal member (though the knowledge that Taiwan's bid for accession was acceptable to WTO members, and that Taiwan might be admitted to the WTO prior to the PRC, was one factor hastening its own willingness to conclude an

---

[17] Susan Shirk, "Luncheon Discussion on the Impact of WTO Entry for Taiwan and China," May 12, 2000, http://hongkong.usconsulate.gov/uscn/state/2000/052101.htm.

[18] Robert B. Zoellick, Remarks delivered to the U.S.-China Business Council, January 31, 2002, http://hongkong.usconsulate.gov/uscn/trade/general/ustr/2002/013101.htm (accessed June 1, 2006).

[19] Deborah Kuo and Ed Chen, "Cross-Strait WTO Entry to Reduce Political Tension: U.S. Official," Central News Agency, February 7, 2002.

[20] Nicholas Lardy, *Integrating China into the Global Economy* (Washington, DC: Brookings Institution Press, 2002).

agreement). Part of the reason for this uneasiness was the distrust of Chen Shui-bian. Regarding Taiwan's forthcoming admission to the WTO, Chinese Minister of Foreign Trade Shi Guangsheng said in March 2001 that Taiwan should be admitted to the WTO under the title "Taiwan, Penghu, Kinmen, and Matsu, simplified to 'Chinese Taipei'," and stated that "when both mainland and Taiwan are WTO members, both will have a cross-strait relationship under one China and a membership relationship in the WTO as well" — a formulation that suggested that somehow Taiwan's admission to the WTO would be under the "one China" formula.[21] Thus, from the beginning, the PRC was unwilling to recognize Taiwan as an equal member of the WTO for fear that such recognition would bolster Taiwan's claim to be a separate state, and, with the interesting exception of the steel dispute case (to be discussed below), the PRC has consistently refused to deal with Taiwan within the WTO framework.

For its part, Taiwan was eager to join the WTO for precisely the reason that Beijing feared — that it would enhance the island's international standing. Thus, Yen Ching-chang, Taiwan's Chief Representative to the WTO, said that "joining the economic United Nations, the WTO, is definitely positive for raising our international status"[22] and Taiwan's Foreign Minister, Tien Hung-mao, noted that by becoming a member of WTO, Taiwan would be able to have increased contacts with other international organizations such as the World Customs Organization, the International Organization of Standardization, the United Nations Commission on Trade and Development, and the World Intellectual Property Rights Organization, all of which have regular interactions with the WTO.[23] Such contacts would obviously raise Taiwan's international profile and create more "space" for Taiwan on the international scene.

---

[21] "Chinese Trade Minister on WTO Entry, Taiwan, India," Xinhua, March 15, 2001 (in BBC Worldwide Monitoring).

[22] Anita Narayan, "China — Taiwan Looks to WTO Entry to Normalize Cross-Strait Trade," *ChinaOnline*, January 2, 2002.

[23] Central News Agency, January 10, 2002.

Nevertheless, Taiwan also hoped that the WTO framework would provide a cover for the two sides to discuss economic issues on an equal basis, a goal that, if accomplished, might allow for a framework for regularizing relations across the strait. Thus, Chen Ming-tong, Vice Chairman of the Mainland Affairs Council (MAC), declared that, "Since Taiwan and mainland China have recently joined the WTO in succession, the two sides should grasp the opportunity to foster mutual trust and goodwill and craft a viable engagement mechanism under the WTO framework to lay a solid foundation for future cross-strait cooperation."[24] Similarly, former Premier Vincent Siew of the opposition KMT argued that "the establishment of an institutionalized system will gradually defuse bilateral conflicts and help build long-term peace, stability and prosperity between the two sides."[25]

For Taiwan, these political and economic goals were inextricably intertwined, and this put the PRC on guard. Thus, while Tang Shubei, former Deputy Head of the Straits Exchange Foundation and current Director of the Research Center on Cross-Strait Relations, urged Taiwan to bring its trade rules into compliance with WTO regulations, and suggested that growing trade pressures would require cross-strait economic cooperation,[26] he also noted pointedly that "cross-strait economic and trade affairs remain China's internal affairs and should be settled by cross-strait consultation." In this regard, he warned that the PRC was resolutely opposed to discussing cross-strait political differences within the context of the WTO (see footnote 26).

Despite mutual suspicion, economic and political pressures worked to ameliorate some of the tensions across the strait. As noted above, as Taiwan was joining the WTO, it loosened restrictions on Taiwan investments in the PRC, the number of PRC products that could be imported into Taiwan, the advertising of PRC products in Taiwan, and — to some extent — the PRC's investment in Taiwan.

---

[24] *Financial Times Information,* January 4, 2002.

[25] "Taiwanese Former PM in Puerto Rico Calls for Free Trade Agreement with China," Central News Agency, April 12, 2002.

[26] Zhu Huaying, "'Seminar on WTO and Cross-Strait Economic and Trade Ties' held in Beijing," Xinhua, January 8, 2002.

This favorable mood was reciprocated by Beijing. On January 24, 2002, Qian Qichen, commemorating the anniversary of Jiang Zemin's "eight points," drew a distinction between the majority of DPP members and a small number of "hard-liners," and invited DPP members to visit the mainland.[27]

Certainly Qian's speech was in response not only to the accession to the WTO, but also, perhaps more importantly, to the DPP victory in the Legislative Yuan elections in December 2001. Nevertheless, the atmosphere surrounding dual accession seemed to prompt a more encouraging attitude from Beijing. Many members of the DPP had already traveled to the mainland, so there was more show than substance to Qian's speech but it, nevertheless, marked a warming attitude on the part of the mainland, and was welcomed as such by Taiwan. Chen Shui-bian reciprocated Qian's remarks by calling for dialogue with China's leadership,[28] and Premier Yu Shyi-kun declared, "There has been no such goodwill gesture for a long time. We welcome it.[29] But as with so many interactions between the two sides, tensions soon emerged when Taiwan Vice President Annette Lu, who is widely disliked on the mainland, decided to challenge Qian's remarks by proposing that she visit the mainland as a women's rights activist. "If Qian is sincere," the Vice President said, "he should let me go there."[30] In response, Beijing's Taiwan Affairs Office stated explicitly that Lu and Chen Shui-bian were "not included in the broad ranks of DPP members" being welcomed to visit the mainland, but rather fell into "another area."[31]

---

[27] Qian Qichen, "Adhere to the Basic Policy of 'One Country, Two Systems,' and Strive to Promote the Development of Cross-Strait Relations," Xinhua, January 24, 2002 (in FBIS CPP20020124000121).

[28] *China Post*, January 29, 2002.

[29] Yeh Ching, "Taiwan's Ruling Party Welcomes Signs of Goodwill from Beijing," Agence France-Presse, January 25, 2002.

[30] Central News Agency, January 25, 2002.

[31] Zeng Jia, "Zhang Mingqing Says Chen Shuibian and Annette Lu Not on List of DPP Members Who May Visit China in Appropriate Capacities," Zhongguo Xinwen She, January 30, 2002 (translated in FBIS CPP20020130000146).

Nevertheless, on January 28, 2002, Taiwan announced that the two sides had agreed to establish a hotline to exchange information regarding crime (criminals frequently violate the law on one side of the Taiwan Strait, and then flee to the other).[32] And, in February, a group of Taiwan businessmen and their families became the first to return to the island from the mainland via Jinmen — an extension of the "mini three links."[33] At the same time, the mainland opened up an indirect air route from Shenzhen to Taiwan via Macau, operating two cargo flights a day.[34] In April, as the ninth anniversary of the Koo-Wang talks in Singapore approached, Koo Chen-fu extended an invitation to Wang Daohan to visit Taiwan, saying that the WTO had created a brand new environment for interaction between Taiwan and China and "provided a new platform for normalizing bilateral relations."[35]

It is thus not surprising that 38 percent of Taiwan residents polled in late January felt that the atmosphere of cross-strait relations had improved, compared with 32 percent who believed it had not. According to the *United Daily News* that conducted the survey, it was the "first time the positive response towards relations with the mainland has exceeded negative viewpoints since April 1993 when preparations for historic cross-strait talks were being made."[36]

Despite these encouraging beginnings, relations between Taiwan and the PRC took a turn for the worse in the summer of 2003, although economic relations, including relations within the WTO, continued to move forward. In May, Chen Shui-bian told *Newsweek* that he was disappointed that the PRC had not responded to his inaugural address in which he had expressed hope that dialogue between the two sides could be resumed.[37] Nevertheless, at the same

---

[32] "Taiwan-China Anti-Crime Hotline Planned in Wake of WTO Entry," Central News Agency, January 28, 2002.

[33] AFX News Limited, February 10, 2002.

[34] Agence France-Presse, March 8, 2002.

[35] "Taiwan's Top China Envoy Invites Mainland Counterpart for Visit," Agence France-Presse, April 17, 2002.

[36] Agence France-Presse, January 28, 2002.

[37] Central News Agency, May 13, 2002.

time, Chen proposed authorizing private organizations to negotiate with the mainland over the opening of the "three links." This was the model used to negotiate air routes between Hong Kong and Taiwan following Hong Kong's return to PRC sovereignty, though Chen noted that the so-called "Hong Kong formula" was just one of several possible options. In proposing that the three links be negotiated by private organizations, however, Chen insisted that Taiwan not be "downgraded, localized, and marginalized" in any talks.[38]

In response, Li Bingcai, Executive Deputy Director of the PRC's Taiwan Affairs Office, said that civil groups could be entrusted to "jump start" talks on the three links, but he added the proviso that the three links must be viewed as "domestic affairs within one country," a criterion that seemed to fly in the face of Chen's demand.[39] Li's offer and conditions were confirmed in July by Vice Premier Qian Qichen.[40]

On July 21, China stepped up pressure on Taiwan by establishing diplomatic ties with the island nation of Nauru, thus reducing the number of nations formally recognizing the Republic of China to only 27. An angry Chen Shui-bian declared that, if the PRC did not respond to his overtures, then Taiwan would have no choice but to "seriously consider walking our own road, walking our own Taiwanese road."[41]

On August 3, Chen Shui-bian escalated his rhetoric further with the most inflammatory speech yet of his administration. Speaking to the pro-independence World Federation of Taiwanese Associations, Chen stated that "Taiwan is not part of someone else, not someone else's local government, and not someone else's province.... Taiwan is an independent, sovereign state. In short, it must be clearly distinguished that both Taiwan and China are a country on either side of the strait (*yibian yiguo*)."[42]

---

[38] Central News Agency, May 10, 2002 (translated in FBIS CPP20020510000094).

[39] *China Daily*, June 25, 2002.

[40] "Qian Qichen Meets Taiwanese Guests," Xinhua, July 5, 2002 (in FBIS CPP20020705000103).

[41] Mure Dickie, "Taipei Warns China over Lack of Response," *The Financial Times*, July 22, 2002.

[42] Office of the President, Taiwan, August 3, 2002 (translated in FBIS CPP20020803000098).

THE STEEL DISPUTE

The conflicting pressures on cross-strait relations were apparent in the handling of the dispute between the two sides on tariffs on cold-rolled steel. On March 23, 2002, China announced that it had tentatively decided to launch an anti-dumping charge against cold-rolled steel exports to the mainland, including those from Taiwan. Continuing to ignore the presence of Taiwan in the WTO, China did not include Taiwan in the list of parties it notified of its actions.[43] China's safeguard action came in the wake of the U.S. decision to impose tariffs of up to 30 percent on imports of foreign steel, which had the effect of diverting cheap steel to the Chinese market. Steel is a major export commodity for Taiwan; in 2001, Taiwan exported 3.5 million metric tons — over US$ 1 billion in value — of steel products to the mainland, accounting for 60 percent of its steel exports.[44] In response to China's investigation, Taiwan's Economic Affairs Minister, Lin Yi-fu, said that China's complaints should be resolved through negotiations under the WTO framework.[45] Reflecting the PRC's unwillingness to see Taiwan treated as an equal under the WTO, a PRC official immediately said that economic and trade problems between the mainland and Taiwan are purely internal affairs and need not go through the WTO.[46]

In June, however, Ablasse Ouedraogo, the Deputy Director-General of the WTO who was then visiting Taiwan, declared that all WTO members are equal in their rights and that members can seek to resolve disputes through the WTO mechanism.[47] Shortly thereafter, Taiwan filed a complaint with the WTO seeking compensation and

---

[43] Guy de Jonquieres, Ken Hijino, and Peter Marsh, "China's Plan to Impose Tariffs on Steel Angers Japanese Exporters," *The Financial Times*, November 7, 2002, 11.

[44] "Beijing Wants Trade Groups to Settle Trade Disputes with Taiwan," China Economic News Service, July 5, 2002.

[45] Central News Agency, March 28, 2002.

[46] "Beijing Rejects Settling Disputes Via WTO," China Economic News Service, March 28, 2002.

[47] Deborah Kuo, "Cross-Strait Trade Disputes Can be Resolved Under WTO Framework," Central News Agency, June 4, 2002.

bilateral consultation with China.[48] In response, MOFTEC Minister Shi Guangsheng said that the two sides should discuss the dispute through trade associations, rather than through the WTO mechanism.[49]

China's position seemed to harden as the date for any consultations approached and after Chen Shui-bian's "*yibian yiguo*" statement. In early September, China's Chief Negotiator, Long Yongtu, declared that as long as the "one China" issue remained outstanding, China would not consult with Taiwan under the WTO framework.[50]

In November, with its investigations completed, the PRC slapped a 23 percent increase in custom duties on five out of nine categories of steel imports as a "safeguard" measure. In response, Taiwan formally requested to hold consultations with the PRC under the WTO framework. According to the WTO rules, any member can request consultations with another member when trade moves affect the first country's interest. Despite the hard-line position outlined by Long Yongtu in September, MOFTEC Minister Shi Guangsheng told *The Financial Times* that "consultations on specific issues can be held between the two sides through their representatives in Geneva." This marked a substantial loosening in the PRC's policy.[51] China had been caught between its desire to prevent legitimizing Taiwan's international status by consulting with it under the WTO framework and its desire to abide by WTO regulations. When push came to shove, the PRC accepted consultations — but not without difficulties.

The PRC continued to push for informal consultations, rather than formal consultations under the WTO framework. Zhang Mingqing of the State Council's Taiwan Affairs Office called for non-governmental organizations to discuss the issue.[52] Moreover, even as China accepted

---

[48] "Taiwan Demands Bilateral Talks with China over Steel Tariff," Japan Economic Newswire, June 20, 2002.

[49] "Beijing Wants Trade Groups to Settle Trade Disputes with Taiwan," China Economic News Service, July 5, 2002.

[50] "Beijing Says WTO Talks Conditional on 'One China' Principle," Global News Wire, September 3, 2002.

[51] Mure Dickie, "Taiwan and China Move Closer to Official Talks," *The Financial Times*, November 25, 2002.

[52] Kyodo News Service, November 27, 2002.

Taiwan's proposal for bilateral consultations, the letter the PRC sent to the Taiwan delegation referred to the Taiwan "Economic and Trade Office," the same term used for the delegations from Hong Kong and Macau, rather than its formal title, the "Separate Customs Territory of Taiwan, Penghu, Kinmen, and Matsu." Taiwan responded by accepting the consultations, but insisting that the PRC use its official title.[53]

Taiwan won the diplomatic jousting at least up to a point. On December 12, the two sides met, but in a hotel rather than in the WTO headquarters. And the leaders of the two delegations were absent, giving the talks a more informal status. Nevertheless, the two delegations met for three and a half hours and the atmosphere was reported to be "very good and cordial." Later Yen Ching-chang, Taiwan's Chief Representative to the WTO, described the talks as a "kind of breakthrough." "Even a few months ago," Yen said, "China emphasized that economic relations with us belonged to domestic affairs... they have undergone quite a remarkable change in this regard."[54] The talks ended inconclusively.[55] Following the WTO judgment against the U.S. for imposing duties on steel imports, the Chinese judged that steel had been dumped on its market, but postponed the application of safeguard duties, effectively removing the issue.[56]

Unfortunately, the steel dumping case marks the only time that China and Taiwan have held consultations under the WTO framework. Officials in Taiwan believe that the temporary shift in the PRC position was due to policy conflict in different bureaucracies in the PRC. Officials in the PRC argue that there was no change of policy; the PRC can have — or not have — informal discussions whenever they want. Other anti-dumping investigations China has launched that have affected Taiwan — including on polyvinyl chloride, Bisphenol A, polyamide fiber, and ethanolamine — have not yet resulted in

---

[53] Global News Wire, December 17, 2002.

[54] Mure Dickie, "China and Taiwan Officials Discuss Trade," *The Financial Times*, December 16, 2002. See also Hui-Wan Cho, "The China-Taiwan Tug of War in the WTO," *Asian Survey* 45, no. 5 (September–October 2005), 736–755.

[55] *Asia Pulse*, December 16, 2002.

[56] "China Delays Anti-Dumping Measures on Imported Steel," *AFX*, May 20, 2003.

consultations between the two sides. Most of these cases are fairly recent, and could potentially be handled in a manner similar to the steel dumping case, but this does not appear likely at this time. It seems that the increasingly tense political atmosphere that has descended on the strait since Chen Shui-bian called for "defensive" referenda in the fall of 2003 and his unexpected victory in the March 20, 2004, election has cast a pall over the progress, tentative as it was, in using the WTO to negotiate economic differences. Taiwan again sought to use the WTO mechanism to achieve parity with the mainland in 2006 by filing an anti-dumping action against the mainland.[57]

INTERNATIONAL RECOGNITION

There is little question that Taiwan's participation in the WTO has increased its ability to interact with other states and thus side-step some of the diplomatic isolation imposed by the PRC. Because of its participation in the WTO, Taiwan has been able to participate in many meetings that would otherwise have been closed to it. For instance, Taiwan participated as a third party in the Dispute Settlement Mechanism that ruled against the U.S. in the steel case.[58] It participated in bilateral discussions with Russia that had applied for WTO membership, and it participated in the Cancun WTO Ministerial Conference in September 2003.[59] Taiwan also participated in a number of seminars sponsored by the WTO, including one in Beijing in which the Vice Minister of Economic Affairs, Chen Ruey-long, participated, marking the first time senior officials from mainland China and Taiwan conferred at a WTO-sponsored symposium. Similarly, two mainland Chinese officials participated in a trade negotiation skills for senior officials seminar that was held in Taiwan in March 2003.[60] In 2004, Taiwan was also able to join the Advisory Center on WTO Law (ACWL), a group formed in 2001 to

[57] *Sing Tao Jih Pao*, September 20, 2006 (translated in FBIS CPP20061003715005).

[58] Central News Agency, July 12, 2003.

[59] Central News Agency, September 13, 2003.

[60] *Asia Pulse*, April 1, 2003, February 13, 2003; Central News Agency, March 15, 2003.

provide legal advice.[61] In the course of negotiations over the Doha Round, Taiwan engaged in over 100 bilateral and multilateral meetings.[62] In addition, the EU opened an office in Taipei, which is a clear sign of the importance of EU-Taiwan trade.

Taiwan's participation in the WTO has also facilitated its negotiation of FTAs, which have become more important after the failure of the 1999 WTO meeting in Seattle. For Taiwan, FTAs are particularly important because China has been very active in negotiating FTAs in Asia, including the ASEAN + 3 Free Trade Area and one that might bring China, Japan, and South Korea together. If Taiwan cannot participate in the regional FTAs, it might find itself economically isolated. Thus, Taiwan concluded its first FTA with Panama in August 2003 (which will give Taiwan access to the North American market, if and when Panama is included in an FTA with North America). It is in active negotiations to conclude an FTA with Singapore and Malaysia, and has pledged to begin discussions with Guatemala and Paraguay.

But in pursuing FTAs, Taiwan has made it clear that it views their political significance just as important as their economic significance. Thus, Taiwan's efforts to persuade Singapore to conclude an FTA using the title "Taiwan" drew a strong rebuke from Senior Minister Lee Kwan Yew. "I think at some time," Lee said, "your government will have to reconsider its position and decide, let's play economics as economics and let's play politics as politics."[63]

Although both Taiwan and China have been questioned about their compliance with WTO commitments, particularly in the area of intellectual property rights (IPR), both have received high praise from international observers for their role in the WTO. Mike Moore, the head of the WTO, said, "I can say that in my time, China has behaved impeccably.... I believe China will emerge as a champion of the new round of trade."[64] An unnamed senior official of the

[61] Central News Agency, May 6, 2004.

[62] Global News Wire, May 18, 2004.

[63] *The Straits Times*, October 15, 2003.

[64] *South China Morning Post*, April 22, 2003.

WTO was quoted as saying that Taiwan and mainland China played "important and statesmen-like" roles in the recently-concluded WTO ministerial conference in Cancun.[65]

CONCLUSION

Accession to the WTO has proven to be a boon to both the PRC and Taiwan. China no longer has to endure the annual extension of MFN (most-favored nation, now known as NTR — normal trade relations) because of the passage of PNTR (permanent normal trade relations), thus removing a contentious issue that always threatened to spill over into trade sanctions or U.S. protectionism. Investment flows into China have continued at high levels, as has China's growth of foreign trade. Perhaps, more importantly, China crossed a sort of psychological Rubicon, whereby it was recognized as one of the major trading nations of the world (it ranks as the fifth-largest trading nation, after all) and correspondingly was invited (though it declined) to participate in the G7 meetings. Moreover, China's WTO accession, together with the formation of FTAs in Asia, has enhanced China's position alongside Japan as one of the economic and political powers of Asia. From a cross-strait perspective, China's accession to the WTO has strengthened trends of recent years by drawing yet more investment and trade from Taiwan.

For Taiwan, the WTO accession marked both economic opportunity and political recognition (albeit, not in the formal sense, that Taiwan appears to want). Although it has increased the island's dependence on the mainland, it has bolstered Taiwan's economy and, therefore, enhanced its economic security. Nevertheless, as Peter Drysdale points out in his chapter in this volume, Taiwan has fallen well short of taking advantage of the opportunities presented. Cross-strait ties (shipping and travel), as well as more open commodity trade and investment, would further enhance Taiwan's economy, but security concerns and political cleavages have so far prevented Taiwan from moving more rapidly on this front.

---

[65] Central News Agency, October 22, 2003.

Nevertheless, WTO membership has allowed Taiwan to interact far more widely and visibly with other WTO members than would otherwise have been possible, and thus Taiwan has been able to reap certain political benefits from membership.

In terms of cross-strait interactions, the WTO accession has created pressures for a continual adjustment of policies governing interaction, as witnessed by Taiwan's revision of its laws governing relations across the Taiwan Strait; the loosening of restrictions on investment; and its cautious approach to opening cross-strait links through the opening of the "mini-links" and charter flights during the Chinese New Year. So far, Taiwan has resisted pressures for the opening of the "three links," but pressures for such links in both the domestic and international business communities are such that Taiwan is likely to have to find a way to open them eventually. Doing so will strengthen Taiwan's economy, though many in political circles appear to fear the psychological impact of such links.

In political terms, the WTO membership has suggested both the pressures to deal with each other, and the failure, for political reasons, to take advantage of this opportunity. The PRC has obviously resisted dealing with Taiwan within the WTO framework, holding that economic conflicts across the strait should be considered within a "one China" context and handled by non-governmental organizations authorized by the respective groups. The PRC has exerted every effort to deny Taiwan the international recognition that it has sought through joining the WTO. The one time China relaxed its approach to permit consultations over its imposition of safeguard measures on steel imports suggests flexibility that might, at some point, regularize cross-strait interactions at a level greater than the "one China" framework that the PRC seeks to impose, and yet less than the formal statehood that Taiwan appears to hope for. Unfortunately, this promising approach was discarded as tensions again mounted between Beijing and Taipei.

This history suggests that as important as economic pressures are, political concerns ultimately dominate. But it also suggests that if, and when political tensions are confined within an acceptable range, there will be an alternative approach that will be available to the antagonists. Perhaps, they will seize the opportunity.

Chapter

7

The Challenges and Opportunities for Taiwan and China in the Financial Sector after Entry into the WTO

Jih-chu Lee

INTRODUCTION

In both Taiwan and China, the financial sector is the weakest sector in the economy. Although they have different degrees of commitment to opening their financial markets, both face stringent challenges following accession to the WTO.[1] In China, it is commonly recognized that there are many economic problems in several different areas, i.e., finance, state-owned enterprises, and agriculture, as well as inequalities and imbalances between urban and rural areas, and so on. Among them, however, the most serious challenge facing the new leadership is in the financial sector, where the problems are interwoven. Because the Chinese leadership lacks experience in dealing with financial complications, any single problem may lead

[1] China and Taiwan entered the WTO in December 2001 and January 2002, respectively.

to crises, causing instability in the economy. Most experts believe that, if an economic collapse were to occur in China, the most likely cause would be a crisis in the financial sector. Therefore, there has been some doubt as to whether China will commit to opening its financial markets in stages.

Despite the challenges, the Chinese government has made some progress in recent years, such as aggressively reducing the NPLs (non-performing loans) of the banking system; improving the financial supervisory mechanism; modifying financial laws; encouraging local Chinese financial institutions to collaborate with foreign banks and inviting foreign financial institutions to acquire shares of local financial institutions; and so forth.[2] The signing of the Closer Economic Partnership Arrangement (CEPA) between China and Hong Kong gives Hong Kong's financial institutions access to the Chinese market on more favorable terms, as compared to other countries. This not only provides a boost for the Hong Kong economy, but it also gives Hong Kong banks an edge over their foreign competitors. The Chinese government believes these will help lower the impact of a further opening of Renminbi (RMB) business to other foreign banks.

In Taiwan, in general, foreign financial institutions have been granted national treatment since Taiwan's entry into the WTO. This means Taiwan's financial institutions have to face competition from foreign counterparts on an equal footing. Due to long-term government protection, excessive political involvement, and an inadequately-planned liberalization policy, the financial industry is not competitive, and has a record of poor performance. Indeed, some influential international magazines have suggested that a potential financial crisis is looming. Thus, Taiwan's entry into the WTO is a serious challenge for financial institutions, given that there are too many small-sized and non-competitive banks in Taiwan's over-banked market.

---

[2] Lee Jih-chu, "Financial Reform in China as well as the Challenges and Opportunities for Taiwanese Banks in China," *Project Report of Council for Economic Planning and Development*, Executive Yuan, Taipei, 2003.

However, coincidentally, China's entry into the WTO provides a timely opportunity for the market expansion of Taiwan's financial institutions. Since the two sides have a common language and culture, when mainland China committed to opening its financial market to foreign banks as a condition to entering the WTO, Taiwan was presented with several advantages. In particular, due to the lag in China's financial development and the inherent advantage of Taiwan's financial institutions, Taiwan's banks could transplant their mature products, which might not be competitive in the markets of the developed countries, to the China market. At the same time, due to their common language and culture, Chinese financial institutions will be able to learn quickly from their Taiwan counterparts and achieve rapid growth. Only when Taiwan's financial institutions could enter China's financial markets did both Taiwan's and China's financial industries stand to gain.

However, because of the sensitive political situation between the two sides, the Taiwan government has many concerns, thus leading it to establish some restrictions on interactions with China. Therefore, Taiwan's financial institutions are establishing themselves in China at a slower pace, and cross-strait financial exchanges and cooperation are sluggish. The recent signing of the CEPA between China and Hong Kong provides a lower threshold and preferential treatment to Hong Kong to access the China market and places serious pressures on Taiwan's financial institutions. But the CEPA also allows foreign corporations that have owned a Hong Kong company for more than one year to apply for CEPA preferential treatment. This encourages Taiwan's financial institutions to buy Hong Kong financial institutions in order to timely enter the China market. Such an arrangement also attracts more Taiwan companies to list on the Hong Kong stock market, rather than on the Taiwan stock market.

After Taiwan's and mainland China's accession to the WTO, there is more room for cooperation in the financial industry. In addition, collaborations between the governments on both sides of the strait may even expand to areas such as stabilizing exchange rates, controlling financial crises, combating financial fraud, and so on.

Unfortunately, due to political considerations, not much progress has been made in these areas over the past several years.

TAIWAN'S ENTRY INTO THE WTO

In general, foreign financial institutions have been granted national treatment since Taiwan's entry into the WTO. This means the Taiwan government can no longer set special restrictions on foreign financial institutions to protect the domestic financial institutions. In other words, Taiwan's financial institutions have to compete with their foreign counterparts on a level playing field. Because Taiwan's financial industry is relatively uncompetitive, as compared with those in the developed countries, the first challenge for Taiwan is to improve the competitiveness of its financial industry and financial structure. At the same time, since with accession, mainland China committed to opening its domestic financial market to foreign countries, the second challenge for Taiwan will be to overcome cross-strait political difficulties to take advantage of the China market, so that Taiwan's financial institutions can be strengthened and provide financial services to Taiwan companies operating on the mainland.

Taiwan's financial system is rather weak, as evidenced by the following characteristics:[3]

1. Over-banking and lack of economies of scale among financial institutions.

As Table 7.1 shows, the five largest banks in Taiwan collectively only account for 38 percent of the total banking assets — a much lower ratio than that of their counterparts in other Asian countries. Furthermore, the average asset scale of the top five banks in Taiwan, compared with their regional and global counterparts, is much smaller (see Table 7.2). There are 5,842 bank branches in Taiwan for a population of only 23 million.

[3] Lee Jih-chu, *Taiwan Financial System and Financial Reform* (Taipei: National Policy Forum, National Policy Foundation, 2002).

Table 7.1 Asset Market Share of the Top Five Banks in Taiwan Compared with Counterparts in Other Asian Countries

	(Unit: %)
Singapore top five banks	93% market share
Hong Kong top five banks	87% market share
Korea top five banks	76% market share
Taiwan top five banks	38% market share

Source: *Morgan Stanley Quarterly Report* (2003).

Table 7.2 Average Asset Scale of the Top Five Banks in Taiwan Compared with Regional and Global Counterparts

World's top five banks	US$ 800 billion to US$ 1 trillion
Regional top five banks	US$ 100 billion to US$ 200 billion
Taiwan's top five banks	US$ 30 billion to US$ 60 billion

Source: *Morgan Stanley Quarterly Report* (2003).

2. Poor profitability and sharply deteriorating asset quality of financial institutions in recent years.

As Table 7.3 shows, the NPL ratio.[4] in Taiwan's banking sector rose from 3.0 percent in 1995 to 8.3 percent in June 2002. Even worse, the NPL ratio for thrifts and rural cooperatives surged from 4.02 percent to 18.2 percent over the same period, against a mere 2.68 percent in June 2002 for foreign banks operating in Taiwan. As Table 7.4 shows, the ROE (returns on equity) and ROA (returns on assets) of Taiwan banks plummeted from 11.5 and 1.0 percent in 1994 to –1.5 and –0.49 percent in 2002, respectively. By contrast, the ROE and ROA of foreign banks in Taiwan increased from 22.2 and 0.93 percent to 30.78 and 1.18 percent, respectively. These statistics reflect, on average, a huge profitability gap between Taiwan banks and foreign banks in Taiwan.

[4] In Taiwan, an NPL is defined as failure to pay interest over six months, in contrast to the international definition of an NPL, which is failure to pay interest over three months.

Table 7.3 The NPL Ratio of Taiwan's Banking Sector (Unit: %)

	Average ratio of all financial institutions	Taiwan banks (including investment and trust companies)	Local branches of foreign banks	Thrifts and rural cooperatives
1995	3.0	2.88	0.82	4.02
1996	4.15	3.74	1	7.1
1997	4.18	3.74	1.07	8.53
1998	4.93	4.41	1.64	10.57
1999	5.67	4.96	3.2	13.7
2000	6.2	5.47	3.22	15.68
2001	8.16	7.70	3.53	16.39
2002-Jun.	8.3	7.75	2.68	18.2

Source: Bureau of Monetary Affairs, Ministry of Finance, ROC (2003).

Table 7.4 Profit Comparison between Domestic and Foreign Banks in Taiwan (Unit: %)

	Domestic banks		Foreign banks in Taiwan	
Time	ROE	ROA	ROE	ROA
1994	11.5	1.0	22.2	0.93
1995	9	0.7	29.6	1.32
1996	9.7	0.7	27.4	1.3
1997	11.4	0.9	33.3	1.52
1998	8	0.6	22	1.01
1999	5.9	0.5	16.72	0.77
2000	4.9	0.39	33.16	1.29
2001	5.5	0.4	32.02	1.19
2002	−1.5	−0.49	30.78	1.18

Source: Central Bank of China, Taiwan (2003).

3. Most Taiwan banks are lacking in innovation, with revenue sources predominantly dependent upon traditional business.

For example, in 2003,Taiwan banks derived 77.7 percent of their revenues from interest rate-related proceeds and only 9.6 percent

Table 7.5 A Comparison of Revenue Sources of Domestic and Foreign Banks in Taiwan (Unit: %)

	Domestic banks	Foreign banks
Interest income	77.7	56.0
Charged fees and commission income	9.64	26.4
Gains on sales of securities	7.19	2.1
Portfolio investment income	1.04	−0.03
Other income	4.4	15.5

Source: Central Bank of China, Taiwan (2003).

from fee income, compared to 56 percent and 26.4 percent, respectively, for foreign banks in Taiwan (Table 7.5).

It is thus not surprising that the international media have repeatedly noted concerns over Taiwan's vulnerability to financial shocks. These weaknesses of Taiwan's financial system have much to do with government policies. The fact that the government does not recognize financial services as an industry has led to excessive intervention on the grounds of maintaining financial stability. At the same time, the government has been reluctant to open up the financial sector to foreign competition.

Efforts to promote competition by allowing domestic institutions to set up new banks since 1990 have been undermined by inadequate exit mechanisms for unsound financial institutions.[5] However the government's preoccupation with preventing bank failures results in "over-banking" and a lack of innovation in Taiwan's banking industry.

Both the government and financial institutions have to confront the harsh reality of unavoidable foreign competition in the post-WTO era.[6] It is encouraging that some financial reforms have been made by the government and some competitiveness enhancements have

[5] Lee Jih-chu, "The Implication of the New Set Up of Taiwanese Private Banks and Its Impact on China's Banking Industry," Conference of China's Bank Privatization, Peking University, 2003.

[6] Lee Jih-chu, "The Challenges of Taiwan Financial System under Global Financial Integration," International Conference on Taiwan's Challenges under Global Economic Integration, National Chengchi University, Taipei, 2002.

been taken by financial institutions. The reform initiatives can be summarized as follows:[7]

1. To improve the competitiveness of domestic financial institutions.

The authority in Taiwan has recently passed three new acts. They are the Financial Institutions' Merger Act, the Financial Holding Corporation Act, and the Financial Asset Securitization Act. The first is aimed at consolidating Taiwan's financial sector so as to take advantage of economies of scale, in turn facilitating the closure of unviable institutions. The second is expected to further increase the economies of scope of the financial sector. Finally, the Financial Asset Securitization Act is intended to benefit the liquidity of Taiwan's financial assets.

2. To dispose of unsound financial assets.

The government now permits the establishment of asset management companies (AMC) to manage asset disposal, in turn improving the financial quality of financial institutions. In addition, the government has reduced the gross receiving business tax in the financial industry and set up a financial restructuring fund with NT$ 350 billion of public money, thus enabling banks to write off bad debts and to exit the market.[8]

3. To establish exit and compensation mechanisms for financial institutions.

The government has passed the Financial Institutions' Merger Act and the Financial Restructuring Fund Act to increase the feasibility of closing unviable institutions.

4 To unify financial supervisory and management systems.

The government set up a new Financial Supervisory Commission in 2004 to integrate regulators of the banking, securities, and

---

[7] Lee Jih-chu, *Taiwan Financial Reform* (Taipei: National Policy Foundation, 2004).

[8] Lee Jih-chu, "The Design of the Taiwan Restructuring Financial Fund: Based on the Korean Experience," National Policy Forum, National Policy Foundation, 2003.

insurance industries. This arrangement will strengthen supervision of businesses in these three industries.[9]

5 To relax financial restrictions and encourage financial innovation.

Due to these improvements, there are conspicuous advancements in the competitiveness of Taiwan's financial institutions and the soundness of its financial system. For instance, 14 financial holding companies can simultaneously provide banking, security, and insurance services through their subsidiary companies. The sizes of these financial holding companies are much larger than that of their previous counterparts. This helps them to achieve both economies of scale and scope, thus strengthening the competitiveness of Taiwan's financial institutions, both domestically and internationally. At the same time, the Financial Supervisory Commission is useful in supervising the financial holding companies.

In addition, the NPLs of the banks declined drastically from a high of 8.16 percent down to 3.12 percent (see Table 7.6). At least 50 poor-performing banks, thrifts, and rural cooperatives were acquired, and exited the financial market, during the past three years. Many new financial instruments have been created, and some non-traditional businesses have grown significantly, such as credit card and asset management businesses.

With respect to cross-strait financial interactions, since both sides have become members of the WTO, the Taiwan government feels that it is now safer for Taiwan's financial institutions to contact their mainland counterparts directly, or to expand business to mainland China. Therefore, it has further liberalized cross-strait financial exchanges, such as allowing financial agencies to be set up across the strait.

The increasing migration of manufacturers from Taiwan to mainland China has highlighted the constraints on financing such

---

[9] Lee Jih-chu, "The Design of Taiwan Unified Financial Regulators," in *Taiwan Financial Reform*, ed. National Policy Foundation (Taipei, Taiwan: National Policy Foundation, 2003).

Table 7.6 The NPL Ratio of Taiwan's Banks

	Taiwan banks		All banks in Taiwan	Taiwan banks	Local branches of foreign banks	Thrifts and rural cooperatives
	Profit before tax	Net worth				
2000	967.8	15 991	6.20	5.34	3.22	15.68
2001	575.9	15 964	8.16	7.48	3.53	16.39
2002	21 045.9	14 228	6.84	6.12	2.36	15.37
2003	2267.5	14 420	5.00	4.33	1.51	13.29
2004	155.4	12 256	3.12	2.78	1.03	10.05

Source: Financial Supervisory Commission.

outward investments because of the absence of Taiwan banks within China. Meanwhile, some businessmen in Taiwan have deliberately increased their financial leverage, resulting in defaults on debts in Taiwan — another factor contributing to the rise of NPLs in the banking sector.[10] By allowing banks to set up offices on the mainland, banks can closely monitor how firms from Taiwan utilize their funding on the mainland and can explore the under-developed mainland markets. Furthermore, by liberalizing the trade finance operations of domestic banking units (DBU) and off-shore banking units (OBU), and by establishing correspondence banking between banks in Taiwan and their mainland counterparts, Taiwan banks will have a larger business scope.

All in all, these positive measures have contributed to the overall competitiveness of Taiwan's financial institutions and the long-term development of Taiwan's financial system, and have provided a basis for future cooperation in cross-strait activities.

[10] Chow Tien-chen, Jih-chu Lee, and Wen-chiey Wang, "A Study of the Financing Sources of Taiwan Businessmen and Establishing Financial Institutions in China," *Project Report of Mainland Affairs Council*, Executive Yuan, Taipei, 1997; Chen Ming-chang, "A Study of the Changes of Attitude of Financing Sources of Taiwan Businessmen in China," Taipei Enterprise Management Society, 2002.

THE COMMITMENTS, IMPACTS, AND REACTIONS OF CHINA'S ENTRY INTO THE WTO

China has made a number of commitments regarding financial services in its WTO agreements. With respect to banking deregulation, foreign banks will be allowed to conduct RMB business with Chinese firms three years following accession. By the end of 2006, foreign banks will be free to conduct RMB business with Chinese citizens. In the insurance sector, casualty and property insurance will be open to foreign competition in major cities within two to three years of accession. Other insurance products, such as group, life, and health insurance, will be open to foreign competition within five years. Within the first two years, foreign insurers may control up to 49 percent of the stakes in joint ventures and, in the following two years, they can set up foreign-owned entities in China. As for securities liberalization, the pace will be more gradual. Foreign securities companies can immediately form joint ventures with Chinese asset management companies to manage domestic pension funds. Such joint ventures, with foreign ownership of up to 49 percent, will be permitted to participate in initial public offerings (IPO) and other investment business, as long as the underlying transactions do not breach capital account restrictions. Foreign companies have been allowed to participate in the domestic A-share markets through so-called QFII (qualified foreign institutional investors) since the end of 2002.

As is the case with Taiwan, China's financial system will be exposed to shocks from foreign competition as a result of these concessions. These shocks will interact with the existing problems in the mainland's financial sector:[11]

[11] Justin Lin, "The Prospective of China's Financial System Reform," China Center for Economic Research, Peking University, Beijing, 2001; Lee Jih-chu, "Financial Reform in China as well as the Challenges and Opportunities for Taiwanese Banks in China," *Project Report of Council for Economic Planning and Development*, Executive Yuan, Taipei, 2003.

1. Serious non-performing loans.

China's big-four state-owned banks are among the 30 largest banks in the world in terms of assets. But their large size does not obscure the fact that they are plagued by high NPL ratios. According to the People's Bank of China, China's central bank, NPLs represent roughly 25 percent of the total assets in the banking sector, or RMB 1.2 trillion. However, estimates by foreign banks and rating agencies are even much higher. For example, Goldman Sachs puts the ratio at 40 percent, and *Business Week* reports that the official NPLs are only one-third of the true bad loans. Standard & Poor's maintains that it would cost as much as 43 percent of China's GDP to re-capitalize the banking system. In comparison, the U.S. government spent only 3 percent of its GDP to clean up the S&L crisis in the early 1990s. It is easy to see how severe the NPL-related problems are in China. These NPLs are caused by government instructions to provide credits to unprofitable state-owned enterprises. As a result, the asset quality of the banks will likely not improve, until the soft-budget constraints of the state-owned enterprises are eliminated.

2. Serious distortion of financial loans.

By almost any conventional measure, such as assets, deposits, and loans, the big-four state-owned banks dominated the market, with a market share of 60–86 percent in 2000 (see Table 7.7). Obviously, this oligopoly market structure lacks competitiveness. As a result, non-state sectors have difficulty securing bank loans. For example, bank lending to non-state sectors (not necessarily to the private sector) only accounts for 15 percent of total lending, whereas these sectors contributed to over 50 percent of industrial production in 2001.

3. Underdeveloped money and bond markets.

Both the money market and the bond market are extremely under-developed. The secondary market for government bonds is illiquid, despite the continued issuance of government bonds. The transaction value of the money market over the GDP has been consistently below 30 percent. The lack of liquidity, as well as the lack of institutional investors, are two of the major challenges in the development of the money market.

Table 7.7 The Market Share of the Big-Four State-owned Banks

	Market Share by Assets		Market Share by Profits		Market Share by Deposit		Market Share by Loan	
	1999	2000	1999	2000	1999	2000	1999	2000
Industrial and Commercial Bank of China	25.71%	26.03%	40.64%	34.83%	33.14%	31.15%	25.77%	26.64%
Agricultural Bank of China	16.53%	14.31%	−0.85%	0.59%	17.76%	17.35%	16.88%	16.37%
Bank of China	19.02%	18.96%	10.44%	11.92%	18.84%	18.61%	14.48%	13.64%
China Construction Bank	15.99%	16.59%	17.72%	17.02%	19.61%	19.28%	12.75%	15.29%
Total	77.25%	75.89%	67.95%	64.36%	89.35%	86.39%	69.08%	71.94%

Source: China Financial Association, *Finance & Banking* (2001).

4. An undisciplined stock market.

Over the past eight years, China's stock markets became the third largest in Asia in terms of market capitalization, trailing behind only Japan and Hong Kong. But China's stock markets are unique, even when compared with other newly-emerging stock markets. The firms' listings are totally determined by the China Securities Regulatory Commission (CSRC), instead of by the Stock Exchanges of Shenzhen and Shanghai. Given this listing mechanism, government intervention is not surprising. Not all shares of listed companies are publicly-traded. With non-traded shares accounting for about two-thirds of the total market capitalization, the government remains the major shareholder of the firms, even after they are listed on the stock exchanges. As a result, in many ways, listed companies continue to behave like state-owned enterprises. The existence of large non-tradable shares facilitates price manipulation. Indeed, the Chinese government's heavy-handed intervention is detrimental to the stock markets.

Finally, China's stock markets have been hit by a series of scandals in recent years. Professor Wu Jinglian, an influential Chinese economist, has billed China's stock market as a giant "casino." Accounting fraud of listed companies is widespread. Such events as the bank run of the Hainan Development Bank, the failure of China Venturetech, and the default of GITIC's external debt, suggest that China's stock market is extremely undisciplined.

5. Immature financial supervisory system.

Over the past ten years, the People's Bank of China has made some progress in setting up financial regulators, streamlining organizations and structures, implementing a legal framework, and improving supervision. However, the inherent weakness of the state-owned banks has resulted in systemic corruption, that often makes supervision politically unfeasible. Financial fraud is rampant.

6. Poor financial activities.

The combination of the big-four state-owned banks having monopolistic positions and the various restrictions imposed on foreign banks has prevented bank competition and innovation. Most banks derive less than 10 percent of their total earnings from fee-related incomes.

Against this backdrop, China's financial system will endure some negative impacts in the post-WTO era:[12]

1. Outflows of deposits and defection of qualified clients from Chinese banks to foreign banks.

In the context of weak competitiveness and extraordinarily high NPLs, the reason Chinese banks can still survive is mainly because foreign banks (158 branches and 214 representative offices in China by the end of 2001) are severely-restricted in their business operations in China. Indeed, only a very few foreign banks in a very few cities can conduct RMB business with multinational corporations today. Chinese depositors cannot deposit savings in foreign banks, and Chinese businesses cannot borrow RMB from foreign banks.

However, the deposit and client bases of the state-owned banks are expected to erode, once the geographic and service restrictions are gradually lifted, as the Chinese government delivers on its WTO commitment. Furthermore, there is no deposit insurance mechanism in China's financial system. Therefore, there is a high possibility of financial instability as China gradually removes the restrictions on foreign financial institutions. This is the reason why Ericsson's decision to shift its accounts from state-owned banks to foreign banks has caused concern among Chinese policymakers.

2. State banks' difficulties in retaining well-qualified personnel.

Foreign banks are undertaking concerted strategies to cherry-pick good employees from the Chinese banks. It is impossible for the state banks to get into bidding wars in the light of the government constraints on the state-owned enterprises. Therefore, state banks will lose even more competitiveness as qualified employees flee. State-owned securities and insurance companies are facing similar challenges.

---

[12] Jing Huande and Xu Jinlian, *China Financial Development Report* (Shanghai: Financial University Press, 2001).

3. China's financial supervisory system will face serious challenges from the deregulation and the liberalization of financial institutions after accession to the WTO.

   Due to the current loopholes, such as the poor regulating skills and supervisory system, regulators were constantly challenged by the financial institutions before WTO entry. In the future, the lifting of financial restrictions will complicate financial services and the more diversified foreign financial institutions will do business in the Chinese market. Both of these changes will make supervision even more difficult.

However, in addition to complicating the challenges facing the Chinese financial system, China's WTO accession also brings some benefits.[13] They are:

1. The acceleration of financial reforms.

   Taking advantage of the requirements of WTO entry, China can ignore domestic resistance to reform and accelerate financial restructuring. In addition to opening and liberalizing its financial markets to foreign financial institutions in stages, according to its WTO commitments, the Chinese government also initiated various reforms and restructuring to improve the soundness of the financial system and financial institutions. These included: 1. actively reducing the NPLs of the major banks, 2. inviting foreign banks to buy into domestic banks, 3. planning to introduce IPOs of major domestic banks on the international stock markets, and 4. allowing foreign institutional investors to participate in the domestic A-share markets through QFII from the end of 2002.

   Anticipating the challenges in the aftermath of WTO entry, in 1999, the Chinese government transferred RMB 1.3 trillion of NPLs from the big-four state-owned banks to four asset management companies effectively backed up by the Ministry of Finance.

[13] Jiao Jin-pu, *The International Competitiveness of China's Banking Industry* (China: Contemporary Economy Publisher, 2002); Lee Ruo-koo, "The Reform of the Chinese Banking System and the Liberalization of Financial Policy," 35th Annual Conference of the Asian Development Bank, 2002.

Recently the government provided US$ 45 billion of foreign reserves to relieve the NPLs of the two major banks (the Bank of China and the China Construction Bank), and US$ 15 billion to the Industrial and Commercial Bank of China. Since then, the NPLs of the four major banks have declined drastically. In addition, the Bank of China and the China Construction Bank plan to issue IPOs overseas; the other two major banks also plan to list on the domestic stock market.

Furthermore, the Chinese government is encouraging foreign investors to take minority stakes in share-holding banks and asset management companies (see Table 7.8). For example, Citibank has formed an alliance with the Shanghai Pudong Development Bank, and HSBC has acquired a 9 percent stake in the Shanghai Bank. In a recent development, Newbridge Capital, a U.S. hedge fund, has acquired about 17.89 percent of the Shenzhen Development Bank. A significant stake in Shenzhen Development Bank will allow Newbridge to drastically change the bank's existing managerial structure. Aggressive moves by foreign investors in a changing banking landscape have forced policymakers to contemplate banking deregulation in such a way that private banks will be allowed in

Table 7.8 Acquisition of Chinese Banks by Foreign Banks in Recent Years

Foreign Banks	Acquisition	%
Commonwealth Bank	Hangzhou City Commercial Bank	19.9
	Jinan City Commercial Bank	11
ING Group	Bank of Beijing	19.9
International Finance Corporation	Bank of Beijing	5
Newbridge Capital Inc	Shenzhen Development Bank	17.89
Standard Chartered	Bo Hai Bank	19.9
International Finance Corporation and Scotiabank Group	Xi'an City Commercial Bank	5
HSBC Group	Bank of Communications	20
Hang Seng Bank	Bank of Shanghai	15.98
International Finance Corporation	China Minsheng Banking Corp. Ltd.	1.08
Citigroup	Shanghai Pudong Development Bank	5

Source: Reuters (June 2005).

certain areas (Zhejiang province, for example), where the private sector is particularly robust.

2. Improving the misallocation of financial assets.

With 70 percent of bank lending diverted into sectors accounting for less than 30 percent of GDP, the result has been an inefficient utilization of capital. Foreign banks participating in RMB business will break down the oligopoly market structure which, in turn, will improve the efficiency of capital utilization.

3. Upgrading the quality of the domestic work force, services, and operating abilities in the financial sector.

The Chinese government has made efforts to bring those who have had international experience into the regulatory agencies. For example, Hong Kong's former Security Exchange Commission (SEC) Chief was hired as Vice Chairperson of the CSRC. It is now common for those who have studied and worked overseas to be recruited into domestic financial institutions or regulatory agencies.

4. Increasing the inflow of foreign capital and improving the effectiveness of the use of capital.

Foreign enterprises in China formerly maintained their financial management organizations in areas outside of China. As more and more foreign financial institutions are allowed to conduct RMB business, local Chinese financial institutions will become healthier due to the competition. This will encourage more foreign capital to be willing to link up with financial institutions in China, thus increasing the inflow of foreign capital and the efficiency of capital utilization.

THE EFFECT OF THE CEPA ON CROSS-STRAIT FINANCIAL INTERACTIONS

In order to revive the economy of Hong Kong, China and Hong Kong signed the CEPA on June 29, 2003, giving Hong Kong financial institutions preferential status over other foreign institutions in access to the Chinese market (see Table 7.9). Furthermore, if a foreigner

Table 7.9 Mainland China's Specific Commitments on Liberalization of the Financial Sectors for the Hong Kong CEPA

Sectors	Specific Commitments
All insurance and insurance-related services	1. To allow groups formed by Hong Kong insurance companies through re-grouping and strategic mergers to enter the mainland insurance market subject to established market access conditions (total assets held by the group over US$ 5 billion; more than 30 years of establishment experience attributable to one of the Hong Kong insurance companies in the group; and a representative office established in the mainland for over two years by one of the Hong Kong insurance companies in the group). 2. The maximum limit of capital participation by a Hong Kong insurance company in a mainland insurance company is 24.9 percent. 3. To allow Hong Kong residents with Chinese citizenship, after obtaining the mainland's professional qualifications in actuarial science, to practice in the mainland without prior approval. 4. To allow Hong Kong residents, after obtaining the mainland's insurance qualifications, and being employed or appointed by a mainland insurance institution, to engage in the relevant insurance business.
Banking and other financial services (excluding insurance and securities)	1. For Hong Kong banks to set up branches or a corporate body in the mainland, the total asset requirement at the end of the year preceding application is to be not less than US$ 6 billion; for finance companies to set up a corporate body, the total asset requirement at the end of the year preceding application is to be not less than US$ 6 billion. 2. There will be no requirement for setting up a representative office in the mainland before a Hong Kong bank establishes a joint venture bank or joint venture finance company in the mainland, or before a Hong Kong finance company establishes a joint venture finance company in the mainland.

(*Continued*)

Table 7.9 (*Continued*)

Sectors	Specific Commitments
	3. For mainland branches of Hong Kong banks to apply to conduct RMB business: a. they should have been operating in the mainland for more than two years. b. in conducting their profitability assessment, the relevant authorities will base their assessment on the overall profitability position of all branches of the bank in the mainland instead of on the profitability position of the individual branches. 4. To allow mainland branches of Hong Kong banks to conduct insurance agents' business after obtaining approval taking effect from November 1, 2004.
Securities	1. To allow the Hong Kong Exchanges and Clearing Limited to set up a representative office in Beijing. 2. To simplify the relevant procedures for Hong Kong professionals applying in the mainland for securities and futures industry qualifications. Hong Kong professionals applying to obtain securities and futures industry qualifications on the mainland need only to undertake training and pass an examination on mainland laws and regulations; an examination on professional knowledge is not required. 3. To allow intermediaries that are licensed with the Securities and Futures Commission of Hong Kong, and which satisfy the requirements of the China Securities Regulatory Commission, to set up joint venture futures brokerage companies in the mainland. The percentage of shareholding owned by Hong Kong licensed intermediaries should not exceed 49 percent (including shareholding of related parties). Requirements with respect to the scope of business and amount of capital, and so forth, of the joint venture futures brokerage companies shall be the same as those for the mainland enterprises.

Source: Trade and Industry Department, Hong Kong (www.tid.gov.hk/english/cepa), Cross-Strait Exchanges and Cooperation in Financial Services in the post-WTO Era.

has held a company in Hong Kong for over one year, that company will be qualified for CEPA treatment. Since Hong Kong's financial institutions are more advanced than their counterparts in Taiwan, and share the same advantages in terms of common language and cultural background, there were tremendous competitive pressures placed on Taiwan's late-starting financial institutions in the China market. These financial institutions are actively lobbying for the Taiwan government to speed up the process of opening up the mainland market to Taiwan financial institutions, as well as seeking a path to China via Hong Kong. It is the CEPA that makes it less attractive for Taiwan businesses in China to issue IPOs in the Taiwan stock market and that makes the achievement of a regional financing center in Taiwan less likely. Given the present situation, the Taiwan government cannot but eventually modify its domestic listing policies for Taiwan companies in China.

In light of the delicate relationship between Beijing and Taipei, if there had been direct financial exchanges between the two sides, the Taiwan authorities would have been worried about accelerating capital outflows to mainland China, as well as about the use of financial means by the Chinese government to destabilize Taiwan's already-vulnerable financial system and to hurt Taiwan's economic development. Therefore, the Taiwan government did not allow direct financial links or reciprocal agencies to be set up until June 2002. But there is some sentiment that a fast-growing Chinese economy and an under-developed banking sector could alleviate the over-banked problem in Taiwan. Furthermore, Taiwan's reluctance to ease cross-strait financial service exchanges makes it difficult for Taiwan banks to closely monitor their customers' financial status in China. Some Taiwan businessmen have taken advantage of this to deliberately default on their domestic debt, thus increasing the NPLs in Taiwan banks.

After accession, both sides of the strait became members of the WTO. The Taiwan government believes that, under the WTO mechanism, it is relatively secure for Taiwan to undergo cross-strait financial interactions; therefore, some further open policies have been adopted.

The Provisions on Financial Transactions between Taiwan and Mainland China, passed in June 2001, enable banks in Taiwan to set up agencies in China, and allow direct financial exchanges of OBUs and DBUs between the two sides. But these steps still lag behind those of other countries. By June 2003, only eight Taiwan banks had set up offices in China. Due to the lack of agreement over the one-China policy, the two sides have not signed a MOU on mutual financial supervision. Therefore, Taiwan banks are limited to opening agencies, not branches, in the Chinese market, in accordance with Chinese laws. However, many Taiwan agencies, trying to catch up with other multinationals, have agreed to become strategic alliance partners with Chinese banks for future cooperation. And some other Taiwan banks have purchased Hong Kong banks to take advantage of the CEPA to access the Chinese market and to circumvent the restrictions of the Taiwan government. Due to similar political considerations, even OBUs were authorized to make loans to Taiwan businesses in China; however, no OBU had actually lent money to Taiwan businesses in China before the end of 2003.

There are also a number of insurance companies and security firms, that have set up offices in China. Some insurance companies have even set up subsidiary companies, because mainland China does not require the signing of an MOU for mutual financial supervision in the insurance industry. Moreover, it is important to note that, although the Taiwan government has not yet authorized its citizens to purchase Chinese stocks, investors from Taiwan have actively poured much money into the Chinese stock market via numerous indirect conduits.

Even after both sides have entered the WTO, based on the most-favored-nation principle, Taiwan must allow Chinese banks to set up operating offices in Taiwan. There are a few Chinese financial institutions that have shown interest in doing so, but, as of this writing, no Chinese firm has been approved by both governments to set up a branch office in Taiwan.

As stated above, Taiwan's financial sector faces difficult challenges due to the slow response of the Taiwan government. This has been especially true since the mainland and Hong Kong implemented the

CEPA. Therefore, in order to raise the competitiveness of Taiwan's financial institutions, the Taiwan government should quickly further liberalize cross-strait financial exchanges, including:

1. Allowing Taiwan's OBUs to conduct RMB business and to extend loans to Taiwan businesses in China.
2. Reducing restrictions on Taiwan banks that apply to invest in China and basing the approval of such applications on bank performance, instead of the size of bank capital.
3. Permitting Taiwan's financial institutions to M&As with financial institutions located in China.
4. Signing MOUs on mutual financial supervision with the Chinese government as soon as possible.
5. Allowing Taiwan companies in China to easily list on the Taiwan Stock Exchange market.
6. Permitting cross-strait financial cooperation and exchanges among businesses and personnel.
7. Permitting Chinese financial institutions to set up branches or agencies in Taiwan.
8. Setting up a "financial alarm system" that will prevent Taiwan's financial system from damage due to instabilities in the Chinese financial system.

THE OUTLOOK FOR CROSS-STRAIT FINANCIAL EXCHANGES AND COOPERATION

Both Taiwan and China are facing increasing foreign competition and pressures following WTO accession. However, the financial systems in both Taiwan and China are robust enough to cope with the shocks unleashed by such foreign competition, if the risks are not managed prudently. With the rapid increases in bilateral trade, investments and swift economic integration between the two sides, cooperation in the financial sectors will be beneficial to both. In addition to the cooperation and exchanges at the financial industry level, actions in other areas such as the following could enhance the stability of each side's financial system. These include:

1. Sharing experiences of financial reform and financial development.

Taiwan's financial system has experienced various phases of deregulation, liberalization, and internationalization. Many of its lessons and experiences in these areas can be helpful to China, particularly considering their common language and culture.

2. Cooperating on a defense mechanism against international financial speculation and attacks.

Both Taiwan and China have amassed large amounts of foreign reserves. It makes sense for Taiwan and China to sign a bilateral swap agreement so that additional liquidity will be readily available if either side is hit by a financial crisis. Indeed, China has signed similar agreements with many regional economies including Thailand — the country that triggered the Asian currency crisis in 1997. Such multilateral swap agreements have proven to be effective in deterring speculative attacks.

3. Extending business strengths by establishing joint strategic alliances.

Financial institutions in Taiwan should be allowed to form strategic alliances with, and to acquire stakes in, their Chinese counterparts. As financial institutions in Taiwan are familiar with Western financial practices, and Taiwan shares a common language and culture with mainland China, if they can make inroads into the Chinese market, their competitiveness in China will be increased. This will help Taiwan to overcome its current problems in the financial industry. At the same time, Taiwan's financial institutions will be the best conduits for China's financial institutions to master modern financial skills and to become more competitive. In addition, in the areas of trade finance, loan syndication, asset management, and consumer banking, Taiwan's experience is also relevant.

4. Cooperating on work force training and exchanges.

Because there are no language and cultural barriers, it is easy for China and Taiwan to learn from each other's experiences. China will require a large pool of financial professionals, and Taiwan will be able to provide necessary training courses.

5. Signing a reciprocal MOU for a financial supervisory agreement.

The signing of a reciprocal MOU for a financial supervisory agreement would make it possible for government regulators on each side to implement supervisory measures over the home country's financial institutions operating on the other side of the strait.

6. Building communication channels and negotiation mechanisms to solve conflicts in the financial sector.

Establishing normal and legitimate communication channels is beneficial to both Taiwan and China. With increasing trade flows across the strait, both sides will be confronted with an increasing number of disputes and misunderstandings. As a result, it is necessary that objective dispute-solving mechanisms be established.

7. Eliminating financial crime through cross-strait cooperation.

In the context of closer contacts and interactions between Taiwan and China, financial crime, for instance, laundering and counterfeiting, has grown rapidly recently. The two sides of the strait should collaborate with each other to punish those who engage in criminal financial activities to ensure normal financial operations.

CONCLUSION

Since the financial sectors on both sides of the Taiwan Strait are the weak links in terms of their international competitiveness, they face serious challenges due to their commitments to open their financial markets after entry into the WTO. On the one hand, China, in particular, which has an unhealthy financial system and lacks experience in dealing with major financial crises, could face severe economic turmoil, if the process of opening up its financial sector is not well-planned. Therefore, the main challenges facing China are to maintain the stability of the entire financial system and to strengthen financial competitiveness, while opening up its isolated domestic financial market.

On the other hand, after joining the WTO, Taiwan has to compete on a level playing field with international financial institutions. Therefore, Taiwan urgently needs to improve the competitiveness of its financial industry. In addition, Taiwan is already showing signs of an over-banked domestic market. Taiwan's financial institutions need to expand outwards. Since they cannot compete in mature North American and West European financial markets, the mainland China market would be a good target for their expansion. Therefore, the second challenge for Taiwan is to initiate an effective way to take advantage of the China market.

In comparison with foreign competitors, Taiwan's financial institutions enjoy certain advantages in China, since the areas share common linguistic, cultural, and historical backgrounds. Furthermore, the financial system in Taiwan is superior to that in China at the present time. Accordingly, China's opening of its relatively-isolated and conservative domestic financial market could provide a valuable opportunity for Taiwan's financial institutions. This also may help Taiwan's financial sector to catch up with the leading Western counterparts. Meanwhile, from China's perspective, financial institutions on the mainland could readily absorb Taiwan's experiences accumulated over the past decades without encountering obstacles in terms of culture or language. Therefore, cooperation would significantly benefit both sides.

Facing the challenges posed by accession to the WTO, governments on both sides of the strait have instituted an array of measures to strengthen their respective financial industries and to upgrade their financial systems. Some substantial achievements have been made. However, due to political considerations, the pace of cross-strait financial exchange is too slow, which is not beneficial to either side. Taiwan might even miss out on the opportunity to explore the China market, and then the opportunity to become a regional financial center.

Moreover, with the rapid increases in bilateral trade and investment, as well as the swift economic integration between the two sides of the strait, financial cooperation could be extended to more important areas, such as the stabilization of the financial systems, or even to currency exchange mechanisms. As a result, a further boosting and enhancing of cross-strait financial cooperation will promote the ability of each side to overcome the challenges of accession to the WTO.

Chapter

8

WTO Accession and its Implications for Agriculture in Taiwan and China

Robert Ash

INTRODUCTION

The challenges of joining the WTO for the farm sectors of China and Taiwan have been essentially the same. Both sectors are among the weakest links in their respective economies. Both have also had to face up to the economic losses, as well as the possible social and political dislocation that a reduction in farm tariffs and non-tariff barriers threatened to precipitate through increased competition from more efficient overseas producers.[1] The scale of such potential losses and dislocations, however, has differed between the two. Against the background of lagging farm income, fiscal exploitation, and widening inter-sectoral and inter-regional differentials that had already

[1] For an insightful analysis of the potential political impact of the agricultural dimension of the WTO agreement, see Joseph Fewsmith, "The Political Implications of the WTO Agreement on Agriculture," in *China's Agriculture in the International Trading System* (Paris: Organisation for Economic Co-operation and Development [OECD], 2001), pp. 125–136.

caused widespread disenchantment and violent protests, the displacement of millions of Chinese farmers, predicted by some analysts, posed an apparent threat to the very authority of the CCP. In Taiwan, the implications of WTO membership were also serious, but less potentially destabilizing. Accommodating a reduction of 100,000 in Taiwan's agricultural population was a serious burden, but one that posed a less dislocative challenge than that facing the mainland Chinese government.[2] The age structure of its farm population, its more comprehensive social security provisions, and the greater cohesiveness of its social fabric, promised to cushion the impact of more intense foreign competition facing farmers in Taiwan.

Analysis of the implications for agriculture from WTO accession must also consider the unique dimension lent by the cross-strait relationship. Market-opening measures associated with joining the WTO, such as reductions in tariffs for farm and fishery products, were likely to result in large-scale inflows of these goods from China to Taiwan. On Taiwan's entry into the WTO in January 2002, the Executive Yuan approved a list of 2,126 products, including 901 agricultural items, which were to be added to the existing list of legal imports from China. Significantly, the list did not include sensitive farm products, the import of which for the time being remained prohibited. Given the pressure that agricultural trade with China was likely to place on Taiwan's farmers, the extent to which Taiwan would be able to continue to exclude agricultural imports from China promised to have an important bearing on the precise consequences for the island's agriculture.[3] So, more positively, would the extent to which the government in Taipei could encourage farmers to shift toward the production of high-value farm products (e.g., tropical fruit) to export to the mainland.

---

[2] Lawrence S. Liu cites Taiwan sources to the effect that the likely impact of WTO accession would be to withdraw 80,000 ha. (9.4 percent of the total arable area) from farm use and reduce the farm population by 100,000 (i.e., by 2.7 percent). See Lawrence Liu, "Enter the Dragons: A Taiwanese Perspective on Cross-Strait Interactions and Taiwan-China's WTO Entry," *China Perspectives*, no. 40 (March–April 2002), p. 54.

[3] Lawrence S. Liu, "Enter the Dragons: A Taiwanese Perspective on Cross-Strait Interactions and Taiwan-China's WTO Entry," *China Perspectives*, no. 40 (March–April 2002).

If Taiwan's farmers viewed post-WTO competition from the mainland with nervousness, the new circumstances promised to offer Chinese farmers, previously barred from selling their goods in Taiwan, new market outlets. From the government's perspective, the exploitation of such markets and the accumulation of an increasing bilateral agricultural trade surplus would help to offset the rising deficits likely to emerge with other countries possessing a competitive edge in farm production.

To what extent the fears of Taiwan's farmers and the hopes of their Chinese counterparts have been realized in the early post-WTO accession period will be considered in the final section of this chapter, which examines emerging trends in cross-strait agricultural trade.

WTO AND AGRICULTURE: THE AGREEMENTS

The following Table 8.1 provides a brief summary of the most important provisions contained in Taiwan's 2001 WTO agreement with respect to the agricultural sector:

The essential thrust of the WTO rules is to open up and liberalize trade as comprehensively and as quickly as possible. Taiwan's negotiators succeeded, however, in securing a longer-than-normal period of adjustment in which to accommodate some of the new regulations. In particular, the provision was made for a "Special Safeguard" (SSG) to be applied to 14 "sensitive" agricultural products. In the event of annual imports of these goods exceeding the stipulated level or of their import price falling to 10 percent or more below the list price, the SSG terms allowed for a special surcharge to be levied in order to mitigate the negative effects that would otherwise ensue.

The agreement provided for the gradual reduction of tariffs on farm and aquatic products not already subject to import restrictions.[4]

---

[4] The emphasis on rice reflected its pre-eminent role in crop production: in 2001, total output of rice was 1.396 m. tonnes, compared with a mere 0.23 m. tonnes of wheat and 0.19 m. tonnes of sweet potatoes. Poultry production is also a vital part of Taiwan's farm economy: in 2001, 32.14 m. ducks and 376.2 m. chickens were slaughtered. See Council for Economic Planning and Development, *Taiwan Statistical Data Book 2002* (Taipei, 2004), pp. 85, 95.

Table 8.1 The WTO Framework Agreement: Major Provisions Affecting Taiwan's Agriculture

Tariffs	End-2001: average tariff on imports of agricultural products: 20.02%. On accession (2002), average farm import tariff to be reduced to 14.01%. Following completion of all scheduled tariff reductions on 1,021 agricultural products for which Taiwan made commitments, average tariff on farm products to be reduced further to 12.86%.
Non-tariff barriers	Taiwan to eliminate area restrictions limiting trade to specified locations in force (end-2001) for 18 kinds of agricultural products (including peaches, lemons, apples, grapes, pears, grapefruit, etc.), and to adopt a policy of free imports. Taiwan to implement tariff-rate quotas on 22 agricultural (including pork belly, chicken meat, animal offal) and fishery products currently (end-2001) subject to import restrictions. For rice, the import quota to be 144,720 m. tonnes* (calculated on brown rice basis) in the first year following accession.**

Notes: * i.e., 8% of the average annual output of rice during 1990–92.
** Other requirements included Taiwan's commitment to international food safety, quarantine, sanitary and phytosanitary standards, and to implementing established procedures "in full conformity with the principle of transparency" in the drafting, implementation, and issuing of sanitary and phytosanitary regulations.
Sources: Government Information Office, *Taiwan* (February 26, 2002); see also Council of Agriculture, *Daomi yinying duice* (Rice Policies) (Taipei: 2001); Council of Agriculture, Executive Yuan (one of several pamphlets issued by the Council of Agriculture on the implications for agriculture of Taiwan's WTO accession).

Additionally, non-tariff barriers (NTBs) would be lifted for agricultural products, including rice and poultry (see footnote 4). Although import quotas would continue to be implemented with respect to rice, other goods were to be subject to tariff quotas, or exempt from quantitative restrictions. In accordance with the Uruguay Round agreement on agriculture, Taiwan was also required to reduce subsidies and other forms of support for farm factors and inputs, the likely cost of which was estimated to be some US$ 3.5 billion (see footnote 4).

The most salient features of China's WTO accession agreement with regard to the agricultural sector contained the following major provisions (see Table 8.2).

Table 8.2 The WTO Framework Agreement and China's Agriculture

Tariffs	Tariffs on agricultural products to be reduced from an average 22% to 17.5% overall by Jan. 2004.[5] Tariff-rate quota (TRQ) system to be established for imports of bulk farm products (incl. wheat, maize, rice, cotton, and soyabean oil). This system to provide for a specified level of imports to be admitted at low duty (10% or less, but 15% for sugar) by 2004. Above-quota imports to be levied at a higher rate. China to eliminate existing TRQ system for imports of barley, soyabeans, rapeseed, peanuts, sunflowers, maize, and cottonseed oil.
Trading rights and distribution	China to facilitate import of most products into any part of China within a 3-year transitional period, at the end of which all entities will enjoy the right to export and import freely (but partial exemptions to this rule for selected products). Some restricted trade (incl. in wheat, maize, rice, and cotton) to be channeled through state trading enterprises. But specific commitments gradually to end monopoly import status confirmed. Foreign enterprises to be permitted to distribute imported agricultural products (incl. grain): to be phased in over 3 years.
Farm export subsidies	Export subsidies on agricultural products to be eliminated.
Domestic farm subsidies	Trade-distorting domestic subsidies to be capped and reduced through multilateral negotiations. Greater transparency to be achieved in formulation of domestic farm support measures.*

Note: * Other provisions of the WTO agreement embraced sanitary and phytosanitary measures. By the terms of the Sino-U.S. bilateral agreement, American producers would continue to enjoy protection against dumping and other "unfair trading practices through the maintenance for 15 years after China's WTO accession of current American anti-dumping methodology (whereby China is treated as a 'non-market economy')." The main points of the U.S.-China Agricultural Cooperation Agreement are summarized in Ching Cheong and Hung Yee Ching, *Handbook on China's WTO Accession and its Impacts* (Singapore: World Scientific, 2003), pp. 201–203.
Sources: Ching Cheong and Hung Yee Ching, *Handbook on China's WTO Accession and its Impacts* (Singapore: World Scientific, 2003). Also useful is Organisation for Economic Co-operation and Development (OECD), *China in the World Economy: The Domestic Policy Challenges* (Paris: OECD, 2002), pp. 750–751, which includes a schedule of TRQs for farm products.

[5] But from 31 percent to 14 percent for U.S. priority products. See Supachai Panitchpakdi and Mark Clifford, *China and the WTO: Changing China, Changing World Trade* (Singapore: John Wiley & Sons [Asia] Pte Ltd., 2002), p. 221. Specific tariff reductions included: from 45 percent to 12 percent (beef); from 40 percent to 12 percent (citrus fruits); from 30 percent to 10 percent (apples); from 50 percent to 12 percent (cheese); from 65 percent to 20 percent (wine); and from 70 percent to 0 percent (beer) (Peter Nolan, *China and the Global Economy* [Basingstokee, UK and New York: Palgrave, 2001], p. 205). Perhaps the single most significant tariff reduction affecting U.S. high-priority products was that on maize, which was scheduled to fall to 3 percent (Ching Cheong and Hung Yee Ching, *Handbook on China's WTO Accession and Its Impacts* [Singapore: World Scientific, 2003], p. 181).

The concerns of China's negotiators regarding the farm sector centered on its enormous size, its weak economic state, and the already widespread social dislocation that existed among the farming community. In 2002, despite over half a century of industrialization that had reduced the contribution of agriculture to GDP to little more than 15 percent, farming in all its forms still absorbed 319.9 million people — over 90 percent of them still tied to crop cultivation.[6] With surplus rural labor — in fact, overwhelmingly farmers — officially thought to number at least 150 million, further large-scale displacement resulting from the WTO accession would exacerbate an already critical situation.

The farm sector's economic weakness has been exemplified by an excessive emphasis on grain production and on the political imperative of maintaining "basic" food (i.e., grain)

[6] The estimate of the farm work force is from the Ministry of Agriculture, *Zhongguo nongye nianjian, 2002* (China Agricultural Yearbook, 2002) (Beijing: Nongye chubanshe, 2003), p. 148, and it differs marginally from the corresponding figure (324.9 m.) in the National Bureau of Statistics, *Zhongguo tongji nianjian, 2002* (China Statistical Yearbook, 2002) (Beijing: Zhongguo tongji chubanshe, 2003), p. 128. Much more intriguing — and potentially very significant for any assessment of the impact of WTO membership on China's agricultural sector — is the implicitly much greater difference between two estimates in the two sources of the total agricultural population (*nongye renkou*): on the basis of information from the Public Security Bureau (*gong'an ju*), Ministry of Agriculture, *Zhongguo nongye nianjian, 2002* (China Agricultural Yearbook, 2002) (Beijing: Nongye chubanshe, 2003), gives a figure of 903 m. (72.1 percent of total population) (p.146) for 2002, compared with an estimate of the *rural* population (*nongcun renkou*) — by definition, a bigger entity than its agricultural counterpart, by virtue of its inclusion of very large numbers of non-agricultural industrial, construction, and service workers, and their families — of only 782.4 m. (p. 97). Acceptance of the Ministry of Agriculture, *Zhongguo nongye nianjian, 2002* (China Agricultural Yearbook, 2002) (Beijing: Nongye chubanshe, 2003), estimate would suggest an even greater impact on the farm sector from China joining the WTO than has been supposed. For a valuable analysis of the nature and extent of surplus rural (agricultural) labor, see also Chinese Academy of Social Sciences, Institute of Rural Development, *Zhongguo nongcun jingji xingshi fenxi yu yuce* (China's Rural Economy: Analysis and Forecast) (Beijing: Shehui kexue wenxian chubanshe, Various Issues) and Ministry of Labor and Social Security. *Zhongguo jiuye baogao, 2003–2004* (Chinese Labor Report, 2003–2004) (Beijing: Laodong shehui baozhang chubanshe, 2004).

self-sufficiency.[7] The benefits of resource reallocation associated with a downward revision of the self-sufficiency criterion from 95 to 90 percent would enhance farm productivity and efficiency.[8] From one perspective, WTO membership promised to assist in this outcome, by encouraging imports of grain that would push China toward a more efficient pattern of resource allocation.[9] Similarly, international competitive pressures would also alleviate other elements of economic malaise in the farm sector, such as stagnating farm incomes, widening inter- and intra-sectoral and/or regional differentials, and increasing farm out-migration.[10] On balance, such gains from the

---

[7] Hu Angang is one Chinese apologist, but not the only one, for the view that China should maintain "a fairly high degree grain self-sufficiency rate which is ... constantly declining [to 90 percent or less]." See Hu Angang, "Lizu guonei, jiben zi gei, shedu jinkou, zujin jiaohuan" (Have a Footing in the Domestic, Have Enough for Self-Sufficiency, Just the Right Amount of Imports, Promote Exchange), *Liaowang* (Outlook), August 26, 1996. See also Fan Gang, "Lun jiejue woguo liangshi gongji wenti de changqi zhanlue yu duice" (On the Long-run Strategy and Short-term Policies for Solving China's Grain Supply Problems), *Zhongguo nongcun guancha* (China Rural Survey), no. 5.

[8] Not that one should merely assume that China's farm system can maintain 95 percent grain self-sufficiency. The record average annual harvest of 505 m. tonnes (1996–1999) might have, and in China did lead to such an assumption. But the subsequent four years, when the average grain harvest fell to 450 m. tonnes (2000–2003), suggest a different judgment.

[9] In general, post-WTO China has the most to gain from increased exports of labor-intensive goods. An expansion of domestic output in associated industries would generate new job opportunities and could facilitate a transfer of labor displaced from the farm sector.

[10] In 2002, 84 m. rural laborers (17 percent of the rural workforce) migrated — 46 percent of them moving beyond their provincial boundaries. See Ministry of Labor and Social Security, *Zhongguo jiuye baogao, 2003–2004* (Chinese Labor Report, 2003–2004) (Beijing: Laodong shehui baozhang chubanshe, 2004), p. 207. The phenomenon of social malaise resulting from the exploitation of farmers has attracted a significant literature, best exemplified by the recent work of Thomas Bernstein and Xiaobo Lü, *Taxation without Representation in Contemporary Rural China* (Cambridge: Cambridge University Press, 2003). Initiatives announced in 2004 (e.g., tax cuts, the extension to farmers of direct subsidies, tightened land regulations, and a commitment to "give more, take less [from] and enliven" farmers) attest to the seriousness with which the government views social and economic difficulties in the agricultural sector.

WTO membership were likely to accrue in the long run, the net short-run impact being less positive.

If Chinese farmers were to meet the challenges of WTO membership successfully, they would require government assistance in order to facilitate production and employment restructuring, alongside renewed farm income growth. Support measures included the allocation of funds and the establishment of farm insurance schemes by local and central governments to support new adjustment mechanisms, and to provide compensation for farmers whose interests had been damaged by WTO accession. Improved agricultural marketing arrangements (including the establishment of a system of standards and quality norms for farm products) also needed to be put into place, if exports were to be increased.

In short, it is not surprising that agriculture was a focus of special concern among Chinese negotiators during the long process of WTO accession. Nor is it surprising that so many observers foresaw the emergence of serious difficulties in the farm sector after China joined the WTO. The remainder of this chapter will focus on these concerns.

IMPLICATIONS OF WTO ACCESSION FOR AGRICULTURE IN CHINA

Trade liberalization following WTO membership demands a reduction in import tariffs and quotas, as well as a reduction in production and export subsidies. If such adjustments raise world market prices,[11] the terms of trade will improve for the net exporters, but worsen for the net importers. China is a net exporter of many farm products, but it

[11] Projections of future agricultural price changes are, of course, intimately linked to underlying assumptions. This is exemplified in the predicted changes to international prices of grains and oilseeds under three scenarios analyzed by Josef Schmidhuber, "Changes in China's Agricultural Trade Policy Regime: Impacts on Agricultural Production, Consumption, Prices, and Trade," in Organisation for Economic Co-operation and Development, *China's Agriculture in the International Trading System*, (Paris: OECD, 2001), pp. 21–51. The following table shows the changing relationship

is also a net importer of other such goods. Because of its central role in the farm economy, however, attention often focuses on grain. An increase in foreign grain shipments to China could become a significant drain on foreign exchange, especially if international grain prices were to rise.

The Chinese Ministry of Agriculture (MOA) has viewed WTO membership as an opportunity to facilitate fulfillment of the strategic goals of reform and opening, including further developing the agricultural sector and rural economy. Closer integration in the world economy does, indeed, promise to assist China in its efforts to modernize the farm sector. Sustained agricultural development is critically dependent on the introduction and application of new scientific techniques over the entire range of farm activities. By facilitating foreign investment, WTO membership can lend support to this highly capital-intensive modernization process.

Accession to the WTO may also facilitate agricultural restructuring, including the rationalization of the structure of traded farm products.[12]

---

between domestic and international prices of cereals and soyabeans during 2000–2002:

	Wheat			Maize			Rice			Soyabeans		
	A	B	C	A	B	C	A	B	C	A	B	C
2000	0.89	1.14	128.4	0.75	0.92	123.1	1.54	1.52	98.9	1.57	2.12	135.0
2001	0.89	1.11	124.7	0.74	1.13	152.7	1.27	1.54	121.3	1.50	2.07	138.0
2002	1.08	1.06	98.1	0.82	1.02	124.4	1.46	1.48	101.4	1.67	2.11	126.3

Key: A=international price (yuan/tonne); B=domestic market price (yuan/tonne); C=index of Chinese domestic market price (A=100).

Sources: Chinese Academy of Social Sciences, Institute of Rural Development, *Zhongguo nongcun jingji xingshi fenxi yu yuce* (China's Rural Economy: Analysis and Forecast) (Beijing: Shehui kexue wenxian chubanshe) (2000–2001, p. 70; 2002–2003, p. 120).

The general, if not universal, picture is one of Chinese prices having fallen, thereby achieving a degree of convergence with international price trends.

[12] This is the theme of an interesting analysis of the likely implications for agriculture of China's WTO accession in the Chinese Academy of Social Sciences, Institute of Rural Development, *Zhongguo nongcun jingji xingshi fenxi yu yuce* (China's Rural Economy: Analysis and Forecast) (Beijing: Shehui kexue wenxian chubanshe) (1999–2000, pp. 52–68).

In particular, it should help generate new sources of farm exports, such as fruits, vegetables, and aquatic and animal-related products, which more closely accord with China's comparative advantage.[13] As the beneficiary of non-discriminatory trade treatment, China should enjoy lower negotiating and transactions costs in formulating commercial farm contracts, as well as gain access to properly-regulated channels of dispute resolution. WTO membership as a *developing* country promised also to confer preferential trade treatment that would encourage closer, more effective cooperation in farm production between China and the rest of the world (including Taiwan).

However, the longer-run gains of the structural adjustment made possible by market-opening measures (including the reduction of tariffs and other barriers), initially, were likely to entail a significant cost to China's agricultural sector by reducing the profitability, output, and income of some farmers, through exposure to overseas competition of their inefficient production of high-cost goods. In particular, tariff reductions and the abolition, or modification, of NTBs would pose serious challenges to farmers using backward technology to generate low-quality products (including processed items).[14]

The effect on agriculture of WTO membership was bound to depend on the extent to which Chinese farmers were exposed to overseas competition as domestic prices were liberalized.[15] One argument

[13] An excellent analysis of China's comparative advantage in agriculture is given by Weng Ming, *Zhongguo nongye jingzhengli yanjiu* (An Investigation into China's Agricultural Competitiveness) (Beijing: Zhongguo nongye chubanshe, 2003).

[14] Post-1978 reforms have made Chinese agriculture increasingly diversified, although crop farming (especially grain cultivation) remains the dominant activity. The impact of WTO membership will not be the same for all branches of farming, nor, in particular, for all crops. Nor will the effects be felt universally throughout the country: the regional dimension of the WTO consequences for agriculture will be very important. See also below.

[15] As long ago as January 1985, the Chinese government made a strategic decision to make farming (including grain production) supply-oriented, not — as previously — demand-oriented. The underlying economic logic was incontestable, but despite warnings about the dangers of farm price volatility under market conditions, the reality of price fluctuations became a pretext for continued government intervention to support farm prices and incomes.

was that, far from resolving such tensions, post-WTO competitive pressures from more efficient foreign producers would make them worse and intensify demands for continuing price protection in vulnerable sectors.[16] But, in 2002, Nicholas Lardy argued that predictions of the economic impact of WTO membership had been exaggerated because of underestimations of the degree of economic restructuring already undertaken by China during the 1990s.[17] For example, in agriculture, the proportion of market-determined farm product prices rose from 6 to 83 percent between 1978 and 1999, while the share of those fixed by the state fell from 93 to a mere 9 percent.[18] In addition, price adjustments were already underway more than two years before

[16] The most vulnerable sector is that of grain, where, in the second half of the 1990s, deliberate government intervention sought to protect farm incomes, even at the cost of domestic prices rising above international levels. For more details, see Hunter Colby, Xinshen Diao, and Francis Tuan, "China's WTO Accession: Conflicts with Domestic Agricultural Policies and Institutions," in Organisation for Economic Co-operation and Development, *China's Agriculture in the International Trading System* (Paris: OECD, 2001), pp. 177–178; see too Xu Xiaoqing, "Changes to Domestic Agricultural Policy after China's Accession to the WTO," in Organisation for Economic Co-operation and Development, *China's Agriculture in the International Trading System* (Paris: OECD, 2001), pp. 161–166. On the eve of the WTO accession, of nine farm products listed by Ma Xiaohe, the Chinese domestic price of only one item (pork) was below the corresponding international level. The prices of the remainder (wheat, rice, maize, soyabeans, oil, sugar, cotton, and beef) exceeded international levels by between 5.8 and 70.2 percent (the average gap was 40 percent). Ma Xiaohe, "Analysis of the Impact of WTO Accession on China's Agriculture," in Ching Cheong and Ching Hung Yee, *Handbook on China's WTO Accession and Its Impacts* (Singapore: World Scientific, 2003), p. 205. (All prices based on estimates for August 2000.)

[17] Nicholas R. Lardy, *Integrating China into the Global Economy* (Washington, DC: Brookings Institution Press, 2002), esp. pp. 22–28. By the mid-1990s, with production costs having risen above the world average, China's wheat, indica rice, maize, rapeseed, and other farm products no longer enjoyed an international comparative advantage and were bound to be hard — even hardest — hit after WTO accession.

[18] Nicholas R. Lardy, *Integrating China into the Global Economy* (Washington, DC: Brookings Institution Press, 2002). The balance was made up of goods, whose prices were "state-guided." Ibid., p. 25.

China's WTO entry, as farmers shifted out of grain cultivation toward the production of less land-intensive and more labor-intensive crops.[19] In 1999, the prices of wheat and maize fell by 20–30 percent, and they continued to fall in 2000.[20] In short,

> [T]he anticipated substantial adjustment required in China's agricultural sector already was under way more than two years in advance of China's entry into the World Trade Organization. Farmers began moving out of grain and into vegetables, fruit, and other crops that were less land intensive in production than grain.[21]

---

[19] Important land-intensive products are grain, oilseeds, cotton, and sugar; their labor-intensive counterparts are fruit, vegetables, meat and animal products, and fish. See also the comment by the Deputy Director of Anhui Agricultural University in Hefei: "Anything that is labor-intensive, you can do cheaper here [in China]. Not just computers and clothes, but broccoli and oranges, too" (Associated Press, May 28, 2002).

[20] Ibid. Data published by the U.S. Department of Agriculture's Economic Research Service (March 2003) showed that the domestic market price of wheat fell by 19.5 percent (red wheat) and 21 percent (white wheat) in 2000; rice prices fell by 16–20 percent; and the price of maize declined by 17 percent. However, the same source showed that market prices of wheat and maize *rose* in 2001, alongside continuing falls in the prices of rice and soyabeans. An article in *China Daily* (February 23, 2002) noted that domestic prices of wheat, soyabeans, edible oil and oil crops, and sugar were 10–70 percent above international levels, whereas prices of meat, vegetables, fruit, and seafood products were between 40 percent and 80 percent *below* international price levels.

[21] Nicholas R. Lardy, *Integrating China into the Global Economy* (Washington, DC: Brookings Institution Press, 2002), p. 25; Note, too, that the expected fall in average tariffs on agricultural goods (from 22 percent to 17.5 percent, 2000–2004) was much more limited than the corresponding fall in industrial tariffs (from 24.6 percent to 9.4 percent) (Organisation for Economic Co-operation and Development [OECD], *China in the World Economy: The Domestic Policy Challenges* [Paris: OECD, 2002], p. 69). It is noteworthy that structural adjustments in the farm sector in anticipation of the WTO accession were reflected in major reductions in agricultural tariffs — from as high as 47 percent (1991) to 23 percent (1996). See Albert P. Park, "Trade Integration and the Prospects for Rural Enterprise Development in China," in Organisation for Economic Co-operation and Development, *China's Agriculture in the International Trading System* (Paris: OECD, 2001), p. 197. Zhu Rongji's announcement (May 1999) that administrative price protection for grain varieties of poor quality and/or in excess supply would gradually be phased out was an explicit recognition of the need for grain area rationalization in advance of joining the WTO. The decision also foreshadowed the reform of the grain distribution system in order to facilitate production in accordance with market dictates.

Policy initiatives in the farm sector, however, were determined by factors other than WTO considerations. The call, in January 2000, to cut domestic production of staple agricultural goods,[22] no doubt, reflected the Chinese government's determination to create a truly market-oriented farm economy and its belief that higher incomes for grain farmers could only be achieved from associated structural adjustments.[23] It also highlighted the importance of securing a more efficient pattern of production, based on regional comparative advantage and designed to meet consumption needs by market means — hence, the withdrawal of protective prices for some cereals,[24] and the announcement of higher prices for higher-quality cereals.[25] In interpreting these initiatives, however, it would be disingenuous not to recognize that, even allowing for their likely contribution toward helping to resolve some of the structural problems faced by agriculture in the run-up to China's WTO accession, they are likely also to have been prompted by the unprecedented grain harvests of the preceding four years.[26]

---

[22] Including a 3.5 percent reduction in grain output.

[23] Concealed in the projected reduction in the grain output was a major contraction in the grain-sown area — 70 percent of it to take place in five provinces (Jiangsu, Anhui, Zhejiang, Hubei, and Sichuan) — including an 8-percent reduction (over 600,000 ha.) in the area under early rice, and a 6-percent cut in the summer wheat acreage. The area adjustments included but also transcended the grain sector, embracing a shift toward non-grain crops, as well as the production of more high-quality grains, more grain for processing, and more feed grain.

[24] Cf. the gradual phasing-out of production and stockpiles of poor-quality early rice and winter wheat in southern China, and of spring wheat in the north. Meanwhile, farmers were warned to expect widening price differences in line with varying qualitative, seasonal, and regional production conditions.

[25] E.g., the sown area of good quality early rice was projected to rise by 14 percent during 2000.

[26] Beijing also explicitly recognized some of the obstacles to implementing successfully such policies, including a lack of capital for agricultural modernization; the absence of effective systems to check output quality; and the inadequacy of means to disseminate new technologies (including information on improved seed varieties). Local reports highlighted failures to differentiate clearly between differing grades of farm products, with consequent adverse effects on farmers' incentives to produce superior farm products. All these deficiencies undermined efforts to make farming

To what extent have the looked-for structural shifts in farming, in fact, taken place? The following figures show the grain sector's share in total sown area, as well as the shares of major individual grain crops in the total grain sown area.

The estimates show that, between 1991 and 2003, the grain-sown area contracted by almost 13 million hectares (11.5 percent) and its share of the total sown area declined from 75 to 65 percent. During the 1991–2000 period, the average rate of contraction was –0.4 percent per year; in the following three years, the corresponding figure was –2.9 percent. For cereals,[27] the same pattern was evident, but even more pronounced (−1.1 percent per year, 1991–2000; −3.4 percent, 2000–2003). One interpretation of these aggregate figures would be to suggest that they reflect rational adjustments to the grain-and cereal-sown areas before and after accession to the WTO — "rational" in the sense of shifting cultivation away from land-intensive crops in which China suffered a comparative disadvantage. Data for 2004 are only preliminary at the time of this writing. Taken at face value, however, they point to a degree of recovery in both grain- and cereal-sown areas. This is attributable, to a large degree, to income-enhancing initiatives for grain farmers, taken in 2004.

Adjustments in areas planted under individual grains highlight efforts made by China in recent years to rationalize its cropping pattern in order, at least in part, to accommodate post-WTO competition from more efficient foreign producers. Between 1991 and 2003 the sown area of uncompetitive, low-value coarse grains ("other" in Table 8.3) fell dramatically.[28] During the same period,

---

responsive to market needs. See also Hunter Colby, Xinshen Diao, and Francis Tuan, "China's WTO Accession: Conflicts with Domestic Agricultural Policies and Institutions," in Organisation for Economic Co-operation and Development, *China's Agriculture in the International Trading System* (Paris: OECD, 2001), p. 178, who showed how, in the late 1990s, local governments sought to circumvent the government's protection price policy "... by downgrading the quality of the farmer's grain ... [or refusing] to purchase all the grain the farmer wishes to sell at the protection price."

[27] I.e., rice, wheat, and maize.

[28] The preliminary estimate for 2004 is anomalously high, and may reflect inaccuracies in sown-area data for one or more of the other grain crops shown in Table 8.3.

Table 8.3 Changes in Grain Cultivation, 1990–2001

	Sown area under following crop categories (m. ha.)								
	All crops	All grains	All cereals	Rice	Wheat	Maize	Soya	Tubers	Other grains
1991	149.59	112.31	94.07	32.59	30.95	21.57	9.16	9.08	8.96
1995	149.88	110.06	89.31	30.74	28.86	22.78	11.23	9.52	6.93
2000	156.30	108.46	85.26	29.96	26.65	23.06	12.66	10.54	5.59
2001	155.71	106.08	82.60	28.81	24.66	24.28	13.27	10.22	4.84
2002	154.64	103.89	81.47	28.20	23.91	24.63	12.54	9.88	4.73
2003	152.42	99.41	76.81	28.70	22.00	24.07	12.90	9.70	2.04
2004	–	101.61	81.50	26.78	21.73	25.58	10.58	10.24	6.70

Sources: National Bureau of Statistics, *Zhongguo tongji nianjian, 2004* (China Statistical Yearbook, 2004) (Beijing: Zhongguo tongji chubanshe, 2004), pp. 486–487; National Bureau of Statistics, *Zhongguo tongji zhaiyao, 2004* (China Statistical Abstract, 2004) (Beijing: Zhongguo tongji chubanshe, 2004), pp. 113, 116. Grain area for 2004 is from National Bureau of Statistics, "Statistical Communiqué on the 2004 National Economic and Social Development," February 28, 2005. Other crop area estimates for 2004 are preliminary, as given by Food and Agriculture Organization (FAO), FAOSTAT database, http://faostat.fao. org/faostat (accessed April 25, 2005).

rice and wheat together lost almost 13 million hectares, although this was partly offset by an expansion of 2.5 million hectares of newly-sown maize.[29] Given that China's comparative advantage in producing labor-intensive japonica rice was likely to survive trade liberalization, it is also significant that its share of the total rice-sown area rose sharply after 1990 (from 16 to 27 percent between 1990 and 2000), whereas that of indica varieties fell from 84 to 73 percent. Such adjustments reveal changes in China's cropping patterns — both within, and by implication, outside the grain sector — that seem to make sense in the context of post-WTO conditions.[30]

[29] Soyabeans were the grain crop whose sown area underwent the most significant expansion of all — by 40 percent during 1991–2002.

[30] Examination of tariff rate reductions associated with China's WTO membership highlights the rationality of shifting out of rice and wheat — crops whose in-quota tariffs were scheduled to drop to a mere 1 percent in 2002 — toward soyabeans

The logic is further underlined in one projection that suggests that, under the impact of forces associated with WTO membership, China's overall grain self-sufficiency will fall from 98 to 91 percent between 2005 and 2020, whereas the self-sufficiency rate for rice will increase from 104 to 109 percent.[31] Implied in these figures is a rise in China's grain imports from 11 million to 49 million tonnes, alongside a tripling of rice exports from 4 million to 12 million tonnes.

References to the economic "logic" of WTO membership reflected in sown area adjustments do not, however, fully capture the complexity of conditions in the grain sector. Even in the absence of China joining the international trading body, the low-return nature of grain farming and the susceptibility of farmers to exploitation[32] by local government officials had already been sufficient to precipitate area adjustments.[33] The reality is invariably more complex than theories based on a *ceteris paribus* assumption, and this is just one instance in which there is an element of coincidence, as well as of causality, underlying the relationship between cropping pattern changes and China's WTO accession.

Tensions between the economic logic of WTO membership, driven by the dictates of comparative advantage, and the policy

---

(that would continue to carry an in-quota tariff of over 20 percent throughout 2002–2004). The expansion of the sown area under maize, whose tariff schedule matched those of rice and wheat, appears to be less logical. This is considered further below.

[31] Linxiu Zhang, "China's Rice Economy and Policy: With Implications to WTO Entry," at www.unep.ch/etu/etp/events/Agriculture/pps_china.pdf (accessed June 1, 2006).

[32] In recent years, the most serious form of such exploitation has been the levying of illegal fines, taxes, and other levies on farmers (see above, note 10).

[33] The end of surging crop output growth under the impact of the earliest farm reforms and the onset of output stagnation in 1985–1999 reflected increasing reluctance by farmers to engage in increasingly less remunerative grain cultivation. The partial recovery of grain production in 2004 had much to do with initiatives — agricultural tax reductions, the extension of subsidies to grain producers, tighter control over arable land, and the liberalization of the grain market — designed to enhance the incomes of grain farmers.

imperative of seeking "basic" grain self-sufficiency[34] are a further complication. Even if sown area adjustments reflect "WTO logic," the profile of China's cereal trade does not accord with the pattern that would have been expected to follow trade liberalization.[35] A marked rise in cereal imports would have been a logical response to the sharp decline in domestic grain output during 2000–2003.[36] Remarkably, however, China remained a consistent net cereal exporter throughout this period.[37] It achieved this by sharply running down its reserves. Given China's continuing comparative advantage in japonica strains, it is not surprising that rice exports should have been sustained. Indeed, as yields improve alongside

[34] In the Chinese usage, "basic" grain self-sufficiency has meant securing at least 95 percent of grain requirements from domestic sources.

[35] Cf. the following estimates of exports and imports of rice, wheat, and maize in 2000–2003 (all figures given in m. tonnes of commercial grain, in contrast to production estimates that are in m. tonnes of raw grain). Data from Ministry of Agriculture, *Zhongguo nongye fazhan baogao, 2003* (Chinese Agricultural Development Report, 2003) (Beijing: Zhongguo nongye chubanshe, 2003), pp. 127–129; National Bureau of Statistics, *Zhongguo nongcun tongji nianjian, 2004* (China Rural Statistical Yearbook, 2004) (Beijing: Zhongguo tongji chubanshe, 2004), p. 250; National Bureau of Statistics, *Zhongguo tongji nianjian, 2004* (China Statistical Yearbook, 2004) (Beijing: Zhongguo tongji chubanshe, 2004), pp. 491, 723, 726; National Bureau of Statistics, *Zhongguo tongji zhaiyao, 2004* (China Statistical Abstract, 2004), (Beijing: Zhongguo tongji chubanshe, 2004), pp. 491, 723, 726.

	Rice			Wheat			Maize		
	Domestic output	Exports	Imports	Domestic output	Exports	Imports	Domestic output	Exports	Imports
2000	187.9	2.96	0.25	99.6	0.19	0.92	106.0	10.48	0
2001	177.6	1.87	0.29	93.9	0.71	0.74	114.1	6.00	0
2002	174.5	1.99	0.24	90.3	0.98	0.63	121.3	11.68	0
2003	160.7	2.62	0.26	86.49	n.a.	0.45	115.83	16.39	0

[36] During these three years, there was a cumulative decline of almost 78 m. tonnes in grain production – enough, at current income levels, to meet the requirements of over 190 m. people.

[37] If, however, China's huge net imports of soya (traditionally considered a grain in Chinese usage) were included in the calculations, its status as a net exporter would be reversed to that of a net importer.

falling per capita consumption, China is likely to remain a net rice exporter. Declines in maize production after 1999 were also less serious than for other cereals, although the continuing high level of exports was only achieved by a significant depletion of stocks.[38] The most striking instance of a lagged trade response to changing domestic production conditions, however, has been that of wheat. In 2002, for example, despite domestic output being at its lowest level since the late 1980s, China remained a net wheat exporter![39] Even in 2003, wheat imports were not significant. This was clearly not sustainable, and with gross imports of 7.5 million tonnes in 2004, China had become the world's largest wheat importer.[40]

In summary, the forces bearing on sown area adjustments in China's grain sector transcend those associated only with accession to the WTO. A priori, other things being equal, the reduction of in-quota rice and wheat tariffs to a minimal level (1 percent)

---

[38] Gerald A. Bange has argued that as income growth continues, and demand for maize for feed and industrial uses rises rapidly, China will "soon re-enter the global market as a significant corn importer." See Gerald Bange, "The Outlook for World Grain and Oilseed Markets" (speech at the Agricultural Outlook Conference, Beijing, July 17–18, 2004). Reports published by the Xinhua News Agency also highlight the unpredictability of trade in maize. In 2002, Xinhua (May 29) noted that "China's large maize consumers, mainly in coastal and southern areas, were turning to maize imports, which were cheaper and better quality" and predicted that net imports of maize would reach 1 m. tonnes in 2002. But a little less than a year later, it reported that China was set to become the second-largest maize exporter in the world, after the U.S., with likely overseas shipments of 10–12 m. tonnes during 2003 (Xinhua, April 16, 2003).

[39] For an excellent analysis of the state of China's wheat economy, see Bryan Lohmar, *China's Wheat Economy: Current Trends and Prospectus or Imports* (United States Department of Agriculture, Economic Research Service, Electronic Outlook Report), May 2004, at www.ers.usda.gov (accessed May 22, 2005).

[40] Imports from U.S. Department of Agriculture Complete Raw Data Files, http://www.fas.usda.gov/psd/complete_files/default.asp (accessed on May 22, 2005). Lohmar argues that as wheat production stabilizes and consumption declines, imports will fall from a high of perhaps 10 m. tonnes (2004-2005) to an average of around 5 m. tonnes. Also relevant is Organisation for Economic Co-operation and Development (OECD), *China in the World Economy: The Domestic Policy Challenges* (Paris: OECD, 2002), p. 71.

was bound to generate higher imports.[41] But far from WTO-permitted import quotas for rice, wheat, and maize having been fulfilled, in 2003, China remained a net exporter of all three cereals. The shibboleth of domestic grain self-sufficiency remained paramount — an attitude reinforced by a belief that stocks were still sufficient to meet the gap between production and consumption. The major policy initiatives of 2004[42] seem, reasonably enough, to have been driven as much by the wish to address the social and potential political consequences of falling incomes among grain farmers as the economic challenges of closer integration in the world economy.

To devote so much space to China's grain sector reflects the continued dominance of cereal cultivation in its farm economy. But other agricultural activities were also bound to be affected by accession to the WTO. For example, even with the benefits of easier adjustment to trade and investment liberalization made possible by the introduction of a new marketing system for cotton at the end of the 1990s,[43] the removal of import quotas was likely to impact on cotton farmers. In the past, imports of raw cotton were constrained by government restrictions, whose removal might have been

[41] Cf. the following estimates (all in m. tonnes) given by Zhang (see footnote 31):

	Actual imports 2000 (see COA website)	TRQ imports, 2002 (Zhang)	Actual imports, 2002 (see COA website)	TRQ imports, 2004 (Zhang)
Rice	0.25	3.76	0.24	5.32
Wheat	0.92	8.45	0.63	9.64
Maize	0	5.70	0	7.20

See Council of Agriculture (COA) (Republic of China, Executive Yuan), *Basic Agricultural Statistics*, at http://stat.coa.gov.tw/dba_as/english/as_root.htm (accessed June 22, 2006); and footnote 31.

[42] I.e., agricultural tax reductions, the extension of subsidies to farm producers, tighter control over arable land, and the liberalization of the grain market.

[43] In 1999–2000, the government's previously monopolistic control over cotton purchases, marketing, and distribution was significantly liberalized. See the Organisation for Economic Co-operation and Development (OECD), *China in the World Economy: The Domestic Policy Challenges* (Paris: OECD, 2002), pp. 67, 72.

expected to bring about a sharp rise in overseas purchases.[44] However, such an increase has not been forthcoming. Although China's physical trade in cotton shifted from a surplus (0.245 million tonnes of net exports) to a marginal deficit (21,850 tonnes of net imports) between 2000 and 2002, the latter figure was still almost 40 percent below both Zhang's TRQ import estimate for 2002, let alone the previous 1997 import peak of 0.75 million tonnes. Only in the wake of a harvest collapse in the North China Plain in 2003 did foreign purchases of raw cotton rise sharply (to account for 20 percent of global imports).[45]

Economic orthodoxy dictates that membership in the WTO would lead Chinese farmers to shift production from land-intensive goods, in which they have a comparative disadvantage, toward more labor-intensive products, in which they enjoy a comparative advantage. Thus, early projections highlighted expected increases in net export earnings resulting from the production of more live animals, meat, fruit, vegetables, cured tobacco, sugar cane, and so forth. The underlying logic is incontrovertible, although the data in Table 8.4 suggest that WTO accession was not the only factor affecting the exports of these goods.

Table 8.4 confirms that exports (in physical and value terms) of goods in which China enjoyed a comparative advantage rose after

---

[44] Ching Cheong and Hung Yee Ching, *Handbook on China's WTO Accession and Its Impacts* (Singapore: World Scientific, 2003), quoted Yu Yongdong and Zheng Binwen (2000) to the effect that almost 5 m. cotton farmers could lose their jobs by 2005 — almost as many job losses as among wheat farmers. It is not clear whether this estimate takes account of the positive impact on domestic production of raw materials (wool and flax, as well as cotton), resulting from greater trade in textile goods associated with WTO membership.

[45] Thus, "import licenses allocating China's TRQ under the WTO were not adequate to cover import demand late in calendar year 2003; there is evidence to suggest that supplemental licenses were issued as early as October, but they were not confirmed officially until December." See James Johnson, Stephen MacDonald, Leslie Meyer, and Carol Skelly, *The US and World Cotton Outlook* (United States Department of Agriculture, February 2004). Net imports for 2004 calculated from data from National Bureau of Statistics, *Zhongguo nongcun tongji nianjian, 2004* (China Rural Statistical Yearbook, 2004) (Beijing: Zhongguo tongji chubanshe, 2004), pp. 249–250.

Table 8.4 Net Exports of Animals, Vegetables, Fruit, Aquatic Products, and Cured Tobacco

	Net exports ('000 tonnes and US$ million)									
	Live hogs		Vegetables		Aquatic products		Fruit (apples, mandarins, and oranges)		Cured tobacco	
	Volume	Value	Volume	Value	Volume	Value	Volume	Value	Volume	Value
1985	2,960	179.4	512.0	225.7	119.6	274.7	107.5	41.7	17.8	30.7
1990	3,000	270.9	893.5	577.7	357.5	1,316.1	128.0	56.7	28.6	49.4
1995	2,530	277.7	1,580.0	1,571.3	610.0	2,087.3	240.7	101.0	56.6	77.3
2000	2,030	230.5	2,450.0	1,576.9	1,200.0	2,267.4	489.0	141.9	93.8	132.1
2001	1,960	219.7	3,170.0	1,914.3	1,540.0	2,588.6	453.3	136.4	134.0	166.6
2002	1,880	213.4	3,600.0	1,887.7	1,630.0	2,872.0	635.4	200.6	135.1	181.9
2003	1,880	214.8	4,320.0	2,195.6	1,580.0	3,332.5	874.5	279.1	134.5	183.9

Sources: National Bureau of Statistics, *Zhongguo tongji nianjian, 1991* (Beijing: Zhongguo tongji chubanshe, 1991), p. 623; National Bureau of Statistics, *Zhongguo tongji nianjian, 1996* (Beijing: Zhongguo tongji chubanshe, 1996), p. 589; National Bureau of Statistics, *Zhongguo tongji nianjian, 2001* (Beijing: Zhongguo tongji chubanshe, 2001), p. 594; National Bureau of Statistics, *Zhongguo tongji nianjian, 2004* (China Statistical Yearbook, 2004) (Beijing: Zhongguo tongji chubanshe, 2004), p. 723.

WTO accession. It also shows that such increases underlined a trend that was already in evidence, even though the rate of expansion accelerated after accession. Between 1990 and 2000, export earnings from the four products (product categories) increased from US$ 2.27 million to US$ 4.35 million (by 6.7 percent per year); during 2000–2003, revenue further increased to US$ 6.21 million (averaging 12.6 percent per year).

Assessing the employment implications of WTO-related structural changes in farm output is extremely difficult. Where those implications are measured, in terms of job losses, assessments of the social impact are even more difficult.[46] The subsistence orientation of farming is also relevant. Not all farm output — especially food — is produced for a market.[47] Where subsistence orientation is strong, the impact of WTO membership, at least in the short run, may be mitigated.

The very different results of attempts to predict the employment effects on agriculture of China's WTO membership highlight the difficulties that surround such exercises.[48] It is beyond the scope of this chapter to give detailed consideration to the potential for job

---

[46] In purely economic terms, the existence of massive surplus labor in farming (overwhelmingly, in grain farming) suggests a negligible opportunity cost of farm job loss. But the social impact of job loss is very different for a young family dependent on its income from farming and with no alternative local employment from that of an elderly person whose son has, or can, find a job in a rural enterprise.

[47] *China Daily*, May 29, 2002, pointed to a national marketing ratio for grain of 30 percent (but with major regional variations — e.g., cf. a corresponding figure of 60 percent in Jilin).

[48] Cf. job losses of 12.8 m. in rice, wheat, and cotton (*China Times*, November 20, 1999); 25.5 m. in rice, wheat, maize, cotton, and oilseeds. Ma Xiaohe, "Analysis of the Impact of WTO Accession on China's Agriculture," cited in Ching Cheong and Ching Hung Yee, *Handbook on China's WTO Accession and Its Impacts* (Singapore: World Scientific, 2003); 9.6 m. throughout agriculture (Yu and Cheng, cited in Ching Cheong and Hung Yee Ching, *Handbook on China's WTO Accession and Its Impacts* [Singapore: World Scientific, 2003]). Yu and Cheng anticipated a 14.2-percent employment loss in the wheat sector alone, implying the loss of 5.4 million jobs. A major difficulty in estimating the employment consequences for China of WTO accession is knowing the precise size of the existing farm labor force; e.g., Thomas Rawski and R. Mead, "On the Trail of China's Phantom Farmers," *World Development*, vol. 26, no. 5 (May 1998), pp. 767–781.

creation, not least because of the need to examine the movement of farmers not only from land-intensive to labor-intensive farm activities, but also from agricultural to non-agricultural rural work.[49] There is also an empirical problem arising from the absence of time-series data showing changes in employment in the various branches of farming (crop cultivation, forestry, fishing, and husbandry).[50] Thus, Table 8.5 merely presents estimates of total agricultural employment since the mid-1990s.

The peak level of agricultural employment was reached in 1991 (341.86 million). Thereafter, the rate of change in farm employment fluctuated; falling until 1996, but then rising again until 1999, after which it once again declined. Some may interpret these figures as lending prima facie evidence of employment adjustments in anticipation of, and under the impact, of WTO accession. But until more detailed data by branch of farming are made available, such a conclusion remains speculative. In the meantime, the potential seriousness of the impact of WTO membership on agricultural employment lies in the scale of the economic and social challenges posed by the massive surplus of farm labor.[51]

---

[49] One major determinant of the employment impact of the WTO accession on the farm sector is the extent to which township and village enterprises (TVEs) can take advantage of the new environment to expand export-oriented production.

[50] E.g., I have not found such data in the Ministry of Labor and Social Security, *Zhongguo jiuye baogao, 2003–2004* (Chinese Labor Report, 2003–2004) (Beijing: Laodong shehui baozhang chubanshe, 2004), nor do they appear to be available in recent editions of *Zhongguo nongcun jingji xingshi fenxi yu yuce* (China's Rural Economy: Analysis and Forecast) or *Zhongguo renkou yu laodong wenti baogao* (Green Book of Population and Labor) both published by Shehui kexue wenxian chubanshe in Beijing.

[51] It is disingenuous to argue that the experience of other countries offers room for optimism in assessing the employment consequences for China; that the share of agriculture in South Korea's total labor force fell from over 50 percent to 11 percent between 1970 and 1997 is instructive. But to argue that such experience suggests that a similar restructuring can "be managed successfully" in China ignores the obvious differences in size in the farm workforces in the two countries. See Organisation for Economic Co-operation and Development (OECD), *China in the World Economy: The Domestic Policy Challenges* (Paris: OECD, 2002), p. 74.

Table 8.5 Employment in Agriculture (Crop Farming, Forestry, Fishing, and Husbandry)

	Total employed persons in agriculture (million)
1990	333.36
1991	341.86
1995	323.35
1996	322.61
1997	324.34
1998	326.26
1999	329.12
2000	327.98
2001	324.51
2002	319.91
2003	312.60

Source: National Bureau of Statistics, *Zhongguo laodong tongji nianjian, 2003* (China Labor Statistical Yearbook, 2003) (Beijing: Zhongguo tongji chubanshe, 2003), p. 26. The figure for 2003 is from National Bureau of Statistics, *Zhongguo nongcun tongji nianjian,* 2004 (China Rural Statistical Yearbook, 2004) (Beijing: Zhongguo tongji chubanshe, 2004), p. 31.

No assessment of WTO membership can ignore its regional impact.[52] There is a presumption that against the background of the high provincial concentration of production of certain farm goods, job losses caused by falling output will impact disproportionately on these regions. That crop production is skewed toward certain regions

[52] E.g., *Renmin ribao* (People's Daily) (February 6, 2002) outlined five measures to help China's farm sector to meet the challenges of the WTO membership. They embody a clear regional dimension to agricultural plans — "major tasks will be centered on high quality wheat production in the Yellow River and Huaihai areas, sweet corn and soyabean production in northeast China and the eastern part of Inner Mongolia, cotton production in Xinjiang Autonomous Region, beef and lamb in the central plains, dairy products in North China, oranges and rapeseed cultivation in the Yangtze River region, and apple cultivation in Shaanxi and the Bohai Gulf region...."

is easily demonstrated. More than half of China's wheat output is produced in just three provinces — Hebei, Henan, and Shandong. Five provinces — Heilongjiang, Jilin, Hebei, Shandong, and Henan — have traditionally accounted for about half of total maize production, as well as for cotton, soyabeans — even rice. Other regions that are unable to meet their own farm requirements may also increasingly resort to imports, rather than relying on an overworked transport system to secure supplies from domestic sources. In short, we may suppose that, with such a high degree of output concentration, the economic and social consequences of declining farm employment associated with China's closer integration in world agricultural markets will be more narrowly-focused on particular regions. Interestingly, however, the evidence of recent years offers neither unambiguous nor unqualified support for this thesis. It is true that the decline in the maize output between 1999 and 2003 was overwhelmingly carried by the five provinces that dominated domestic production. By contrast, however, the three provinces that, in 1999, had supplied half of China's wheat output accounted for less than one-third of the output decline during the same period.[53] In short, the extent to which the regionalization of farm production damages economic and social development remains to be seen.

ASSESSING THE IMPLICATIONS OF WTO ACCESSION FOR AGRICULTURE IN TAIWAN

As shown in Table 8.6, the profile of agriculture and its position in the national economy changed more profoundly in Taiwan than it did in China after the 1950s.

---

[53] Relevant data can be found in the National Bureau of Statistics, *Zhongguo tongji nianjian, 2000* (Beijing: Zhongguo tongji chubanshe, 2000), p. 387; National Bureau of Statistics, *Zhongguo tongji nianjian, 2004* (China Statistical Yearbook, 2004) (Beijing: Zhongguo tongji chubanshe, 2004), p. 491. They show that wheat output in Hebei, Shandong, and Henan fell by 14.3 percent, compared with a national decline of 24.1 percent (1999–2003). In the case of the five major maize-producing provinces (Heilongjiang, Jilin, Hebei, Shandong, and Henan), the corresponding decline was 15.2 percent, compared with a corresponding national figure of 9.6 percent.

Table 8.6 The Declining Contribution and Changing Composition of Agriculture in Taiwan

	Farm output as % of GDP	Farm sector's share of fixed capital formation (%)	Farm population as % of total population	Farm workers as % of total employment	Composition of agricultural production (%)				Farm exports as % of all exports	Farm imports as % cf all imports
					Farm crops	Forestry	Fishing	Livestock		
1952	32.22	20.46	52.37	56.06	68.60	6.50	9.10	15.80	67.00*	33.57*
2000	2.09	0.70	16.52	7.80	45.41	0.07	24.94	29.57	2.21	5.42

* Data for 1964. (But Council for Economic Planning and Development, *Taiwan Statistical Data Book 2002* [Taipei, 2004], p. 214 showed that raw and processed agricultural goods accounted for 91.9 percent of total exports in 1952).

Source: Taiwan Provincial Government, Department of Agriculture and Forestry, *Taiwan Agricultural Yearbook*, 2002.

Comparisons with China are instructive. Official Chinese statistics indicate that, in 2002, the agricultural population[54] still accounted for 72 percent of China's total population — significantly higher than at any point in post-1949 Taiwan.[55] One has to go back almost 40 years to find a time when agriculture's share in Taiwan's total employment (45 percent) and GDP (14.6 percent) matched those of Chinese farmers today. Not since 1984 has the farm sector's share of export earnings or import spending been as high as it was in mainland Chinese in 2003.

However, such comparisons should not lead us merely to assume that the implications for Taiwan's agriculture from the WTO accession have been negligible. As the experiences of many countries show — including those of two of Taiwan's neighbors (Japan and South Korea) — the small size of the farm sector is no guarantee that closer integration in the global economy will be reflected in the absence of any significant social or economic consequences. In addition, the removal of artificial barriers on cross-strait farm trade, as required by WTO rules, has been a source of heightened political concern for Taiwan in the face of cheaper agricultural exports likely to be forthcoming from mainland China.

The demographic characteristics of farming in Taiwan are central to any assessment of the impact of WTO membership on

---

[54] I.e., *Nongye renkou.* See Ministry of Agriculture, *Zhongguo nongye nianjian, 2003* (China Agricultural Yearbook, 2003) (Beijing: Nongye chubanshe, 2003), p. 146. The fact that the share of China's *rural* population (*nongcun renkou*) in the total population is officially estimated to have been 60.91 percent in the same year highlights the difficulty of obtaining an accurate estimate of the urban-rural composition of the Chinese population. National Bureau of Statistics, *Zhongguo tongji nianjian, 2003* (China Statistical Yearbook, 2003) (Beijing: Zhongguo tongji chubanshe, 2003), p. 97. Highlights the difficulty of obtaining an accurate estimate of the urban-rural composition of the Chinese population.

[55] I do not have access to 2002 data for Taiwan, but, in 1999, farm families — defined as families in which at least one person was engaged in crop cultivation or livestock-raising — accounted for just 12.1 percent of all families in Taiwan. Council of Agriculture, *Nongye tongji nianjian, 2000* (Agricultural Statistics Yearbook, 2000) (Taipei: Executive Yuan, 2001), p. 308.

the rural community. The most recent farm census[56] suggests some of the social and economic vulnerabilities of Taiwan's agricultural sector in the run-up to accession in 2000.[57] It shows, for example, that the average age of both the farming population and farm workers was old and getting older,[58] whereas the gender ratio among farmers was also more highly-skewed toward men than for the total population.[59] In addition, literacy and the educational levels of the

[56] I.e., Directorate-General of Budget, Accounting and Statistics, "Agricultural, Forestry, Fishery and Husbandry Census," at visit http://eng.dgbas.gov.tw/lp.asp?CtNode=1632&CtUnit=782&BaseDSD=7 for further details.

[57] As in Japan and South Korea, what might be termed the "cultural" implications of WTO accession for agriculture should not be ignored. The *Taipei Times* (July 9, 2000) observed, "the development of farming villages is not just about winning competition in agricultural markets. The economic development of agriculture is just one aspect of reconstruction. A lack of consideration about cultural ... and ecological issues will make for an incomplete reconstruction strategy and leave these areas at the mercy of the market economy.... Compared with industrial societies, farming villages have special lifestyles and value systems.... They bring forth a new type of consumerism that is about much more than buying merchandise." Issues such as these have come to the fore in Taipei (e.g., cf. President Chen Shui-bian's advocacy of "agri-tourism" and "recreational agriculture") in a way in which they have not done so in China, where the purely socioeconomic consequences of WTO accession have been the major preoccupation. When Taiwan first embarked on talks to join the GATT in 1990, officials "used 'rice culture' to defend its policy of banning rice import: rice was the foundation of Taiwan's stability" (Deutsche Presse Agentur, cited in *Taipei Times*, April 22, 2002). The same source quoted a former Council of Agriculture director (Sun Ming-hsien) to the effect that "rice supply concerns national grain security. Taiwan could face a food crisis if it relies on foreign countries for its grain supply. More importantly, rice paddies replenish ground water. When they are gone, Taiwan could become a desert."

[58] In 2000, the average age of "farm directors" engaged in crop farming and animal husbandry was 58.6, and 85 percent of all such persons were older than 45. Since 1990, the number of farmers who are 65 years of age and above has risen by 68.7 percent (Directorate-General of Budget, Accounting and Statistics, "Agricultural, Forestry, Fishery and Husbandry Census," at http://eng.dgbas.gov.tw/lp.asp?CtNode=1632&CtUnit=782&BaseDSD=7 for further details).

[59] Males constituted 59.25 percent of the farm household population, compared with 51.13 percent for the total population (Directorate-General of Budget,

farm population were lower than among other social groups.[60] Given the political parties' geographical affiliations — political and economic — the regional implications of WTO accession deserve attention as well: in 2000, 78 percent of farms were located in central and southern Taiwan, compared with only 17 percent in the north and a mere 5 percent in the east.

On the eve of WTO accession, crop farming remained the single most important agricultural activity in Taiwan, accounting for about 45 percent of total value output. Next in importance were animal husbandry (30 percent) and fishing (25 percent). Forestry was of negligible importance. In value terms, crop cultivation was dominated by fruit farming, followed by vegetable and rice growing.[61] However, data from the 2000 Agricultural, Forestry, Fishery and Husbandry Census show that rice farming was still the single most important employment activity among Taiwan's farmers, followed by fruit and vegetable cultivation.[62] Concealed in these estimates is the finding that only 18 percent of farm households were engaged full-time in agriculture. Of the 82 percent that pursued farming on a part-time basis, the overwhelming

Accounting and Statistics, "Agricultural, Forestry, Fishery and Husbandry Census," at http://eng.dgbas.gov.tw/lp.asp? CtNode=1632&CtUnit=782&BaseDSD=7 for further details; Council for Economic Planning and Development, *Taiwan Statistical Data Book 2002* (Taipei, 2004), p. 22.

[60] 10.49 percent (but 5.49 percent for males, 16.02 percent for females). In addition, about one-third of men and women in the farm household population had received only primary school self education. Ibid.

[61] Council of Agriculture (Republic of China, Executive Yuan), *Basic Agricultural Statistics*, at http://stat.coa.gov.tw/dba-as/english/as_root.htm (accessed June 22, 2006).

[62] 43.9 percent of farm households engaged in rice cultivation, compared with 18.9 percent and 13.95 percent in fruit and vegetable cultivation respectively. Only 2.39 percent of farm households were engaged in raising livestock and poultry, although these activities contributed a disproportionately-higher share of farm value-output, highlighting the higher levels of average labor productivity associated with them. The Census was undertaken by the Directorate-General of Budget, Accounting and Statistics (DGBAS) (for details, see www.dgbas.gov.tw/census~n/one/agr_ total89en.htm).

majority — some 89 percent — picked non-agricultural activities as their main source of employment.[63]

All these factors posed major challenges for Taiwan's agriculture in the wake of WTO accession. The existence of a poorly-educated and aging agricultural labor force militates against efficiency improvements in farming. Part-time farmers are less likely to undertake capital and human investment in activities that typically account for no more than 20 percent of their time and effort. There is also a perception that farmers in central and southern Taiwan, where agricultural production is concentrated, are resistant to technological change and other forms of farm modernization.[64] Finally, a structural aspect of Taiwan's farming — its tiny scale — deserves mention. In 2000, 721,161 farm households cultivated an arable area of 851,000 hectares, generating an average farm size of a mere 1.18 hectares.[65] In the face of foreign competition based on highly-efficient, capital-intensive practices, farming on such a small scale seemed untenable. In addition, in trying to meet such challenges, policy options and adjustment mechanisms were necessarily constrained by the government's commitment to uphold WTO requirements, including the elimination of protectionist trade

[63] Directorate-General of Budget, Accounting and Statistics, "Agricultural, Forestry, Fishery and Husbandry Census," at http://eng.dgbas.gov.tw/lp.asp?CtNode=1632&CtUnit=782&BaseDSD=7 for further details. The onset of a severe economic recession in 2001 was an added complication for Taiwan. With unemployment running at more than 5 percent, instead of being able to reduce farm employment in 2002 (20,000 farmers had been expected to leave the land), the government had to accommodate a return to the countryside of some 29,000 workers. See also Lin Shiang Neng, "The Prospects of Agricultural Development after the Accession to WTO (2)," at http://www.npf.org.tw/PUBLICATION/TE/092/TE-R-092-008.htm.

[64] E.g., see Kevin Chen in *Taipei Times*, November 26, 2002, p. 10.

[65] Directorate-General of Budget, Accounting and Statistics, "Agricultural, Forestry, Fishery and Husbandry Census," at http://eng.dgbas.gov.tw/lp.asp?CtNode=1632&CtUnit=782&BaseDSD=7 for further details. The same source shows that by 2003 the average farm size had fallen to 1.16 ha.

barriers, the removal of import bans in place of import quotas, and the implementation of tariff reductions.[66]

There was widespread agreement that, within the agricultural sector, the group likely to be most severely affected by Taiwan's WTO accession would be the 317,000 households engaged in rice farming.[67] Before Taiwan joined the WTO, rice cultivation was inefficient, characterized by its small scale, attendant high costs, and lack of international competitiveness. Its survival under such conditions had been mainly attributable to the government's willingness to restrict imports, provide guaranteed prices to rice producers,[68] and even to facilitate sizable rice exports.[69] Such was the background against which predictions were made that the rice-sown area might contract by between 30,000 and 50,000 hectares in the wake of WTO accession.

---

[66] By the end of 2002, an import ban on 23 items had been replaced by import quotas, and some 90 percent of agricultural products consumed in Taiwan were opened to imports; price support subsides were cut; and tariffs on farm imports were reduced to 14.1 percent, compared with 20.02 percent in 2001 (Government Information Office website, www.gio.gov.tw/taiwan-website/5-gp/q&a/page_ 08.htm [accessed October 2002]; Lin Shiang Neng. "The Prospects of Agricultural Development after the Accession to WTO (2)," at http://www.npf.org.tw/PUBLICATION/ TE/092/TE-R-092-008.htm).

[67] By the terms of its WTO accession, Taiwan undertook to permit rice imports on the basis of a tariff-free minimum market access quota of 144,720 tonnes (brown rice equivalent), or about 8 percent of domestic consumption during the base-year period of 1990–1992. Imports would be raised by 2 percent per year until restrictions had been entirely eliminated. See Sophia Huang, "Taiwan's Trade Barriers to Recede with WTO Accession in Sight," Economic Research Service, *Agricultural Outlook* (November 2001).

[68] Domestic prices were far higher than international prices. E.g., in 1998–2000, the average farm-gate price of local non-glutinous rice was 18.8 yuan/kg., whereas retail prices of polished rice were between NT$ 29 and NT$ 34. By contrast, the international price (FOB) of Thai rice was just NT$ 6/kg. Council of Agriculture, *Daomi yinying duice* (Rice Policies) (Taipei: Council of Agriculture, Executive Yuan, August 2001), p. 1.

[69] In 2000, over 166,000 tonnes of cereals (overwhelmingly rice) were exported, earning Taiwan US$ 491.8 million. Council of Agriculture (Republic of China, Executive Yuan), *Basic Agricultural Statistics*, at http://stat.coa.gov.tw/dba_as/english/as_root.htm (accessed June 26, 2006).

Table 8.7 Rice Production in Taiwan

	Total output (brown rice) ('000 tonnes)	Total sown area ('000 ha.)	Average yield (kg/ha.)
1995	1,686.5	363.5	4,640
1996	1,577.3	347.8	4,536
1997	1,662.7	364.2	4,565
1998	1,489.4	357.7	4,164
1999	1,558.6	353.1	4,414
2000	1,540.1	339.6	4,535
1998–2000 average	1,529.4	350.1	4,368
2001	1,396.3	331.6	4,210
2002	1,460.7	306.8	4,760
2003	1,338.3	272.1	4,918
2001–2003 average	1,398.4	303.5	4,608

Source: Council for Economic Planning and Development, *Taiwan Statistical Data Book 2002* (Taipei, 2004), p. 85.

Table 8.7 summarizes rice production in Taiwan on the eve and in the aftermath of joining the WTO.

The figures suggest that against the background of an already-declining trend in both total output and sown area since 1997, WTO membership had a further significant impact on Taiwan's rice economy.[70] Against the baseline average (1998–2000), total sown area contracted by almost 47 million hectares during the next three years (2001–2003), while total production declined by 131 million tonnes (brown rice equivalent). It is interesting that between 1998–2000 and 2001–2003, the rice sown area fell by 13.3 percent, whereas the contraction in total output was about 8.5 percent. In other words, average yields improved by almost 5.5 percent. To what extent the rise in land productivity was attributable to efficiency improvements associated with WTO membership deserves further consideration.

[70] Note, however, that after joining the WTO, Japan became a new outlet for Taiwan's rice: see Central News Agency (Taipei), November 14, 2003, which reported a preliminary agreement whereby Japan would import Taiwan rice.

As early as April 2002, rice imports had already forced a major contraction in the rice-sown area.[71] Rice producers' initial response was to reduce prices, although reports spoke of considerable price instability as a result of farmers' confusion about what constituted a "fair price."[72] The government, meanwhile, undertook to buy up unsold locally-produced rice at a "reasonable" price, although such price-support measures were not wholly successful. In November 2003, some 150 rice farmers gathered outside the Legislative Yuan and the Council of Agriculture to protest low government purchase prices for rice and to demand increased cash subsidies.[73] To what extent the agreement reached with the WTO in July 2004, providing for cuts in domestic farm production subsidies, will affect Taiwan's rice economy remains to be seen.[74]

Rice farming is not the only activity that has been affected by the WTO membership. Table 8.8 highlights some of the adjustments that have taken place in other branches of agriculture before and after 2001.[75]

The declining production of grains, other than rice, was in evidence for some years before Taiwan joined the world trading

---

[71] *Taipei Times,* April 12, 2002 stated that 100,000 ha. of rice fields had been left fallow, and by July, some 70,000 tonnes of rice had been purchased from the U.S., Japan, Thailand, and Australia (*Taipei Times*, September 26, 2002). It was also reported that, in March 2002, 300 groups representing rice farmers and rice millers had set up a "Taiwan Rice Development Association" – a "self-help organization" designed to help them adjust to WTO membership (*Taipei Times*, April 12, 2002).

[72] *Taipei Times,* September 26, 2002. Import prices varied from NT$ 49/kg (Thai rice) to NT$ 250/kg (Japanese rice). Domestic rice typically retailed at NT $32–36/kg.

[73] The farmers claimed that rice-growing costs were NT$ 23/kg, compared with the government purchase price of NT$ 16.6/kg (*Taipei Times,* November 1, 2003). The farmers were quoted as complaining that "2 kilos of rice is selling for less than a packet of cigarettes. Half a kilo isn't worth a marinated egg."

[74] *Taipei Times,* August 2, 2004.

[75] It would be facile merely to assume that post-2000 changes simply, or necessarily, reflect the impact of WTO accession. A finding that recurs throughout this chapter is that changes occurring in recent years were already under way in the 1990s. In Taiwan's case, the onset of an economic recession in 2001 was a major complicating factor.

Table 8.8 The Changing Profile of Farm Production in Taiwan (1995–2003)

	Coarse grains							
	TOTAL	Sweet potatoes	Maize*	Sugar cane**	Fruit	Vege- tables	Flowers and plants***	Hogs
1995–1997 average	753.9	202.5	369.5	4,251.3	2,513.8	3,013.8	124.5	1,427.2
1998–2000 average	511.5	201.2	207.7	3,236.5	2,491.6	3,229.2	117.8	1,064.5
2001–2003 average	464.6	193.3	174.3	1,949.7	2,695.6	3,200.4	111.5	1,124.6

Notes: * Includes maize for food and animal feed.
** Refined sugar cane.
*** Excl. orchids – figures in million dozens.
Except for flowers and plants, all figures in '000 tonnes.
Source: Taiwan Provincial Government, Department of Agriculture and Forestry, *Taiwan Agricultural Yearbook*.

body, and has continued, albeit at a decelerating rate, since 2001. Taiwan was once one of the world's main producers and exporters of sugar in the 1950s and 1960s, generating an output of over 1 million tonnes on its 100,000 hectares of sown area. Under the pressures of industrialization and falling international prices, the sown area had fallen by almost two-thirds by 2000. This downward trend continued and by 2003 less than 30,000 hectares were planted (most of it controlled by the Taiwan Sugar Corporation).[76] Trade liberalization has, meanwhile, made Taiwan a free market for almost all fruits and vegetables.[77] Table 8.8 highlights the continued buoyancy of vegetable production. As for fruit, although imports

[76] Sown-area estimates are available in Council for Economic Planning and Development, *Taiwan Statistical Data Book 2002* (Taipei, 2004), p. 88.

[77] The exceptions are young coconut, oriental pears, pomelos, dried longan, and longan pulp, bananas, pineapple, mangoes, and persimmons, all of which remained subject to TRQs. The most important vegetable subject to import restrictions was dried shiitake mushrooms (the subject of a trade dispute between China and Japan in 2001).

were expected to depress the prices of locally-produced goods, production has risen, with the output of both citrus and other varieties reaching peak levels in 2003.[78] Finally, despite the potential vulnerability of high-cost livestock production to overseas competition, no major branch of animal husbandry seems to have suffered unduly as a result of foreign competition in the aftermath of WTO accession.[79]

From more detailed annual data in Table 8.9, I have tried to investigate the extent to which recent changes in domestic farm production are reflected in Taiwan's foreign trade in agricultural goods.

From these figures, it is possible to calculate Taiwan's changing agricultural trade balance as shown in Table 8.10.

Overall, Taiwan's farm trade balance showed a modest improvement in the three years after 2000, although it remained in substantial deficit due mainly to sizable imports of cereals.[80] But it is noteworthy that recent changes have reflected trends that were already in evidence after the mid-1990s. Disaggregated data highlight important changes affecting trade in specific farm activities, as Taiwan's farmers sought to shift production toward higher-value activities in which they enjoyed a comparative advantage (not least, consumer-ready farm and horticultural products).[81]

---

[78] Star performers were pineapples and persimmons; major losers were apples and grapefruits. In January 2004, it was reported that the Taiwan External Trade Development Council would intensify its efforts to promote the production and export of high-value fruits (e.g., wax apples). See *Taipei Times,* January 7, 2004.

[79] The production (by implication, sown area) adjustments referred to here can usefully be examined in relation to the changing structure of relative prices in Taiwan. An index of wholesale prices (2001=100) shows the following index numbers for 2003: all agriculture, 106.74; farm crops, 100.29; forestry, 115.96; livestock, 120.63; and fisheries, 104.09. Council of Agriculture (Republic of China, Executive Yuan), *Basic Agricultural Statistics,* at http://stat.coa.gov.tw/dba_as/english/as_root.htm (accessed June 22, 2006).

[80] In 2003, cereal imports accounted for 52 percent of total crop imports (and 25 percent of the value of such imports).

[81] Disaggregated data also show a 150-percent rise in the value of exports of livestock, poultry, meat, and offal. But this likely reflects a recovery from the depressed levels of production associated with the serious outbreak of foot-and-mouth disease in Taiwan in 1997.

Table 8.9 Taiwan's Agricultural Foreign Trade

EXPORTS					
	Total	Crop farming	Livestock	Fisheries	Forestry
1995–97	1,694.0	689.2	403.0	416.9	184.9
average	(5,038.2)	(796.1)	(2,630.5)	(1,356.4)	(255.2)
1998–2000	1,581.0	768.6	223.6	454.3	134.5
average	(3,179.0)	(674.3)	(1,263.8)	(1,079.6)	(131.2)
2001–2003	1,720.6	849.4	206.5	552.7	111.9
average	(3,139.0)	(670.0)	(1,131.6)	(1,226.5)	(111.1)
IMPORTS					
1995–97	20,143.0	13,679.2	838.0	511.3	5114.5
average	(9,893.9)	(5,419.9)	(1,938.9)	(690.1)	(1,845.0)
1998–2000	17,992.7	12,136.6	986.1	397.5	4472.5
average	(7,671.8)	(4,311.0)	(1,619.1)	(577.9)	(1,163.8)
2001–2003	18,081.9	12,874.9	841.2	396.8	3,969.0
average	(7,237.5)	(4,255.5)	(1,558.9)	(499.7)	(923.2)

Notes: Output shown as '000 tonnes; export value (US$ m.) given in parentheses.
Source: Taiwan Provincial Government, Department of Agriculture and Forestry, *Taiwan Agricultural Yearbook*.

Space constraints preclude a detailed consideration of changes in living standards in Taiwan's farm sector. However, an analysis of farmers' price terms of trade is useful. At the most general level, evidence suggests improvements in the terms of trade between 2000 and 2003.[82] But, at a more disaggregated level, there are some telling indicators of deteriorating conditions facing some groups of farmers. For example, the Council of Agriculture shows that, alongside a rise of 2.6 percent in the average price of daily necessities during 2001–2003, prices received by crop farmers fell by 4.6 percent – and

[82] The general index of prices received by farmers was 104 in 2003 (2000=100), while that of prices paid by farmers was 103. Calculated from Council of Agriculture (Republic of China, Executive Yuan), *Basic Agricultural Statistics*, at http://stat.coa.gov.tw/dba_as/english/as_root.htm (accessed June 22, 2006).

Table 8.10 Taiwan's Agricultural Trade Balance

	TRADE BALANCE (EXPORTS MINUS IMPORTS +/−)				
1995–97 average	(−4,855.7)	(−4,623.8)	(+691.6)	(+666.3)	(−1,589.8)
1998–2000 average	(−4,492.8)	(−3,636.7)	(−355.3)	(+501.7)	(−1,032.6)
2001–2003 average	(−4,098.5)	(−3,585.5)	(−427.3)	(+726.9)	(−812.1)

All figures in US$ m.

by 3.5 percent for livestock farmers. The Council of Agriculture data show that, in contrast to a slight rise in per capita non-farm income during this period, farmers' average income fell marginally. In 2003, farm income was about 3 percent lower than the peak 1999 level; expressed as a proportion of non-farm income, it was almost 5 percentage points lower than its highest relative level in 1995. Such figures take no account of the differentiated effect of the income decline among different farming occupations.

CONCLUSION — DUAL WTO ACCESSION AND CROSS-STRAIT AGRICULTURAL TRADE

The increased exposure of China and Taiwan to international competition as a result of their dual accession to the WTO poses many challenges to their respective agricultural sectors. Ultimately, the most important benefit of their WTO membership is the impetus that it may give to agricultural restructuring and intensified economic reform. The direct gains reflect the orthodox dictates of the principle of comparative advantage and the shift from lower-return, land-intensive farm operations toward higher-return, labor-intensive activities. In China's case, if WTO membership facilitates more exports of non-agricultural — but not necessarily non-rural — labor-intensive products, the associated process of industrial restructuring may generate new job opportunities, and thereby enhance the transfer of labor displaced from farming.[83] However, the sheer scale of China's farm population, the existence of up to 150 million surplus farm workers, and the high level of discontent felt by farmers subject to economic exploitation whose incomes have increasingly fallen behind those of other groups, are factors that also highlight the dangers that WTO membership might bring, if it causes an intensification of such problems.

In Taiwan, the threats posed by the negative consequences of WTO membership are less urgent. Compared with the mainland, Taiwan is not only small, but also enjoys higher levels of social and economic development. For example, in 2001, Taiwan's farm population was 3.69 million. In China, only two provinces — Tibet and Qinghai — had agricultural populations that were smaller than this.[84] In the same year, rough calculations suggest that the GDP of Taiwan's primary sector was about the same as that of Yunnan, around 70 percent of that of Fujian, and one-third of the corresponding figure for Shandong (the Chinese province with the highest primary sector GDP).[85] Such comparisons lend a useful perspective to this chapter's analysis, although not to the extent of suggesting that the agricultural implications of WTO accession for Taiwan are negligible. The experiences of South Korea and Japan offer evidence

[83] Such an argument must be treated cautiously. With 150 million surplus farm workers, a rapid rise in food and other agricultural imports could impose an unsustainable burden of adjustment on farmers, whose alternative employment opportunities may become increasingly-constrained. Note that the success of any program of large-scale labor reallocation will demand active and costly government intervention in order to coordinate and accommodate the changes.

[84] See Council of Agriculture (Republic of China, Executive Yuan), *Basic Agricultural Statistics,* at http://stat.coa.gov.tw/dba_as/english/as_root.htm (accessed June 22, 2006) and Ministry of Agriculture, *Zhongguo nongye nianjian, 2002* (Chinese Agricultural Yearbook, 2002) (Beijing: Nongye chubanshe, 2003), p. 141. The agricultural populations of Beijing, Tianjin, and Shanghai were about the same as that of the whole of Taiwan!

[85] I made these calculations using the World Atlas method on the basis of primary sector data in the Council for Economic Planning and Development, *Taiwan Statistical Data Book 2002* (Taipei, 2004) and the National Bureau of Statistics, *Zhongguo tongji nianjian, 2002* (China Statistical Yearbook, 2002) (Beijing: Zhongguo tongji chubanshe, 2002).

to the contrary, as does the attention that the government on Taiwan has given to agricultural issues in recent years in the face of farmer protests against deteriorating conditions supposedly attributable to the impact of trade liberalization. In September 2004, President Chen Shui-bian's announcement that the Council of Agriculture was to be upgraded to full ministerial status in order to promote "sustainable [agricultural] development" highlighted, more than symbolically, the importance that the government still attached to the farm sector.[86]

The nature of the impact on agriculture from joining the WTO was foreseeable, if not quantifiable, in both China and Taiwan. A significant finding of this chapter is that planners in both Beijing and Taipei sought, through their respective policies, to anticipate the impact on the farm sector of WTO accession — hence, for example, the price and tariff adjustments undertaken by the Chinese government in advance of joining the WTO. A plethora of predictive analysis and guidance issued by the Council of Agriculture similarly demonstrates the concern of the government in Taiwan about possible economic and social consequences of membership.

More recent initiatives by the Taiwan government have sought to accommodate some of the pressures of WTO membership. For example, an important stabilization measure was the establishment in 2003 of a NT$ 300-billion special budgetary fund designed to help Taiwan farmers who have been adversely affected by agricultural imports.[87] This was in addition to the adoption of the Agricultural Financial Law (July 2003) and the proposed establishment of a national agricultural bank to help meet farmers' financial needs.[88] In January 2004, it was also announced

[86] Cf. also Premier Yu Shyi-kun's description of agriculture as the "mother of industry" and his commitment to promote agricultural development through "biotechnology ... farm tourism and [more effective] market strategies" (*Taipei Times*, September 21, 2004).

[87] *Taipei Times*, February 23, 2003.

[88] Note, too, an increased emphasis on "agri-tourism" and "recreational agriculture" as new income-earning outlets for farmers in the post-WTO environment. A more critical note was sounded in a comment by Tu Jenn-Hwa (National Taiwan University), who pointed out that notwithstanding government appeals to Taiwan farmers to innovate in anticipation of WTO entry, the share of the Council of

that additional funds of NT$ 23.5 billion would be made available for compensation against losses incurred by farmers as a result of WTO entry.[89]

The manipulation and disregard of official rules are other ways in which WTO members have sometimes tried to combat the negative consequences of accession and to protect their own self-interests. In this regard, the findings of the U.S. government's two annual reports on China's WTO compliance are quite revealing.[90] Both acknowledge China's timely implementation of tariff reductions with respect to farm products, thereby facilitating wider market access for U.S. farmers. But other actions taken — in some cases, not taken — by the Chinese government were blamed for raising barriers to such access. These included the "capricious practices" of Chinese customs and quarantine officials; recourse to inappropriate biotechnology regulations; failure to remove trade-inhibiting and scientifically unsustainable sanitary and phytosanitary measures; and the maintenance of "a generally opaque regulatory regime." Even allowing for some progress in resolving such problems during 2004, it is likely that issues such as these will continue to bedevil China's trade in agricultural products with the U.S. and other countries in the foreseeable future.[91]

Agriculture's budget devoted to agricultural R&D had fallen from 7.3 percent (1994) to 4 percent (1998) and an expected 3.7 percent in 2003 (*Taipei Times*, November 4, 2002).

[89] *Taipei Times*, February 10, 2004.

[90] U.S. Trade Representative, *Report to Congress on China's WTO Compliance*, 2003/2004, at www.ustr.gov/assets/Document_Library/reports_Publications/2003/asset_upload_file425_4313.pdf and www.ustr.gov/assets/Document_Library/reports_Publications/2004/asset_upload_file281_6986.pdfWorld_Regions/North_Asia/China/ (accessed May 22, 2005).

[91] Written testimony presented by the U.S.-China Business Council to the Office of the U.S. Trade Representative (September 2004) noted that "[m]any tariff rate quotas (TRQs) continued to be monopolized by state-owned trading companies, particularly in agriculture, despite China's WTO commitments to license and make allotments available to non-state traders. ... [C]ontinuing use of sanitary and phytosanitary standards in agricultural commodity trade as a non-tariff trade barrier ... raised very serious concerns over the past year," at www.uschina.org/public/documents/2004/09/tpsc_testimony.pdf (accessed May 22, 2005).

Empirical evidence presented in this chapter highlights the considerable impact, now and in the future, of WTO accession on the farm sectors in China and Taiwan. In interpreting such evidence, there are two important qualifications to make. The first, quite simply, is that an assessment of the full impact of WTO membership, even several years after accession, remains premature. Since December–January 2000–2001, both China and Taiwan have been in a transitional, adjustment phase of their membership, and only after they have been exposed to the full force of international competition will the true extent of the influence on their farm sectors become apparent.[92] The second is that tempting though it is to view farm performance and policies in China and Taiwan through the prism of the WTO, other issues have been equally instrumental in bringing about change.[93] In short, the analysis of the impact on farming of WTO accession should not succumb to the false logic of *proper hoc, ergo hoc,* and merely assume that changes that have taken place since joining the WTO are attributable to membership.

Finally, what of the impact of dual accession on cross-strait agricultural trade and cooperation? Traditionally, Taiwan's farm trade has been dominated by the U.S. and Japan. On the eve of the WTO accession, the U.S. was already the main source of imported

---

[92] Thus, "[t]he full effect of Taiwan's WTO accession will not be felt until at least after 2004, when some products that are under TRQs will be fully liberalized. In the short run, quotas on many products will restrict their import growth potential." See Sophia Huang, "Taiwan's Trade Barriers to Recede with WTO Accession in Sight," Economic Research Service, *Agricultural Outlook* (November 2001). Huang's comment applied equally to China.

[93] In China, measures implemented in 2004 — tax cuts (including the eventual abolition of the general agricultural tax), the unprecedented extension of *direct* subsidies to grain farmers, grain market liberalization, and more effective controls over land transfers — are all primarily aimed at addressing continuing social malaise, rather than the economic problems associated with WTO membership.

agricultural products for several decades,[94] whereas Taiwan's chief export destination for farm goods was Japan.[95] By contrast, the government maintained strict controls over farm imports from the mainland until January 2002, when the Bureau of Foreign Trade issued a list of 2,126 items (including 901 agricultural products) that were added to the list of goods that could be legally imported from China.[96]

Since the late 1980s, cross-strait interactions have added a critical dimension to Taiwan's external economic relations, leading Taiwan to become increasingly trade-dependent on China. Between 1990 and 2000, Taiwan's total trade dependency ratio vis-à-vis the mainland more than doubled.[97] Concealed in this finding was a low import, but high export rate of dependence. Most strikingly, Taiwan's reliance on the mainland as an export market increased from 6.5 percent (1990) to 17.9 percent (2001).[98]

[94] Taiwan first became a significant importer of farm products in the 1970s. In 1979, the value of farm goods imported from the U.S. exceeded US$ 1 b. for the first time; it exceeded US$2 b. in 1993, and reached almost US$3 b. in 1996. In 1997–2000, the average annual value of farm imports from the U.S. was US$2.1 b., accounting for around one-third of the total. In 2000, Taiwan was the fifth-largest market for U.S. agricultural products, after Japan, Canada, Mexico, and South Korea. See Sophia Huang, "Taiwan's Trade Barriers to Recede with WTO Accession in Sight," Economic Research Service, *Agricultural Outlook* (November 2001).

[95] Japan accounted for 33.5 percent of Taiwan's agricultural exports, followed by Hong Kong (24.5 percent) and the U.S. (12.4 percent) (*Taipei Times*, November 29, 2002).

[96] The final list embraced almost 5,700 products, or 44 percent of all those under Taiwan's tariff schedule. See Nicholas R. Lardy, *Integrating China into the Global Economy* (Washington, DC: Brookings Institution Press, 2002), p. 166.

[97] From 4.2 percent to 12.1 percent, according to estimates of cross-strait trade published by the Mainland Affairs Council (MAC) in Taipei, and global foreign trade figures provided by the Department of Statistics (Ministry of Finance). See www.mac.gov.tw/english/index1-e.htm for the MAC data (accessed May 22, 2005); also Council for Economic Planning and Development, *Taiwan Statistical Data Book 2002* (Taipei, 2004), p. 210.

[98] See www.mae.gov.tw/english/index1-e.htm (accessed May 22, 2005). Also Council for Economic Planning and Development, *Taiwan Statistical Data Book 2002* (Taipei, 2004), p. 210.

There is strong prima facie evidence that since accession to the WTO, Taiwan's trade dependence on the mainland has intensified. In 2004, for example, China accounted for 18 percent of Taiwan's global trade — a rise of six percentage points since 2001. During the same period, Taiwan's bilateral export dependence increased by almost eight percentage points to reach 25.8 percent. Meanwhile, the share of Taiwan's imports originating from China also rose sharply: from 5.5 percent (2001) to 9.9 percent (2004). But to what extent Taiwan's increasing trade, and especially export dependency, should be interpreted as having strengthened or weakened Taiwan's economic vulnerability vis-à-vis the mainland is less unambiguously answered. The safest observation is that they highlight the continuing process of economic integration between the two sides.

Unfortunately, I have been unable to find comprehensive estimates of post-accession bilateral trade in agricultural products.[99] At a global level, Taiwan's agricultural trade account has consistently been in deficit since 1974. Having peaked at US$ 5.9 billion in 1997, it subsequently declined to US$ 3.8 billion in 2001. In the next two years, the farm trade deficit once again widened, increasing by almost 19 percent between 2001 and 2003. Even so, the 2003 deficit — US$ 4.54 billion — was 24 percent below the 1997 peak figure. From the same global perspective, the deterioration of China's agricultural trade account has been much more dramatic: in 2004, China recorded a farm trade deficit of US$ 5.5 billion, compared with surpluses of US$ 5.7 billion and US$ 2.5 billion in 2002 and 2003. However, the shift from surplus to deficit was less a reflection of WTO-related pressures, and more one of declining domestic grain harvests and a severe depletion of domestic grain stocks associated with quite different factors.

In terms of bilateral trade relations, late 2004 fears that Taiwan would be inundated by Chinese farm imports in the wake of WTO

[99] But *Taipei Times,* September 14, 2000, reported that in 2000 Taiwan suffered a deficit of US$ 250 million in its agricultural trade with China.

Table 8.11 Exports of Agricultural Products from Taiwan to Japan, the U.S., Hong Kong, and China

	Exports of farm products from Taiwan to the following							
	Japan		Hong Kong		United States		China	
	Export value (US$ m.)	As % value of Taiwan's total farm exports	Export value (US$ m.)	As % value of Taiwan's total farm exports	Export value (US$ m.)	As % value of Taiwan's total farm exports	Export value (US$ m.)	As % value of Taiwan's total farm exports
2001	1,020	33.6	744	24.5	376	12.4	49	1.6
2002	1,080	34.2	742	23.5	344	10.9	66	2.1
2003	1,160	37.3	585	18.8	311	10.0	170	5.4
2004 Jan.–Sept.	1,010	–	[See under China]	–	270	–	610*	–

* Incl. Hong Kong

Source: Data for 2001–2003 from Council of Agriculture;[100] data for 2004 from Central News Agency (Taipei), November 3, 2004.

[100] I am grateful to Ms. Lily Hsu (formerly director, Administrative Decision, Taipei Representative Office in the UK) for providing me with these data.

accession do not seem to have been realized.[101] As Tables 8.11 and 8.12 show, changes in farm trade between Taiwan and the mainland during 2001–2003 were characterized by rises in both exports to and imports from China. At the same time, there was quite a sharp contraction in exports of Taiwan farm products to Hong Kong in 2003.

As a result of increased shipments to the mainland, between 2001 and 2004, China rose from eighth to fourth place as an export destination for Taiwan's farm products. In 2003, the value of such shipments increased by 62 percent — the single largest rise among all Taiwan's trading partners; and, in 2004, mainland China absorbed 9.2 percent of all exports of agricultural products from Taiwan.[102] Meanwhile, concealed in the estimates shown in Table 8.12, is the finding that as a source of farm imports, China rose from seventh to fourth place between 2001 and 2003. The net outcome of the changes shown in Tables 8.11 and 8.12 was a small deterioration in the Taiwan's balance of agricultural trade vis-à-vis China.[103]

However, the evidence presented here remains inconclusive and any conclusions that are drawn from it are necessarily premature. At the time of writing, the mutual importance of both China and Taiwan as agricultural trading partners has clearly increased, although not to the extent of changing the primary geographical direction of each country's trade in farm products. As was the case before WTO accession, for example, Japan, the U.S., and Hong Kong

---

[101] Chinese sources argue that part of the reason lies in Taiwan's violation of WTO rules and its continued implementation of a discriminatory trade policy vis-à-vis the mainland. E.g., see *China Daily*, August 20, 2004, which also refers to China's determination to promote exports of competitive products, including farm goods, to Taiwan.

[102] See China News Agency, April, 29, 2005, which also noted that in 2004 Japan remained the largest market for Taiwan's farm products, accounting for 40 percent of all exports.

[103] Taiwan's trade deficit vis-à-vis the mainland rose from US$ 211 million to US$ 242 million between 2001 and 2003. During the same period, its farm trade surplus vis-à-vis China and Hong Kong fell from US$ 533 million to US$ 343 million.

Table 8.12 Imports of Agricultural Products from the U.S., Australia, Japan, Thailand, and China

	Imports of farm products to Taiwan from the following									
	United States		Australia		Japan		Thailand		Mainland China	
	Import value (US$ m.)	As % value of Taiwan's total farm imports	Import value (US$ m.)	As % value of Taiwan's total farm imports	Import value (US$ m.)	As % value of Taiwan's total farm imports	Import value (US$ m.)	As % value of Taiwan's total farm imports	Import value (US$ m.)	As % value of Taiwan's total farm imports
2001	2,420	35.3	548	8.0	432	6.3	336	4.9	260	3.3
2002	2,420	33.6	583	8.1	461	6.4	375	5.2	370	5.1
2003	2,568	33.0	529	6.8	–	–	–	-	412	5.3

Source: See Table 8.11.

remain the three largest markets for Taiwan's agricultural goods.[104] Official Chinese sources have expressed their readiness to promote cross-strait agricultural cooperation, including facilitating increased imports of Taiwan farm products. But recent reports indicate that China has used artificial barriers to impede such imports, just as it has to inhibit American imports of agricultural goods. The selective imposition of high duties has also eroded the competitiveness of Taiwan farmers in the production of some goods.[105] In fairness, Taiwan, too, has yet to permit genuinely direct trade with the mainland in some basic farm products — above all, rice. In short, there are major problems still to be overcome before the true impact on cross-strait farm trade arising from WTO membership becomes clear.

[104] Thus, Lee Chin-lung (Chairman, Council of Agriculture) said on April 29, 2005: "China is neither the biggest nor the only market for Taiwan agriculture" (China News Agency, April 29, 2005).

[105] A report of April 10, 2005 noted that "[t]he combination of high duties and Taiwan's higher labor costs means that local [i.e. Taiwan] agricultural goods are 3–5 times more expensive than similar items in Chinese stores. ... Based on its WTO commitments, China has opened its markets to 35 different kinds of fruit, but its market is still closed to 23 of the 35 from Taiwan because of quarantine issues....", at www.etaiwannews.com/Taiwan/politics/2005/04/10/1112099851.htm (accessed May 1, 2005).

Chapter

9

The Impact of the WTO on Taiwan's and China's Electronics Industries

Charles Trappey

The emergence of the electronics industry in China and Taiwan occupies a unique place in industrial history. Within less than half a century, industrial shifts and technology transfers have occurred between Asia, Europe, and America, followed by the development of global enterprises that are creating intellectual property at an unprecedented rate. The amount of money involved (upward of US$ 3 billion to construct a single 12-inch wafer fabrication facility)[1] and the strategic nature of electronic products are creating concern that China's and Taiwan's trade policies are driving the migration of technology, and are causing a threat to the manufacturing, research, and design capabilities of other countries.

China and Taiwan are taking advantage of the market forces that resulted from the WTO membership and, as a result, are adding to the global electronics supply chain through linkage, innovation,

[1] J.I. Lieberman, *White Paper: National Security Aspects of the Global Migration of the U.S. Semiconductor Industry*, Airland Subcommittee, U.S. Senate, Armed Services Committee, June 2003.

design, and the creation of intellectual property. The WTO discipline has helped Taiwan to create a knowledge-based economy, and has enabled China to work toward a future service-based economy — events that are significantly impacting global economic growth.

The direction taken by China to build an electronics infrastructure (science parks with autonomy, incentives, and services) follows the formula for building Taiwan's Hsinchu Science and Industrial Park in the early 1970s. As a result, the central control of the Chinese Communist Party over this industrial sector is experiencing a shift from the ministries to quasi-state commercial entities.[2] Electronics industry trade problems remain to be resolved both in China and Taiwan. China's value-added taxes (VAT) and standards; the closed-door approach to China's foreign direct investment in Taiwan's electronics industry; the lingering issues over direct flights; and the constrained cross-strait movement of labor information and capital, are inconsistent with the spirit and intent of the WTO.

This chapter presents the issues and the impact of the WTO on the electronics industry. The first section presents the history of the electronics industry to highlight how the WTO discipline has accelerated growth by building confidence in foreign direct investment. The second section presents the trade changes following WTO accession. Sections 3 and 4 describe the WTO issues for China and Taiwan respectively. The chapter concludes with the view that Taiwan, as a new democracy, has too many groups working against each other and, as a result, it often fails to take the steps needed to boost intellectual property protection, and to educate and to enforce the WTO discipline. China, on the other hand, has too few groups. However, these groups hold significant wealth, power, autonomy,

---

[2] C.V. Trappey, "The Vision Becomes a Reality: Interview with Dr. Shu Shen Shou," in the *Taiwan Electronics Industry* (CD-ROM), 2000. Dr. Shu was the former President of the National Tsing Hua University, Hsinchu (1970–1975), a National Science Council Commissioner that planned the Hsinchu Science Park, and Chairman of the Industrial Technology Research Institute from 1976–1987. Dr. Shu played a leading role in setting the industrial policy for Taiwan's high-tech industry. During his later years, Dr. Shu transferred the same ideas and insights to colleagues working at the National Tsing Hua University in Beijing, which created China's technology and science park policies.

and influence, which can counter the goals and objectives of the WTO. As both China and Taiwan make progress under the WTO, it is very likely that a balance among the influential groups will be achieved over time, and that China and Taiwan will emerge as the world's largest manufacturing base for the electronics industry.

THE HISTORY OF THE ELECTRONICS INDUSTRY IN CHINA AND TAIWAN

The history of the development of the electronics industries of China and Taiwan began in the 1950s when China and Taiwan were building international alliances. During the 1960s, when China underwent the Cultural Revolution, Taiwan was creating its first Original Equipment Manufacturing (OEM) factories. The 1970s were a very fortunate time for China as global markets began to open. Taiwan began to develop its own name-brand computers and to invest in larger-size electronics companies. In the 1980s, China began to attract foreign direct investment and Taiwan created its first global-scale electronic enterprises. During the 1990s, China established its first OEMs and Taiwan succeeded in completing a globally-linked and comprehensive electronics supply chain. By the year 2002, after China and Taiwan entered the WTO, the greatest changes of all began to occur. Both economies were linked through a globally-integrated supply chain. Furthermore, innovation, design, and the creation of electronics intellectual property continued to accelerate on both sides of the Taiwan Strait.

The 1950s: Building Alliances

Taiwan and China were pursuing two completely different paths of industrial development during the 1950s. China formed a critical alliance with the Soviet Union (the Treaty of Friendship, Alliance, and Mutual Assistance),[3] which strengthened transportation

[3] Ministry of Foreign Affairs, "Conclusion of the Sino-Soviet Treaty of Friendship, Alliance and Mutual Assistance," 2000, http://www.fmprc.gov.cn/eng/ziliao/3602/3604/t18011.htm (accessed October 2003).

routes, provided assistance, and offered recommendations for the restructuring of the Chinese economy,[4] with a particular emphasis on military strategy and buildup for actions against Tibet, South Korea, and Taiwan. During these early years, money was raised to buy electronics technologies that could be used to build radio broadcasting and television facilities, as well as to construct the first Chinese vacuum tube computer in 1958.[5] China's computer and overall electronics development at the time was far behind that of the USSR or the U.S. By comparison, the U.S. had already developed the high-level programming language FORTRAN in 1954, and IBM had successfully launched its first commercial computer, the 701 EDPM, which had been developed as part of the Korean War effort in 1953.[6]

Taiwan, on the other hand, was benefiting from its close ties with the U.S., which included military support to defend Taiwan during the Korean War. Aid during the 1950s amounted to over US$ 4 billion, which facilitated the development of a manufacturing and educational infrastructure.[7]

One of Taiwan's first branded electronic motor manufacturers, the Teco Electric and Machinery Company, was launched during this period. By July 1958, the National Chiao Tung University Institute of Electronics was offering a two-year graduate program leading to a Master's of Science degree in electrical engineering, while China was preoccupied with political movements. Academic institutions were closed and intellectuals were sent to the countryside. Even under these circumstances, China managed, in 1958, to launch the

---

[4] USC-UCLA Joint East Asian Studies Center, "Conversation between the Soviet Union's Joseph Stalin and China's Mao Zedong," December 16 1949, www.isop.ucla.edu/eas/documents/mao491216.htm (accessed October 2003).

[5] L.I.C. Chiu, *Development of the Electronics Industry in Mainland China* (Taipei: Council for Economic Planning and Development, Chung Hwa Institution for Economic Research, Industrial Technology Research Institute, 1991).

[6] M. Bellis, *The History of Computers, What You Need to Know About Inventors*, http://inventors.about.com/library/blcoindex.htm (accessed October 2003).

[7] PBS, *Commanding Heights, Taiwan Economics*, http://www.pbs.org/wgbh/commandingheights/lo/countries/tw/tw_economic.html (accessed October 2003).

Changhong Machinery Factory, which is China's largest color TV manufacturer today.[8]

The 1960s: The Cultural Revolution and the Rise of Taiwan's OEMs

Taiwan achieved several important milestones during the 1960s. First, in 1961, with special funding from the United Nations, the Ministry of Education opened the Telecommunication and Electronics Training Center (TETC) in Hsinchu. The TETC established the technological foundation for the electronics industry by introducing computer technology, initiating television broadcasting, and manufacturing the island's first transistors and solid-state lasers.

China was also making advancements in electronics. However, most electronics developments were military-related and associated with the growing military-industrial complex of state-owned firms. A second-generation transistor computer was built, wired and wireless communications were advancing, and technology was being transferred from the military to develop televisions, with Changhong Machinery playing a leading role. The militant phase of the Cultural Revolution that began in 1966, however, completely upset the development of the electronics industry, and it was not until after Mao Zedong's death that the electronics industry made significant gains.

During the same period, Taiwan was pursuing a market-oriented approach by creating export-processing zones to attract foreign capital and companies. A special industrial zone was set up in Kaoshiung in 1966 to facilitate the export of domestically-manufactured goods, thus reducing the trade deficit.[9] Kaoshiung Electronics Company and Phillips Taiwan set up facilities in the Hsinchu Science Park, and were the first to package integrated circuits. Although direct aid from the U.S. had ended, Taiwan received a loan of US$ 150 million from

---

[8] http://en.changhong.com/product/20020528/202_1523.jsp (accessed October 2003).

[9] M.M.K. Lin and C.V. Trappey, "The Development of Taiwan's IC Industry," *IEEE Transactions on Components, Packaging and Manufacturing Technology* 20, no. 4 (1997), 235–242.

Japan,[10] thereby creating closer cooperation with Japanese firms. Among some of the early Japanese firms to enter the Taiwan market were Panasonic and Sanyo, and shortly thereafter, electronics industrial production and exports entered a boom period, with Taiwan producing Original Equipment Manufacturing (OEM) transistor radios and color televisions for export.

Moreover, some of Taiwan's most famous brand-name appliance companies were started during the 1960s. These companies began to compete with Taiwan's long-established Tatung Company, which, during the 1950s, was exporting electric fans, and leading in the local development of rice steamers, televisions, and air conditioners. The Kolin Company that remains a leading producer of innovative household products opened its doors in Sanchung with only NT$ 2 million capital.[11] Sampo Corporation was established in 1962, starting out as a supplier of resistors and capacitors, and later manufacturing a full range of electric appliances.[12] As a result of efforts by these companies and other market innovators, the Chung Hwa Institute reported that, during the 1960s, exports of electronic products from Taiwan had surpassed the US$ 1 billion mark (see footnote 5).

The 1970s: China's Market Opening and the Emergence of Electronic Designs in Taiwan

Shortly after the end of the Cultural Revolution, China renewed efforts to build a super high-speed computer. Very important and critical changes occurred at the end of the 1970s that favorably changed the environment for foreign direct investment. China's National People's Congress opened the doors in 1979 by passing the first laws on the

---

[10] http://www.pbs.org/wgbh/commandingheights/lo/countries/tw/tw_full.html (accessed June 12, 2006).

[11] www.kolin.com.tw/english/history/index.asp (accessed October 2003).

[12] www.sampo.com.tw/english/careers/company/detail.asp?ArticleAuto=37 (accessed October 2003).

formation of joint ventures.[13] Historically, the attraction of capital to China began with the resolution of the debate within the Chinese Communist Party, which juxtaposed Mao Zedong's approach of self-reliance to the global-minded internationalist approach of Deng Xiaoping who, beginning in 1979, stressed the modernization of agriculture, defense, science and technology, and industry.[14]

Taiwan was experiencing difficult times during the 1970s as the first global oil crisis of 1973 caused a 23 percent rise in domestic prices, an inflation rate of 41 percent, and a decline in the economic growth rate to a mere 1 percent.[15] Diplomatic relations were severed between Taiwan and the U.S., but the spirit of economic cooperation was maintained with the formation of the American Institute in Taiwan (AIT), and the active involvement of the U.S.–Taiwan Business Council and the American Chamber of Commerce, which helped maintain trade and business relationships with U.S. electronics firms holding substantial investments in Taiwan.

During the 1970s, Taiwan's agricultural sector was also in decline, and although the manufacturing sector had grown into a major contributor to the economy, Taiwan's overall exports were badly hit by inflation. The government sought new ways to stimulate the economy by increasing public spending. Funding was provided to the Industrial Technology Research Institute to build the Electronic Research and Service Organization (ERSO), the launch point for the IC manufacturing industry, which provided the basic laboratories and personnel for the transfer of technology. A key milestone for ERSO was a 1976 project with RCA to transfer integrated circuit technology. The project was instrumental in demonstrating the feasibility

---

[13] V. Simone and A.T. Ferara, *The Asian Pacific Political and Economic Development in a Global Context* (White Plains, NY: Longman, 1995).

[14] I.G. Cook and Y.J. Wang, "Foreign Direct Investment in China: Patterns, Processes, and Prospects," in *Dynamic Asia: Business Trends and Economic Development in Pacific Asia*, ed. I.G. Cook, M.A. Doel, R.Y.F. Li, and Y.J. Wang (Brookfield, VT: Ashgate, 1998), 177–208.

[15] C.V. Trappey and H. Chen, "The Integrated Circuit Industry: A Technological Powerhouse," in *Made by Taiwan*, ed. Chun-Yen Chang and Po-Lung Yu (Singapore: World Scientific, 2001).

of industry and government working together to build Taiwan's electronics sector.

During 1979, regulations governing the establishment of science and industrial parks were promulgated, and the first IC industries began to build facilities in Hsinchu. Also, in this decade, Taiwan's scientists created the island's very own integrated circuit; increased the production of color televisions beyond the one million units per year mark; and established a wide range of consumer electronic-related manufacturing specialties, including watches, electric fans, rice cookers, and basic electronic components manufactured to order for a growing number of international firms. Finally, the 1970s marked the beginning of Taiwan's Original Design and Manufacturing (ODM) industry, the encouragement of small and medium enterprises, and the beginning of China's acceptance of foreign investment. Acer, entering the Taiwan market as Multitech, had started off as an electronics trader and component designer, but, by 1979, it designed and created Taiwan's first computer for mass export.

The 1980s: China Attracts FDI and Taiwan Builds Science Parks and Global Enterprises

The 1980s marked the emergence of China's electronics industry as a market force. Changes started across the board, led largely by the economic reforms of Deng Xiaoping. Under Deng's leadership, the pace of technology transfer, particularly for information, electronics, and communications technology, moved at an unprecedented speed. In these years, China also benefited from foreign investment. Simone and Ferara (see footnote 13) stress the importance of foreign direct investment in boosting technology transfer. Woolridge[16] shows that China was the world's largest recipient of foreign direct investment (FDI) during the 1980s.

With this support, China began to transfer technologies from military complexes, opening up defense science techniques to the

[16] A. Woolridge, "Survey of Multinationals: Managing in the Frontier," *The Economist*, June 24, 1995.

public, in order to restructure the electronics research base toward the development of commercial products. Shanghai and Beijing were established as electronics centers and special economic zones were opened in Shenzhen, Zhuhai, and Shantou. According to Cook and Wang (see footnote 14), China adopted a progressive approach to bring in foreign capital, focusing initially on the creation of joint ventures to attract capital from overseas Chinese in Hong Kong and Macau. A new regulation of the China State Council, the Provisions for the Encouragement of Foreign Investment, made the operation of foreign joint ventures more transparent and allowed foreign-invested companies to operate with greater autonomy from the local bureaucracies. In 1988, with the issuance of the Provisions for the Encouragement of Investment by Taiwan Compatriots, plans were made to allow capital flow from Taiwan.[17]

As a result of these provisions, the door was open for the inflow of foreign capital and technology to build the Chinese electronics industry. Some of the first results included the creation of the Galaxy high-speed calculator, the production of the Great Wall computer (1,000 units in 1987), and the acceleration of television production that was at the level of 10 million units in 1986. By 1988, the production of televisions exceeded 200 million units, as China became the third-largest television manufacturer in the world (see footnote 5). Large foreign investors were drawn to the market, with Philips, NEC, and Motorola setting up IC manufacturing facilities in 1989.

The end of the 1980s marked a turning point for China's electronics industry that had entered into a new age of openness and international trade, and the government began its first negotiations with the members of the General Agreements on Tariff and Trade (GATT).

During the 1980s, Taiwan was affected by the global recession, a decline in diplomatic ties, a fall in demand for its products, and a decrease in private investment. Despite these bad times, Taiwan made its greatest strategic jump forward into IC manufacturing and design.

[17] "Mainland Expands Protection for Taiwanese Investors," *Economic Daily News*, December 13, 1999.

With government backing, the United Microelectronics Corporation (UMC) was established, representing a first step in moving the electronics industry from IC packaging into IC manufacturing. Taiwan continued to adjust its industrial structure by promoting the information and electronics industry through incentives and regulations. For example, the regulation on "Encouraging Investment Conditions and Requirements" had a positive effect on the investment climate and helped to build the electronics sector, in spite of the global recession.

When the U.S. telephone monopoly was dismantled, the newly-formed regional companies began to send orders to Taiwan firms to manufacture telephone parts and telecommunications equipment. Orders from the "Baby Bell" companies helped UMC and others in the Science Park to survive a difficult start-up period during adverse economic conditions. The Taiwan Semiconductor Manufacturing Company (TSMC), established in 1987, began the island's first IC design business and created a dedicated semiconductor foundry industry. With the formation of UMC and TSMC, the foundation for the IC industry was completed. Taiwan had become a growing global electronics force, making computers, home appliances, PC peripherals, and communications devices, with the combined ability to create products that boosted demand and increased overall IC production.

Further, the successful manufacture of video recorders, telephones, digital switchboards, electronic calculators (exceeding 1 million units in 1981), hard disk drives, and printers created greater interest in the emerging Science Park, not only increasing foreign investment, but also attracting large numbers of well-trained scientists and engineers, educated abroad and living overseas, back to Taiwan.

Finally, during the 1980s, Taiwan became the world's sixth-largest computer producer. Computers produced in Taiwan at this time included the MR-10 super mini-computer and the 80386 minicomputer. Kimpo became the world's largest contract manufacturer of handheld calculators, and the company's largest shareholder launched Quanta Computer. Other companies launched were MiTAC International Corporation, founded in 1982, which began as an exclusive manufacturer of PCs. Acer (Stan Shih), Mitac (Mathew Miao), Quanta (Barry Lam), UMC (Robert Tsao), and TSMC

(Morris Chang) became the bellwethers establishing the direction of the Taiwan electronics industry for the 1990s.

The 1990s: The Rise of China's OEMs and Taiwan's Global Supply Chain

During the 1990s, Taiwan aggressively expanded the electronics industry through technology transfer and by adding support industries to the supply chain. By the end of the 1990s, Taiwan had achieved a comprehensive domestic electronics industry with a fully-integrated supply chain covering design houses, masking firms, IC fabrication plants, wafer manufacturers, chemical suppliers, packaging plants, testing firms, substrate providers, and lead-frame manufacturers. The industry had reached the point of self-sustainability, in terms of research capability, as well as the ability to generate intellectual property. The number of managers who returned to the Hsinchu Science Park increased from 422 in 1980 to 4,108 in 2000. The returnees were mostly educated abroad, bilingual, and holding masters and Ph.D degrees.[18] The government established three new priorities for technology transfer during the 1990s: opto-electronics (light emitting diodes [LED] and components, displays, storage, and communications), printing technology (laser, fax, and printers), and projection display technologies.

By the end of the 1990s, investment commitments had reached almost US$ 80 billion, setting a record for growth and occupying all of the land in the Hsinchu Industrial Park. The IC firms began planning and building facilities in the Tainan science-based industrial park.

China began to close the gap with Taiwan for OEM appliance manufacturing through Hong Kong trade during the 1990s. The emphasis was placed on tape recorders, televisions, calculators, and electronic components. While Taiwan was making great strides

[18] C.Y. Chang and P.L. Yu, "The Development of Taiwan's IC Industry: An Overview," in *Made by Taiwan*, ed. Chun-Yen Chang and Po-Lung Yu (Singapore: World Scientific, 2001).

in advanced research and development for integrated circuits and optoelectronics, the trend of outsourcing OEM manufacturing to China grew as the output of Taiwan's home appliance industry began to decline. The shift of OEM manufacturing from Taiwan to China, particularly for electronic components and products, was accelerated by investments from Taiwan's electronic companies that were seeking lower labor costs and larger markets during the 1990s. The investments continued to grow and, by 2002, the year of WTO membership, the annual investment flow from Taiwan to China into the electronics sector had nearly doubled.[19] The investment phenomena, caused in part by the OEM electronics manufacturing shift, may be thought of as the natural development of the Chinese and Taiwan electronics industry over the past decade. Nonetheless, as shown by the investment statistics, WTO membership certainly served as a catalyst for the merger of the electronics manufacturing base.

2000 and Beyond: Linkage, Innovation, Design, and the Creation of Intellectual Property

Taiwan's objective for the next ten years is to foster the design and creation of branded intellectual property (silicon software or Sci-Soft) based on Taiwan's existing strengths in the areas of hardware and manufacturing of electronic components (silicon hardware or Sci-Hard).[20] Taiwan has developed one of the most comprehensive semiconductor supply chains in the world, with an infrastructure that includes design houses, semiconductor and other component manufacturing facilities, masking process plants, testing companies, and a wide range of component packaging lines (see Figure 9.1).

---

[19] Ministry of Economic Affairs, Investment Commission, "Statistics on Overseas Chinese and Foreign Investment, Outward Investment, and Indirect Mainland Investment, the Republic of China," June 2003.

[20] C.Y. Chang and C.V. Trappey, "The National Sci-Soft Project," *Applied Surface Science*, no. 216 (2003), 2–7.

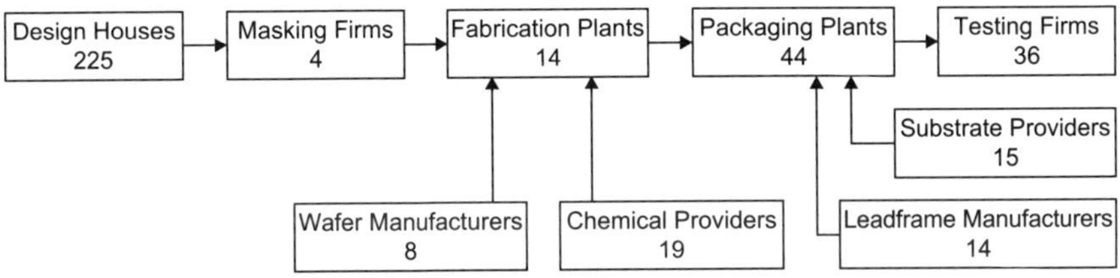

Figure 9.1 Taiwan's development of a comprehensive semiconductor supply chain[21]

Companies comprising the semiconductor supply chain are globally-linked and are integral to the worldwide production of electronic parts, components, and equipment. The state of development for the semiconductor industry has reached a high level of efficiency, with Taiwan's foundries ranked first among competitors and holding 76 percent of the global market share. Fabless design houses are ranked second (after the U.S.) and hold a 20 percent market share, while testing and packaging are ranked first with a 35 percent market share.

Taiwan's electronics industry has experienced success in the area of electronics manufacturing and foundry-based production of semiconductors since the 1980s. However, innovative design and the creation of brand-name products have not reached the desired level of development. Of course, it can be argued that the economics of branding are not worth it for Taiwan's OEM and ODM firms, since branding will only alienate overseas clients. However, with the rapid growth of electronics design houses, there is a drive to create high-value intellectual property (mostly for semiconductors and components) that is sold as an essential part of global consumer electronic goods.[22]

[21] Figure 9.1 shows 225 design houses for the year 2003. This number is about twice the number reported in 1999, indicating the addition of about 25 new design houses per year over the last four years. Data provided by the Information Technology Information Systems, Industrial Technology and Research Institute (ITIS/ITRI), 2003.

[22] National Chiao Tung University President Chang Chung Yen (architect of the National Sci-Soft Program) refers to this strategy as "Made in Taiwan (MIT) everywhere, made in Taiwan all of the time." His formula for success is Brand Name: Taiwan, Silicon Solution=Taiwan, Silicon System=MIT, Manufacturing → Design.

The previous limitation to branding was that not enough of Taiwan's electronics companies were driving the designs for global consumer products and contributing to the core underlying technology used in the creation of these products.[23] Over time, Taiwan's design houses are expected to lead the third wave of industrial development, whereby companies will directly contribute to the overall design, manufacture, and marketing of brand-name electronic products and consumer goods, in addition to the creation of IP for components. With the promotion of design capability and the creation of intellectual property via the Sci-Soft project, Taiwan's electronics firms better safeguard their investments — an outcome that benefits both economies in the long run.

Post-WTO, Europe, Japan, Korea, the U.S., and Taiwan are accelerating the transfer of design and manufacturing technology to the China market, each according to their specialty. The impact on Taiwan is that the industry's traditional OEM role has dramatically changed businesses are now facing new challenges and entrepreneurs are recognizing new opportunities. Sci-Soft addresses this post-WTO marketplace dynamic through the strategic restructuring of industrial development. Whereas the past emphasis was on contract-based production, the new emphasis is placed on the design of system-on-chips and product components, and the final step will be to emphasize the marketing of Taiwan's global brand products (see footnote 20).

The creation of a knowledge-based economy does not mean a complete shift from one manufacturing strategy to another. Rather, the Sci-Soft strategy builds on the existing industrial infrastructure and utilizes extant industrial strengths.[24] As the world electronics market develops, shifts in production invariably occur and manufacturing facilities move to take advantage of markets, materials, and labor. Mainland China is showing increased manufacturing development, whereas other regions in Asia are seeing a boom in service and intellectual property development. That is, manufacturing growth in one area is complemented by the growth

[23] C.V. Trappey, *The Taiwan Electronics Market* (Taipei: Hwa-Tai Publishing, 2000).
[24] www.eic.nctu.edu.tw/SOC/button.htm (accessed August 2002).

of knowledge-based economies in other areas. China began semiconductor production from mid-range technology (0.25 micron), and will migrate to 0.14 micron trench capacitor technology at SMIC through agreements with Infineon and 0.11 micron memory production with Japan's Elpida this year.[25]

The manufacturing advances in China are complementing and supporting the market shifts in Taiwan. Taiwan is phasing out mid-range manufacturing and is producing chips, using advanced processes at the 0.13 and 0.09 micron levels. In addition to these changes, the Taiwan semiconductor industry is shifting toward the creation of intellectual property — the innovation behind the products manufactured in the increasingly-sophisticated and expensive semiconductor fabrication facilities. Further, the creative design of integrated circuits and the ability to build a system on a chip by integrating blocks of intellectual property are fueling the growth of Taiwan's knowledge-based economy.

These changes to the economy are encouraged and supported by the National Sci-Soft Project with funding from the Ministry of Economic Affairs (MOEA). The Taiwan government has allowed indirect investment from Taiwan to China, and the investments have facilitated the creation of a stronger downstream electronics industry market, supply chain, and manufacturing base. Figure 9.2 depicts the scale of the approved investment from Taiwan.[26] After Taiwan's accession to the WTO in 2002, investment in the electronics sector in China exceeded US$ 2.5 billion and continues to

[25] Semiconductor Manufacturing International Corporation (SMIC) currently has three fabrication facilities in Shanghai and one fabrication facility in Beijing. The Beijing facility is capable of producing 3,000 12-inch wafers per month. Grace Semiconductor Manufacturing was founded by Jiang Zemin's son, Jiang Mianheng, and Winston Wong, the son of Wang Yung-ching, the chairman of Taiwan's largest business group, Formosa Plastics, and is the next largest semiconductor facility in China with similar production capabilities. See http://english.peopledaily.com.cn/200208/08/eng20020808_101159.shtml, http://www.elpida.com/en/news/2003/06-05.html (accessed June 10, 2006).

[26] Ministry of Economic Affairs, Investment Commission, "Statistics on Overseas Chinese and Foreign Investment, Outward Investment, and Indirect Mainland Investment, the Republic of China," June 2003.

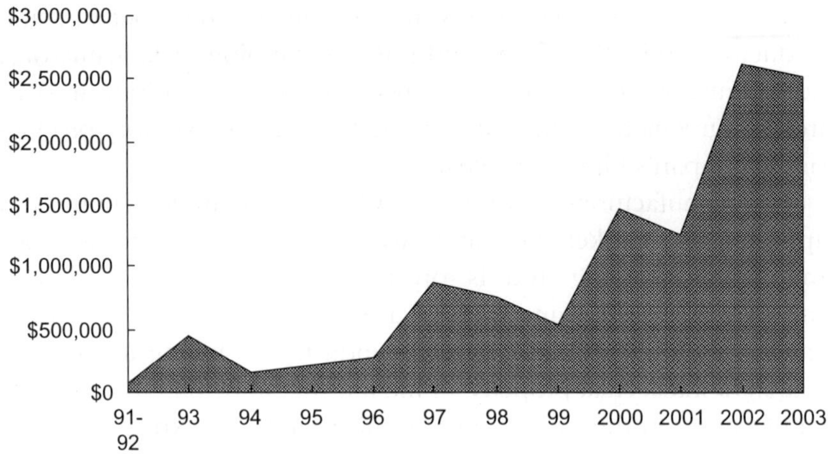

Figure 9.2 Approved indirect mainland electronic and electronic appliance investment from Taiwan (US$ 1,000)

account for roughly a one-quarter of all approved investments to China. The numbers do not reflect the total scale of investment by Taiwan in the China electronics market since there is a continuing unapproved outflow of capital.

The investment flows, both approved and unapproved, have helped to create the consumer electronics manufacturing base in the Pearl River Delta (Guangdong province) and the emerging high-technology parks and semiconductor wafer manufacturing facilities in the Shanghai area (Jiangsu province). There are currently over 70 science and industrial parks with an electronics focus located throughout China.[27] Most of these parks are based on the model used to build Taiwan's first high-tech park. Tax holidays are used to attract companies; equipment and facilities are shared, on-site job training is offered; social services (banks, schools, and retail outlets) are provided; and government offices are available to handle customs and administration.[28]

[27] Research by author, 2003.

[28] Site visits to science parks in Shenzhen and Shanghai by the author, June 2001.

WTO ACCESSION FOR CHINA AND TAIWAN

China faced many more problems than Taiwan in its accession to the WTO, since it has been gradually transitioning toward a market economy from a strict command economy.[29]

Thus, China's ministries and agencies had to commit to a transition from the old role of directing and controlling enterprises. Whereas Taiwan was introduced to the GATT discipline in 1992 and had a developed legal system by the time of accession, China had to agree to focus on the implementation and enforcement of laws, regulations, and other measures to promote the smooth functioning of markets.

The greatest commitment of the WTO required that China's state-owned enterprises (the foundation of the electronics industry) face greater accountability and the full force of global competition. The result has been a significant transfer of power from government officials to leaders of quasi-state commercial entities,[30] as well as the formation of a large number of wholly-owned foreign firms and global technology joint ventures producing over US$ 23 billion worth of integrated circuits.[31] According to the Semiconductor Industry Association, China's State Development Planning Commission is making the structural changes to satisfy the domestic demand for integrated circuits and within five to ten years will have sufficient technology to reduce the production gap with the developed countries.

As part of its WTO accession package, China joined the WTO Information Technology Agreement and agreed to reduce tariffs on

---

[29] U.S. Trade Representative (USTR), "Background Information on China's Accession to the World Trade Organization," 2001, http://www.ustr.gov/Document_Library/Fact_Sheets/2001/Background_Information_on_China's_Accession_to_the_World_Trade_Organization.html?ht=(accessed June 7, 2006).

[30] U.S. Information Technology Office (USITO), "Written Comments to the U.S. Government Interagency Trade Policy Staff Committee in Response to Federal Register Notice 03-18467 Regarding China's Compliance with its Accession Commitments to the World Trade Organization (WTO)," September 10, 2003.

[31] D. Hatano, "Fab America — Keeping U.S. Leadership in Semiconductor Technology," Semiconductor Industry Association, Silicon Valley Tax Directors Group Congressional Staff Visit, August 27, 2003.

most IT products by 2005.[32] During the year 2004, most IT tariffs in China had either fallen below 6 percent or had been eliminated. Almost all finished electronic product tariffs are now zero, with some IT components remaining at 3 percent to 9 percent.[33] Since China cannot import IT components tariff-free, local companies are at a competitive disadvantage relative to foreign imports of finished IT goods.[34] Local pressure is building to remove the remainder of the tariffs.

Upon accession to the WTO, Taiwan reduced its overall tariff rate to below 5 percent, with about two-thirds of the tariff reductions to be made upon accession. The remaining items were to be reduced by the end of 2002, with limited exceptions on a small class of items, which were scheduled for reduction during 2004. For consumer electronics, such as color television sets, video cassette recorders, and compact disc players, Taiwan reduced tariffs to 10 percent.[35] For heavy household electronic goods, such as air conditioners, washing machines, and dryers — goods that were traditionally sold through a few dominant retail chains — the tariff reductions have opened up the market with sales through over 200 hypermarkets and Do It Yourself (DIY) stores at extremely competitive prices. With the tariffs on household electronics goods and consumer electronics reduced to about half, the marketplace was opened to a wide variety of brands and price promotion strategies. Computers, peripherals, displays, and monitors have also fallen in price, not only for final products, but also for components, since Taiwan eliminated tariffs on 25 different semiconductor products. Thus, the tariff reductions have had an

---

[32] Taiwan was an original party to the agreement, whose members contributed over 80 percent of all world trade in IT products; World Trade Organization, "Ministerial Declaration on Trade in Information Technology Products," Singapore, December 9–13, 1996.

[33] American Chamber of Commerce, "2002 White Paper: American Business in China," People's Republic of China, 2002.

[34] American Chamber of Commerce, "WTO Implementation Report," People's Republic of China, Fall 2002.

[35] N. de Spiegeleire, "A Rough Guide to Taiwan's WTO Accession, Sector-by-Sector Effects and Implications," American Chamber of Commerce, April 2000, 20–21.

impact, not only on the manufacturers, but also positively on the end-consumers in the Taiwan marketplace.

The WTO accession has had a great impact on China's FDI inflow and Taiwan's FDI outflow. Post-WTO, China continued to be the world's largest recipient of FDI in 2002. The Organisation for Economic Co-operation and Development reported that China's FDI rose to US$ 52.7 billion, exceeding the FDI to the U.S. At least half of the 2002 FDI originated in Hong Kong, with unaccounted amounts coming from Taiwan and "round-tripping" investments from China. Round-tripping investments are investments that flow out of China and into Hong Kong (or the Virgin Islands or the Cayman Islands) and then back into China to take advantage of investment incentives offered to non-mainland investors. The Bank of China estimated in 2003, that Hong Kong's share of FDI into China may have dropped to 20 percent from an average of 50 percent over the last 15 years, and will continue to decline under the WTO.[36] However, there are no official statistics nor consensus about the amount of round-tripping investments into China.

The WTO membership has helped to place China's investment environment in a very positive light, particularly against the bleak and volatile backdrop of a global economic slowdown, corporate scandals, and geopolitical risks in 2002. In addition to the positive image, structural reforms related to China's WTO entry can be credited for the increase in FDI inflows.

Such changes in policies and structural reforms have historically led to a surge in China's FDI.[37] However, China's FDI has been different from other developing economies (and most similar to Taiwan's history of FDI) where the government did not direct the

---

[36] "China Ahead in Foreign Direct Investment," *OECD Observer*, no. 237 (May 2003); Hong Kong Trade Development Council, "Foreign Direct Investment in China," Economic Forum, content provided by the Bank of China Group, January 2003, http://www.tdctrade.com/econforum/boc/boc030101.htm (accessed June 7, 2006).

[37] E.M. Graham and E. Wada, "Foreign Direct Investment in China: Effects on Growth and Economic Performance," in *Achieving High Growth: Experience of Transitional Economies in East Asia*, ed. P. Drysdale, Y. Huang, and M. Kawai (New York: Oxford University Press, 2003).

capital into state-owned enterprises. China's inland provinces are dominated by state-owned enterprises, but most of the FDI is flowing into the coastal provinces, and a large portion is being used to develop technology-based electronics firms, where there is no existing competition. Thus, significant amounts of China's post-WTO FDI, like Taiwan's pre-WTO FDI, has been directed toward the creation of human capital within science parks that rely on college-trained engineers and managers. For the most part, the FDI is not used to create low-wage jobs but to develop an electronics sector with a comparative advantage.

WTO ISSUES: AGGRESSIVE POLICIES TO DEVELOP AND PROMOTE DOMESTIC IT PRODUCTION

Both China and Taiwan have made many changes to government operations to comply with the WTO. However, China has made far more changes than Taiwan. Because the mainland acceded to the WTO in December 2001 without all of its laws and regulations in compliance with WTO obligations, there remains a long list of issues to be settled. For China, the issues of greatest concern to WTO members are the indirect subsidies in the form of substantial rebates on the value-added tax (VAT) charged on Chinese-made chips.[38] Taiwan, on the other hand, is considered a participant (but not a target) in the dispute given its large investment in Chinese industries. Further, China has made systemic reforms in the areas of transparency, notice and comment, and the uniform application of laws and judicial review. Section 3 looks at these changes and the WTO issues that remain to be resolved in China.

China's Drive toward Transparency

The American Chamber of Commerce in China (AmCham PRC) reported (see footnote 33) that more than 50 laws and administrative

[38] A. Batson, "China's Policies On Chips Meet Vocal Foreign Opposition," Dow Jones Newswires, June 5 2003, http://webreprints.djreprints.com/765510630487.html (accessed June 1, 2006).

regulations, and more than 1,000 ministerial regulations that were inconsistent with the WTO regulations, have been amended or repealed. The Ministry of Foreign Trade and Economic Cooperation (MOFTEC)[39] has issued a document called "Sectoral Guidance Catalog for Foreign Investment," which classifies investments as encouraged, restricted, or prohibited. The list demonstrates the extent to which the electronics industry is being promoted since China's accession to the WTO. Very little in the way of information technology products or manufacturing equipment is prohibited. AmCham PRC further noted that the MOFTEC document was issued jointly by the State Development Planning Commission (SDPC) the State Economic and Trade Commission (SETC), and MOFTEC. The document is important as it relaxes restraints on foreign participation, and these changes are in accordance with the WTO accession agreement.

China has opened a WTO Enquiry and Notification Center and this center can be accessed through the official MOFCOM website (www.mofcom.gov.cn). In comparison, the official bureaucratic structure and procedure for establishing electronics firms in China is still much more complicated than those in Taiwan, as are the structures for monitoring and enforcing WTO rules. The organization in China that investigates anti-dumping issues and answers inquiries about imports, anti-subsidies, and other protective measures is managed by the Fair Trade Bureau of Imports and Exports (Figure 9.3).

China has been more effective than Taiwan in training companies and officials about the WTO, largely through the contributions and participation of foreign governments and trade associations. MOFCOM and SETC work together on WTO education, with MOFCOM taking the lead on briefing the SDPC, the State Administration of Industry, and the Publicity Department of the Chinese Communist Party, and the SETC briefing state-owned enterprises (SOEs). The SETC and MOFCOM have jointly created a project with the National School of Administration to train general managers and consultants. The AmCham PRC report indicates that

[39] MOFTEC is now called the Ministry of Commerce, MOFCOM.

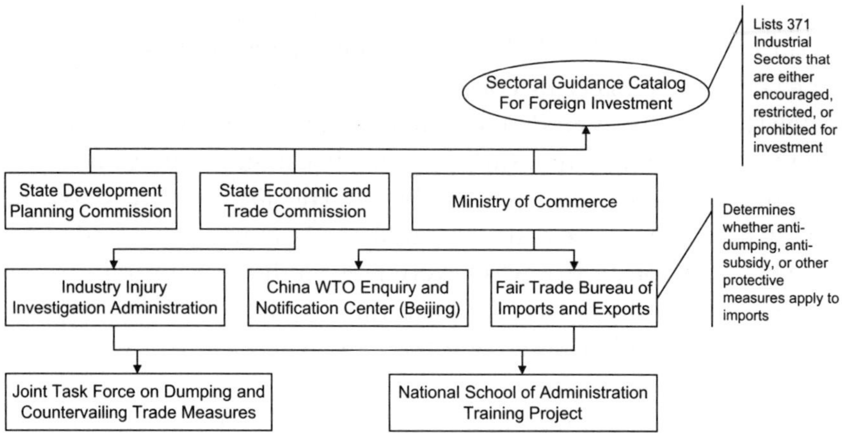

Figure 9.3 Electronics investment is encouraged by the sectoral guidance catalog and electronics dumping issues are covered by a Joint Task Force of the MOFCOM and the SETC

the U.S. Trade Development Agency has regularly sponsored WTO requirements and implemented training seminars, as well as developed WTO training software. The EU has provided funding for WTO legal affairs and financial services (US$ 14.7 million), and the Asian Development Bank has funded the creation of a legal education program at the Peking University Law School. In comparison, Taiwan still has too few programs, and insufficient funding and external assistance for training government leaders, businesses, and business associations about Taiwan's WTO accession and issues.[40]

China's Customs Valuation

China agreed to its obligations under the WTO agreement relating to customs valuation upon accession, without any transition period. The accession agreement reinforces China's obligation not to use

[40] Taiwan launched a World Trade Organization (WTO) Center under the Chung-hua Institution for Economic Research (CIER) with 20 staff and initial capital of about $2 million U.S. dollars. See J. Ho, "Government Launches Think Tank for Trade Issues," *Taipei Times*, September 10, 2003. Available at www.taipeitimes.com/News/biz/archives/2003/09/09/2003067164 (accessed June 1, 2006).

minimum or reference prices as a means for determining customs value, and it calls on China to implement the World Customs Organization Decisions on Valuation of Carrier Media Bearing Software for Data Processing Equipment and Treatment of Interest Charges in Customs Value of Imported Goods within two years after accession.[41]

Foreign electronics firms complain that China is using reference pricing (a means used when the stated transaction price is believed by the importing government to be inaccurate), instead of the actual transaction price (Figure 9.4). Although the press does not report reference pricing problems experienced by Taiwan firms in China, a survey was circulated to determine if electronic components shipped from Taiwan to China were being subjected to reference pricing.[42] The research measured whether it was more likely for a Taiwan firm to forgo reference pricing if it was characterized as a compatriot firm (a firm that lists itself as a Chinese company without Taiwan business ties, but built with Taiwan capital). Further, the research sought to determine if there was a difference in the way compatriot firms are treated from foreign WTO members (Taiwan firms listed under the same legal name in Taiwan and China).

The survey indicated that if a firm chose to be listed as a same-name Taiwan firm, then it was more likely to experience problems with customs. Even if a firm was listed as a Chinese company, it did not escape problems with customs and to make matters worse, it was subjected to frequent demands for the transfer of technology. Thus, although Taiwan firms in China do not appear to be receiving preferential treatment over foreign firms, the strategy to pursue compatriot firm status to gain market advantage appears ineffective.

---

[41] U.S. Trade Representative (USTR), "Background Information on China's Accession to the World Trade Organization," 2001, http://www.ustr.gov/Document_Library/Fact_Sheets/2001/Background_Information_on_China's_Accession_to_the_World_Trade_Organization.html?ht=(accessed June 7, 2006).

[42] C.V. Trappey, "A Survey Circulated to 91 Individuals Enrolled in MBA and EMBA Programs in Taiwan," September 2003.

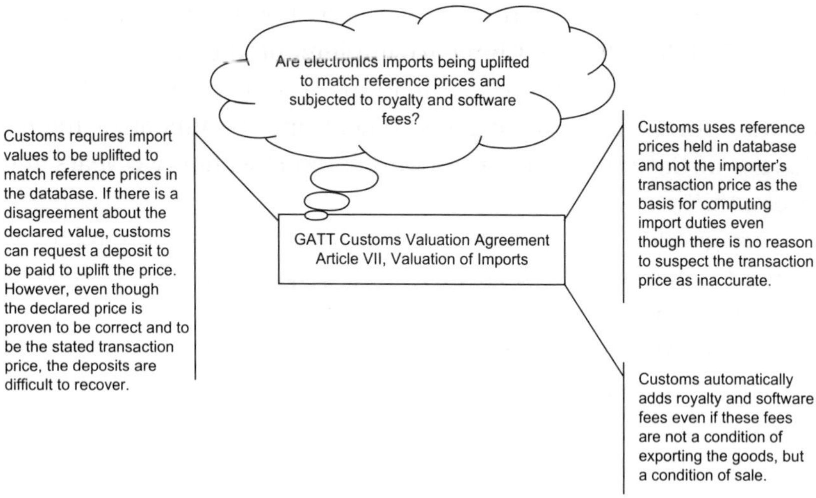

Figure 9.4 Uplifting import values to match reference prices in Article VII

Technical Barriers to Trade

Under GATT Article III, the use of internal taxes and charges, laws and regulations, or requirements cannot be used to protect domestic production. Thus, China's accession to the WTO means the government will operate with transparency; use the same technical regulations, standards, and conformity assessment procedures for both imported and domestic goods; and use the same fees, processing periods, and complaint procedures for both imported and domestic goods. Therefore, if a foreign firm is manufacturing semiconductors in China, then GATT Article III protects the foreign firm in China, and allows equal treatment for procurement of goods and services, marketing and manufacturing requirements, and the pricing of available goods and services by transportation, energy, and telecommunications authorities. Pursuant to this, a foreign semiconductor fabrication facility cannot be charged more for power or electricity, should not be unfairly subjected to tariffs, and cannot be held up by transportation companies to create an unfair advantage for local semiconductor manufacturers.

Researchers at the Beijing office of the U.S. Information Technology Office (USITO) noted that there is growing concern over trading rights for foreign-funded enterprises, and a disassociation between trading and distribution rights. The issues of logistics and transportation of electronics goods and components, as well as the taxation of these goods, are at the forefront of the challenges submitted to the WTO by the U.S. in 2004.[43]

The Semiconductor Industry Association (SIA),[44] American Chamber of Commerce (see footnote 33), the U.S. Information Technology Office,[45] and Senator Lieberman[46] all argued that there is growing protectionism in the Chinese semiconductor industry and technical barriers to trade are a leading cause of concern. The AmCham PRC report noted that China is using indirect subsidies in the form of rebates on the value-added tax on commodities and a variety of electronic products, including semiconductors, to discriminate against imports. That is, if a foreign firm wants to import semiconductors to use in a locally-made phone, then the imported semiconductors will not receive a significant or equivalent refund on the value-added tax as a local firm. AmCham PRC says the Chinese government has set up a task force under MOFCOM to study the VAT as applied to semiconductors. Given the number of

---

[43] Semiconductor Industry Association and Dewey Ballantine, "China's Emerging Semiconductor Industry: The Impact of China's Preferential Value-Added Tax on Current Investment Trends," October 2003.

[44] The SIA says that the VAT is "an aggressive policy to promote domestic manufacturing. The SIA has observed that 17 percent is considered the normal VAT for chips, but amounts over 3 percent to 6 percent are rebated for chips made in China. See D. Hatano, "Fab America — Keeping U.S. Leadership in Semiconductor Technology," Semiconductor Industry Association, Silicon Valley Tax Directors Group Congressional Staff Visit, August 27, 2003.

[45] U.S. Trade Representative (USTR), "Background Information on China's Accession to the World Trade Organization," 2001, http://www.ustr.gov/Document_Library/Fact_Sheets/2001/Background_Information_on_China's_Accession_to_the_World_Trade_Organization.html?ht=(accessed June 7, 2006).

[46] J.I. Lieberman, *White Paper: National Security Aspects of the Global Migration of the U.S. Semiconductor Industry*, Airland Subcommittee, U.S. Senate, Armed Services Committee, June 2003.

associations, trade organizations, and U.S. senators working to bring the issue to WTO arbitration, substantial rebates on the VAT have become the most controversial electronics trade practice under investigation.

Standards

The Protocol on the Accession of the PRC,[47] Part 1, Section 2(C) 1, states that WTO members are to be provided access to and the opportunity to comment on "all laws, regulations and other measures pertaining to or affecting trade in goods, services, TRIPs or the control of foreign exchange before such measures are implemented or enforced." This is a very interesting case in point for Taiwan electronics firms. Do Taiwan firms want to be seen by China as a foreign entity or as a compatriot firm and take a side that may impact their competitive advantage over foreign firms? Notably, the amount of foreign competition in the China electronics market has risen.

If the Taiwan government takes the position as a WTO member to see and comment on drafts of regulations, then it has to uphold and promote regulatory practices, which may limit market practices that give advantages to China's domestic firms and compatriots. Taiwan firms have not been observed taking a stand with U.S. and European trade associations to break down unfair trade practices in China, and, sooner or later, will have to choose a side.

Furthermore, Taiwan firms are not actively commenting on the Certification and Accreditation Administration (CNCA) Compulsory Product Certification System,[48] a system that directly impacts the China Compulsory Certification (CCC) for verifying electronic product safety and electromagnetic emissions. The American Chamber of Commerce[49] has voiced concerns that electronics products being sent to China's designated laboratories (often affiliated with research

---

[47] www.wto.org/english/thewto_e/acc_e/protocols_acc_membership_e.htm (accessed June 2003).

[48] www.cqc.com.cn/ccc/regulationseng.pdf (accessed June 2002).

[49] American Chamber of Commerce, "WTO Implementation Report," People's Republic of China, Fall 2002.

institutes engaged in producing similar products to those being tested) are possibly causing IP violations by copying products, instead of testing and certifying products.

Taiwan, acting under the International Standards Organization (ISO) and the Notification of Acceptance to the WTO Related to the Code of Good Practice for the Preparation, Adoption, and Application of Standards (notification under Paragraph C of the WTO Technical Barriers to Trade [TBT] Code of Good Practice) will need to continue active involvement in the Committee on Technical Barriers to Trade.[50] There are emerging electronics standards for wireless communication devices and semiconductors, mobile phones, radios, televisions, and CD players, which will directly impact Taiwan's competitiveness and the application of the WTO rules will help make these standards fair to all members.

TRIMS: Trade-Related Investment Measures

Upon accession to the WTO, China agreed to eliminate local content requirements and technology transfer requirements. Even though China agreed under TRIPS not to require companies to transfer technology as a condition of investment, survey results showed that there were Taiwan firms being pressed to supply technology.[51] These issues can best be identified by Taiwan trade associations notifying the Taiwan government and WTO trade officials. However, given the ongoing struggle between electronics businesses and associations versus the government, little is being said or reported officially.[52] Whether or not technology transfer is being used to

---

[50] http://www.gtwassociates.com/answers/GTBTM29.pdf (accessed June 13, 2006).

[51] C.V. Trappey, "A Survey Circulated to 91 Individuals Enrolled in MBA and EMBA Programs in Taiwan," September 2003.

[52] The most publicized struggle between business, government, and political parties was illustrated by the Taiwan Semiconductor Manufacturing Company's interest to invest in the China semiconductor market. After a two-year struggle that increased the cost and reduced the opportunity of the strategic investment, press coverage continued to question the decision. See Taiwan News, "TSU Condemns Decision on TSMC China Plant," January 24, 2003,

facilitate the approval of Taiwan investment in China, or to influence the recommendations for project loans from Chinese banks, requires further investigation.

TRIPS: Trade-related Intellectual Property Rights

China has agreed to adhere to internationally-accepted norms to protect and enforce the intellectual property rights of foreign companies and individuals in China. As shown in Section 2, China is in the process of modifying the full range of intellectual property laws and regulations, including those relating to patents, trademarks, trade secrets, integrated circuits, and copyrights. The laws concerning semiconductor masks, IC layout design, and discrete semiconductors have been changed, and companies can apply for intellectual property protection. However, violations continue, particularly the reverse engineering of chips and reproduction using the original company's name and trademark.[53]

Moreover, the American Chamber of Commerce (see footnote 34) reported that the prosecution of patent infringement claims can be difficult, since courts lack the technical ability to prosecute the misappropriation of trade secrets. Amcham PRC further pointed out that there are also uncertainties about the applications for patents. The primary issue of concern is whether or not Chinese citizens employed by a foreign firm in China must receive government approval before assigning patent rights to the firm for inventions developed by the employee during the course of employment.

---

www.taiwanheadlines.gov.tw/20030124/20030124p3.html (accessed July 2003); U.S. Trade Representative (USTR), "Background Information on China's Accession to the World Trade Organization," 2001, http://www.ustr.gov/ Document_Library/ Fact_Sheets/2001/Background_Information_on_China's_Accession_to_the_World_ Trade_Organization.html?ht=(accessed June 7, 2006).

[53] U.S. Information Technology Office (USITO), "Written Comments to the U.S. Government Interagency Trade Policy Staff Committee in Response to Federal Register Notice 03-18467 Regarding China's Compliance with its Accession Commitments to the World Trade Organization (WTO)," September 10, 2003.

TAIWAN'S WTO ISSUES

The European Chamber of Commerce in Taiwan (ECCT) established a WTO committee immediately after Taiwan's accession in January 2002.[54] The purpose of the committee is to protect European business interests in Taiwan and to expand market opportunities for European businesses. The ongoing monitoring of Taiwan's WTO compliance begins with the designation of a consulting firm to identify WTO issues. After analyzing Taiwan's WTO commitment and the impact on European businesses, the members will either hire a law firm to take action, or align with WTO practice groups to lobby for change. The ECCT continues to monitor compliance problems through committee action, and reports and collaborates with ECCT trade officers to produce monthly alert reports that are forwarded to the EU, ECCT members, the Taiwan government, and lawyers enforcing compliance.

The general conclusion reached by the ECCT is that, to date, the Taiwan authorities have, for the most part, complied with the reduction in tariffs in accordance with the WTO agreement. The commitments to reducing non-tariff barriers have also, by and large, been complied with. However, there are indicators that domestic interest with the WTO is starting to wane and that the compliance program is being frustrated by a lack of attention. The European Chamber of Commerce notes that full compliance is necessary for Taiwan to make the case for entry into free trade agreements. There are several areas of concern for European industries, but the most watched is the protection of intellectual property.[55] The technical

---

[54] European Chamber of Commerce in Taiwan (ECCT), "ECCT-WTO Committee Position Paper," January 2003.

[55] The position of the Americans is the same. In a recent speech, the Director of the American Institute in Taiwan said "Last June, the LY [Legislative Yuan] considered draft revisions to the Copyright Law. Had those revisions been passed intact, Taiwan could have declared a major IPR victory. Most people here believe the law has been strengthened. Unfortunately, last-minute changes made to the bill by LY members fatally weakened the text. In some respects, the revised Copyright Law is a step backward for IPR protection. Foreign investors have consequently taken note

non-tariff barriers to trade, such as quantity, safety, environmental, or other standards to exclude foreign goods, are also causing concern among foreign chambers of commerce. The non-tariff barriers could potentially be used to obstruct trade in the area of electronics trade between China and Taiwan. The two areas of concern being monitored that are related to electronics are the following:

- Under the WTO agreement, there is a mandate stipulating the free flow of persons for temporary business visits. Further, the length of stay of mainland China visitors is not consistent with that for other countries' visitors.[56] Given the growing importance of the cross-strait electronics industry, there should be fair treatment and reciprocal treatment to encourage trade development.
- Technical barriers to trade, such as using unreasonable restrictions on quality, safety, environmental factors, or standards, can all potentially be used to unfairly restrict the flow of electronic goods. The WTO Technical Barriers to Foreign Trade (TBT) can potentially be used to prohibit consumer electronics imports by China or Taiwan, but to date, no violations have been reported.

---

that Taiwan, a WTO member for nearly two years, has been unable to pass legislation consistent with its commitments under TRIPS, and the people of Taiwan, who are needed to press for improvement, still do not know the new law's failings" (D. Paal, director, the American Institute in Taiwan, "Leveraging Taiwan's Talents Through IPR Protection," World Trade Law Association Asia-Pacific Regional Conference, October 18, 2003, http://www.ait.org.tw/en/news/pressrelease/viewer.asp?ID=2003101801&GROUP=PR [accessed June 10, 2006]).

[56] Council for Economic Planning and Development, "Length of Stay in Taiwan Increased for Mainland Chinese Employees," *Industry of Free China* (Taiwan New Economy News) 92 (September 2002), 75; The Mainland Affairs Council sets the maximum length of stay for Chinese employees of multinational enterprises in Taiwan to three years. Regulations are posted at http://www.mac.gov.tw/english/index1-e.htm (accessed June 10, 2006). Taiwan firms are not granted the same rights as multinational firms. This places local firms at a great disadvantage to build a knowledge-based economy by limiting access to engineering and science talent from China.

CONCLUSION

The conclusion links the positive trade policy changes in China and Taiwan with the WTO accession and the new economy philosophy. Had there been no WTO-influenced organizational and policy changes in China and Taiwan, the investment environment would have been quite different at the end of the 2001 and Asia would be a very different place today. Quite simply, the WTO opened the doors for investors by accepting China as a member. Had the doors been closed, the investment flow would not have been large enough to create the comprehensive electronics industry supply chain that exists today. There continue to be trade conflicts and challenges to the post-WTO electronics industry, but nothing serious enough to stem the flow of investment.

As a new democracy, Taiwan has too many groups working against each other and, as a result, it occasionally fails to take the steps needed to boost intellectual property protection and enforce WTO discipline. China, on the other hand, has too few groups, but the WTO has helped to create new groups with significant wealth, power, autonomy, and influence. The new power groups, however, do not always work consistently toward the goals and objectives of the WTO, and in the case of VAT and standards are working aggressively to secure their interests and to protect the market from competition. However, as both Chinese and Taiwanese electronics firms make headway under the WTO, it is very likely that a balance will be achieved and the electronics industry in greater China will emerge as the world's largest.

NEW ECONOMY MARKET FORCES

The new economy reflects the gains in economic performance that can come about as a result of increased technical innovation, organizational change, and improved public policies.[57] Information

[57] White House, "The Clinton-Gore Administration: Sustaining America Prosperity — Highlights of the 2001 Economic Report of the President," January 12 2001, http://clinton5.nara.gov/WH/new/html/Fri_Jan_12_113936_2001.html (accessed June 1, 2006).

technology acts as a catalyst to the gains, since new hardware, software, and communication capabilities increase the economic potential. The 2001 Economic Report of President Clinton shows that entrepreneurs further stimulate change to business organizations through business reconfiguration and new business creation. New businesses bring in new ways of managing human resources, new production strategies, changes in channel relationships, and new financing models and business restructuring. The WTO can be considered an important driving force of the new economy, since it advocates structural reform, the fast diffusion of information and communication technology, the acceleration of trade across borders, and the building of a global workforce.

China's and Taiwan's WTO accession has made it possible for both to play a significant role in the global new economy. Therefore, in the post-WTO era, Taiwan and China will realize greater economic integration, face increasing competitive pressure (that causes business change and development), experience technological and social change, and benefit from increased information and knowledge flows. Further, the economic growth in both regions has stimulated consumer demand in China and Taiwan. The Chinese and Taiwanese electronics industries, and, in particular, sectors related to information and communications technology, exemplify the progress that can result from engaging the new economy philosophy.

Without the WTO, it is unlikely that either member would be reaping the current levels of economic benefit and innovation growth. The economic benefits have clearly changed China's electronics industry, whereby the emphasis is now placed on the development of human capital, as well as the development of the technology infrastructure. Taiwan has, likewise, benefited from the increasingly competitive environment that has caused industry to shift to a knowledge-based service economy targeting electronics innovation and design. With the ongoing simultaneous development of the electronics industry in China and Taiwan, the emergence of strong information and communications sectors, the building of global brands, and with the participation in the WTO, the electronics marketplace of greater China is changing the global electronics supply chain. Since the 1970s, China and Taiwan have built up an ICT industry, using similar policies and strategies. With cross-strait electronics supply chain integration, encouraged by WTO entry and its related policies and regulatory changes, the greater China region is poised for continued and accelerated growth.[58] Further, the Information Technology Agreement of the WTO is creating a global ICT market with China and Taiwan offering their competitive advantages — China with its promising market and affordable labor and Taiwan with its capital, technology, and ability to integrate design and manufacturing services for the global electronics market. Overall, the creation of wealth through industrial development and strategic cross-strait links, combined with the discipline of complying with the guidelines of WTO principles, will certainly help to sustain the world's fastest growing electronics marketplace and production base in the history of the electronics industry.

[58] Institute of Information Industry (III), "1980~2004 Production Values of Electronics and Information Industry in China," *III MIC Marketing Information Report*, March 2005; The III MIC report indicated the annual growth of China electronics production was 20.5 percent, 15 percent, and 41.2 percent, respectively, between 2001 and 2004. In 2004, the production value reached RMB 2,655 billion (approximately US$ 330.9 billion).

Chapter

10

The Impact of Accession to the WTO: The Case of the Automobile Industry

Chwo-Ming Joseph Yu

INTRODUCTION

This chapter examines the automobile industry and addresses the following two questions:

(1) What has been the impact of WTO membership on this sector in Taiwan and China?
(2) What kind of cross-strait cooperation has been created due to common membership, and what further cooperation might be expected in the future?

In order to understand the impact on the auto sector, we have to address this issue in the context of the global auto industry. Thus, after the introduction, Section 2 presents an overview of the world automobile industry and the joint ventures formed by major automakers in China; Section 3 describes the market characteristics in Taiwan and China; Section 4 assesses the impact of WTO accession; Section 5 depicts the joint ventures between automakers from

Taiwan and China; Section 6 summarizes the development of cross-strait cooperation for firms in the automobile industry; and the last section concludes the chapter.

THE WORLD AUTOMOBILE INDUSTRY AND INTERNATIONAL JOINT VENTURES IN CHINA

Overview of the World Auto Industry

As the markets in developed countries matured, the opening of markets, high economic growth rates, and positive attitudes toward consumption in developing countries led the major automakers to accelerate their efforts at internationalization. The hectic and very expensive business of securing markets abroad and building foreign capacity has divided the world's automotive industry into three tiers:[1]

1. The first tier of large, profitable firms, e.g. General Motors, Ford, Toyota, Volkswagen, and Honda, are undertaking most of the foreign direct investments and acquisitions of smaller firms;
2. The second tier, including Chrysler, Mercedes-Benz (the automotive arm of Daimler-Benz), Renault, Nissan, and Fiat, has sought or negotiated alliances with one another to increase their coverage of global markets and to compete with the first-tier companies. Examples of such alliances are the Renault-Nissan alliance and the merger of Daimler and Chrysler; and
3. The third tier of firms, consisting of nameplates, such as Volvo, Mazda, Kia, and Mitsubishi, which already have lost, or stand to lose in the future, their independence as they become subsidiaries of other companies.

Global rationalization has compelled smaller auto companies to join forces with one another and, in some cases, to be taken over in whole or in part by larger auto firms. Table 10.1 clearly illustrates this development. The trend implies that the automobile industries

[1] L.S. Hiroka, *Global Alliances in the Motor Vehicle Industry* (Westport, CT: Quorum Books, 2001).

Table 10.1 The Major Automakers

Company	Units produced in 2000 and 2002 (million)	Remarks
General Motors (group)	8.1 8.3	Including Opel, Vauxhall, Saab, Holden, Daewoo, Isuzu, etc.
Ford (group)	7.3 6.7	Including Volvo, Jaguar, Land Rover, Mazda, etc.
DaimlerChrysler (group)	6.5 6.3	Including Mercedes, Smart, Mitsubishi, etc.
Toyota (group)	6.0 6.6	Including Daihatsu and Hino
Volkswagen (group)	5.1 5.0	Including Audi, Bentley, Seat, Skoda, etc.
Renault-Nissan (group)	5.1 5.0	Including Dacia
PSA (group)	2.9 2.3	Including Peugeot and Citroën
Fiat (group)	2.6 2.1	Including Alfa Romeo, Lancia, Ferrari, etc.
Honda	2.5 3.0	
Hyundai (group)	2.5 2.6	Including Kia

Source: Calculated from www.oica.net/htdocs/main.htm

in Taiwan and China, both newcomers in terms of making cars and less competitive internationally, will likely seek alliances with major carmakers from other countries.

Joint Ventures of Major Automakers in China

The downturn in the European and U.S. markets, coupled with their high production costs, has forced automakers to look toward low-cost centers such as China for their auto component needs. China has a cost advantage, primarily due to its lower labor, product, and processing costs, plus its large and yet untapped market.[2] In this section, we focus on manufacturing cooperation, either through licensing or joint ventures, among the top six automaker groups in China.

Working with foreign automakers is a relatively-new phenomenon in China. The birth of three joint ventures, Beijing Jeep, Guangzhou Peugeot, and Shanghai Volkswagen, in the 1980s marked the beginning of such cooperation.[3] But years of learning still have not reduced the time required for foreign firms to find Chinese partners. For example, Ford spent two years negotiating with Chongqing Chang'an Automobile Co. to form a US$ 98 million joint venture to produce passenger cars.[4]

The cooperative agreements of the major automakers in China are listed below:

1. General Motors (GM)

GM ventures in China include: Shanghai GM (50 percent ownership); Jinbei GM (50 percent ownership); Pan Asia Technical Automotive Center; Liuzhou Wuling Motors Co., Ltd. (34 percent ownership); and one joint venture in Yantai (Shandong province) (25 percent ownership and 50 percent by Shanghai GM). In addition, GM owns 49 percent of Isuzu that has two subsidiaries, in Jiangxi and Chongqing, for light truck production, and it has provided capital to Guangzhou Auto to make buses (see footnote 3). GM has successfully brought a series of its products into China and, with more than 21 parts-making affiliates there, it has ambitious programs both in China and in its plans to serve Asian markets by its production base in China (see footnote 1). In fact, GM shipped Chinese-made Buick vans to the Philippines in 2003.[5] In addition, GM's plan to increase twenty-fold

[2] S. Cody and A. Zhou, "An Overview of the Automobile Industry in China," www.chinastrategic.com.

[3] H. Li, "World Automobile Giants' China Strategies in the 21st Century," *People's Daily*, January 16, 2002.

[4] "Ford Gets Foothold in China's Market," *People's Daily*, April 26, 2001.

[5] H. McDonald, "Made in China," smh.com.au, October 18, 2003.

the amount of auto parts sourcing from China for global production has motivated some U.S. parts suppliers to invest in China.[6]

2. Ford

Ford currently has more than ten sales agencies, over 40 service facilities, and two global accessory sales agencies, as well as a technology training center in China. In terms of automobile manufacturing, it has Jiangling Motor Company (29.96 percent ownership) and Chang'an Ford Automobile Co. (50 percent ownership). In addition, Mazda that is 24.5 percent owned by Ford set up a joint venture with a subsidiary of the First Automobile Works (FAW) in China in 2002. Despite being the first U.S. automaker to enter the Chinese market in 1978, Ford apparently lags behind in its market development in China (see footnote 3).

3. DaimlerChrysler (DC)

Beijing Jeep (42.4 percent ownership), the first auto foreign joint venture in China, formed by Chrysler and Beijing Auto in 1983, marked DC's entry into China. DC formed a joint venture (35 percent ownership) with Yaxing-Benz Limited in Yangzhou to produce buses and signed a technology transfer agreement with Anhui Ankai Automobile Co., Ltd. to produce a deluxe vehicle. But as a group, DC lacks a long-term plan to penetrate the Chinese market (see footnote 3).

On the positive side, Mitsubishi Motors that is 37.3 percent owned by DC has a successful joint venture in China. China Motor, of which Mitsubishi has 19.62 percent ownership, has formed a joint venture (50 percent ownership) with South East Auto Industry, Ltd. in Fuzhou (the second largest light sedan producer in China). Due to the success of this joint venture, DC and South East Auto Industry, Ltd. have agreed to invest more than US$ 50 million to establish a plant in Fuzhou to manufacture Benz autos.[7]

---

[6] J. McCracken, "Automakers and Trade: Flood of Auto Parts," *Detroit Free Press*, February 12, 2004.

[7] "China Motor, DaimlerChrysler Plan Joint Venture," *People's Daily*, June 12, 2001.

4. Toyota Motor Co., Ltd.

Toyota has two production ventures in China: Sichuan FAW (45 percent ownership) and Tianjin Toyota Motor Co., Ltd. (50 percent ownership). It is also involved in parts manufacturing ventures, such as Tianjin Fengjin Auto Parts Co., Ltd. (90 percent ownership); Tianjin Toyota Forging Co., Ltd.; Toyota Motor Technical Center; Tianjin Jifeng Auto Parts Co., Ltd. (30 percent ownership); and Tianjin Toyota Motor Engine Co., Ltd. (50 percent ownership). In fact, in 2005, the Toyota Group had 12 wholly-owned subsidiaries or joint ventures in China.[8]

The general perception has been that Toyota lags far behind its European and American counterparts in China (see footnote 3). However, the announcement by Toyota and the First Automobile Works Group (FAW) of the formation of a long-term cooperative relationship in August 2002 placed Toyota in a new competitive position. After the announcement, FAW merged with Toyota's joint ventures in China, re-establishing FAW as a giant Chinese corporation.[9] Toyota estimated that, after working with FAW, its auto production in China might reach 170,000 units in 2005[10] and, in fact, reached 131,000 units.

To expand its market share in southern China, Toyota is negotiating with Shanghai Automotive Industry Group (SAIC) and Guangzhou Automobile Industrial Group (that has joint ventures with Honda and Isuzu) for two potential production cooperation ventures. Toyota's goal is to hold a 10 percent market share by 2010.[11]

5. Volkswagen (VW)

VW remains the largest auto producer in China, with Shanghai VW (50 percent ownership); FAW-VW (40 percent ownership); and FAW

[8] www.toyota.co.jp/en/about_toyota/manufacturing/worldwide.html.

[9] "Fujian to Become Major Auto Base in 10 Years," *People's Daily*, January 18, 2001.

[10] J. Lian, "Toyota Will Produce 170,000 Cars in 2005," *China Commercial Times*, December 25, 2002 (in Chinese).

[11] Z. Song, "Toyota Fighting Hard to Get 10% of the Market," *Jingji ribao* [Economics Daily], July 4, 2003 (in Chinese).

(Audi), a licensing agreement between 1988 and 1997 (see footnote 1). VW intends to introduce advanced manufacturing techniques and product technologies into China, and to bring its two Chinese ventures, as well as accessory systems, into its global networks of purchasing, product R&D, and marketing (see footnote 3). From a strategic point of view, VW has established a strong platform in China for manufacturing, as well as for exporting to other Asian nations. In 2003, VW started exporting Shanghai-made Passat luxury cars to Southeast Asia.[12]

6. Renault-Nissan

Renault is not active in China. The announcement of its intention to cooperate with Sanjiang (in Hubei province) to assemble light buses was its first project in China (see footnote 3). However, through Nissan, that is 44.4 percent owned by Renault, and Yulong that is 25 percent owned by Nissan and owns 34.28 percent of China Motor, Renault is still situated in the Chinese market.

Nissan's initial contact with China was a technological support agreement with FAW to produce small-sized trucks in 1984, lasting until 1993. Thereafter, a production venture, Zhengzhou Nissan (5 percent ownership), was established. Nissan has ties with two other Chinese automakers because Yulong has formed Aeolus with FAW, and China Motor has formed South East Auto Industry, Ltd. with the Fujian Automobile Industry Group.

To highlight its commitment to the Chinese market, Nissan agreed to form a 50-50 joint venture with Dongfeng Motor in September 2002 to increase sales, and to speed up the introduction of new models. Nissan will also provide the joint venture with management know-how, such as sales planning, distribution, quality management, marketing, and finance.

Foreign automakers are thus active leading players in the Chinese market. As shown in Table 10.2, 97 percent of the market was dominated by foreign alliances and 3 percent by 20 local carmakers

[12] H. McDonald, "Made in China," smh.com.au, October 18, 2003.

Table 10.2 Dominant Joint Ventures in China's Auto Industry

Joint venture	Local partner	Foreign partner in 2000 (%)	Year	Market share
Shanghai-VW	SAIC	VW	1985	35.6
FAW-VW	FAW	VW	1985	17.8
TAIC	Tianjin Automotive** Industry Group	Daihatsu Toyota	1987	14.9
DPCA	Dongfeng	Citroën	1992	8.9
	Chang'an Suzuki	Chang'an Automobile Suzuki	1993	6.9
Shanghai GM	SAIC	GM	1998	5.0
Guangzhou	Honda Guangzhou Auto	Honda Group	1998	4.9
Beijing Jeep	Beijing Automobile Industry Group	Daimler Chrysler	1984	1.0
Total*				97.0

*For the remaining 3 percent, FAW had 2 percent and 19 other local firms together had 1 percent.
**51 percent owned by FAW.
Source: P. Gao, "A Tune-up for China's Auto Industry," *McKinsey Quarterly*, no. 1 (2002).

in 2000.[13] This may cause public concern because the automobile industry, as a pillar industry, must be controlled by national firms. However, the relative success of the joint projects to introduce foreign capital and technology in the 1980s reinforces the interest and confidence of both the government and producers.[14] Thus, the consensus is that joint ventures with foreign firms must be set up on a "win-win"

[13] P. Gao, "A Tune-up for China's Auto Industry," *McKinsey Quarterly*, no. 1 (2002).
[14] W. Zhang and R. Taylor, "EU Technology Transfer to China: The Automobile Industry as a Case Study," *Journal of the Asia Pacific Economy* 6, no. 2 (2001), pp. 261–274.

basis: besides creating jobs and generating tax revenues, local firms should share decision-making powers regarding business development, channel development, and distribution of profits.[15]

Market Characteristics

After examining the market size and the characteristics of the leading automakers in Taiwan and China, we can understand the reason why automakers from Taiwan invest in China and why Chinese automakers work with foreign firms.

Market Size

After reaching a height of over 480,000 units in 1997, the total demand for cars in Taiwan, including sedans and commercial vehicles, became saturated and started to decline. The market size was 420,000 in 2000, 347,000 in 2001, and 399,000 in 2002. In terms of local production, the volume was 350,000 in 2000, 288,000 in 2001, and 343,000 in 2002[16] (see Table 10.3). Increased foreign competition, after WTO accession and overcapacity, makes it inevitable that Taiwan automakers will look for overseas markets.

In China, the volume of cars sold was 1,580,000 in 1997; 1,628,000 in 1998; 1,830,000 in 1999; 2,069,000 in 2000; 2,340,000 in 2001; 2,360,000 in 2002; and 4,391,000 in 2003.[17] Local car production also increased significantly over time: 2,321,000 units in 2001, 3,287,000 units in 2002, and 4,444,000 units in 2003. The rapid growth of the market (e.g., more than 10 percent annual growth

---

[15] D. Lee, "SAIC Plans to Locate Production Base in Yunzhou," *China Commercial Times*, October 20, 2002 (in Chinese); "China's Auto Industry at the Crossroad," *People's Daily*, May 16, 2001.

[16] C. Chu, "The Automobile Industry," *Polaris Securities Special Investment Issue* (October 2002), 10–29 (in Chinese).

[17] Xinhua, "China's Auto Sales Expected to Top 5 Million Units in 2004," *People's Daily*, January 20, 2004.

Table 10.3 Market Size in Taiwan

	1998	1999	2000	2001	2002
Local production (volume)	397,396	362,550	356,545	291,307	345,211
%	83.8	85.6	84.8	83.9	89.5
Imports (volume)	76,684	60,940	63,918	56,113	53,671
%	16.2	14.4	15.2	16.1	13.5
Total (volume)	474,060	423,490	420,464	347,420	398,882

Sources: C. Chu, "The Automobile Industry," *Polaris Securities Special Investment Issue* (October 2002), pp. 10–29 (in Chinese).
www.ttvma.org.tw/cht/industrial-survey.php#1

from 1999 to 2001) and local production in recent years can be attributed to the following factors (see footnote 16):

- Because of the high costs associated with smuggling cars, locally-produced cars have been substituted for smuggled imports.
- The building up of an infrastructure, especially highways, has increased the demand for cars.
- The steady rise in income pushes up the demand for cars as well. The experience of other countries shows that the auto market takes off when per capita income reaches US$ 4,000. In the coastal cities (e.g., Shanghai), the average income was more than US$ 4,000 in 1998. Currently, passenger cars account for 30 percent of car sales, compared to 70 percent in the developed countries, suggesting the potential for future demand for passenger cars.

As shown by statistics, the number of cars sold in China is five times that in Taiwan and one-seventh that sold in the U.S. But the penetration rate is low — fewer than ten passenger cars per 1,000 people, compared with 250 in Taiwan and more than 500 in Germany and the U.S. per 1,000 people (see footnote 13). With WTO accession, better infrastructure, new sales and distribution channels, and the increasing number of Chinese who purchase high-end consumer items, it is expected that the auto market in China will take off (see footnote 16).

Major Players

1. In Taiwan

The goal of the government in Taiwan had been to build a national automobile industry, but it gradually came to realize the difficulties inherent in such an effort. As a result, the protection of the automobile industry has been gradually reduced, and restrictions on car imports and entry of foreign carmakers have been eased. For example, tariffs on small cars were reduced from 60 percent in 1986, to 45 percent in 1988, to 40 percent in 1990, and to 30 percent in 1992.[18] The "Policies to Develop the Automobile Industry in 1985" significantly relaxed the restrictions on foreign ownership of local automakers.[19] The "Strategies to Develop the Automobile Industry in 1992" further encouraged automakers to be technologically-independent and to become more international in focus. Furthermore, protective measures were gradually removed, in anticipation of WTO entry.

There are ten automakers in Taiwan, the first four accounting for 90 percent of sales in 2002, and because some automakers also import cars, total imports accounted for about 14 percent of sales. As shown in Table 10.4, capacity utilization is low. All automakers work with foreign automakers, including Mitsubishi, Nissan, Toyota, VW, Ford, Opel, and Daewoo, either through licensing agreements or equity arrangements. In the past, due to the small size of the domestic market, the unavailability of key components, and the limited investment in R&D, Taiwan automakers focused more on the domestic market. Fully understanding the implications of WTO entry, these automakers have now invested more in design, quality, and overseas expansion, and they have been trying to persuade foreign partners to help them to export.[20] As a result, the international competitiveness of Taiwan's automakers has been enhanced.

---

[18] C. Chang and C. Wu, "Miracle and Mirage: The Development of the Automobile Industry in Taiwan," in *Structure and Competitiveness of Taiwanese Firms*, ed. W. Chang (Taipei: United News Publishing Co., 2002), pp. 143–186 (in Chinese).

[19] China Credit Corporation, *Taiwan Industry Report: The Vehicle Industry* (Taipei: China Credit Corporation, 1994) (in Chinese).

[20] K. Cheng, "Time to Fight for the Auto Industry in Taiwan?" *Financial News*, no. 236 (November 2001), pp. 327–331 (in Chinese).

Table 10.4 Profiles of Automakers in Taiwan

Makers	Annual capacity (cars)	Cars sold in 2000*	Car production in 2002	Market share in 2002	Foreign partner
China Motor	120,302	90,965	93,973	28.9%	Mitsubishi
Yulong Motor	120,000	71,426	56,006	17.2%	Nissan
Kuozui	110,000	82,142	91,126	27.9%	Toyota, Hino
Ford Lio Ho	110,000	58,696	60,013	16.2%	Ford, Mazda

* Including cars imported from foreign partners or parent firms.
Source: *Vehicle Industry Monthly* (in Chinese).

Among the four automakers, Kuozui and Ford Lio Ho are not publicly-traded firms. Kuozui, in which Toyota and Hino have a 56.7 percent joint ownership, is producing for both the local market and export market. Ford Lio Ho, in which Ford has 80 percent ownership, is a marketing and production subsidiary. Ford Lio Ho has demonstrated its design capability by participating in several Ford new car development projects, and the headquarters has announced that the car designed by the subsidiary may be produced in China and other Asian countries.[21]

YULONG MOTOR CO., LTD.

Yulong, the first automaker in Taiwan, was 25-percent owned by Nissan until 2003. In its early years, Yulong relied on Nissan for technology, but, over the years, it has built up its own capabilities in car design and manufacturing. Starting in 2000, according to a news release, the firm has been pursuing a strategy of "developing international markets while continuing to develop the domestic market."

To solidify its relationship with Nissan, Yulong was split into two companies, Yulong (the original name) and YLN, in

[21] M. Shen, "Taiwan as a Springboard to Other Asian Countries," *China Commercial Times*, November 4, 2002 (in Chinese).

May 2003.[22] Yulong, with no Nissan ownership, will focus on original equipment manufacturer business (OEM business), very similar to the role played by the Taiwan Semiconductor Manufacturing Corporation (TSMC). Therefore, Yulong can produce cars for Nissan or other automakers. Because Yulong owns car dealerships, as well as runs car rentals and car financing businesses, it can sell cars for, or provide services to, any other automaker. On the other hand, YLN, 60-percent owned by Yulong and 40-percent owned by Nissan, will be in charge of all activities related to Nissan in Taiwan and China, including: (1) in Taiwan: purchasing, R&D, and marketing of Nissan cars; and (2) in China: operating Aeolus and selling cars made by Dongfeng Motor, a joint venture between Nissan and Dongfeng.

CHINA MOTOR CORPORATION

The Yulong Group, including Yulong Motor and Taiyuan Textiles, owns 34.28 percent of China Motor; Mitsubishi owns 19.62 percent. Through Yulong and Mitsubishi, China Motor is connected with DaimlerChrysler and Renault-Nissan.

As the market leader in Taiwan, especially in light commercial vehicles, China Motor's international expansion goal is to set up a manufacture-to-sale network in some emerging markets. The firm has engaged in the following activities abroad:

- Setting up a joint venture in China — the South East Auto Industry, Ltd. It is one of the fast-growing auto manufacturers on the mainland. In 2000, its two-shift capacity was 60,000 units, and in 2004 production capacity reached 160,000.
- Participating in Mitsubishi's component complementary system — the Mitsubishi Asian Car-Freeca (KZ) Project. China Motor is supplying 25 percent, 35 percent, and 98 percent, respectively, of complete knocked down (CKD) parts to Mitsubishi's affiliates in Indonesia, the Philippines, and Vietnam.

[22] Z. Song, "Yulong Becoming an OEM Supplier," *Jingji ribao* [Economic Daily], May 21, 2003 (in Chinese).

- Exporting of light commercial vehicles to the Middle East, Central and South America, and the U.S.
- Cooperation with foreign firms. It has signed a technical agreement with Premier Automobiles Limited in India to manufacture commercial vehicles.

To prepare for international competition, the four firms have engaged in efforts to reduce costs through different means, such as standardization of parts, pooling of purchasing orders, assisting suppliers to reduce costs, and increasing production efficiency.[23]

Unlike highly-integrated operations where all parts and works-in-progress are developed and manufactured in-house by Chinese automakers, one unique strength of the Taiwan automobile industry is the close cooperation between automakers and suppliers, which allows for lower transaction costs, and is conducive to product and process innovations. The experience of Toyota illustrates the advantage of such a relationship. Toyota has developed a network system, whereby it is at the center and is surrounded by independent suppliers whose primary customer is the automotive company. Strong ties between Toyota and its suppliers enable these firms to share trade secrets regarding future car designs and engineering modifications (see footnote 1). Though similar close relationships between automakers and suppliers generate competitive advantages for Taiwan firms, to maintain these advantages abroad the Taiwan automakers have to take some of these suppliers with them when they make foreign investments.[24] A good example is China Motor, that took 29 suppliers with it when it invested in China.

2. In China

In 1994, the Chinese government identified the automobile industry as a pillar industry in its national industrial policy for the 1990s.

[23] M. Shen, "Carmakers Successfully Reach the Goal of Cost Reduction," *China Commercial Times*, November 18, 2002 (in Chinese).

[24] C. Yu, "Restructuring of Production Networks in Foreign Countries: The Case of Taiwanese Firms," in *Foreign Direct Investment*, ed. J. Chen (NY: Macmillan Press, Ltd., 2000), pp. 96–114.

The goal was to foster national pillar industries through structural adjustments, mergers, and acquisitions.[25] The 1994 Industrial Policy of the Automobile Sector specified that:[26]

- Preferred automakers are allowed to be listed in the stock exchange markets, to issue bonds, to borrow money from banks, and to have access to foreign capital.
- The goals are to form two or three large automobile-related conglomerates, and six or seven automobile-production groups.
- A foreign firm can form only one joint venture, with less than 50 percent ownership, for the production of the same category of cars.

With the implementation of this policy, the auto industry has been undergoing restructuring through asset transfers and stock exchanges, based mainly on the three groups, namely, First Automobile Works Group (FAW), Dongfeng Motor Corporation (Dongfeng), and Shanghai Automotive Industry Corporation (Group) (SAIC).[27]

FIRST AUTOMOBILE WORKS GROUP (FAW)

The core of the FAW is China FAW, which, set up in 1953, was the pioneer in car manufacturing in China. Over the years, FAW has merged with or acquired majority control of several automakers, including Tianjin Auto Group in 2002. Currently, with assets of RMB 80 billion and 126,000 employees, FAW has 29 wholly-owned subsidiaries, 14 affiliated subsidiaries, and a technical center. To strengthen its technological capabilities and accelerate the development of new models, FAW has established ties with major automakers, such as GM and VW (see Figure 10.1). A major agreement

[25] W. Zhang and R. Taylor, "EU Technology Transfer to China: The Automobile Industry as a Case Study," *Journal of the Asia Pacific Economy* 6, no. 2 (2001), pp. 261–274.

[26] Y. Cheng, "The Industrial Policies in China," *Fortune China Monthly*, August 1994 (in Chinese).

[27] "China's Auto Industry at the Crossroad," *People's Daily*, May 16, 2001.

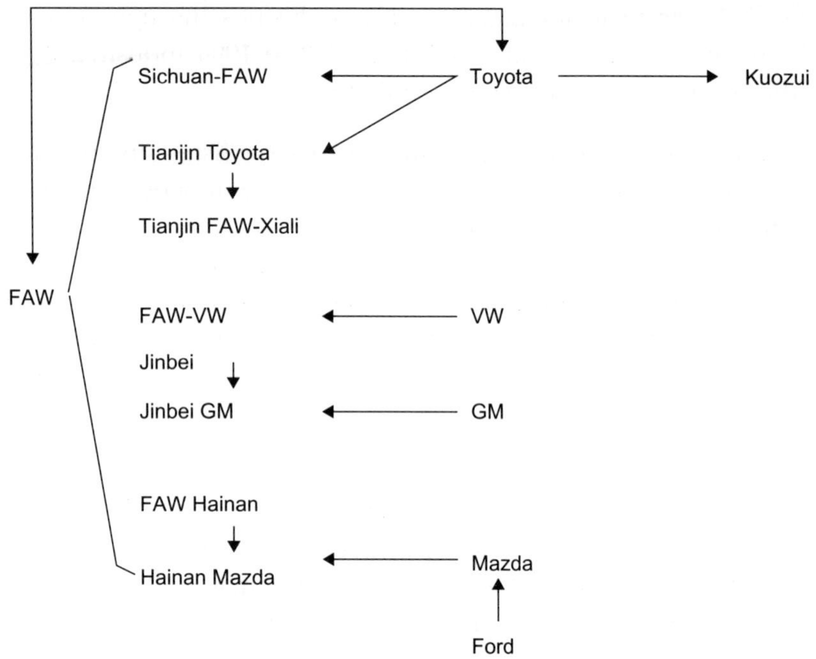

Figure 10.1 Joint ventures of First Automobile Works Group

was signed with Toyota on August 29, 2002 to establish a strategic and long-term cooperative relationship for business in China.[28] Together, the two auto companies agreed to move forward with preparations for the production of three types of vehicles: mini-vehicles, medium/large luxury sedans, and medium/large luxury class sport utility vehicles.[29] FAW produces cars of all sizes for a variety of uses (i.e., sedans, buses, and trucks), and has production facilities nationwide, including the Northeast, Tianjin, Shandong, the East, Southwest, and Hainan and Shenzhen. FAW has set up sales offices abroad in Asia, Africa, Europe, and South and North America to promote international sales. In 2002, sales reached 580,000 autos. FAW aims to reach annual production of one million autos and to fulfill the dream that "every Chinese family owns a car."

[28] "Auto Giant Being Reborn after Reform," *People's Daily*, September 13, 2002.

[29] www.toyota.com

SHANGHAI AUTOMOTIVE INDUSTRY CORPORATION (GROUP) (SAIC)

SAIC manufactures and distributes passenger cars, buses, tractors, motorcycles, heavy-duty trucks, and auto parts and components. With more than 60,000 employees and an annual production capacity of 400,000 sedans, SAIC has been ranked no.1 among the 500 largest domestic industrial enterprises in China for years and is one of the 20 pilot enterprises supported by the government.

Since 1984, due to China's reform and opening policy, SAIC has been attracting and utilizing foreign capital, and introducing and absorbing world advanced technology. SAIC has formed 57 joint ventures with automakers from 11 countries, including Germany, the U.S., Japan, the United Kingdom, France, and Italy (see Figure 10.2).[30] By utilizing advanced technologies and management innovations, exploring new markets, shaping new competitive advantages, and taking initiatives, SAIC has been preparing for the challenges created by China's accession to the WTO. In 2001, SAIC's revenue reached RMB 98 billion, with the sales volume of its passenger cars exceeding 300,000 units and a market share of 43 percent of the domestic market.

SAIC has implemented four projects, focusing respectively on customer satisfaction, overall innovation, global operations, and people-oriented management, to improve its competitiveness. With the goal of becoming one of the world's top 500 firms by the end of the next five-year period, SAIC continues to adjust its product lines, develop both domestic and international markets, and cultivate its own R&D capabilities.

DONGFENG MOTOR CORPORATION (DONGFENG)

Dongfeng entered the market of auto manufacturing, selling, and services as a group company in 1981. The core of Dongfeng, the Second Automobile Works, was established in 1969 as a showcase

[30] C. Lee, "Taiwan as a Springboard to Enter China," *China Commercial Times*, April 21, 2002 (in Chinese).

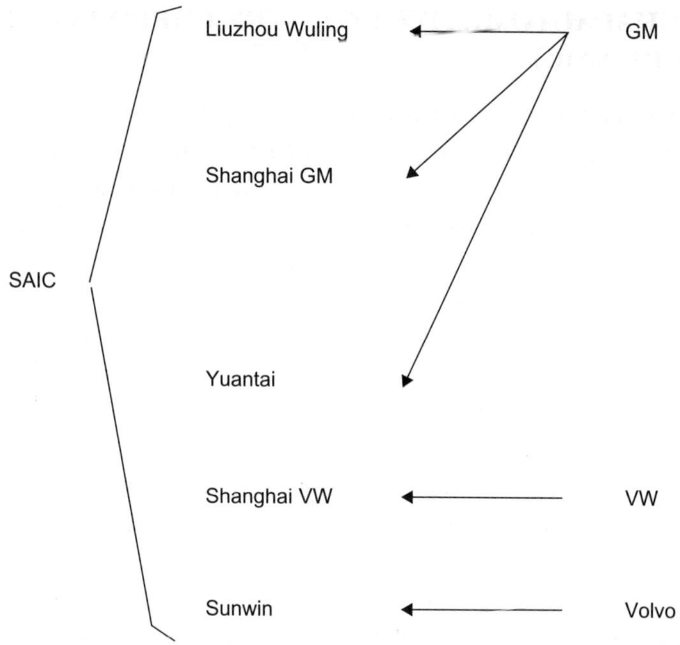

Figure 10.2 Joint ventures of Shanghai Automotive Industry Corporation

for the Chinese people's efforts in auto manufacturing. Over the years, Dongfeng has gained capabilities to produce cars, trucks, and buses. It has more than 120 subsidiaries (two of which are publicly-traded firms), and an annual production capacity of 5,060,000 cars. Starting in the 1990s, Dongfeng began working with international automakers, such as the PSA group (see Figure 10.3).[31] A notable development was the creation of a joint venture company, Dongfeng Motor Co., Ltd., with Nissan in September 2002, which incorporates all of Dongfeng's buses, trucks, and commercial vehicles, in addition to a full range of Nissan passenger vehicles.[32] In 1999, Dongfeng

[31] D. Bai, "Dongfeng Signs Cooperative Agreement with Peugeot and Citroën," *China Commercial Times*, October 25, 2002 (in Chinese).

[32] C. Kung, "Cooperation between Nissan and Dongfeng Sends Strong Signal for the Restructuring of State-owned Enterprises," *China Commercial Times*, September 24, 2002 (in Chinese); "Dongfeng, Nissan Sign Joint Venture Agreement," *People's Daily*, September 19, 2002.

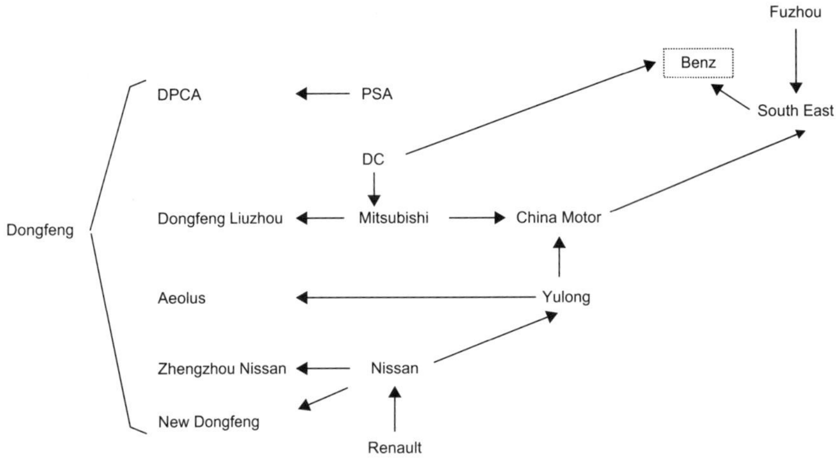

Figure 10.3 Joint ventures of Dongfeng Motors Corporation

employed 105,000 workers, held assets of RMB 51.9 billion, sold more than 200,000 autos (265,000 autos in 2001) with a sales volume reaching RMB 26.1 billion. Dongfeng has exported autos to more than 40 countries. Dongfeng's goal is to be internationally competitive, to control 20 percent of the domestic market, and to have sales reaching RMB 100 billion within five years.

In addition to these three automaker groups, there are other local automakers competing in the industry. These automakers, either privately-owned groups (such as Geely Group and Shanghai Brilliance Group), or government-owned groups (such as Fujian Automobile Industry Group, Chang'an Auto Corporation, Guangzhou Auto Group, and Beijing Automobile Industry Group), are improving their technologies and bringing out new models by working with foreign automakers (see Figure 10.4).

According to the country's original program, China will have three plants producing large autos, three plants producing small autos, and two plants producing mini-cars. A new round of establishing auto joint ventures with foreign firms, marked by the entry of GM into China in 1998 and aiming to produce cars for different groups of users, has intensified competition among automakers.[33]

[33] B. Xiao, "Changes in China's Automobile Industry This Year," Trade.com, May 20, 2002.

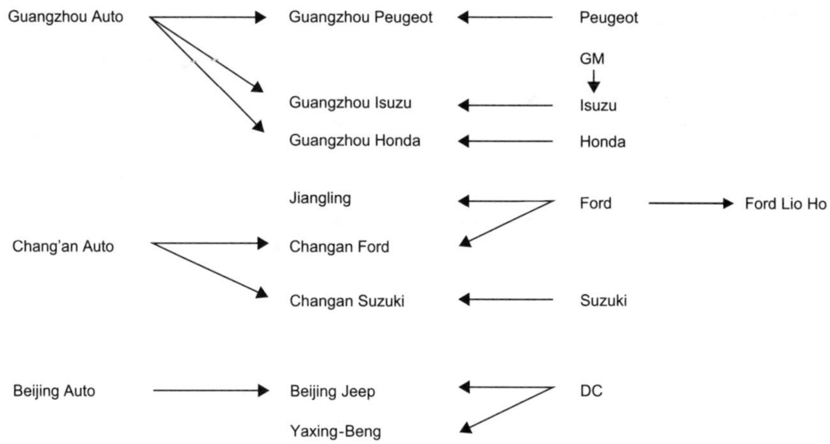

Figure 10.4 Other joint ventures

As a result of the loosening up of government policies, an increase in the various kinds of auto manufacturers and producers of different auto products is gaining steam. According to initial statistics, 12 light and mini-type automobile producers have begun, or are preparing to manufacture sedans; cargo vehicle producers are moving to produce passenger cars; and medium- to heavy-duty vehicle producers are moving to produce light vehicles (see footnote 33).

THE IMPACT OF ACCESSION TO THE WTO

In both Taiwan and China, a negative impact on the automobile industry was expected after WTO entry. However, the reality is that automakers have handled this challenge well. We will first describe the expected impact and then discuss the actual impact.

Expected Impact of WTO entry

Taiwan, applying to the WTO as the Separate Customs Territory of Taiwan, Penghu, Kinmen and Matsu,[34] agreed to make the

[34] "WTO Entry Expected to Impact Prices," *Taiwan Headlines*, November 16, 1999. WTO, "Report of the Working Party on the Accession of the Separate Customs Territory of Taiwan, Penghu, Kinmen and Matsu," WT/ACC/TPKM/18, October 5, 2001.

following changes in its automobile industry as a condition for accession:

1. Reduce tariffs on small cars from 30 percent to 17.5 percent over a period of eight years.
2. Revise the three-tier commodity tax on imported cars:
   —Maintaining the current rate of 25 percent for cars with engines smaller than 2,000 cc;
   —Reducing the rate to 35 percent for cars with engine sizes between 2001 cc and 3600 cc;
   —Gradually reducing the rate for cars with engines larger than 3600 cc from 60 percent to 35 percent.
3. Eliminate local content and sourcing requirements immediately after accession.
4. Eliminate restrictions on car importing areas, particularly for cars imported from Europe, immediately after accession and change to impose tariff quotas.
5. Allow production and importing of cars with diesel engines two years after accession.
6. Eliminate the reduction in the commodity tax due to investments in design engines, auto bodies, and so forth, three years after accession.
7. Reduce tariffs on automobile parts from 14.58 percent to 8.93 percent by 2004.

The government claimed that the WTO entry would increase Taiwan's international competitiveness, despite initial setbacks for some domestic industries, such as the agricultural and livestock sectors, as well as the heavy electric, paper-processing, and household electrical appliance manufacturing industries. The automobile industry that had been protected under the government's umbrella was expected to suffer significantly.[35] Fewer restrictions and more flexibility on imports would increase competition among

[35] "WTO Accession Said to Boost Taiwan's Competitiveness," *Taiwan Headlines*, September 20, 2001.

automakers and suppliers of automobile parts in Taiwan. But the Industrial Development Bureau predicted that four local automakers, namely China Motor, Yulong, Kuozui, and Ford Lio Ho, could survive the anticipated intense competition after Taiwan entered the WTO.[36]

China agreed to implement the following measures regarding automobiles and parts:[37]

1. To unify its laws, regulations and standards for domestic and imported automobiles and parts;
2. To formulate, publish and implement laws and regulations, and standards, in order to establish a transparent system, under which all laws and regulations would be applied, so as to accord imported products treatment no less favorable than that accorded to like products of national origin.

In addition, the following major concessions for accession were made by the Chinese government:[38]

1. Tariffs:
   - Auto tariffs would be gradually reduced from between 80 percent and 100 percent to 25 percent by the end of 2006.
   - Tariffs on automobile parts would be gradually reduced from 35 percent to 10 percent.
   - Tariffs for completely knocked-down kits or semi-knocked down kits, if imposed, would be less than 10 percent.
2. Import quotas for cars would be increased annually by 15 percent and would be phased out by 2005.
3. No limitations on models and types for car production would be imposed after the second year of accession.
4. Minimum investments needed for approval by the government would be increased over time: US$ 60 million after the first year;

[36] "Four Carmakers Will Survive WTO Entry," *Taiwan Headlines*, June 14, 2001.

[37] WTO, "Report of the Working Party on the Accession of China," WT/ACC/CHN/49, October 1, 2001.

[38] www.chinability.com/WTO.htm#auto%20package

US$ 90 million after the second year; and US$ 150 million after the fourth year of accession.

5. Foreign, non-bank financial institutions would be permitted to provide auto financing.
6. By 2006, there would be no restrictions on importing and exporting cars; owning vehicle wholesalers or retailers; and providing repair/maintenance services.
7. Local content and sourcing requirements would be eliminated immediately after accession.
8. Import or investment approvals would no longer be tied to technology transfer, R&D, the provision of offsets, or export-performance requirements.
9. Better intellectual property protection for technology transfer would be provided, and requirements mandating that the Chinese partner in a joint venture gain ownership of trade secrets, after a certain number of years, would be eliminated.

As in the case of Taiwan, the Chinese entry into the WTO implied more imports of both autos and components, lower prices for consumers, and more competition for domestic automakers. Some automakers, such as Toyota and Honda, realizing that a huge, complex market like China is best targeted by well-planned and strategically-located facilities that complement their exports from factories in Japan, will continue to invest even without the signing of the accord (see footnote 1). However, other international automakers, because of the less risky market after WTO entry, will be more aggressive in setting up manufacturing plants, mostly through joint ventures with local automakers in China.

Chou, Wang, Chen, and Kuo[39] applied a multi-regional computable general equilibrium model to analyze the impacts of liberalization of

---

[39] J. Chou, S. Wang, K. Chen, and N. Kuo, "Trade and Direct Investment Across the Taiwan Strait: An Empirical Analysis of Taiwan and China's Accession into the WTO," paper presented at the meeting on Industrial Development and Cooperation between Taiwan and China under the Framework of WTO, National Chengchi University, Taipei, December 17, 2002.

global trade in services and commodities in the aftermath of WTO accession by Taiwan and China. The impact was assessed within different scenarios (Table 10.5). Table 10.6 shows the impact on output, exports, and imports for the motor vehicle sector. Scenarios A and B are static simulations in which the capital accumulation effect is not considered. A comparison of the four scenarios suggests that: 1. freer cross-strait trade and direct investment policies would reduce domestic output and increase imports in Taiwan; and 2. the negative impact on the automobile sector, especially the drastic increase of imports, would be reduced by the capital accumulation effect for China.

In general, it was anticipated that the total output of the automobile industry in Taiwan, either for cars or parts, would be reduced after WTO accession. Seetoo and Yu[40] stated that: 1. past experience shows that with a 1 percent reduction of import tariffs for cars, local production of cars suffered a 1.56 percent loss of market share; 2. the lifting of import quotas, mainly applied to some exporting countries, increases the negative impact; and 3. the lifting of local content laws reduces the incentives for local firms to develop key components, and some parts suppliers would be forced to exit the market, due to competition from imported parts.

Due to protection by import tariffs, quotas, and other non-tariff barriers, China's auto industry is not internationally competitive. Official statistics indicate that, in 2003, there were 123 vehicle plants, among which only two had an annual output of more than 500,000 units, eight with more than 100,000 units, and 95 with fewer than 10,000 units.[41] In order to be competitive internationally, the annual production capacity of a plant should be more than one million units.[42] According to research conducted by the

[40] D. Seetoo and C. Yu, "The Impact of Joining the WTO on the Automobile Industry," 1996 report of the Association of Taiwanese Vehicle Manufacturers, Taipei (in Chinese).

[41] "China to Restructure Auto Industry," *China Daily*, August 18, 2003. "Government to Rationalize Auto Sector," *China Daily*, October 19, 2003.

[42] N. Xia, "China's Automobile Industry to Take the Brunt of Impact of WTO Entry," Trade.com, October 16, 2000.

Table 10.5 Simulation Design

Simulation specifications	Static—Scenario A	Static—Scenario B	Steady-state—Scenario C	Steady-state—Scenario D
Post-accession trade liberalization	Yes	Yes	Yes	Yes
Direct cross-strait transportation	No	Yes	No	Yes
Cross-strait investment liberalization	No	Yes	No	Yes

Notes:

1. Post-accession trade liberalization: reductions in barriers to trade in commodities and services.
2. Direct cross-strait transportation: the lifting of transportation barriers imposed by the Taiwan government (reduction of transportation costs by 40 percent).
3. Cross-strait investment liberalization: the lifting of regulations imposed by the Taiwan government on direct investment activities in mainland China.

Source: J. Chou, S. Wang, K. Chen, and N. Kuo, "Trade and Direct Investment Across the Taiwan Strait: An Empirical Analysis of Taiwan and China's Accession into the WTO," paper presented at the meeting on Industrial Development and Cooperation between Taiwan and China under the Framework of WTO, National Chengchi University, Taipei, December 17, 2002.

Table 10.6 Simulation Results for the Motor Vehicle Sector (Unit: %)

	Scenario A	Scenario B	Scenario C	Scenario D
Taiwan				
Output	−9.26	−11.57	−8.67	−10.45
Exports	17.77	10.98	18.92	12.95
Imports	24.16	26.21	24.10	26.29
China				
Output	−1.47	−1.71	2.78	4.23
Exports	−8.21	−12.08	2.89	3.64
Imports	8.28	10.99	5.51	6.81

Source: J. Chou, S. Wang, K. Chen and N. Kuo, "Trade and Direct Investment Across the Taiwan Strait: An Empirical Analysis of Taiwan and China's Accession into the WTO," paper presented at the meeting on Industrial Development and Cooperation between Taiwan and China under the Framework of WTO, National Chengchi University, Taipei, December 17, 2002.

State Council Development Research Center, the following changes were expected in the automobile industry due to accession to the WTO (see footnote 42):

- 15.1 percent reduction in output
- 14.5 percent reduction in employment
- 15.1 percent increase in imports
- 7.8 percent reduction in exports

Thus, although the Sino-U.S. agreement on China's entry to the WTO provided a five- to six-year buffer period for the automobile industry, the competitive pressures on local automakers would still be heavy.

Impact after WTO Entry

1. In Taiwan

Immediately after accession, the automobile market, as well as the automakers in Taiwan, in 2002 did better than expected due to two reasons:[43] first, as automakers tried to win market share by engaging in cut-throat competition, reduced prices increased the affordability of cars for consumers; second, as automakers tried to lure consumers by introducing various new models, the demand for cars was stimulated, which led to more sales.

Moreover, attracted by the potential in China, automakers began investing there. To develop their mainland business, automakers have been relying on Taiwan's expertise, and have started recruiting new employees for expatriation to China.[44] Examples are: Ford Lio Ho sent personnel trained in purchasing, product development, and production in Taiwan to China and increased recruiting in Taiwan; GM

[43] M. Shen, "Sales Targets in 2003 Vary Among Firms," *China Commercial Times*, January 4, 2003 (in Chinese).

[44] M. Shen, "Taiwan Becoming More Important as International Automakers Moving to China," *China Commercial Times*, June 2, 2003 (in Chinese); M. Shen, "Moving Westward, Recruiting More People," *China Commercial Times*, October 8, 2002 (in Chinese).

transferred executives in marketing and product development from Taiwan to China and recruited other personnel for future relocation to China; Yulong sent personnel trained in marketing and production to China, and recruited people trained in R&D, marketing, production, and technical support for the operations in China; and China Motor recruited people trained in R&D, marketing, production, finance, information systems, and technical support, with the understanding that they will be expatriated to China in the near future.

In fact, several foreign automakers have used similar strategies in restructuring operations in Taiwan. For example, in 2002, DaimlerChrysler, Volvo, and Honda set up subsidiaries or branch offices in Taiwan, instead of working with local importers/agents (see footnote 30). The objective is to use Taiwan as a springboard to penetrate the Chinese market: armed with the knowledge about how to sell cars to Chinese and business personnel cultivated in Taiwan, it will be easier for these firms to enter China in the future.

Realizing that the control of marketing and channels is important to success, China Motor has asked Shung Ye Motors and Fortune Motors, two auto dealers with which it has equity investments, to start operating in China. Shung Ye Motors has sales subsidiaries in Shanghai and Beijing, and Fortune Motors has sales subsidiaries in Dongguan and Tianjin.[45]

After Taiwan became a member of the WTO, the government gradually took action to fulfill its commitments in the automobile industry[46] by taking the following measures: reducing tariff rates as promised; simplifying the commodity tax structure for cars; eliminating local content restrictions; applying a tariff quota system for vehicle imports; and reducing tariffs on automobile parts. As a result, except for a few complaints on the import restrictions for automobile parts from China,[47] WTO compliance seems not to be problematic for Taiwan.

---

[45] M. Shen, "China Motors' Selling Arms Moving to China," *China Commercial Times*, October 18, 2002 (in Chinese).

[46] M. Lin, "WTO Entry: Two Years After," *Taiwan Business Topics* (January 2004), pp. 42–43.

[47] C. Yuan, "Foreign Firms Complaining about Import Restrictions for Goods from China," August 11, 2002, Southen.com (in Chinese).

2. In China

By 2002, China's WTO accession in late 2001 was primarily manifested in an increase of imported cars and their varieties (see footnote 33). The tariff on imported cars was generally expected to be cut from 12 to 15 percent.[48] In addition to import quota increases, the import tariffs for cars of 3000 cc or above were slashed to 50.7 percent from 80 percent, and for those smaller than 3000 cc, the rate was reduced to 43.85 percent from 70 percent in 2002.[49] Domestic car prices are expected to fall because of the significant increase in imports and the cost reductions due to the economies of scale of local producers. However, car prices in 2002 did not drop as drastically as expected due to the strong domestic demand.[50]

China's auto industry has survived the gloomy predictions of an influx of cheap foreign vehicles in the first year after WTO membership. The entry of foreign automobiles did not affect the domestic industry as severely as many had feared in 2001.[51] For one thing, the tariffs for imported cars were still too high, and people still preferred to buy locally-produced foreign cars, such as Buicks made by Shanghai GM.[52] Analysts in China credited the government for smoothly phasing in the liberalization policies and automakers in China are confident about their competitiveness in meeting the challenges created by the full WTO commitments.[53]

However, in contrast to Taiwan, China's WTO compliance remained problematic in the view of foreign automakers. For example,

---

[48] Y. Li, "Foreign Car Makers Eager to Enter Chinese Market," *People's Daily Online*, December 18, 2001.

[49] B. Xiao, "Changes in China's Automobile Industry This Year," Trade.com, May 20, 2002.

[50] C. Kung, "Car Prices Will Not Go Down in the Short-run," *China Commercial Times*, November 18, 2002 (in Chinese).

[51] "Auto Industry Forges Ahead after China's WTO Entry," *People's Daily*, December 12, 2002.

[52] C. Huang, "Heavy Taxes for Car Buyers in China," *Money Magazine*, December 2, 2002 (in Chinese).

[53] China.com.cn, "Why the Impact Has Not Been Severe After WTO Entry?" March 2, 2004 (in Chinese).

Ford commented that:[54] "WTO compliance in 2002 has not gone well. Key areas of concern are import quotas, vehicle standards and certification, auto financial services, local content requirements and distribution rights." It was felt that the areas of non-compliance with WTO commitments appeared to be symptomatic of slow implementation at local levels, or due to misunderstandings of what needed to be done and the huge task of opening the market.[55]

Acknowledging that China has gradually fulfilled its WTO obligations, Terence Stewart,[56] in testimony before the U.S.–China Economic and Security Review, concluded, after observing the disappointing results of 2003: "I would have to give China a grade of no better than C in meeting its WTO commitments." He specifically indicated three problems for the auto industry: 1. auto financing has not been opened up to foreigners; 2. limits on autos and auto parts have not been relaxed according to the WTO commitments; and 3. there are restrictions on selling imported and China-made autos from the same location.

In a positive development, China announced that, beginning in 2004 (i.e., one year ahead of schedule), it would permit certain U.S. automakers to import U.S.-produced cars and to establish their own exclusive networks to sell and service U.S.-produced cars in China.[57] This development effectively ends the auto quota system for U.S. automakers.

Joint Ventures between Firms in Taiwan and Firms in China

Firms in Taiwan invest in China because of its large market size and production resources. In addition, cultural affinities allow Taiwan

[54] www.ford.com

[55] S. Collinson, "China Must Do More to Meet WTO Commitments: U.S. Chamber of Commerce," September 16, 2003, quickstart.clari.net

[56] T.P. Stewart, "China and the WTO: Compliance and Monitoring," statement of Terence P. Stewart, Esq., Managing Partner, Law Offices of Stewart and Stewart, before the U.S.–China Economic and Security Review Commission, February 5, 2004.

[57] U.S. Trade Representative, *Report to Congress on China's WTO Compliance*, December 11, 2003.

firms some advantages over other foreign firms that usually have better technologies. Chinese firms welcome foreign firms, including firms from Taiwan, because they bring in capital, know-how, and technology, plus potential help in penetrating international markets. The following describes two joint ventures, Aeolus Automobile and South East Auto Industry, Ltd., formed by automakers from Taiwan and China.

Formed in 2000, Aeolus Automobile is a joint venture between Dongfeng, Yulong (40 percent ownership), and Guangzhou Ja Yun Bao Automobile, in which Dongfeng has the controlling share.[58] A subsidiary of Dongfeng, Aeolus, produces new sedan models that the state has approved for Dongfeng. After signing a licensing agreement with Nissan, Aeolus now produces Nissan sedans and engines, including the Aeolus Bluebird No. 1, 2, 3, and will produce other Nissan models in the future. Sales of Aeolus in 2003 increased to 50,000 cars. Aeolus competes with other automakers based on its efficient operations and high-quality work, and was among the top ten sedan makers in China in 2004.

South East Auto Industry, Ltd. is a joint venture formed in 1995 by China Motor and Fujian Automobile Industry Group. The venture benefits both parties: it gives China Motor entry into the Chinese market; it gives the Fujian government an opportunity to build itself into one of the country's important auto manufacturing bases within ten years.[59] The production capacity of South East was 60,000 units in 2002, 83,000 in 2003, and it reached 160,000 in 2004. Its sales record has been impressive: 47,000 cars in 2002 and 84,000 cars in 2003. The objective is to reach sales of 250,000 cars to be among the top five automakers in China.[60] The success of South East encouraged the Fujian Automobile Industry Group, China Motor, and DaimlerChrysler to form a 50:25:25 venture

[58] M. Shen, "The Yulong Group Strides in China," *China Commercial Times*, January 14, 2003 (in Chinese).

[59] "Fujian to Become Major Auto Base in 10 Years," *People's Daily*, January 18, 2001.

[60] M. Shen, "The Grand Scheme of Yulong in Taiwan and China," *China Commercial Times*, December 5, 2002 (in Chinese).

to produce Benz commercial cars for 7 to 11 and 13 to 17 passengers.[61]

As indicated in a previous section, Taiwan suppliers will follow their clients abroad. Auto parts suppliers did, indeed, follow their customers (i.e., China Motor and Yulong) to invest in China and made additional investments in hopes of serving China's large market. The quality and prices of Taiwan parts suppliers have won praise by customers, such as automakers and maintenance shops,[62] and China operations have increased the profits of some suppliers significantly.[63] One example is the Tong Yang Group (TYG), the largest producer of plastic auto parts in Taiwan. In China, the TYG had three parts ventures (i.e., Chongqing Dajiang Yuqiang, with 65.38 percent ownership; Nanjing Tong Yang, with 65 percent of ownership; and Fuzhou Tong Yang, with 100 percent ownership), and four joint ventures with Japanese firms (i.e., Tianjin Mitsubishi, 37.5 percent ownership; NBC (Panyu Nasa), 40 percent ownership; Changchun Dun Yang NBC, 40 percent ownership; and Tianjin NBC, 40 percent ownership) in 2002 (see footnote 16). In addition, TYG and a subsidiary of FAW announced the formation of Changchun Fawer Tong Yang to produce plastics parts, with TYG owning 51 percent of the venture in December 2002.[64] Operations of suppliers from Taiwan in China have enhanced the competitiveness of automakers in both China and Taiwan.

In comparison to automakers, auto parts suppliers from Taiwan seem to be more active in the post-WTO era. They make more investments in China to cope with the growing demands by automakers.[65]

---

[61] M. Shen, "Yulong, DaimlerChrysler, and Fujian Automobile Industry Group Forming a Joint Venture," *China Commercial Times*, March 22, 2003 (in Chinese).

[62] D. Lee, "MIT Parts Well Known in China," *China Commercial Times*, February 28, 2003 (in Chinese).

[63] H. Du, "Parts Suppliers Gaining in China," *China Commercial Times*, April 15, 2003 (in Chinese).

[64] H. Du, "Tong Yang and FAW Form a Joint Venture," *China Commercial Times*, December 25, 2002 (in Chinese).

[65] "Auto Parts Makers Continue Investing in China," *Economic Daily*, May 25, 2005 (in Chinese).

For example, in addition to Changchun Fawer Tong Yang, TYG has added five more plants in China (i.e., Harbin Hafei Tong Yang in 2003; NBC (Wuhan), Chongqing Dajiang Yuqiang, and Wuhu Youth Tong Yang in 2004; and Nanjing Niyang in 2005). As a result, auto parts makers with operations in China enjoy high profit margins.[66]

Developments Associated with Accession to the WTO

In the context of the global automobile industry, we know that firm size, in terms of number of cars sold and produced, is an important indicator to gauge competitiveness. The industry is dominated by a few firms and these firms have been trying to form alliances with firms in other nations. The reality for automakers in Taiwan is: because they are either owned by foreign firms (e.g., Ford or Toyota) or controlled by foreign firms (e.g., Nissan or Mitsubishi), when making important strategic decisions, such as investing in China, they have to take into account the views of foreign firms. At the same time, the reality for Chinese automakers is: because major segments of the market are served by joint ventures with foreign firms, they have to develop other advantages in serving the local markets to ensure their independence. Cooperation between automakers from Taiwan and China may create advantages for both parties.

The common membership in the WTO gives firms in Taiwan and China equal and fair opportunities to penetrate one another's home market. We likely will see more cooperation between these firms in different types of value activities along the value chain in the future (Figure 10.5). We have already seen cooperation between automakers and parts makers. Apparently, firms can also cooperate in other activities along the value chain, such as car distribution and financing.

The value of a car is created by the work of many people involved in the value chain, and each step adds to its value. The most important part in the process is generated by the workers in the automobile factory. In addition, the value of a car is created

[66] C. Chu and P. Wan, "Competition among Three Major Auto Parts Makers," *Money Magazine*, April 21, 2003 (in Chinese).

Parts (purchasing, importing, and manufacturing) → Parts inventory management → R & D and design → MIS → Assembly → Painting → Marketing and selling → Channel → Financing → Services

Figure 10.5 Value chain of the automobile industry

through the integration of other participants in the process, including designers, market researchers, salesmen, the financing industry, the insurance industry, the physical distribution industry, and many others. It is estimated that the value-added in the manufacturing process accounts for only about 40 percent of the total value of an auto. About 60 percent of the value is contributed by other value activities or participants. Thus, it is possible for automakers or service providers from Taiwan and China to form alliances in areas other than car production (Figure 10.5).

A very positive development is the passage of the Car Financial Companies Act by the Chinese government on October 3, 2003, which allows local and foreign firms to run car loan businesses. Because only 20 percent of car buyers bought cars with loans, the potential market is high. Foreign automakers, all running car loan businesses in other markets, are evaluating the timing of entry. One effective way is to work with local financial institutions to enter the market. It was rumored that GM was negotiating with a local financial institution[67] (in fact, GM-SAIC Auto Finance Co. obtained the approval from the China Banking Regulatory Commission to start operations in 2004).[68] Presumably firms in Taiwan, with their understanding of the consumption behavior of Chinese car owners, will be good partners with local Chinese firms.

In fact, Taiwan firms have taken the initiative beyond car production. Yulong has encouraged its dealers in Taiwan to set up operations in China.[69] At the same time, South East Auto has helped its

[67] D. Lee, "Stay Put for Forming Car Financing Companies by Foreign Carmakers," *China Commercial Times*, October 11, 2003 (in Chinese).

[68] "GM Obtains Approval for Auto Finance," *People's Daily*, August 6, 2004.

[69] D. Lee, "Taking Control of Channel Development Becomes the Trend," *China Commercial Times*, October 25, 2002 (in Chinese).

distributors expand operations to include parts supply and services. The distributors for China Motor in Taiwan have also invested in China to provide selling and service functions. The result has been very positive (see footnote 58): distributors from Taiwan sold 4,500 cars in 2002 and 15,000 cars in 2003.

Chronologically, the development process between Taiwan and Chinese firms in the automobile industry probably follows the pattern listed below:

1. Before WTO entry

Taiwan automakers invest in China because of the attractiveness of the market potential. The following developments have been observed:

- Taiwan firms invest in China to produce cars and they either follow their foreign parents or follow the foreign technology;
- Suppliers invest in China to produce parts, mainly to satisfy the needs of Taiwan automakers in China, and gradually develop local customers (i.e., local and foreign automakers);
- Lower production costs, or gains from economies of scale, enable suppliers to export parts to Taiwan and other countries.

As expected, Taiwan automakers (i.e., Yulong and China Motor) and suppliers (such as TYG and TYG Brothers Industries Co.) have invested in China. These firms benefited significantly from their operations in China. However, without common WTO membership, parts trade between Taiwan and China was very limited.

2. WTO entry

With both Taiwan and China entering the WTO, trade liberalization led to more trading activities. Development proceeded according to the following pattern:

- More parts, mainly produced by Taiwan producers in China, export to Taiwan and cars manufactured in China, either by foreign firms or Taiwan firms, gradually increase their export volume to Taiwan;

- Chinese parts suppliers and automakers begin exporting to Taiwan;
- Chinese automakers set up offices in Taiwan, mainly to handle import activities and to know the market;
- There is more intensive trading across the Taiwan Strait, either in cars or parts, and more sharing of ideas and interaction between people on the two sides;
- Automakers move into other areas of value activities, such as distribution, maintenance, insurance, and finance, mostly by working with local firms with complementary capabilities (e.g., a Chinese automaker has a service agreement with a Taiwan distribution chain in Taiwan; a Taiwan automaker forms an auto financing company with a Chinese bank in China; or a Taiwan automaker forms an auto insurance company with a foreign insurance company in China).

Among the five types of activities listed above, only parts of the first and fifth have been realized. Though more parts suppliers have invested in China and some distributors from Taiwan have provided selling and service functions in China, we have observed limited trade in the automobile sector. In addition, 66 items associated with cars and parts still could not be imported from China in 2005.[70] Because of the political conflicts between Taiwan and China, WTO membership has not generated a significant volume of trade between Taiwan and China in the automobile sector, which is a sensitive sector in most countries. Two recent developments, one with a negative and one with a positive impact on trade, deserve attention. First, though small (i.e., US$ 30.2 million), auto parts imported from China increased by 116.6 percent from 2003 to 2004. The Chinese National Federation of Industries (in Taiwan) has voiced concern for its members about the negative impact of imports on local industries.[71] Second, pressures from the EU and the

---

[70] W. Ding, "The Government Is Inclining to Modify the Restrictions on Trucks Imported from China," *Economic Daily*, May 4, 2005 (in Chinese).

[71] Chinese National Federation of Industries, "Be Aware of the Imports from China," August 15, 2005, www.cnfi.org.tw (in Chinese).

American Chamber of Commerce have pushed the government in Taiwan to review its policies on cars and parts imported from China. On balance, it is believed that more relaxed policies on trade in the automobile sector will be adopted.

Foreign firms have contributed to the intensity of trade and investment activities between Taiwan and China. For example, the American Chamber of Commerce in Taipei[72] has urged the government to build aggressively on economic synergies with China. It appears that foreign automakers have been conducive to the integration of the automobile sectors in Taiwan and China. Fully understanding the market potential in China and the ability of people from Taiwan to work with Chinese employees and consumers, foreign automakers have staffed their China operations with employees working in their Taiwan affiliates or subsidiaries. They even transferred the managers from Taiwan to become high-level executives in China.[73] Some automakers (such as GM) have positioned China as an export base to neighboring Asian countries, and some (such as Ford and Toyota) plan to design and market the same cars in Taiwan and China.[74] These automakers have exercised their global positions to influence the trade policies and have facilitated current flows of human resources, capital, and parts between Taiwan and China. The opening up of car imports from China by the government in Taiwan will not be too long in coming.

Under the WTO framework, if the two sides can gradually and progressively formulate mutually-acceptable policies, the degree of integration of the automobile sectors in Taiwan and China and the long-run cross-strait cooperation between firms can be expected. Though this positive development depends on the political climate, as well as the interactions between Taiwan and China, international

---

[72] American Chamber of Commerce in Taipei, "2005 Taiwan White Paper," *Taiwan Business Topics* (May 2005), wp1–wp48.

[73] M. Shen, "Ford Relying on Taiwanese to Run the Show," *China Commercial Times*, November 29, 2003 (in Chinese).

[74] M. Shen, "Taiwan Becoming More Important as International Automakers Moving to China," *China Commercial Times*, June 2, 2003 (in Chinese).

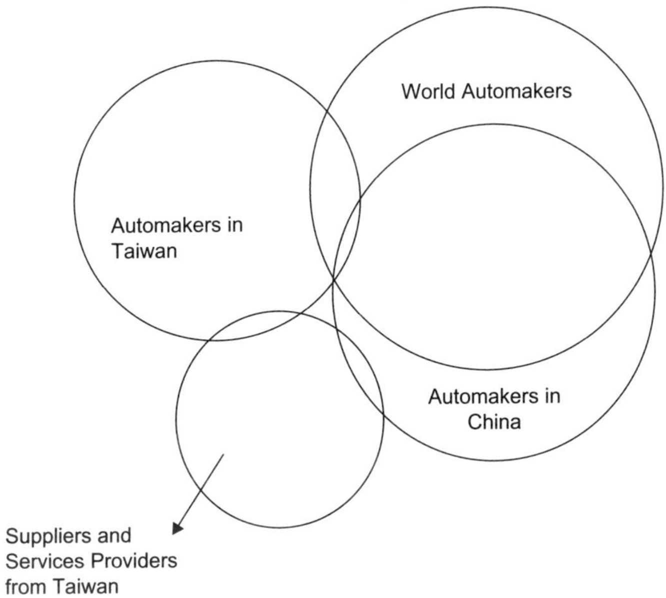

Figure 10.6 Relationships among automakers

pressures, especially those from foreign firms (such as automakers), definitely can facilitate this process. Therefore, we will witness more cooperation among automakers, parts suppliers, and service providers from Taiwan, China, and other nations (Figure 10.6).

CONCLUSION

The economies in Taiwan and China are affected by accession to the WTO. This chapter has three major findings: (1) Because the major automakers in Taiwan and China have formed joint ventures with foreign automakers, the auto industries in Taiwan and China have been gradually integrated into the global automobile industry; (2) Automakers in Taiwan and China have faced the challenges created by WTO entry, though foreign automakers have complained about China's WTO compliance record; and (3) common membership in the WTO has increased limited parts trade in the automobile sector, despite the unresolved conflicts between Taiwan and China.

In anticipation of WTO entry, automakers in Taiwan began to invest in China and automakers in China began to form joint ventures with foreign automakers. With WTO entry, more foreign automakers have entered China. Regardless of nationality, all automakers eye China for markets — China can be used as a base to export parts and autos to neighboring countries. Indeed, some automakers have already started exporting cars from China.

Parts suppliers from Taiwan seem to be more active in responding to the WTO challenge. Before 2002, they followed their clients to invest in China and after 2002 they formed joint ventures with foreign and local firms in China. For them, serving clients in China is more important than shipping parts back to Taiwan.

If Taiwan and China can find a solution to their problems under the WTO framework, more cross-strait cooperation between firms in the value chain of the automobile industry can be expected. Though Taiwan firms have already had operations in China in car assembly, distribution, and parts manufacturing, and firms in the automobile industry can benefit from more trade liberalization, these firms are not taking an initiative in this direction. Interestingly, foreign firms, especially automakers, which have gained by cross-strait exchanges of resources, can be instrumental in liberalizing direct cross-strait transportation and cross-strait investments, and can be catalytic in helping Taiwan and China to reap the benefits of the WTO regime in the automobile sector.

Chapter

11

Postscript

Steven M. Goldstein

The expression *"plus ça change, plus c'est la mĕme chose"* (the more things change, the more they stay the same) aptly sums up much of the analysis by the authors in this volume. Membership in the WTO, they suggest, has had only a marginal impact on the thriving economic relationship that developed before dual accession and has continued to flourish in the years that have followed. Moreover, an examination of the cross-strait economic relationship since the completion of these chapters suggests that the factors they identify as initially limiting the impact of common membership remain in effect four years after accession. In this postscript, we first highlight the arguments presented in this volume regarding the limited impact of dual accession, and then turn to a brief discussion of subsequent developments.

To be sure, during these years, cross-strait production chains have grown dramatically, accompanied by increased Taiwan investment on the mainland, as well as greater cross-strait trade. According to one estimate, the two-way trade has grown from US$ 37.4 billion in 2002 to US$ 71.7 billion in 2005, with Taiwan enjoying a surplus of

US$ 31.9 billion.[1] Moreover, in 2005, Beijing estimated that cumulative investment in the mainland had reached US$ 89.6 billion, although most estimates place the figure at closer to US$ 100 billion.[2]

Yet, the striking conclusion that emerges from the contributions to this volume is that at best the WTO regime has played only a marginal role in the growth and the management of these thriving cross-strait economic links. For example, in his study of the automobile industry, Joseph Yu notes that most of the gains that have accrued to Taiwan companies have been a result of their ties to multinational corporations. Yu argues that of the five potential benefits that the island's companies might have gained from dual accession, only two have been realized. Similarly, Jih-chu Lee highlights the lost opportunities for the financial industry on both sides of the strait, which have resulted from the failure to fully realize the possibilities offered by dual accession.

The reason for this is quite simple: although both sides have exhorted the other to adhere to the terms of the WTO regime, neither has been willing to do so itself.

Thus, Connie Guang-Hwa Yang concludes her chapter by noting that "Taiwan has a separate trade regime for its trade with the PRC, which is not completely guided by WTO rules, but rather directed by the assessment of the authorities in Taiwan of the cross-strait and global environment." Likewise, Chi Schive notes the "vast differences between Taiwan's current regulatory system for cross-strait economic links and a WTO-conforming framework." Arguing that neither side had reached an agreement with the other at the time of accession, Taiwan has continued to practice non-conforming behaviors, such as restricting imports from the mainland, limiting the movement of persons across the strait, and banning mainland investment in most of the island's service industries.[3] This is a policy that Drysdale and Xu

---

[1] www.chinabiz.org.tw/chang/Eco/156-2005-10/156-06.xls, accessed on March 16, 2006; *Asia Times*, March 23, 2006.

[2] *Asia Times*, March 23, 2006.

[3] An example of this justification can be found in FBIS, "Taiwan Urged to Clarify Cross-strait Trade Policy at WTO," Central News Agency (Taipei), February 15, 2006.

argue is damaging the island's economy, and ultimately limiting its role in the future economic system of Asia.

While Taiwan has sought to limit its openness to the mainland, Beijing has pursued the opposite course — skirting full compliance with the WTO regime in its own way. As noted in the introduction, mainland policy has sought to maximize the benefits available to TIEs, perhaps violating the principles of national treatment or most-favored nation in the interest of increasing its political leverage among Taiwan business people.

Yet China is not so generous when it comes to dealings within the WTO organizational framework. From the moment of Taiwan's application to the GATT in 1992, China's leaders were concerned about the implications of possible claims of international recognition that were implicit in the island's membership in the international organization. As Joseph Fewsmith demonstrates, Beijing has belied any expectations that the WTO might become a forum for resolving cross-strait differences. Fearing that any dealings with Taiwan would only enhance its international position, the mainland avoided contacts with the island's representatives and used every opportunity — from disputing its title in the organization to preventing its accession to the Government Procurement Agreement — to diminish Taiwan's status within the organization. Fewsmith concludes his discussion by noting that, thus far, the story of cross-strait relations in the WTO "suggests that as important as economic pressures are, political concerns ultimately dominate."

If we turn to an examination of recent trends in cross-strait economic relations, it is clear that the dominance of political concerns remains the central characteristic of cross-strait economic relations. Generally, Taiwan has continued to maintain an economic regime in its dealings with the mainland that does not conform to WTO requirements. Restrictions on imports remain, investment opportunities open to other WTO members are closed to mainland entities, and Taiwan companies (unless in partnership with a foreign company) are prevented from taking full advantage of concessions that were made by the mainland upon accession. Still, as we shall see below, Taipei persists in its attempts generally to expand its role within the organization; to engage the mainland within the WTO framework; and to call for China's adherence to the organization's regulations in its dealings with the island.[4]

Similarly, the mainland continues to use selectively the opportunities afforded by common membership in the WTO to advance its own priorities in the cross-strait conflict. Politics has remained central, with Long Yongtu, China's Chief Representative to the WTO talks, pledging in 2005 that, if Taiwan could "truly recognize the '1992 consensus,' it would bring about a completely new situation in cross-strait trade and economic cooperation under the WTO framework."[5]

Absent such recognition by Taiwan, the mainland has sought to avoid any dealings with Taiwan within the WTO and to diminish the island's status within it. Although a March 2006 anti-dumping action initiated by Taiwan towel producers brought a mainland response, for the most part Beijing has rejected Taipei's attempts to contact China within the WTO framework, even as China has decried the island's continued non-conforming limitations on cross-strait trade and investment.[6] Skirmishes have continued over mainland attempts to limit the use of any nomenclature in organization documents (such as the internal telephone directory) that might suggest sovereign status for the island's government, and the mainland has persisted in its opposition to Taiwan's accession to the Government Procurement Agreement.[7]

However, it was in the wake of the dramatic trips by Taiwan's opposition leaders to the mainland in the spring of 2005 that the contrasting uses of the WTO in cross-strait trade became most apparent.

---

[4] For example, in late March 2006, Taipei pledged to go through the WTO to protest alleged Chinese trademark infringement in the naming of teas (*Taiwan News*, March 23, 2006).

[5] FBIS, "Taiwan Urged to Clarify Cross-strait Trade Policy at WTO," Central News Agency (Taipei), February 15, 2006.

[6] After the government in Taiwan started the anti-dumping investigation, the mainland sent representatives to Taipei to justify pricing procedures (*Financial Times*, March 2, 2006).

[7] FBIS, "Taiwan Protests WTO Member Directory Changes," Central News Agency (Taipei), March 23, 2006.

Soon after the passage of the Anti-Secession Law in March 2005, Chinese Prime Minister Wen Jiabao announced that the import of Taiwan fruits would receive preferential treatment.[8] As the visits by KMT Chairman Lien Chan and People First Party (PFP) James Soong materialized, the governments on the two sides of the strait approached the issue in a manner consistent with past trajectories. For the mainland, these preferential regulations were presented in a manner consistent with earlier unilateral concessions granted to Taiwan business people. Avoiding any contact with the government in Taipei or any reference whatsoever to the relationship between these concessions and the WTO trade regime, Beijing carefully coordinated the offer on fruit imports with the new united front efforts toward the KMT and the PFP. Preferential tariffs for Taiwan fruit became simply another example of cross-strait economic policies in the service of politics, which avoided the WTO framework.

The response from Taiwan was equally predictable and equally selective in its uses of WTO practices. As in the past, although it was unwilling to conform to the organization's regime in its own trade policies, Taipei was eager to enhance its standing vis-à-vis the mainland by using that regime to settle trade issues. Thus, in response to possible pressures on Taiwan business people in the wake of the Anti-Secession Law, the government pledged to "seek justice" through the WTO, should their interests be threatened.[9] In addition, it sought to use that organization to negotiate further the mainland's offer regarding preferential treatment for fruit imports, even as some Taiwan commentators questioned whether such targeted concessions were even permissible under WTO regulations.[10] Not surprisingly, Taipei's demands and reservations were ignored by the mainland.

---

[8] FBIS, "Cross-Strait Farm Exchanges Uncertain Despite Beijing Overture," Central News Agency (Taipei), April 5, 2005.

[9] FBIS, "Cross-Strait Disputes Difficult to be Handled Under the WTO Framework," Central News Agency (Taipei), April 8, 2005.

[10] FBIS, "MAC Won't Oppose Private Cross-strait Exchanges: Vice Chairman," Central News Agency (Taipei), April 8, 2005; "TT Editorial Questions PRC Motives in Lifting Tariffs on Taiwan Fruit," *Taipei Times*, May 16, 2005.

True to past form, this issue was resolved outside the organization's trade regime.

In all, our examination of the interactions of the two sides within the WTO since 2002 suggests that the separation of economics from politics in the relationship between Taiwan and the mainland should be qualified when it comes to their dealings within this important international organization. It also suggests that the frequently-expressed optimism that growing economic ties across the strait will foster an easing of political tensions ignores the lessons of the past, which demonstrate the power of politics in shaping the economic context, rather than vice-versa.

Index